OXFORD PHILOSOPHICAL TEXTS

David Hume

An Enquiry concerning Human Understanding

OXFORD PHILOSOPHICAL TEXTS

Series Editor: John Cottingham

The Oxford Philosophical Texts series consists of authoritative teaching editions of canonical texts in the history of philosophy from the ancient world down to modern times. Each volume provides a clear, well laid out text together with a comprehensive introduction by a leading specialist, giving the student detailed critical guidance on the intellectual context of the work and the structure and philosophical importance of the main arguments. Endnotes are supplied which provide further commentary on the arguments and explain unfamiliar references and terminology, and a full bibliography and index are also included.

The series aims to build up a definitive corpus of key texts in the Western philosophical tradition, which will form a reliable and enduring resource for students and teachers alike.

PUBLISHED IN THIS SERIES:

Berkeley *A Treatise concerning the Principles of Human Knowledge* (edited by Jonathan Dancy)
Berkeley *Three Dialogues between Hylas and Philonous* (edited by Jonathan Dancy)
Hume *An Enquiry concerning Human Understanding* (edited by Tom L. Beauchamp)
Hume *An Enquiry concerning the Principles of Morals* (edited by Tom L. Beauchamp)
Leibniz *Philosophical Texts* (edited by R. S. Woolhouse and Richard Francks)
Mill *Utilitarianism* (edited by Roger Crisp)

FORTHCOMING TITLES INCLUDE:

Frege *Philosophical Writings* (edited by Anthony Kenny)
Hume *A Treatise of Human Nature* (edited by David Fate Norton and Mary J. Norton)
Kant *Groundwork for the Metaphysics of Morals* (edited by Thomas E. Hill and Arnulf Zweig)
Kant *Prolegomena to Any Future Metaphysics* (edited by Günter Zöller)
Locke *An Essay concerning Human Understanding* (edited by S. Nicholas Jolley)
Spinoza *Ethics* (edited by G. H. R. Parkinson)

DAVID HUME

An Enquiry concerning Human Understanding

EDITED BY
TOM L. BEAUCHAMP

OXFORD
UNIVERSITY PRESS

OXFORD

UNIVERSITY PRESS

Great Clarendon Street, Oxford OX2 6DP

Oxford University Press is a department of the University of Oxford.
It furthers the University's objective of excellence in research, scholarship,
and education by publishing worldwide in

Oxford New York

Auckland Cape Town Dar es Salaam Hong Kong Karachi
Kuala Lumpur Madrid Melbourne Mexico City Nairobi
New Delhi Shanghai Taipei Toronto

With offices in

Argentina Austria Brazil Chile Czech Republic France Greece
Guatemala Hungary Italy Japan Poland Portugal Singapore
South Korea Switzerland Thailand Turkey Ukraine Vietnam

Oxford is a registered trade mark of Oxford University Press
in the UK and in certain other countries

Published in the United States
by Oxford University Press Inc., New York

Editorial introduction and apparatus. © Tom L. Beauchamp 1999

The moral rights of the authors have been asserted
Database right Oxford University Press (maker)

First published 1999

British Library Cataloguing in Publication Data

Data available

Library of Congress Cataloging in Publication Data

Hume, David, 1711–1776.
[Philosophical essays concerning human understanding]
An enquiry concerning human understanding / David Hume; edited by
Tom L. Beauchamp.
(Oxford philosophical texts)
Includes bibliographical references and index.
1. Knowledge, Theory of—Early works to 1800. I. Beauchamp, Tom L.
II. Title. III. Series.
B1481.B43 1999   121—dc21   98–54454

Typeset by SNP Best-set Typesetter Ltd., Hong Kong
Printed in Great Britain
on acid-free paper by
Ashford Colour Press Ltd, Gosport Hampshire

ISBN 978-0-19-875248-6

12 13 14 15 16 17 18 19 20

Contents

PART 1

Introductory Material

How to Use this Book

This edition of *An Enquiry concerning Human Understanding* contains several editorial materials intended to assist students in understanding the historical background of the work and its most difficult passages.

Part 1 is comprised of introductory materials. The Editor's Introduction explains Hume's intellectual context, as well as the structure, content, and arguments in this *Enquiry*. The Introduction concentrates on the major topics and arguments in the work and is arranged to disclose its analytical structure. It is followed by a section of suggested supplementary readings, arranged topically. Most of the readings listed are recent attempts to explicate Hume's philosophical writings, but also included are various editions of Hume's philosophical works and early modern writings in the relevant areas of philosophy. A short note following the suggested readings explains the origin and editorial basis of the text used in this edition.

Part 2 contains the text itself. This part begins with an Advertisement, or notice, that Hume published late in life. This Advertisement expresses some of his views about the importance of his later work in philosophy, including *An Enquiry concerning Human Understanding*. Next is the text of the *Enquiry*, which is presented in a form designed to be particularly congenial for students. Each portion of the text that is annotated in Part 3 (in the back of the book) is marked in the text by a small dagger (†). Hume's cryptic footnote references are filled out by editorial insertions (in brackets). Finally, numbers appear in the margin at the beginning of each paragraph of the text. These marginal numbers are introduced by the editor to afford a universal reference system that allows precise citation without reference to the page numbers of this or any other edition. This style of reference by section and paragraph numbers is subsequently used in the Introduction, the Annotations, and the Glossary of the present volume (for all of the works of Hume).

Part 3 includes additional aids. The first is the Editor's Annotations to the text of the *Enquiry*. The previously mentioned daggers in the text correspond to each annotation (designated by paragraph number within sections). These notes explain difficult concepts, references, and passages in the text. At the beginning of the annotations for each section of Hume's text is a brief editorial synopsis of the content of that section. These concise overviews of the content of the section contrast with the Intro-duction, which treats key themes and arguments in the work in greater depth. Translations of all passages in a foreign language are also supplied, as is information on sources that Hume identifies or to which he alludes.

Also included in Part 3 is a Glossary. It clarifies terms that carried dif-ferent meanings when Hume wrote than they do today. This Glossary explains or defines only words and phrases used by Hume. A list of Ref-erences is also found in Part 3. The authors and works it contains are all cited in this volume either by Hume or by the editor. The list is markedly different from the supplementary readings, despite some overlap in his-torical sources.

Students may choose to use this editorial material in several ways. One strategy is to begin reading without consulting the editorial material, only using that material when there is need for a definition (as found in the Glossary) or an explication of a portion of the text (as found in the Anno-tations). However, this approach will not be best for every student. Many students will seek to understand features of the work that are treated in the Introduction before they begin the text. In short, one can use the several editorial aids as one sees fit.

List of Abbreviations

ann.	the annotation(s) at
c.	century or centuries
DIS	*A Dissertation on the Passions*
Ed. Intro.	Editor's Introduction to the present volume
EHU	*An Enquiry concerning Human Understanding*
EPM	*An Enquiry concerning the Principles of Morals*
Letters	*The Letters of David Hume*, ed. J. Y. T. Greig, 2 vols. (Oxford: Clarendon Press, 1932)
NHR	*The Natural History of Religion*
THN	*A Treatise of Human Nature*

Editor's Introduction

An Enquiry concerning Human Understanding (*EHU*) is David Hume's attempt to introduce his philosophy to a European culture in which many educated people read original works of philosophy. This audience came to appreciate his genius, but many readers found it difficult to accept positions that Hume advanced about the limited powers of human understanding, the attractions of scepticism, the compatibility of free will and determinism, and weaknesses in the foundations of religion. Hume's philosophy was highly controversial in the eighteenth century and remains so today.

1. Early Life and Publishing History

Born in Edinburgh in 1711, Hume went to college there at a very young age. He soon became fascinated with philosophy. Shortly after leaving college he experienced a pivotal moment in his philosophical development:

when I was about 18 Years of Age [1729], there seem'd to be open'd up to me a new Scene of Thought, which transported me beyond Measure, & made me, with an Ardor natural to young men, throw up every other Pleasure or Business to apply entirely to it. . . . I cou'd think of no other way of pushing my Fortune in the World, but that of a Scholar & Philosopher.[1]

There were setbacks in the path of cultivating this 'new Scene of Thought'—that is, plan for a new system of philosophy—but by 1737 Hume had produced a draft manuscript of a lengthy work, which he entitled *A Treatise of Human Nature*.

1.1. The 'Failure' of the Treatise

When this three-volume work was published in 1739–40,[2] Hume hoped for a respectful reception by able scholars. He knew that the work was

---

[1] Mar. or Apr. 1734, to a doctor, in *The Letters of David Hume*, 1: 13 (hereafter *Letters*). All materials cited in footnotes are listed in the References.

[2] Two volumes of the *Treatise* (*THN* 1, on the understanding, and *THN* 2, on the passions) were published in Jan. 1739. The final volume (*THN* 3, on morals) was published in Nov. 1740.

bold and that boldness is often a mark of philosophical genius. However, the book was strenuous reading, and its doctrines were deplored by many critics. Hume once said that his book 'fell *dead-born from the Press*; without reaching such distinction as even to excite a Murmur among the Zealots'.[3] The book was more noticed than this comment suggests, but typically Hume met with intolerant and undiscerning criticism. He soon lamented his decision to publish the *Treatise* and began to reflect on how he might recast his philosophical views.[4] *EHU* was the first stage in this recasting.

1.2. *The Writer of Essays*

There was, however, an important interim period after the *Treatise* and before *EHU*, and Hume's development during this period is vital for understanding the structure and content of *EHU*. Hume was an admirer of the elegant prose of essayists such as Joseph Addison.[5] Shortly after completing the *Treatise* he wrote several essays that he hoped would engage the literate community in Britain. His *Essays Moral and Political* (1741–2) did communicate effectively and became a publishing success.[6] By 1745 Hume had formed a conception of himself as a man of letters with a goal of writing philosophy in a clear and elegant style.

As he distanced himself from the *Treatise*, Hume concluded that he could improve his style without fundamentally modifying his philosophical theses. He then 'cast . . . anew'[7] the three books of the *Treatise* as separate publications employing the essay style. Various parts of Book 1 were significantly revised and released for publication in 1748, eventually under the title *An Enquiry concerning Human Understanding*.

1.3. *The* First Enquiry

Hume's book is not merely a restyled version of the *Treatise*: it is an original work with a large body of entirely new material. Now often called

---

[3] 'My Own Life' 6 (cited by paragraph number), in *Letters*, 1: 2.

[4] Hume later said he was 'carry'd away by the Heat of Youth' (Mar. or Apr. 1751, to Gilbert Elliot of Minto, in *Letters*, 1: 158). Late in life he formally disavowed *THN*, calling it a 'juvenile work'; see the Advertisement (p. 83), first printed in Jan. 1776 and appended to unsold and new copies of his *Essays and Treatises on Several Subjects*.

[5] See *EHU* 1.4 for comments on Addison's pleasing style.

[6] See also *Political Discourses* (1752), which Hume called 'the second Part of my Essays' ('My Own Life' 9, in *Letters*, 1: 3). The success of his essays may explain Hume's frequent use of literary features and examples in *EHU*, a style not found in *THN*.

[7] 'My Own Life' 9, in *Letters*, 1: 3.

the *First Enquiry*,[8] it was written as a collection of essays centred on human understanding, although some essays were more focused on this theme than others. When Hume recalled the *First Enquiry* in his autobiography, he stated that it was 'at first but little more successful than the Treatise of human Nature'.[9] Over time, however, it gained in reputation and was issued in ten new editions during Hume's lifetime.[10]

Eventually Hume became a philosopher and literary figure of great renown, but he was never a professor or a writer in the cloistered environment of a university. He was, in different periods of his life, secretary to a British general, keeper of the Advocates' Library in Edinburgh, embassy secretary and chargé d'affaires of the British embassy in Paris, and under-secretary of state in the Northern Department of the British government in London. Hume died in Edinburgh in 1776, near the end of a period now known as 'the Enlightenment'.

2. Cultural and Intellectual Background

The philosophical, scientific, and theological controversies of the Enlightenment influence the arguments in every section of *EHU*. The term 'Enlightenment' now refers to some principal European intellectual and cultural currents in and around the eighteenth century; it was used at the time by writers convinced that centuries of darkness and confusion were giving way to enlightenment in many fields of learning.[11]

Advances in science and religious conflict during and after the Reformation were among the chief influences on Enlightenment thinking. They inspired leading figures to question many traditional beliefs, including foundational religious doctrines and major philosophical

---

[8] The first title placed on this work was *Philosophical Essays concerning Human Understanding*. In 1756 this title was changed to *An Enquiry concerning Human Understanding*. Book 2 of *THN* was recast in 1757 as an essay 'Of the Passions', soon given the title *A Dissertation on the Passions*. Book 3 was heavily revised and published in 1751 as *An Enquiry concerning the Principles of Morals*—Hume's *Second Enquiry*.

[9] 'My Own Life' 8, in *Letters*, 1: 3.

[10] In its third edition *EHU* began to be published together with several other works in a collected edition, *Essays and Treatises on Several Subjects*. This 1,000-page edition collected all of the philosophical, political, and literary works that Hume wished to reissue as revised editions.

[11] The 'Scottish Enlightenment', in particular, refers to roughly a 100-year period beginning just before Hume was born. The term 'Enlightenment' was never used to refer to a purely philosophical movement, but philosophical developments were influential in law, medicine, science, history, literature, and other fields of learning.

systems. Several Enlightenment philosophers, including Hume, viewed their activities as advancing the earlier scientific and philosophical work of figures such as Francis Bacon (1561–1626), Galileo Galilei (1564–1642), Thomas Hobbes (1588–1679), René Descartes (1596–1650), John Locke (1632–1704), Isaac Newton (1642–1727), and G. W. Leibniz (1646–1716).

Newton's programme of experimental research and discoveries of scientific laws in astronomy had an extraordinary impact on virtually all fields of learning. His work and that of other experimentalists promoted a confidence in the capacity to understand and control the powers of nature. Many figures, including Hume, thought that this work in the physical sciences had begun to unlock some of nature's intimate secrets. It was widely believed that new discoveries in other domains would result from the same kind of careful and controlled reflection. For example, some philosophers believed that the human mind could be examined scientifically, and some held that universal laws could be discovered that would serve as models of social and political governance. Faith in progress was the Enlightenment's driving force, and Newton was its symbolic inspiration.

Many philosophers began to search for a scientific framework that would correct excessive speculation in philosophy and eliminate guesswork. They also opposed intolerance and dogmatism in religion. Hume vigorously supported a scientific philosophy and denounced many aspects of traditional philosophy and organized religion, especially the zealous and the doctrinaire. His arguments in *EHU* show the influence of philosophers such as Locke and the experimental and data-compiling methods of the new science introduced by figures such as Newton, Robert Boyle (1627–91), and Robert Hooke (1635–1703), who had made impressive strides in the explanation of natural phenomena and the discovery of scientific laws. Like these figures, Hume distrusted tradition and authority, while maintaining confidence in the powers of philosophy and the new science to generate a proper intellectual climate for dispassionate investigation. *EHU* is, in some respects, the quintessential Enlightenment book. It incorporates a confidence in science, a daring attempt at new discoveries about the human mind, an opposition to superstition and fanaticism, an emphasis on human nature, a restrained scepticism about traditional views of knowledge and belief, and a mood of reform and critique.

Hume profited from several predecessors (most notably Locke) who held that we must examine the human mind to ascertain its capacities and limits before we can hope to provide answers to great philosophical questions about the nature of God, the world, and the soul. In the *Treatise* Hume said that his attempt 'to explain the principles of human nature' required him to propose a philosophy and system of the sciences 'built on a foundation almost entirely new'.[12] He regarded the bulk of ancient and modern philosophers as having an inflated, even pretentious, faith in the powers of human reason. Many of these philosophers thought that, using reason alone, they could establish the existence and nature of God, identify the most basic entities that comprise the universe, and grasp eternal truths of morality. Today we think of some prominent Continental philosophers as the chief proponents of such views, but in Hume's time rationalist theories were also prominent in Britain.[13] Even Locke and George Berkeley (1685–1753), with whom Hume is in some respects closely aligned, talked confidently of God and the ultimate entities or properties in the universe.

Indeed, the overwhelming body of philosophers thought that reason can penetrate beyond what can be known on the basis of experience. They are Hume's opposition, and every section of *EHU* carries the message that these philosophers are overly confident. Hume's alternative emerges near the end of *EHU*: of advantage to philosophy and humankind, he says, is 'the limitation of our enquiries to such subjects as are best adapted to the narrow capacity of human understanding' (12.25). He cultivates this theme of the limitations of human understanding at every opportunity. It is the cement of his work in this book, the reason for its title, and the pivotal concept for reining in the enormous optimism of Enlightenment thinking.

3. Two General Features of Hume's Philosophy

Two general features of Hume's philosophy affect virtually every section of *EHU* and most of his philosophy: his experimental approach to the study of human nature and his theory of mental faculties.

---

[12] *THN*, Introduction 6.

[13] The Continental rationalists included Descartes (1596–1650), Gottfried Wilhelm Leibniz (1646–1716), and Baruch Spinoza (1632–77). British rationalists included Ralph Cudworth (1617–88), Samuel Clarke (1675–1729), and William Wollaston (1660–1724). Each was mentioned by Hume in some book. In general, a rationalist holds that the basis of knowledge is found in propositions of reason that possess a necessity like that of mathematical axioms.

3.1. *An Experimental Science of Human Nature*

Hume's philosophy is commonly depicted as an empiricism, which is the theory that experience, not pure reason, is the source of all information about matters of fact. Hume undeniably commended experience and criticized speculative reason, but the term 'empiricism' should be used with caution. It is not a term he used, and an empiricist theory of knowledge is not the stated objective of *EHU*. Hume's primary ambition was to study the mind in the way in which other natural events are studied.

This naturalistic study of the mind, as it is now called, is of the first importance in understanding his work. In the Introduction to the *Treatise* Hume depicted this study as a 'science of human nature', that is, a systematic explanation of human understanding, belief, passion, motivation, and other dimensions of the mind. He thought that this science could provide laws that could be confirmed with as much confidence as the laws of physics. Hume mentions this project of a science of human nature in the first sentence of *EHU* and pursues it throughout the book.

The Enlightenment ideal of a scientific philosophy was influential when Hume wrote, but methods of applying scientific techniques to the mind were not well developed. Hume claimed in the *Treatise* to follow an 'experimental method', an idea he invokes in *EHU* when he says that he seeks 'experimental conclusions' (4.19). His understanding of *science* and *experimental method* is not entirely clear, but we know that he was influenced by the principles of scientific method published by Boyle and Newton, who wrote about the roles of observable phenomena, hypotheses, and experimental accuracy. Newton rejected speculative explanations, demanded controlled observations, and formulated scientific laws. When he formulated the laws of gravitational attraction, Newton knew that the idea of gravitation was obscure and did not claim to experience or observe gravitational 'forces' or 'powers'. Instead, he formulated general laws of gravitation that were limited to descriptions of the ways in which bodies behave.

Hume hoped to develop a science of human nature that followed this model of describing behaviour and discovering laws. He hoped to discover laws of the inner human world of perception, desire, feeling, belief, reasoning, and inference. Since the forms of observation and experimentation employed in the natural sciences cannot be directly transferred to a psychological science, different methods must be utilized in examining the mind.

'Experimentation' does not signify a single strategy or method for

Hume. Sometimes when he says that his science is experimental, he means that it must involve careful observation and generalization. Hume liked to amass observational information about human mental functions and then use this data to develop theories about the mind. For example, he carefully studies the various functions of the imagination and then devises a theory about how this faculty differs from faculties such as the understanding.

Hume also proposes that his experimental science must engage in activities that we usually associate today with the word 'experiment', namely, experimentation designed specifically to test, discover, or prove something. However, he does not think of this work in terms of the carefully controlled experiments conducted in the laboratory sciences. He thinks in terms of cautious thought experiments in which we gradually refine tentatively held general principles. In one strategy he tries to vary the conditions under which a phenomenon occurs in the mind in order to observe and then theorize about the outcomes of the various conditions. For example, he considers different circumstances of personal and family success in order to discover the conditions under which a feeling of pride arises in the mind. His goal is to discover the nature and causes of feelings of pride.

In another strategy Hume intentionally brings several different ideas or propositions before the mind in order to see which do and which do not stimulate a belief. He thinks he can determine the difference between belief, disbelief, fiction, uncertainty, and the like. What differences occur in the mind, he asks, when we feign a train of fictional events in a realistic manner, by contrast to when we remember a train of events that we believe actually occurred?[14] This strategy of thought experimentation is designed to capture the psychological characteristics of belief—and ultimately to develop a theory of belief.

Among the most important of Hume's experimental conclusions is that the mind moves from one idea to the next in accordance with three 'principles of association' that are features of human nature (3.2). These principles are discussed in this Introduction in §4.4, 'The Association of Ideas and Principles of Connection'.

3.2. Faculties of the Mind

Hume's interest in human nature and the mind led him to discuss the roles and functions of several mental faculties, the most prominent being

---

[14] See *EHU* 5.10–11. The answer to this question is discussed in this Introduction, §5.6.

the understanding, reason, the senses, the imagination, and the passions.[15] Hume sometimes confuses readers by treating *understanding* and *reason* as virtually synonymous and by ascribing functions to the imagination that he elsewhere seems to attribute to the understanding.[16] None the less, these faculties have distinguishable functions in his philosophy.

The *understanding* is the faculty of probable inference (that is, inductive inference or inference from cause to effect). It can also be described as the faculty of factual reasoning or reasoning from experience. As the title *An Enquiry concerning Human Understanding* indicates, study of this faculty is the nucleus of the work.

Reason is the faculty of immediate intuition and demonstration. It can also be described as the faculty of demonstrative reasoning. Perhaps Hume's most consistent account of 'reasoning' is that there are two types: (1) demonstrative (the discovery of relations of ideas in pure reasoning), and (2) factual (the discovery of matters of fact in experience). (See this Introduction, §5.1, and the annotations at 4.1.) The first type of reasoning is clearly the province of reason, but Hume commonly attributes the second type to the understanding and sometimes even to the imagination. This usage confuses many readers. It seems tidier to regard the second form of reasoning as the province of the understanding, a usage followed in this Introduction and generally followed in *EHU*, where Hume seldom mentions the faculty of reason except to indicate what this faculty does not do.

By the *senses* Hume means the various sensory capacities: auditory, visual, olfactory, etc. Through these modalities we assimilate information about the world. The senses are not to be understood as the concepts that we use to identify what is received in sensory experience: the hearing of a sound is different from the intellectual identification of the sound that has been heard.

The *imagination* is the faculty of creating and connecting items that are not present to the senses. This faculty recombines the ideas acquired in experience. In particular, the imagination combines ideas on the basis

---

[15] This list should not be taken as a complete catalogue of Hume's faculties of the mind. He mentions other faculties, including memory and will.

[16] Numerous vagaries accompany Hume's use of these terms, especially 'reason'. Hume in various passages treats reason as comprised of one or more of the following faculties: (1) a priori reasoning; (2) demonstrative reasoning; (3) immediate intuition; and (4) probable or factual reasoning. Hume also describes reason as a faculty that simplifies principles. For additional details, see Winters, 'Hume on Reason'; and Norton, *David Hume: Common-Sense Moralist, Sceptical Metaphysician*, 96–8 n. 4.

of other previously possessed ideas. For example, it creates the idea of a centaur from ideas it possesses of the human body and the horse's body. For many philosophers the only work of the imagination is to create such imaginary or unreal items. For Hume, however, the imagination is given an additional role: it is the faculty responsible for the mind's representation of much of what is taken to be real. For example, Hume accounts for the origin of our idea of and belief in material bodies through the work of the imagination. The imagination thus plays a role in creating both what is real and what is fictional, but its ideas always come from one of two sources: the external senses or an internal awareness of the mind's activity (5.10).

Finally, the *passions*—which Hume often calls *sentiments*—are comprised of emotions, feelings, and desires. Hume contends that particular passions are caused in persons by previous impressions or ideas. For example, we fear, hope, grieve, love, and hate based on some prior experience, such as witnessing a shocking event or having a love affair. Many figures in the history of philosophy have denigrated the passions as deceptive states that control human actors, while viewing reason as an enlightening and distinctive human trait that does not threaten human freedom as the passions do.[17] In Hume's philosophy, however, passion often appropriately motivates action, while reason and understanding are in the service of passion.

Hume's philosophy expands the scope of the imagination and the passions while contracting the role assigned in other philosophies to understanding and reason. One of the hallmarks of *EHU* is Hume's thesis that the understanding and reason cannot be allowed to range beyond experience in the way some of his predecessors (the rationalists mentioned previously) had maintained. They held that reason is capable of grasping fundamental truths about the natural, mental, and moral worlds in a manner analogous to the way in which reason grasps mathematical truths. Hume thinks that this belief cannot be sustained by a proper examination of reason, understanding, and experience.

Hume argues that reason and the understanding are impotent to prove the existence of the external world, to prove the existence of God, and

---

[17] Many philosophers before Hume had disapproved of behaviour driven by passion. Plato (5th–4th c. BC), the Stoics, St Augustine (4th–5th c. AD), Spinoza, and others viewed the passions as irrational and sometimes overpowering influences needing the disciplined control of reason. The ancients sometimes depicted the passions as a kind of madness or misconception, whereas many moderns treated the passions as confused perceptions and judgements.

to prove that there are forces and powers in nature. However, reason and the understanding are not altogether impotent. The understanding enables us to develop the science of human nature, and the understanding allies with reason to make distinctions, judge of matters of fact, draw conclusions, correct biases, and help create social practices. Part of the genius of Hume's philosophy is his attribution of thought and reflection to reason and the understanding, while insisting that these faculties are less powerful than has generally been believed. Whether Hume succeeds in his arguments is, not surprisingly, highly controversial.

4. Philosophy of Mind

Hume states in Section 1 that a philosophy of mind, including the faculties previously discussed, is central to his study of human nature:

It is remarkable concerning the operations of the mind, that, though most intimately present to us, yet, whenever they become the object of reflection, they seem involved in obscurity. . . . It becomes, therefore, no inconsiderable part of science barely to know the different operations of the mind, to separate them from each other, to class them under their proper heads, and to correct all that seeming disorder, in which they lie involved. . . . [This is a] mental geography, or delineation of the distinct parts and powers of the mind . . . (1.13)

In Section 2, 'Of the Origin of Ideas', and Section 3, 'Of the Association of Ideas', Hume leaves no doubt that the category of *ideas* is central to his theory of mind. Locke and a few philosophers before Hume regarded all human thought as resting on experiences that furnish ideas. For example, a person who thinks about whether a steaming hot cup of coffee is too hot to drink employs ideas that are based on the person's experiences. The person has memories of touching heated cups, seeing the rising of steam, feeling a burned tongue, etc. Locke presented human understanding as the realm of these ideas, and Hume begins his philosophy with a similar approach.

4.1. Impressions and Ideas (Section 2.1–3)

In both *EHU* and the *Treatise* an introductory section (the 'Introduction' in the *Treatise*) is followed by a section on 'the origin of ideas'. In both works Hume relies on a basic distinction between two forms of perception (where perceptions are understood as the items of our mental world): impressions and ideas. Impressions are original perceptions—the items in experience that appear directly to the mind, such as colours, sounds, figures, and feelings. Ideas are derived from impressions and become stored resources for remembering, imagining, thinking, reflecting, and symbolizing.

Hume says that ideas *copy* impressions. For example, a stored image of something a person once observed is an idea. As copies, ideas typically do not reach the 'force and vivacity' of the original impressions. 'The most lively thought is still inferior to the dullest sensation' (2.1) even when the thought has reached the peak of its vigour, such that we can almost feel or see what we originally perceived. For example, suppose you have an impression of a sailing boat. When you later think about your experience of perceiving the sailing boat, the idea of the sailing boat is based entirely on the memory of your awareness at the time of that perceptual experience. All awareness is based on such impressions in Hume's philosophy. There are both outer perceptions, or what we usually think of as sensory experiences, and inner perceptions, which are mental experiences such as feelings of elation, depression, agitation, and anger.

Hume thought the difference between impressions and ideas so obvious that it 'requires no nice discernment or metaphysical head to mark the distinction' (2.2). However, his views are more complicated than this comment suggests. He begins Section 2 by analysing the 'less forcible and lively' character of ideas. Soon after invoking the thesis that ideas are always less lively, he challenges it: when the mind is 'disordered by disease or madness', he says, ideas can appear as lively as impressions, with 'such a pitch of vivacity, as to render these perceptions altogether undistin-guishable' (2.1). How, then, can we distinguish ideas and impressions?

Hume's answer seems to be that a diseased or mad person with vivid ideas has lost perceptual reliability. If this is his view, his criterion of *live-liness* as a way of distinguishing ideas from impressions needs supple-mentation in terms of a criterion of *reliability*. Hume seems on several occasions in *EHU* to be looking for ways of distinguishing reliable beliefs from unreliable ones. We will return to this problem in §4.3, 'Meaning and Meaninglessness'.

4.2. Simple and Complex Ideas (Section 2.4–8)

If a person lacks a form of sensation such as sight, the person can have no impressions from that sense, and therefore can have no correspond-ing ideas. For example, a congenitally blind person has no ideas of colour and a congenitally deaf person no ideas of sound. None the less, Hume did not think that every idea is acquired directly from experience. Ideas arise from dreams, inaccurate memories of events, indoctrination, and the like. Through the imagination we combine ideas into more complex ideas, which may not have corresponding impressions:

When we think of a golden mountain, we only join two consistent ideas, *gold*, and *mountain*, with which we were formerly acquainted. A virtuous horse we can conceive; because, from our own feeling, we can conceive virtue. . . . When we analyze our thoughts or ideas, however compounded or sublime, we always find, that they resolve themselves into such simple ideas as were copied from a precedent feeling or sentiment. (2.5–6)

Our imagination supplies us with many complex ideas like 'virtuous horse', 'golden mountain', and 'centaur' that are not direct copies of corresponding impressions, but that can be broken down into component simple ideas with corresponding impressions. Underlying this thesis is a distinction between memory and imagination. We remember horses, but imagine virtuous horses. In imagination we 'unite' virtue 'to the figure and shape of a horse' that memory provides.

Hume challenges his readers to produce an idea that cannot be explained within this framework, and then quickly responds to his own challenge. In a much-discussed passage he ponders a counter-example to the principle that ideas always derive from correspondent impressions. He asks us to imagine a person who has never seen a particular shade of blue but grasps other shades of blue and understands how the colour chart gradually descends from the deepest to the lightest colours. Hume asks whether it is 'possible for him, from his own imagination, to supply . . . that particular shade'. Hume acknowledges that the person can supply the shade, which indicates that simple ideas are not always derived from 'correspondent impressions'. However, he dismisses this counter-example as 'so singular' that it deserves little attention. He says it does not alter the 'general maxim' that it appears to counter (2.8).

Many philosophers believe that this counter-example does threaten basic principles in Hume's philosophy and that he dismisses it too quickly. The missing shade of blue cannot be broken down into simpler ideas, and the example seems to confront Hume's 'general maxim' with an unexplainable case. For this reason critics maintain that Hume fails to show that all ideas must derive from impressions. Is there a way to meet this criticism? Perhaps his theory of meaning can supply an answer.

4.3. Meaning and Meaninglessness (Section 2.9)

Hume presents the distinction between impressions and ideas as a *factual* part of his science of human nature. He then uses the distinction to construct a powerful *evaluative* principle about reliable ideas: ideas for which there are no corresponding impressions are mere inventions and fictions that sometimes seem to represent what is real and, when formed as propositions, seem to state what is true. However, these ideas have no corresponding reality or truth any more than there exists a golden mountain or a virtuous horse. Hume uses this line of thought to distinguish fact from fiction and truth from falsity, and it also gives him an account of language and meaning: 'When we entertain . . . any suspicion, that a philosophical term is employed without any meaning or idea (as is but too frequent), we need but enquire, *from what impression is that supposed idea derived?* And if it be impossible to assign any, this will serve to confirm our suspicion' (2.9).

Hume maintains that terms such as 'substance' have been employed in philosophy without clear meaning and that resultant controversies are burdened by these meaningless terms. The meaning of a term is the 'determinate idea, annexed to it' (2.9). To discover the source of the idea's meaning involves tracing the idea to its impression-source. If the term does not signify some idea traceable to an impression, Hume considers the term meaningless. 'Substance' is an example of a meaningless term; 'winged horse', by contrast, is not meaningless, simply imaginary.

Hume proposes that adherence to the maxim that 'we need but enquire, *from what impression is that supposed idea derived?*' will help philosophy banish undue speculation and associated jargon, especially concerning 'nature and reality' (2.9). For example, Hume discusses 'the idea of God, as meaning an infinitely intelligent, wise, and good Being' and points to the impressions that give rise to this idea (2.6). Once we understand the sources of this idea, we will be in a position to assess claims that persons make about God. In tracing an idea's origins and meaning we take the first step towards assessing the truth or falsity of propositions that employ the idea. If a term has no 'meaning or idea', this fact will become clear.

Some philosophers after Hume developed this general strategy as an empiricist principle of meaning: a term has a meaning (or is meaningful) only if it refers to something that can be experienced or refers to ideas that can be analysed into items that can be experienced; whether or not something has been experienced, it can be. This principle has the potential to help Hume overcome the problem of the missing shade of blue discussed earlier. The term 'blue$_x$' (designating the missing shade) is meaningful as long as the shade to which it refers can be experienced, even if a person has never actually had an impression of it. 'Blue$_x$' is meaningful because that to which it refers can be experienced by perceivers who possess reliable sensory capacity.

Whether Hume accepted this application of his principle is unknown; but if he did, it might explain why he did not regard the counter-example of the missing shade of blue as a serious threat to his general account of the origin of ideas and the meaning of terms. Perhaps he thought the imagination could create the idea of the missing shade in a context of colour-shading in which it was known that the created idea could be corroborated in experience by finding an actual example of the missing shade.

4.4. The Association of Ideas and Principles of Connection (Section 3.1–18)

Hume maintains in Section 3 that certain ideas are naturally combined in the mind. The ideas are related by 'principles of connexion among ideas' that operate without any intention to make the connections. This section provides another example of the theory that the mind is to be understood naturalistically.

Hume argues that the mind has 'natural propensities' to connect ideas: 'Different thoughts or ideas of the mind . . . introduce each other with a certain degree of method and regularity. . . . I do not find, that any philosopher has attempted to enumerate or class all the principles of association' (3.2). Hume classifies these principles as *resemblance, contiguity,* and *causation*. His thesis is that the mind moves naturally from one idea (or impression) to another idea that resembles it, is contiguous to it, or is its cause or effect. For example, why do I think of my parents when I look at a picture of them? Because there is a resemblance between them and the picture. Why do I think of a school when I think of a particular playground? Because the one is geographically contiguous with the other. Why do I think of pain when I think of my recent wound? Because wounds cause pain.

Before Hume, Locke had searched for some 'natural Correspondence and Connexion' between ideas.[18] Hume's innovation was to seek *univer-*

---

[18] Locke, *Essay* 2.33.5.

sal principles that explain how otherwise loose and disconnected ideas are associated in a regular manner. He assigns the imagination a central role. The imagination has the capacity to freely reorder and recombine ideas, but it also has a very different capacity to routinely associate some ideas with others. He takes this capacity of mechanical association so seriously that in the last line of his *Abstract* of the *Treatise* he refers to the principles of association as 'the cement of the universe', meaning that, were it not for these principles, all ideas in our minds would be unassociated and independent.

In the remaining paragraphs of Section 3 (3.4–18), Hume applies these ideas about association and connection to the connectedness and unity found in literary and historical works. He maintains that the writer of these compositions has a definite plan or object. The events or actions that the writer relates are connected in the imagination; and the work has a 'certain unity' created by a connecting principle (3.6, 10). The connecting principle among the various events forming the subject differs in accordance with the different designs of the writer. Some writers use the connecting principle of *resemblance*. For example, the events depicted might resemble each other in that they are all miracles. Writers, especially annalists and historians, also employ the connecting principle of *contiguity in time and place* to connect the depicted events (3.7–8). For example, historians generally structure their accounts so that events immediately follow one another in time, and often in close geographical proximity. Too much distance in either time or place destroys the connection between events. Finally, Hume argues that the most common type of connection among the different events is *causation*: writers trace the causes and effects in a chain of events, each major link of which the writer endeavours to capture in the narration (3.9).

The connecting principles in historical and literary compositions therefore turn out to be the same as the connecting principles in the mind: 'the three connecting principles of all ideas are the relations of *Resemblance, Contiguity,* and *Causation*' (3.18).

5. Epistemology

Philosophers have long examined what we know and the ways we think and reason. Epistemology is the branch of philosophy concerned with the basis and limits of knowledge, the justification of claims to knowledge, the assessment of scepticism about knowledge, and the proper roles of experience and reason. Hume explores these topics throughout *EHU*. He attempts to show that all beliefs about the world derive from experience and are probable rather than certain.

Hume was at times careful and at times loose in his use of the term 'knowledge'. In his early writings, especially the *Treatise*, he generally followed philosophers like Descartes in confining the word 'knowledge' to statements that are certain and unrevisable. He applied the term 'probable' to factual statements or beliefs that could be amended or corrected and that are not certain. However, by the time he wrote *EHU*, Hume was using the term 'knowledge' in a more ordinary sense, which allows that something can be known even though it is not known with certainty. Some propositions, like 'The sun will rise tomorrow', are known with a strong probability or near certainty. Whether called knowledge or probability, Hume insists several times that the wise person proportions belief to the evidence. Belief rooted in good evidence will 'reasonably beget a pretty strong degree of assurance' (10.4). This evidence, and belief properly proportional to it, is the goal of science and all factual investigation.

Hume's concern in *EHU* is less with the meaning of 'knowledge' and more with two related topics: (1) a distinction between intuitively or demonstratively certain 'relations of ideas' and non-demonstrable but probable 'matters of fact'; (2) inferences from what has been observed to what has not yet been observed. The second topic dominates his discussion.

5.1. Relations of Ideas and Matters of Fact (Section 4.1–2)

Hume introduces the distinction between relations of ideas and matters of fact at the beginning of Section 4:

All the objects of human reason or enquiry may naturally be divided into two kinds, to wit, *Relations of Ideas* and *Matters of Fact*. Of the first kind are the sciences of Geometry, Algebra, and Arithmetic; and in short, every affirmation, which is either intuitively or demonstratively certain. . . . Propositions of this kind are discoverable by the mere operation of thought, without dependence on what is any where existent in the universe. . . .

Matters of fact . . . are not ascertained in the same manner . . . *That the sun will not rise to-morrow* is no less intelligible a proposition, and implies no more contradiction, than the affirmation, *that it will rise*. We should in vain, therefore, attempt to demonstrate its falsehood. (4.1–2)

Hume's examples of these two types of 'objects of human reason or enquiry' take the form of propositions about facts and propositions about relations of ideas. He offers both logical and epistemological criteria of the differences between these propositions.

A LOGICAL CRITERION

As the above quotation indicates, Hume believes that the negation (denial) of a statement of relation of ideas is a contradiction, whereas the negation of a statement of fact is not a contradiction. For example, the negation of 'A triangle has three sides' (that is, 'A triangle does not have three sides') is a contradiction. Hume claims that this contradiction logically cannot occur in the case of matters of fact. For example, the negation of 'This building has three sides' (that is, 'This building does not have three sides') is not a contradiction. It may be false to say 'This building does not have three sides', but it is not contradictory.

EPISTEMOLOGICAL CRITERIA

An epistemological criterion is stated in terms of how we come to know or believe statements. Hume says that statements of the relations of ideas are 'either intuitively or demonstratively certain'. By 'certain' Hume does not mean merely that we have no doubt about a proposition; we often do not doubt mistaken statements that we should doubt, and this fact does not render them certain. He means that a statement is certain when we are justified 'by the mere operation of thought' in not doubting its truth. We know these statements without reference to what exists in the world; these statements are therefore known a priori. For example, the statement 'A triangle has three sides' is known to be true merely by grasping the meaning of the terms involved.

Statements about matters of fact are not known by the mere operation of thought and are neither intuitively nor demonstratively certain. The truth or falsity of these statements depends on the underlying evidence, which is gained by experience. A statement such as 'The sun will rise tomorrow' is not true merely by the meanings of words or by a priori relations. We do not and cannot have the same grounds for assurance that the sun will rise tomorrow as we have for the truth of a proposition in mathematics. It is *probable* that the sun will rise tomorrow, not *certain*.

Many epistemologists before Hume, notably Descartes, had searched for a foundation of certainty for their philosophical system. Sceptics, by contrast, typically doubt that such certainties can be found. Hume accepts a piece of each theory by acknowledging certainty in statements of relations of ideas while insisting that matters of fact are at best merely probable. He thought that many philosophers before him had made the mistake of claiming certainty, and therefore knowledge, when they could claim only some level of probability. This position makes him a sceptic about claims of certainty in matters of fact as well as a sceptic about philosophical systems that rest on such claims of certainty.

5.2. Matter-of-Fact Inference as Causal Inference (Section 4.3–5)

Once he has introduced the distinction just discussed, Hume addresses only matters of fact in the remainder of Section 4. He emphasizes causal reasoning or causal inference, now often called inductive inference. His transition sentence shows the connection between the distinction and the new topic: 'It may, therefore, be a subject worthy of curiosity, to enquire what is the nature of that evidence, which assures us of any real existence and matter of fact, beyond the present testimony of our senses, or the records of our memory' (4.3). Hume argues in Section 4 that no rational principle or argument provides a sure foundation for the inferences we make from past or present evidence to future existence.

Much of what we know about the world is based on our senses and our memory. For example, when reading books we experience impressions of words, colours, shapes, etc. We identify these impressions through ideas stored in memory. Beyond sensation and memory we have many ideas and beliefs for which we have no direct perceptual confirmation. For example, we believe that the sun will rise tomorrow, that heavy objects will always fall to the ground when dropped, and that all stars will be in motion. On what are these beliefs based, Hume asks, since they cannot be confirmed through past or present perceptions and memory?

He gives an initial answer near the beginning of Section 4: 'All reasonings concerning matter of fact seem to be founded on the relation of *Cause* and *Effect*. By means of that relation alone we can go beyond the evidence of our memory and senses' (4.4). Hume is claiming that whenever we assert something about events in the world that exceeds the boundaries of memory and present perception, we are reasoning from causes to effects or from effects to causes. For example, asserting that sunlight and rain will bring a good summer crop requires an inference from past experience of sunlight and rain (as causal conditions) to a future circumstance of crops that we have not yet experienced. Hume thinks that all inferences about matters of fact are ultimately causal inferences.

5.3. Causal Inference Based on Experience, not on Reason (Section 4.6–13)

Hume next offers an analysis of the basis of belief in cause–effect relations and of how this belief leads to causal inferences:

the knowledge of this relation is not, in any instance, attained by reasonings *a priori*; but arises entirely from experience, when we find, that any particular objects are constantly conjoined with each other. Let an object be presented to a man of ever so strong natural reason and abilities; if that object be entirely new to him, he will not be able, by the most accurate examination of its sensible qualities, to discover any of its causes or effects. ADAM, though his rational faculties be supposed, at the very first, entirely perfect, could not have inferred from the fluidity and transparency of water, that it would suffocate him, or from the light and warmth of fire, that it would consume him. (4.6)

Adam could know nothing about the effects of water merely by feeling it or seeing it—or by using capacities of pure reason to think about it. Nor can we. We learn about the many effects of water by experiencing those effects. No one could know without experience that water will clean dirty clothes, that waves will erode seashores, or that hot springs under the earth can erupt and shoot water in the air. These beliefs are not based on relations of ideas and are not demonstrable. However, the more vividly and frequently we experience a connection between two types of event, the more confidently we expect the first event to be followed by the second.

Hume's opposition to rationalist philosophies, as sketched previously, is evident in this argument. He is concerned to show that human capacities for obtaining knowledge and probable belief are more limited than his rationalist predecessors had maintained. Several beliefs are constitutive of the rationalist model that Hume attacks. Though the rationalists did not articulate their beliefs about causation in careful and detailed arguments, the following are the pivotal rationalist beliefs that Hume rejects:

1. Causes contain their effects.
2. Causes entail their effects, just as premisses entail conclusions.

3. Causes entail their effects because there is a necessary connection between them.

To illustrate the first belief, consider Descartes's question 'how could the cause give [reality] to the effect unless it *possessed* it?'[19] Descartes here implies that causes already contain their effects, but Hume regards effect-events as different from anything actually contained in the cause-events. For example, if a person drops a drinking-glass on the floor, the effect of shattered glass does not seem to have been contained in the causal conditions of this outcome (a shaky hand, a hard floor, the nature of brittle glass, etc.).

To illustrate the second belief, consider the causal judgement 'If a rattlesnake injects venom into a person, the person will quickly feel ill'. We believe this general law, and experience supports our belief, but the conclusion that a person will feel ill does not follow logically or rationally. The premiss 'a rattlesnake injects venom into a person' does not (merely by logic) entail 'the person will quickly feel ill'. This conclusion only 'follows' after experience with rattlesnake bites.

By contrast, consider this line of reasoning:

If a figure is a triangle, then the figure has three sides.
This figure is a triangle.
Therefore, this figure has three sides.

This argument has one intuitively certain premiss and one indisputable premiss, and the conclusion follows logically. The premisses entail the conclusion. Hume claims that causal reasoning is not like this model of demonstrative reasoning, even if their structures are superficially similar. Effects are not entailed by causes, and causal relations are known only by experience.

We need not address the third rationalist belief about necessary connection just yet. It plays a central role in Hume's general treatment of causation, which is discussed below. Enough has been said to indicate that Hume thinks that no *logically* necessary connection exists between causes and their effects.

5.4. The Problem of Induction (Section 4.14–23)

Once Hume has established that all factual inferences rest on cause–effect relations, he considers whether these inferences have a solid foundation.

---

[19] Descartes, *Meditations* 3; italics added.

The major question in Section 4, Part 2 is, *What is the foundation of all conclusions from experience?* This problem is now commonly referred to as the 'problem of induction'.[20] Hume's analysis is a development of his thesis that matters of fact are neither intuitively certain nor demonstrable. He argues that inductive reasoning (that is, causal or factual inference) is not a product of reason and therefore cannot provide demonstrations. Section 4, Part 2 is perhaps the most important portion of *EHU*, and we will trace the line of argument in some detail.

THE PROBLEM OUTLINED

How does experience of past events warrant or provide a foundation for beliefs about similar future events? Hume notes that we commonly rely on the principle that future events will resemble past events of the same type. For example, if blocks of ice always chip and crack under forceful thrusts with an ice pick, we assume that this causal fact will not change in the future. We assume that we have well-founded, reliable information about the past and that nature will not change its patterns. But what supports these beliefs?

To appreciate Hume's problem, consider a standard form of inductive inference: From (1) 'All examined cases of X have been followed by Y', we sometimes conclude (when numerous cases have been examined) that (2) 'All Xs are followed by Ys'. Two examples are: from (1a) 'All examined deep surgical incisions have been followed by scars', we conclude that (2a) 'All deep surgical incisions are followed by scars'; and from (1b) 'All examined swans have been white', we conclude that (2b) 'All swans are white'. A gap exists between (1) and (2) in each case. Given that we are reasoning solely from observed cases, how do we reliably draw conclusions concerning the next case or all cases? In Hume's own example of the nourishment we gain from bread, on what basis does it follow that the next piece of bread we eat will nourish us?

We sometimes reach mistaken conclusions when we reason in this inductive manner. For example, we find a black swan or we eat contaminated bread. Hume therefore inquires about the foundational premiss or 'medium' that supports inductive inferences. He mentions several promising propositions that at first seem capable of serving as a suitable premiss or medium:

---

[20] Instead of 'induction' Hume uses expressions such as 'experimental conclusions' and the 'long course of uniform experiments' (see 4.19–21).

1. 'Similar causes have similar effects'.
2. 'Nature is uniform'.
3. 'The future will resemble the past'.
4. 'The future will be conformable to the past'.

If any one of these propositions could be shown to be correct, induction would be warranted, and we would know the basis of sound causal inference. Any proof of these propositions, Hume argues, must rely either on *demonstrative* arguments (deduction from relations of ideas using the faculty of reason) or on *probable* arguments (induction from matters of fact using the faculty of understanding). Can either do the work?

NO CONNECTING PROPOSITION IS PROVABLE DEMONSTRATIVELY

The needed argument cannot be demonstrative, Hume argues, because it is possible that nature will change or that our beliefs are incorrect, and what is possible cannot be demonstrated to be false. Hume denies that a medium or connecting proposition can be definitively established by any form of demonstrative argument: 'That there are no demonstrative arguments in the case seems evident; since it implies no contradiction that the course of nature may change' (4.18).

NO CONNECTING PROPOSITION IS PROVABLE INDUCTIVELY

The argument cannot be probable without begging the question. That is, a probable argument would reach its conclusion by assuming what is at issue and in need of proof. Such reasoning presupposes the principle that nature is uniform, a principle itself derived from probable reasoning.

[A]ll our experimental conclusions proceed upon the supposition, that the future will be conformable to the past. To endeavour, therefore, the proof of this last supposition by probable arguments, or arguments regarding existence, must be evidently going in a circle, and taking that for granted, which is the very point in question. (4.19) . . . Where is the medium? . . . the inference is not intuitive; neither is it demonstrative . . . To say it is experimental, is begging the question. (4.21)

In sum, Hume presents us with a dilemma: because all reasoning is either inductive or demonstrative, any reasoning in support of induction must follow one of these two models. A priori or demonstrative reasoning fails because a denial of the four connecting propositions (e.g. 'Nature is uniform') fails to produce a contradiction; and induction or causal inference (matter-of-fact reasoning) fails because the conclusion that 'Nature is uniform' is itself reached by inductive inference.

CONCLUSION

Many interpreters of Hume have maintained that his *psychological* claims about reason, the understanding, and the imagination in Section 4 are part of a deeper *epistemological* thesis that causal inferences from experience are not rational and cannot be justified. This interpretative question about the nature of Hume's scepticism about induction cannot be explored here. Fortunately, all that needs to be remarked for our purposes is that Hume is offering some kind of sceptical critique of inductive inference and is maintaining that reason does not underlie or support inductive inference. Having reached this conclusion, he is poised to explain how a mental faculty other than reason leads us to suppose that the future will resemble the past. This subject is addressed in Part 1 of Section 5.

5.5. Sceptical Solution of Sceptical Doubts (Section 5.1–8)

Hume assigns to Section 5 the intriguing title 'Sceptical Solution of these Doubts' (the doubts raised in Section 4, entitled 'Sceptical Doubts concerning the Operations of the Understanding'). Because the mind lacks the support of reason in inductive inference, it must be driven by another 'principle of equal weight and authority' in human nature (5.2). The principle Hume identifies is the psychological mechanism of custom or habit. Hume's 'sceptical solution' to his earlier 'sceptical doubts' about induction is that whenever experience has conditioned us to expect a type of outcome, the propensity we have developed to expect the outcome is 'the effect of *Custom*', not reason (5.5).

Hume does not claim in Section 5 that he can justify a medium (connecting proposition) or provide a demonstration of inductive inference. He offers only a psychological explanation of the mechanisms of inductive inference and of our confidence in it. Custom, he says, is a principle of human nature more instinctual than rational. Customary associations are based on repeated experience of cause–effect relations. When a person experiences repeated cases of events of type X (for example, the blade of the guillotine falling on a person's neck) followed by events of type Y (for example, death), the perceiver comes to expect that whenever an instance of X occurs, an instance of Y will occur. This expectation is the psychological basis of all forms of inductive inference.

Hume does not conclude that inductive inference is worthless or that we should avoid use of inductive inference because it rests merely on custom. He maintains that such inference is a normal, indeed vital, function of the mind. Without the influence of custom, which leads us to expect that future events will be similar to past events, we could not engage in science or form factual beliefs. Whether Hume means this line of argument to constitute a practical justification of induction is unclear, but he is serious in his claim that induction is our best guide in life's affairs (as it is for non-human animals—see this Introduction, §5.8).

5.6. Belief (Section 5.9–20)

We have discussed Hume's argument that 'All belief of matter of fact or real existence' is derived from causal inferences. In Part 2 of Section 5 he undertakes to discuss the nature of belief itself, which, he says, is a matter of an idea being felt in a certain way: 'the difference between *fiction* and *belief* lies in some sentiment or feeling, which is annexed to the latter, not to the former, and which depends not on the will' (5.11). Hume characterizes this sentiment or feeling as follows: 'belief is nothing but a more vivid, lively, forcible, firm, steady conception of an object, than what the imagination alone is ever able to attain. This variety of terms, which may seem so unphilosophical, is intended only to express that act of the mind, which renders realities, or what is taken for such, more present to us than fictions' (5.12).

As an example of Hume's point, consider what happens when reading a fine history of an actual war (the Second World War, say), by contrast to a fictional recounting of a war. Reading the history leads to a very different feeling about the events portrayed than does the reading of a fictional narrative of imagined events in a war (*Star Wars*, say). Belief consists in an idea accompanied by this feeling about the reality of the events, a feeling which is noticeably different from the feelings that accompany purely imaginary or fictional creations.

Hume's theses about the 'peculiar sentiment' involved in belief and the fact that it 'depends not on the will' are more significant than first appearances might suggest. To believe a proposition is to judge it to be true. But on what basis is this judgement made? Is belief purely a mental feeling of a person, or is some proposition attached to the mental state? Can we will to believe something? Is a belief determined in the mind by rational or by non-rational factors?

These are profoundly important philosophical questions, and Hume offers at least brief answers. In describing belief as the having of an idea accompanied by a non-rational sentiment, Hume is distancing his views from philosophers such as Descartes who claim that sound beliefs come from sound reasoning and that assent can be freely imparted or withheld. Hume thinks that once we see the psychological mechanisms that lead us to beliefs, we will be impressed with the fact that reason has no determinative role to play. Beliefs, then, are mental states controlled by non-rational factors. We can control the evidence on which beliefs are formed, but not the formation of belief itself.

Hume's argument about belief in Section 5 again derives from his project of a naturalistic explanation of the mind. He is explaining the nature of belief and how persons come to form beliefs; he is not examining whether these beliefs are justified. Eventually, however, he will argue that some of our basic beliefs are based on fictions of the imagination. For example, our belief that colours are in natural objects, rather than in our own mind, is based on a powerful fiction. Hume does not mean that persons who have these beliefs are aware that their beliefs are founded on fictions. He means only that we can have false beliefs, unjustified beliefs, and the like. Even if false or unjustified, they are beliefs none the less. The goal of Hume's philosophy is often not to justify one set of beliefs in preference to another, but to explain why and how the beliefs are formed through mechanisms of the mind.

5.7. Probability and Probable Belief (Section 6)

We have seen that Hume regards demonstration and induction as two forms of 'reasoning'—indeed, the only two forms. No demonstrative certainty ever attaches to inductive or probabilistic thinking, but high probabilities do sometimes amount to 'proofs'.[21] Probability judgements are guided by factual evidence of frequencies of occurrence and express a person's level of confidence that a specific outcome will occur.

Various philosophers before Hume associated probabilistic thinking with reasonableness in the sense that reasonable persons think in terms of probabilities when under conditions of uncertainty. Although he does

---

[21] For the distinction between proof and probability, see n. 10 in the text and the annotations on that note. See also Hume's use of the contrast between proofs and probabilities in his treatment of miracles in Section 10.

not employ the language of 'reasonableness', Hume does maintain that custom, which is regulated by probabilities, is justifiably regarded as 'the great guide of human life' (5.6). He also defends the view of Cicero and Locke that the probable is credible, and, when used properly, is generally reliable.

Locke and Hume thought of the mind as almost mechanically clocking the frequencies of events and forming corresponding degrees of belief in their recurrence. As the probability of an event, such as rain falling from dark clouds, increases, 'our belief or expectation of the event [will be] more steady and secure' (6.2). There appears 'that reliance or security, which constitutes the nature of belief and opinion' (6.3). As the probability decreases, so does confidence in an event's occurrence. We can assign some probability to effects that occur in a lower range of frequency even when they are not actually expected. Hume offers examples from games involving throws of dice to illustrate this point. He concludes that there are many degrees of probability and, correspondingly, many degrees of confidence that certain outcomes will in fact occur.

5.8. *Reason and Belief in Animals (Section 9)*

In Section 9 Hume's accounts of causal inference, probabilistic reasoning, and belief are extended to the domain of non-human animals. Many philosophers have postulated that non-human animals do not reason and that the possession of reason distinguishes humans from animals. Descartes even argued that animals have no minds; they are machines that lack even sensation and passion. Hume, by contrast, finds that we share numerous biological and mental capacities with other animals, including, most noticeably, the capacity of causal reasoning. He acknowledges that humans are far superior to other animals in capacities of reasoning, but he sets out to show fundamental similarities in experience, memory, and inference:

Animals, as well as men, learn many things from experience, and infer, that the same events will always follow from the same causes. . . . The ignorance and inexperience of the young are here plainly distinguishable from the cunning and sagacity of the old. . . . In all these cases . . . the animal infers some fact beyond what immediately strikes his senses; and this inference is altogether founded on past experience. (9.4)

Hume maintains that non-human animals are analogous to humans in their ability to experience pain and fear, their patterns of learning and inferring, and their emotional and cognitive abilities. Like Darwin a century later, Hume claims that these differences are generally of *degree* rather than *kind*. None the less, humans do seem unique in their capacities of morality, criticism, politics, law, religion, and the like, and Hume occasionally hints that these capacities render humans different in kind, not merely different in degree. He thinks that animals lack the capacities to participate in the rich array of cultural activities found in human communities, and he never attributes the high-level capacity of demonstrative reasoning to animals. Accordingly, Hume confines his attention to the weaker thesis that many animals love, hate, enjoy, suffer, and the like, just as they make causal inferences. He also maintains that the passions of animals are directed at many of the same objects at which human passions are directed. For example, animals learn, as do we, that certain objects are to be feared, and they then direct their fear at those objects.

For many philosophers today language and self-consciousness are more critical factors than reasoning in differentiating humans from non-human animals. Some of these philosophers take language to be central to all forms of thought and self-consciousness to be a necessary condition of autonomy or personhood. Hume made no clear pronouncement on these issues. His legacy is an outspoken defence of causal reasoning and belief-formation in animals. Perhaps his most significant contribution was to move as far as anyone before him to a naturalistic explanation of human and non-human minds, an explanation that used similar categories for the human and the non-human.

Prior to Hume most philosophers had conceived of human beings as fashioned in the image of God—or, at least, as occupying a status above non-human animals in the hierarchy of nature. Humans alone were regarded as using reason to form knowledge and to determine appropriate actions. Hume attempted to undermine this conception by arguing that humans are more closely aligned with the animal kingdom than the kingdom of God. Humans are as much a part of the natural realm as are the other animals.

6. Metaphysics

In addition to causal inference, Hume is interested in causation itself. In Sections 7 and 8 he explores this topic, focusing in particular on the 'necessary connection' (the power, force, or necessity) that joins a cause to its effect. He calls on his arguments about belief, knowledge, and inference to address two metaphysical issues, one about causal necessity and the other about liberty and necessity. His science of human nature is here extended to mental causation, the causation of human action, and freedom of the will.

6.1. Causal Necessity (Section 7)

In Section 7 Hume considers whether there is a necessary connection between cause and effect, a relation he takes to be identical to the cause's power to produce an effect. His arguments represent a profound shift of direction in the history of philosophy. Many of Hume's predecessors had supposed that the causal relation is properly analysed in terms of a particular cause's inherent power, efficacy, or agency—or, as some philosophers had held, in terms of God's power and agency. In contrast, Hume thinks that we have no means of detecting the power, efficacy, or agency of causes or of God.

EXPERIENCE ESSENTIAL FOR THE DETECTION OF CAUSES

Hume believes that nothing that we can observe in an object or event prior to experience of it provides a reason to expect any sort of effect to follow from it. Here is a contemporary example of his point: workers in chemical manufacturing plants sometimes work with compounds about whose health effects in humans little information is available. Call one of these compounds C_{12}. What could one conclude about the health effects of C_{12} merely by seeing, tasting, or touching the compound? Nothing. Imagine that several workers in the chemical plant who work with this compound begin to report that they are suffering from headaches, dizziness, memory lapses, and nausea. Research must be conducted to determine whether these effects are caused by exposure to the chemical compound. Investigators might carefully study people who have repeatedly become dizzy after working with the compound, and they would study what happens when animals breathe the compound in concentrated doses. By gathering this information about C_{12}, a good possibility exists of establishing a causal connection. But nothing can be determined about the effects that C_{12} produces in the human system until we have this kind of experience with the compound. The same conclusion holds for tobacco and forms of radiation that we now know to be associated with adverse health effects.

OUR INABILITY TO DETECT NECESSARY CONNECTION IN EXPERIENCE

We can discover *causes* by experience, but can we discover *necessary connections* by experience? Among Hume's favourite examples of the problem of finding necessary connections is the impact between two colliding billiard balls. As one ball rolls towards another, we see motion, then contact, hear a distinctive smack, and feel certain that the second ball will speed away from the first ball. Do we, in addition, observe any power or necessary connection between the two balls? Hume thinks not, and he believes that his point applies to all cases of causation. Wherever he turns to find an example of necessary connection in nature, none emerges: 'We only find, that the one [event] does actually, in fact, follow the other. The impulse of one billiard-ball is attended with motion in the second. This is the whole that appears to the *outward* senses' (7.6).

THE NATURE OF NECESSARY CONNECTION

These conclusions rely in part on Hume's claims in Section 2 about impressions and the meanings of words. The meaning of a term is the idea 'annexed to it' (2.9). He says in Section 7 that he wants to 'fix, if possible, the precise *meaning*' of the terms *necessary connection, power,* and the like in order to remove some part of the obscurity that has surrounded philosophies that employ these notions (7.3). Hume is convinced that we do have an idea of necessary connection and that its origin is somewhere in impressions. He therefore pursues the following philosophical project: 'let us examine its impression . . . let us search for it in all the sources, from which it may possibly be derived' (7.5). The pursuit of this impression takes up the bulk of Section 7 (all of Part 1 and a significant portion of Part 2).

Hume presumes that the idea of causal necessity is linked to the belief that, given a particular set of conditions, only one outcome can be expected in the circumstances. If we thought that two or more mutually exclusive outcomes could occur in a particular circumstance, we would not use the language of 'cause' and 'necessary'. Rather, we would say that an outcome is possible or probable—in the sense of 'probable' discussed previously. Saying that two objects or events are necessarily connected is our way of proclaiming the impossibility, given nature's uniformity, that one type of object or event will not be succeeded by another type of object or event.

But is this *uniformity* in nature all there is to *necessity* in nature? Hume's answer, as we will now see, is that necessary connection is more than uniformity and that it has a source very different from the one most of us have presumed.

THE NATURE OF CAUSATION

To reach this conclusion, Hume starts by identifying some observable features in the relation between cause and effect: the effect succeeds the cause and there is a constant or repeated relationship of succession between that type of cause and that type of effect. He argues that necessary connection is not an empirical relation like these relations. Necessary connection is not found in the events themselves, but found in the mind's inference from the cause to the effect. We are aware of necessary connection in inward, not outward, perception. The feeling of the mind's movement in the act of causal inference *is* the impression of necessary connection.

This causal inference can occur only after we have experienced objects or events a sufficient number of times to establish the customary association emphasized in Section 5. Repetition of conjoined events creates and reinforces this association. For example, when we see an instance of a type of event with which we are already familiar (a pebble being dropped in a pond, say), we immediately expect another event (a circular rippling effect). An event of one type leads a person to infer that an event of another type will occur because the person has been mentally conditioned to expect this outcome. The feeling of the transition in the mind is the impression of necessary connection, and the idea of necessary connection is a copy of this impression. The impression and idea are all we know about necessary connection.

At one point in his search for the meaning of 'necessary connection' Hume considers the possibility that this idea might have no impression-source at all and therefore might be meaningless (7.26). However, after raising this possibility, he quickly dispels its overly sceptical implications: 'When we say, therefore, that one object is connected with another, we mean only, that they have acquired a connexion in our thought, and give rise to [causal] inference' (7.28). Hume calls this conclusion 'extraordinary', but insists that it can be confirmed by any careful observer.[22]

---

[22] Hume does not suggest that we make a mistake in using the language of 'necessary connection'. A mistake occurs only if a person erroneously believes that necessity is in the events. Necessity appears to be in events only because we mentally project it outward onto the events: 'as we *feel* a customary connexion between the ideas, we transfer that feeling to the objects; as nothing is more usual than to apply to external bodies every internal sensation, which they occasion' (*EHU* n. 17).

TWO DEFINITIONS OF 'CAUSE'

Once he has specified the idea of necessary connection (his primary goal in Section 7), Hume presents one of the most widely discussed parts of his account of causation. He offers two definitions of 'cause', one of which emphasizes constant conjunction and the other of which emphasizes a conveyance or transfer of thought (7.29):

[Df1] we may define a cause to be *an object, followed by another, and where all the objects, similar to the first, are followed by objects similar to the second.*[23]

[Df2] another definition of *cause* [is] . . . *an object followed by another, and whose appearance always conveys the thought to that other.*

These two definitions of 'cause' raise interpretative problems. Some of Hume's expositors maintain that he holds a 'regularity theory' of causation grounded exclusively in the first definition. Others maintain that he holds a modified 'necessity theory' of causation based on the second definition. Still others hold that the two distinct definitions are both foundational in his system. Although this debate cannot be pursued here, it is possible that his first definition is more suitable as a definition of causes as experienced by the 'outward senses', whereas his second definition is more suitable as a definition of causes as we experience them in outward and inward perception. Hume's interest in both topics may explain why he presents two definitions rather than one.

The two definitions may also illuminate another philosophically important aspect of Hume's theory. Many sequences of events that are constantly conjoined in experience are not instances of causation. For example, the chimes in a college tower may always be activated immediately after a particular student's wristwatch strikes the hour, yet there is no causal connection between the two events. For a connection to be causal, there must not only be evidence of constant conjunction, but

---

[23] Following this first definition Hume immediately adds: 'Or in other words, *where, if the first object had not been, the second never had existed.*' This gloss on the first definition of 'cause' does not seem equivalent to the definition itself—a textual unclarity that has spawned conflicting scholarly commentary. For further detail, see ann. 7.29.

It is surprising that, after devoting an entire section to the meaning of 'necessary connection', Hume makes no explicit mention of it in these two definitions. This omission is puzzling in light of Hume's insistence at 8.25 that a definition of 'cause' must include necessary connection as a 'part of the definition'—a point that he also propounds in *THN* 2.3.1.18 (cf. 2.3.1.4 and *Abstract* 32). The omission of this notion in his formal definitions can perhaps be explained by Hume's inclusion of '*conveys the thought*' in his second definition. The comparable definition in *THN* 1.3.14.35 mentions a mental determination.

evidence sufficient to effect the belief that the two types of event will always be conjoined. Hume's first definition states the factual basis for belief that a regularity in nature may be causal, but says nothing about causal belief itself. The second definition could be taken as stating the psychological basis (the mental conditions of causal inference) necessary for belief that any observed sequence is a causal sequence.

In the end Hume may have thought that he did not need to favour one definition over the other, because his larger project in *EHU* is a naturalistic account of the human mind. The metaphysical task of saying what causes really are may have been less central than the project of constructing a theory of the mind and causal inference. Hume's account of human liberty will help us test this hypothesis.

6.2. Liberty and Necessity: The Freewill Problem (Section 8)

In Section 8, entitled 'Liberty and Necessity', Hume examines human choice and action in a manner consistent with his treatment of natural events in previous sections. Much in this section is an application of the theory of necessary connection to human actions. Although human choices and actions often seem irregular and unpredictable, Hume supposes that the world is everywhere law-governed and predictable. Just as there is no necessary connection in or between events, there is no necessary connection in or between human events such as motives and actions. There is, however, a constant conjunction between motives and actions, and in this sense motives cause actions.

This view has sometimes been called determinism—that is, the position that all events, including human actions, are determined by prior causes. Every event is related to a prior event in such a way that it would violate a law of nature for the prior event to occur and the subsequent event not to occur. The thesis that every event is caused suggests that no choices or actions are free in the sense that they could have been other than they were, a conclusion that challenges the belief that persons may be praised or blamed for what they do. The 'long disputed' (8.2) problem of 'necessity and liberty' is thus really two problems, one metaphysical and the other ethical. The metaphysical problem is whether human actions are causally determined by prior conditions. The ethical problem concerns the implications of determinism for blame and excuse, systems of punishment, and other features of the moral life.

Philosophers who discuss whether we act freely have generally responded in one of three ways:

1. Not everything is determined, and therefore freedom is possible.
2. Everything is determined, and therefore freedom is impossible.
3. Everything is determined, and free will is possible.

Hume defends a version of the third position, which is often called 'compatibilism' and which Hume calls a 'reconciling project' (8.23). He insists that determinism is a correct theory and that an adequate theory of freedom actually requires determinism. Hobbes, Locke, and Leibniz defended forms of compatibilism prior to Hume, and in this respect Hume's account is not novel. None the less, his account is innovative and has often been praised as the most persuasive compatibilism of the seventeenth and eighteenth centuries.

Hume is addressing the conceptual, metaphysical, and ethical problems that underlie this classical issue, and he also provides a psychological account of how the mind functions in making ascriptions of moral praise and blame. These strands are intertwined in his analysis, but we will distinguish them here.

CONCEPTUAL PROBLEMS

Hume begins Section 8 with the need for 'exact definitions' of key terms in order to eliminate 'ambiguous expressions'. He defines 'liberty' and 'necessity' in a way that allows for a person's being both free and determined: 'Liberty' is '*a power of acting or not acting, according to the determinations of the will*' (8.23) in circumstances in which an actor is not constrained to choose one way or another. 'Necessity' is causal necessity, and Hume again insists that 'Beyond the constant *conjunction* of similar objects, and the consequent *inference* from one to the other, we have no notion of any necessity, or connexion' (8.5; cf. 8.21).[24] In response to the question 'Are actions free or determined?', Hume's definitions position him to maintain that actions are free when a person wills them in the absence of constraining conditions that make him or her do other than

---

[24] Hume later makes explicit use of the two definitions of 'cause' delineated in Section 7. He cites them to distinguish two definitions of 'necessity' (8.27): 'Necessity may be defined two ways, conformably to the two definitions of *cause*, of which it makes an essential part. It consists either in the constant conjunction of like objects, or in the inference of the understanding from one object to another. Now necessity, in both these senses, (which, indeed, are, at bottom, the same . . .)'. Many commentators have noted that these two senses are not at bottom the same. However, Hume's reasons for giving two definitions are understandable. His first definition describes only the external impression-sources (impressions of constant conjunction), whereas the second definition cites both the external and the internal impression-sources. From this perspective, there are two definitions and two meanings of both 'cause' and 'necessity'.

what he or she wills to do. Actions are determined—that is, necessitated—in all cases, because every effect, including volitions and actions, has a cause.

Some critics of Hume's theory maintain that his definition of 'liberty' is inadequate. They think that a person does not act freely unless there is no causal determination of the will. A person acts freely only if in the same circumstances (with the same incentives, motives, character, etc.), the person could have chosen more than one way, had the person in fact chosen under these conditions to do so (thus showing that incentives, motives, and the like are not causally determinative). Hume does not believe that there is liberty in this sense. He thinks this account entails a denial of universal causation (the will being *uncaused*) and is inconsistent with moral responsibility.

Hume maintains that this great 'dispute' rests largely on an ambiguity in the meaning of terms. It is 'merely verbal'. Once proper meanings are attached to 'liberty' and 'necessity', the controversy will be closed—or at least closed to further investigation by the human understanding (8.2–3, 22–3).

METAPHYSICAL PROBLEMS

In Hume's account, persons perform free actions when they do what they have willed without constraint. Using his theories of necessity in the causal relation—in particular, his view that necessity is only in the mind of an observer, not in the actions of an agent—Hume maintains that laws of nature do not constrain persons or force persons to do something. We cannot transcend the laws of nature, but the laws do not necessitate.

Hume regards the notion of a free action that is uncaused as having no basis in our considered beliefs. He thinks we believe that all events are caused and that the actions of persons flow from prior and often identifiable conditions in those persons—for example, their actions flow from their 'motives and character' (n. 18). We understand and explain a person's 'voluntary actions' by citing the person's motives, and 'the same motives always produce the same actions' (8.7). What other explanation of action could there be? Not chance, Hume says, because actions would then be random and out of our control.

THE ETHICS AND PSYCHOLOGY OF ASCRIPTIONS OF
PRAISE AND BLAME

Hume maintains that actions are caused by 'character, passions, and affections' (8.31). Because these causal conditions are internal and unimposed, rather than external and imposed, the resultant actions are ours and we can be held responsible for them. Only if the actions are ours can we, from a moral point of view, be praised, blamed, rewarded, or punished. Hume thinks it would be ridiculous to say that a person could be held responsible if the person's hand were to strike the face of another person either by chance or because someone else caused the hand to move. He concludes that the uncaused acts of will that some philosophers claim to be possible actually leave actors without responsibility for their actions, thereby undermining the foundations of morality.

Hume specifies two conditions that must be present for liberty and for us to approve or disapprove, praise or condemn, excuse or blame, credit or reproach, and forgive or punish. These conditions are (1) absence of constraint and (2) causation of action by a person's own motives, passions, or states of character. This appears to be a conceptual and moral thesis about the proper conditions of liberty, approval, and blame, not merely a psychological thesis.

At the same time Hume offers a related psychological thesis of substantial importance for his science of human nature. Perhaps his clearest statement is the following: 'The mind of man is so formed by nature, that, upon the appearance of certain characters, dispositions, and actions, it immediately feels the sentiment of approbation or blame' (8.35). To hold someone responsible is, psychologically, to feel this sentiment. One feels the sentiment whenever a quality of mind or character in the person being evaluated causes that sentiment to arise. For example, if a person intends to do me unjustified harm, I will hold the person responsible and feel the sentiment of blame directed at that person. In the absence of such a motive in another person, no sentiment of blame or ascription of responsibility will arise.

This naturalistic account of the mind gives Hume a psychological basis for arguing that judgements of liberty are compatible with judgements of necessity and that persons are in fact praised or blamed whenever something in their character is the object of a certain kind of moral sentiment.

EXPLANATIONS OF ACTION

A naturalistic explanation of freely willed actions follows directly from Hume's theory of causation and his psychological theories about motive and action: 'The philosopher, if he be consistent, must apply the same [causal] reasoning to the actions and volitions of intelligent agents' as he does to 'reasonings concerning external objects' (8.15, 17). Hume argues

41

that we learn from many contexts of human actions, such as 'wars, intrigues, factions, and revolutions' (8.7), that there is 'a uniformity in human motives and actions', just as we learn of uniformity 'in the operations of body' (8.8). He believes that there is a constant conjunction between motives and actions in human behaviour and that human nature remains the same over time in its principles and operations.

> The same motives always produce the same actions: The same events follow from the same causes. Ambition, avarice, self-love, vanity, friendship, generosity, public spirit; these passions, mixed in various degrees, and distributed through society, have been, from the beginning of the world, and still are, the source of all the actions and enterprizes, which have ever been observed among mankind. . . . Mankind are so much the same, in all times and places, that history informs us of nothing new or strange in this particular. Its chief use is only to discover the constant and universal principles of human nature . . . (8.7)

Since such causal inferences should be as secure in the human domain as the natural domain, we can expect to establish universal principles of human nature and a scientific psychology (8.7–9).

Some philosophers find this analysis dogmatic, unduly speculative, and incompatible with Hume's demands for a science of human nature. They hold that the alleged universal and general principles that Hume says 'history discovers' are as much a mystery today as they were in Hume's time. It is easy to construct general statements that connect particular motives and actions, but the trouble with these candidates—as Hume acknowledges (8.12)—is that they are invariably false, because they all have exceptions. If phrased to exclude all exceptions, they seem vacuous.

For example, consider an explanation of a person's descent down a roof-ladder: the action is explained by the person's belief that his hat is on the ground below and by his desire to retrieve the wind-blown hat. It is easy to generalize this singular statement into a lawlike statement to the effect that whenever persons wish to retrieve their wind-blown hats from the ground and believe that descending a ladder will enable them to do so, they will descend the ladder. This general statement is plainly not a causal law. Persons might ask other persons to retrieve their hats or conclude that retrieval of the hat is not worth the descent.

Hume's response to this criticism and counter-example would presumably rest on his general strategy of making a comparison between human actions and natural phenomena. For example, he describes human action through analogies to irregular events in the human body and variations in the weather:

> in the human body . . . irregular events [sometimes] follow from any particular cause; the philosopher and physician . . . know, that a human body is a mighty complicated machine: That many secret powers lurk in it, which are altogether beyond our comprehension: . . . therefore the irregular events . . . can be no proof, that the laws of nature are not observed with the greatest regularity in its internal operations. . . . The internal principles and motives may [likewise] operate in a uniform manner, notwithstanding these seeming irregularities; in the same manner as the winds, rain, clouds, and other variations of the weather are supposed to be governed by steady principles . . . (*EHU* 8.14–15)

From this perspective, we should treat conclusions about relations between motives and actions as rough-and-ready approximations of underlying causal relations that are hidden from view. Our evidence is 'imperfect', but our ignorance does not exempt us from preserving the same causal commitments in the explanation of human action that we accept in the explanation of natural phenomena.

Given these commitments Hume appears to be proposing a search for laws of human action that are more precise than any regularities yet established. If these attempts to provide genuine laws were to continue to meet with failure, even as the conditions of scientific inquiry approach the optimum, Hume would presumably have no recourse but to allow that there apparently are no precise laws relating actions to reasons, motives, beliefs, and desires.

However, there are many levels on which the search for laws might proceed, as Hume points out: 'philosophers, observing, that, almost in every part of nature, there is contained a vast variety of springs and principles, which are hid, by reason of their minuteness or remoteness, find, that it is at least possible the contrariety of events may not proceed from any contingency in the cause, but from the secret operation of contrary causes' (8.13). It may be premature to give up on the causal explanation of human actions merely because no lawlike motive–action connections have been discovered. One alternative would be to argue that the laws governing human behaviour do not describe causes and their effects in terms of motives and actions, but in terms of brain-states and movements. This strategy would be consistent with Hume's programme, but he does not mention it in *EHU*.

These problems are important for Hume. Unless he can render plausible his programme for the explanation of human action, it is doubtful that he can claim to have shown that there is a 'necessity' in human conduct of the sort he insists on throughout Section 8.

7. Philosophy of Religion

EHU contains two fascinating journeys into the philosophy of religion: Section 10, 'Of Miracles' (a criticism of the foundations of revealed religion), and Section 11, 'Of a Particular Providence and of a Future State' (a criticism of the foundations of natural religion). A profound scepticism about religion is apparent in these sections.

Hume's views present a challenge to what was in his time the primary theological defence of the Christian religion: reports of miracles in scripture and philosophical arguments for the existence of God. Hume maintains that these defences of religion surpass the bounds of human understanding and reason, and he proposes that we confine belief to evidence gained in experience. These strategies of argument in *EHU* are by now familiar.

7.1. Evidence for Miracles (Section 10)

Many writers before and during Hume's lifetime investigated whether belief in miracles is justified. Issues of the historical credibility of reports of miracles were at the forefront of the discussion, and a tangled controversy had arisen regarding appropriate criteria for assessing historical evidence. An example of the critics of miracle reports is English divine and free-thinker Thomas Woolston (1670–1733). In *Discourses on the Miracles of our Saviour* (1727–9), he maintained that there are many absurdities and improbabilities in scriptural reports of miracles, especially in the gospel narratives. In 1733 Woolston died in prison, where he had been confined on a charge of criminal blasphemy for his views on miracles. Hume was developing his views on miracles around this time, and soon wrote an essay on miracles. He omitted this essay from the *Treatise*, fearing it would be offensive, but then published it as Section 10 of *EHU*. His principal conclusion is that the evidence for miracles is suspect and that the doctrines of particular religions are unsupported by testamentary reports of miracles.

THE DEFINITION OF 'MIRACLE'

Hume defines a miracle as a transgression (or violation) of a law of nature through a divine intervention (*'a particular volition of the Deity'*; n. 23). Miraculous events must actually violate a law—that is, a causal regularity in nature—whereas the 'marvellous' merely violates *expectations* of lawful behaviour. Hume appreciates that many generalizations about regularities in nature that people formulate are not truly laws of nature. An event that violates what is believed to be a law, but in fact is not a law, is not a miracle under his definition.

Many theologians have argued that a miracle does not occur in the natural order and therefore cannot violate the natural order. In this conception, a miracle is brought about by a cause (namely, God) that transcends the order of nature. Hume might respond that it is unintelligible to suppose that an event could occur in nature, as miracles do, without itself being part of the natural order. For example, if God parted the Red Sea to assist in the exodus from Egypt, it is hard to explain how the Red Sea is not part of the natural order even if God is not part of the natural order. This conceptual matter is important, because it shows that Hume may be conceptually at odds with some of the theologians he is criticizing.

THE PROBLEM OF UNRELIABLE TESTIMONY

When persons report that they have observed a miracle, under what conditions, if any, are their reports credible? Hume proposes that several considerations play a role in assessing the credibility of a person's testimony. One consideration is what he calls the *authority* of the person. A person who is well situated to make a report, has experience in such matters, and understands that evidence is needed in order to justify claims is more likely to give an authoritative and credible report than a person who lacks these credentials. A second consideration is the reliability of a person's *character*. Persons who are honest, impartial, and sober of judgement are generally credible, whereas persons 'of a doubtful character' cause us to 'entertain a suspicion' about their reports (10.7).

Reports of miracles would therefore have initial credibility if the persons making the reports had the requisite authority and character. However, in Part 2 of his essay Hume denies that there has ever been credible testimony for miracles.[25] Typically, witnesses to miracles have

[25] See the transition paragraph (10.14) at the beginning of Part 2, where Hume says that he has supposed in Part 1 that testimony could amount to an 'entire proof'—a 'concession'

not been persons of 'such unquestioned good sense, education, and learning' or of such 'undoubted integrity' as to place them beyond the suspicion that they might be deluded, out to deceive others, or swayed by an ill-considered faith (10.15). Hume maintains that once all the evidence for and against belief in miracles is weighed, it is, on balance, inadequate to sustain reports of miracles. To reach this conclusion, which he defends primarily in Part 2, Hume relies on an argument about the proof of miracles that he defends primarily in Part 1.

THE 'PROOF' OF MIRACLES

Hume asks whether there can be sufficient evidence to constitute a proof that a miracle occurred. In answer, he presents the following argument:

1. A wise person 'proportions belief to evidence' (10.4).
2. Evidence is based on experience of the frequency with which events are constantly conjoined (from unexceptionable or uniform conjunctions, to conjunctions that almost always occur, to conjunctions that rarely occur).
3. Strong evidence defeats weak evidence.
4. The strongest evidence is found in *proofs*, which are based on well-documented experimental evidence of unexceptionable regularities in nature (laws of nature).
5. Weaker evidence than that in *proofs* is found in *probabilities*, which are based on evidence ranging from events that almost always happen to events that rarely happen.
6. Human testimony short of a proof rests on evidence that is weaker than the evidence supporting a proof.
7. The wise person will believe a proof rather than a conflicting conclusion based on weaker evidence.
8. A report of a miracle is a report of a violation of a law of nature.
9. There exists 'a uniform experience' against every report of a violation of a law of nature that amounts to 'a direct and full *proof* . . . against the existence of any miracle' (10.12).

    Therefore, the wise person will believe the strong evidence supporting the law (a well-founded proof) rather than testimony of a miracle, which rests on weaker evidence (a less well-founded probability).

he will not make in Part 2, where he attempts to show that 'there never was a miraculous event established on' adequate evidence.

Hume sometimes indicates, especially in Part 2, that evidence from miracle stories is never strong enough to warrant belief in miracles. At other times, especially in Part 1, he seems to allow that under ideal conditions testimony for a miracle by credible persons might merit acceptance. The following is a celebrated passage in which Hume states what he calls a 'general maxim': 'no testimony is sufficient to establish a miracle, unless the testimony be of such a kind, that its falsehood would be more miraculous, than the fact, which it endeavours to establish: And even in that case, there is a mutual destruction of arguments, and the superior only gives us an assurance suitable to that degree of force, which remains, after deducting the inferior' (10.13).

There has been scholarly disagreement over the meaning of this difficult passage. One plausible interpretation links Hume's maxim directly to the arguments about induction and probability in Sections 4–6, as well as to the nine-step proof just outlined: we must weigh the evidence for the accuracy of a person's testimony that a miracle occurred against the evidence for the law that the miracle violates. Credible testimony can, in principle, conflict with reliable induction from experience; ultimately, credibility attaches to that which is most probable. If the credibility of the testimony—e.g. by a group of physicians who witness a miraculous cure—is greater than the reliability of the evidence—e.g. against the possibility of cures for an 'incurable disease'—the testimony has force in supporting the claim of a miracle. In this way, claims of miracles can counterbalance evidence for laws of nature whenever the weight of testimony given by solid witnesses is substantial by comparison to the weight of the evidence for a law.

Consider, as an example of Hume's point, the 'testimony of the apostles' to the 'miracles of our Saviour' with which he begins Section 10. Suppose each apostle is a person of good character and authority who never reports on events unless competent to do so and never misrepresents facts. Although the apostles were eyewitnesses to the reported events and knew Jesus well, the claim that he fed a multitude of people with a simple plate of continually multiplying loaves of bread and fish defies anything we know about the production and consumption of food. To decide what merits belief in this case, one would have to weigh the credibility of the apostles' reports against the evidence for the proposition that food cannot be spontaneously replenished. Relying on probabilities is unavoidable in this assessment, but it is possible that the evidence for the reliability of the apostles' reports is more substantial than the evidence for a law that renders improbable what they report.

In weighing the state of the evidence one could also decide that the apostles' reports, on balance, have less support than the law of nature that was allegedly violated. The testimony may lack a sufficient number of credible witnesses, may descend from persons with a clear bias, or may have been reported for the first time many years after the alleged events took place. Hume thinks we will generally come to a sceptical conclusion if we carefully weigh all the evidence, but his maxim seems to leave open the possibility that the weight of the evidence could fall in either direction.

RELIGIOUS CLAIMS AND RIVAL MIRACLES

Hume also argues that 'a miracle can never be proved, so as to be the foundation of a system of religion' (10.36). He notes that many religions rely on reports of miracles to support their unique claims, but he thinks these religions all run into a problem of rival miracles: when two religions generate conflicting claims, the claims of both religions cannot be true, although both can be false. 'Evidence' for the miracles in one religion therefore undermines the claims in rival miracles promoted by other religions.

Hume also challenges the religious belief that God causes miracles. Hume here relies on the arguments about causation that he advanced in Sections 4–7: because we cannot experience a constant conjunction between the volition of the deity and a causal outcome, we have no basis for the claim that God is the cause. (See related arguments for this thesis in Section 11.) However, Hume does not conclude that miracles cannot occur or even that we cannot experience miracles. He merely points to the high standard of evidence necessary to support the conviction that a report of a miracle is reliable.

7.2. *Evidence of Divine Providence (Section 11)*

In the section entitled 'Of a Particular Providence and of a Future State' Hume considers some pillars of Western monotheistic religious beliefs other than doctrines of scripture and reports of miracles. Even some of the most influential figures of the Enlightenment, including Hugo Grotius, John Locke, and scientifically oriented philosophers in the early Royal Society, accepted a 'natural religion' in which the existence and activities of God were thought to be demonstrated by philosophical argument. Sceptical of these claims, Hume focuses in Section 11 on beliefs about a God who intervenes to provide for human creatures.

This section is partially composed as a dialogue in which a 'friend who loves sceptical paradoxes' either states Hume's arguments or puts them in the mouth of the ancient philosopher Epicurus. The friend's message is similar to views Hume himself expresses in other writings, and therefore they can be safely assumed to represent his own views. The central conclusion reached in the section is that no known evidence supports traditional beliefs about God's providence, whereas some evidence calls these beliefs into question.

At the time Hume wrote, many theists believed in the immediate operation of God's providence. God was believed to control death, drought, floods, and other threats to human life and flourishing. By contrast, deists denied such a *particular* providence, holding instead that a sovereign God originally established unalterable universal laws to govern nature and that thereafter God did not interfere with the established laws by particular acts of providence. Deists believed that these laws provide the primary and perhaps sole evidence for the existence of God, whereas theists looked to nature for evidence of God's providence. Theists were suspicious of deistical reasoning and suspected irreligion in anyone who ascribed all current events to natural causes rather than to divine guidance.

In this section Hume may seem to be writing about ancient rather than contemporary philosophical and religious systems. However, he is using ancient figures as a device of argument and means of communicating with his audience; the ancients are not a major focus of his philosophical concerns, which are primarily directed at seventeenth- and eighteenth-century natural theologians. Hume appears to criticize primarily the philosophical theologians of the Judaic, Christian, and Islamic religions.

THE ARGUMENT FROM DESIGN

Philosophers and theologians in these and other traditions had for centuries argued that nature shows evidence of a supremely wise and benevolent creator and that each component part of the universe is well designed and works to good ends. They believed that human reason can discover evidence of God's design, providence, and benevolence. According to the argument from design, the universe resembles a machine fashioned by a fine machinist or a work of art created by a fine artist. The resemblance is sufficiently strong that it is reasonable to postulate a designer of the universe whose powers account for the order and complex interactions that we experience. This argument is analogical: intricate machines such as watches are analogous to the intricate machinery of the universe, and therefore they probably resemble each other in having a designer.

PROBLEMS WITH THE ARGUMENT FROM DESIGN

Hume maintains that this argument from apparent order to a designer outstrips the evidence and runs into several moral and theological problems. These problems centre on (1) causation, (2) analogy, and (3) the existence of evil and disorder.

1. Hume invokes his earlier argument that our understanding of causal relations depends on experiences of constant conjunctions between cause and effect. In the case of the argument from design he maintains (in the imaginary speech by Epicurus) that we cannot obtain experience of the cause—that is, the creator or designer of the universe. We are naturally curious about the cause or causes of the universe, but we have no basis on which to infer the cause because we have no experience of the beginnings of universes. We know causal relations only by constant conjunctions, whereas the universe is a unique object with unknown and inaccessible causes:

I much doubt whether it be possible for a cause to be known only by its effect. . . . It is only when two *species* of objects are found to be constantly conjoined, that we can infer the one from the other; and were an effect presented, which was entirely singular, and could not be comprehended under any known *species*, I do not see, that we could form any conjecture or inference at all concerning its cause. (11.30)

2. Hume regards the analogy between the origin of natural objects and the origin of designed objects as too remote to support the claim of similarity required for the argument from design. Even if we were to posit a divine source of order in the universe, we could attribute to that divine source only that which can be inferred by strict analogy from effects in the universe as it exists. Thus, we could attribute to God (or multiple gods, perhaps) only that measure of wisdom, power, and creativity reasonably inferable from the universe. This analogical basis for knowledge of God seems to preclude inference to omniscience, omnipotence, and moral traits such as justice and benevolence in acts of design and providence.

3. Hume also maintains that the many features of the universe from which we draw pleasure and satisfaction are counterbalanced by the evils, disorders, and hardships of life, all of which appear contrary to the plan of a wise, superintending God. These evils, disorders, and hardships might all be explained if certain features of the world (such as laws of nature) prevent God from acting benevolently, but this thesis modifies the usual

conception of God in religious traditions and is too speculative to contain merit (11.17).

Hume twice uses the language of 'the religious hypothesis' (11.18 and 11.27) to represent the suppositions that he opposes in Section 11. 'Hypothesis' is often a negative word for him, suggesting undue speculation. It appears that he has had the central features of the religious hypothesis under discussion in Sections 10 and 11 and has found the hypothesis without foundation. By the end of Section 11 Hume has again brought to the foreground his conviction that experience rather than reason is the proper source of causal beliefs. The speech put in the mouth of Epicurus captures the point succinctly (11.23): 'The experienced train of events is the great standard, by which we all regulate our conduct. . . . In vain would our limited understanding break through those boundaries. . . . [T]he subject lies entirely beyond the reach of human experience.'

8. Scepticism

Hume's contemporaries commonly regarded him as a sceptic, as do many philosophers today.[26] We saw in §§ 5.5 and 7.1–2 of this Introduction that Hume's account of the narrow limits of human reason and understanding suggest that he is a sceptic about induction and about natural and revealed religion. In Section 12 Hume considers which forms of scepticism, if any, are justified.

Early in his career, Hume seemed to encourage the interpretation of his philosophy as sceptical. He wrote in the *Abstract* of his *Treatise*, for example, that

the philosophy contain'd in this book is very sceptical, and tends to give us a notion of the imperfections and narrow limits of human understanding. Almost all reasoning is there reduced to experience; and the belief, which attends experience, is explained to be nothing but a peculiar sentiment, or lively conception produced by habit. Nor is this all. When we believe any thing of *external* existence, or suppose an object to exist a moment after it is no longer perceived, this belief is nothing but a sentiment of the same kind. . . . [The book]

---

[26] At the time Hume wrote, sceptics were understood as philosophers who maintained that no certainty exists about anything, that even the best methods of reasoning leave us shy of the truth or fail to resolve conflicting claims to the truth, and that a person should suspend judgement rather than accept dogmatic beliefs. Today the term 'scepticism' is applied more broadly to many forms of doubt about claims to know. It remains an important question in Hume scholarship to what extent he is a sceptic, what type of sceptic he is, and the particular claims about which he is sceptical.

concludes, that we assent to our faculties, and employ our reason only because we cannot help it.[27]

Thus encouraged by Hume himself, many readers have interpreted him as sceptical of our ability to justify our most fundamental beliefs by appeal to either reason or the understanding.

However, interpreting the nature and depths of Hume's scepticism is difficult. He distinguishes several types of scepticism, disparages most, and never clearly associates himself with any one school. He maintains that many sceptics cannot successfully rid themselves of the very beliefs that they criticize. For example, sceptics closeted in their studies can plausibly deny that tables exist in an external world, yet find themselves unable to doubt that tables exist as soon as they sit down to dinner. This paradoxical thesis that we lack adequate justification for beliefs that we inevitably hold is a key ingredient in Hume's response to the lure of scepticism.

8.1. Ancient Scepticism: Academics and Pyrrhonians (Section 12.21–5)

Hume waits until the last section of *EHU* to examine scepticism in depth. Mid-way through this section he compares and assesses two groups of influential ancient sceptics: the Academics and the Pyrrhonians. He entitles Section 12 'Of the Academical or Sceptical Philosophy', a choice of title that suggests to some readers that he associates Academic scepticism with his own view. But is this reading the correct one?

Pyrrhonism was a robust scepticism that originated in the teachings of Pyrrho of Elis (4th–3rd centuries BC) and his followers. Pyrrho attacked the dogmatism and system-building of schools such as the Stoics and presented a scepticism based on the refusal to accept positive beliefs about non-evident matters.[28] He allegedly thought that any belief that seemed plausible could be counterbalanced by an opposite belief that also seemed plausible; no criteria of proof or judgement decisively determine which arguments or conclusions are correct.[29] Pyrrhonists reasoned that one should cease being teased and frustrated by the goal of discovering what

---

[27] *Abstract* 27.

[28] According to Diogenes Laertius, *Lives of Eminent Philosophers* 9.11.62–9 (2: 474–91, esp. 474–5).

[29] Sextus Empiricus, *Outlines of Pyrrhonism*, bk. 1, chs. 1–4, 7–8, 10–12, 27–8, 33; bk. 2, chs. 4–9, 12, 15. Pyrrho's views appear to have been first formulated systematically by Aenesidemus, but the only recorded texts are those of Sextus. His works provide Pyrrhonian argu-

is worthy of belief and instead suspend judgement and belief in virtually all matters.[30]

Hume exhibits some admiration for the Pyrrhonists' views about the limits of human understanding and reason. Like them, he starts with what appears (that is, perceptions) and expresses reservations about many judgements that reach beyond appearances. He also thinks that Pyrrhonism can serve a useful philosophical purpose by deflating undue philosophical pride and pretentiousness (12.21–4). In his *Abstract* of the *Treatise*, Hume attributes monumental weight to Pyrrhonian reasoning: 'Philosophy wou'd render us entirely *Pyrrhonian*, were not nature too strong for it.'[31] Again in *EHU* he emphasizes the philosophical attractions of Pyrrhonian principles, noting that it is 'difficult, if not impossible, to refute them' (12.21).

However, Hume says that he is no Pyrrhonian. He says that we are not capable of suspending beliefs generated by the constitution of our nature. Moreover, a science of human nature is an inquiry into what should be believed, and Pyrrhonists, in Hume's understanding of their philosophy, back away from such inquiry. Hume likewise doubts that a suspension of judgement would lead to any practical good, even were it possible: 'All discourse, all action would immediately cease; and men remain in a total lethargy, till the necessities of nature, unsatisfied, put an end to their miserable existence' (12.23). The great 'subverter of Pyrrhonism', says Hume, is the practical demand of ordinary life (12.21).

Hume contrasts Pyrrhonism with Academic scepticism, a philosophy that emerged in the Academy, the great school or 'university' founded by the Athenian philosopher Plato (5th–4th centuries BC). Academic sceptics were aware of and learned from Pyrrhonian writings, but they particularly esteemed the teachings of Plato's mentor Socrates (5th century BC) regarding how little is definitively known and how much can be questioned. In contrast to the Pyrrhonists, the Academic sceptics accepted the search for truth as a proper philosophical goal. They presented methods to draw out and assess the arguments on all sides of a problem, and they were prepared to accept probabilities as a credible basis for judgement.

---

ments commonly accepted as the standard formulation, and they were very influential in European philosophy after their publication in the 16th century.

[30] *Outlines of Pyrrhonism*, bk. 1, chs. 13 ff., 20–3.

[31] *Abstract* 27. It has often been said that Hume misrepresents the Pyrrhonists. They, like Hume, insist on open, non-dogmatic inquiry. No position is taken in this Introduction on the proper understanding of Pyrrhonism.

In this philosophy, Hume says, Pyrrhonism's 'undistinguished doubts are, in some measure, corrected by common sense and reflection' (12.24).

8.2. Excessive and Moderate Forms of Scepticism (Section 12.1–5, 26–34)

Despite his modest admiration of Pyrrhonism, Hume denounces it (12.21) along with the method of sceptical doubt in Descartes's philosophy (12.3).[32] Both forms of scepticism strike Hume as 'excessive', because they question everything, including the trustworthiness of the very human faculties that we use to form beliefs. Hume objects that we must rely on these faculties even to formulate sceptical doubts. Excessive scepticism therefore promotes an incoherent form of universal doubt.

Hume distinguishes these deficient scepticisms from the 'more *mitigated* scepticism, or ACADEMICAL philosophy' (12.24). A mitigated scepticism subjects beliefs to critical scrutiny and investigates the limits of the powers of human mental capacities to support these beliefs. It insists on clear principles and proceeds only by sure steps to review and re-review conclusions and their consequences. This kind of scepticism helps us appreciate the 'only methods, by which we can ever hope to reach truth' and serves as a 'necessary preparative to the study of philosophy' (12.4). To be appropriately sceptical, then, is to attend to the evidence on all sides, to eliminate prejudice, and to remain open to new discoveries and insights.

8.3. Scepticism with Regard to Reason (Section 12.17–22)

Whatever the nature of his sympathies for Academic scepticism, some commentators believe that Hume is himself a deeper sceptic, especially with regard to reason.[33] One basis of this interpretation is Hume's per-

---

[32] Descartes sought certain knowledge. He maintained that every proposition is to be treated as provisionally false and every faculty as deceptive until we find a substantial premiss that is certain beyond doubt. This philosophical doubt is *methodical* as a technique for arriving at certain knowledge. It is *sceptical* because it requires a satisfactory justification in order to overcome doubt. See *Meditations on First Philosophy* 1 (esp. 2: 15).

[33] The heading to this section is borrowed from *THN* 1.4.1, 'Of Scepticism with regard to Reason'. Hume does not use this title or specifically mention scepticism about reason in *EHU*, but the passages cited below are taken by many readers to be his continued scepticism about reason in *EHU*.

sistent ambition to reduce functions traditionally attributed to reason to the imagination, passion, or instinctive mechanisms. Typical passages in *EHU* are the following:

[Induction or causal inference] is an operation of the soul, when we are so situated, as unavoidable as to feel the passion of love, when we receive benefits; or hatred, when we meet with injuries. All these operations are a species of natural instincts, which no reasoning or process of the thought and understanding is able, either to produce, or to prevent. (5.8)

[E]xperimental reasoning itself, which we possess in common with beasts, and on which the whole conduct of life depends, is nothing but a species of instinct or mechanical power, that acts in us unknown to ourselves; and in its chief operations, is not directed by any such relations or comparisons of ideas, as are the proper objects of our intellectual faculties. (9.6)

This reduction of reason and other faculties to mere instincts has seemed to many commentators an overt scepticism about reason.[34]

Hume had presented at least two developed arguments in the *Treatise* (1.4.1.5–6) for scepticism with regard to reason, but no trace of these arguments remains in *EHU*. Instead Hume restates some ancient sceptical problems about whether space and time are infinitely divisible. He does so in order to prove that reason without recourse to experience encounters severe difficulties and is 'thrown into a kind of amazement and suspence' (12.18). 'Absurdities and contradictions' regarding whether time and particles of matter are or are not infinitely divisible so confound reason that we are driven to a scepticism about all abstract reasonings (12.2). Beyond these somewhat indeterminate conclusions about the weakness of pure reason, Hume says little in *EHU* about scepticism regarding reason.

None the less, Hume's many uses of the term 'reasoning' suggest that he is not a sceptic about all forms of reasoning.[35] He never denies that we engage in complicated forms of reasoning in mathematics and the comparison of ideas (the proper province of 'reason'); nor does he doubt that we engage in subtle forms of scientific and other causal reasoning (the proper province of 'understanding'). He considers such 'accurate and just reasoning' the only solution to the errors of abstruse philosophy, metaphysical jargon, and popular superstition and errors (1.12).

---

[34] In *THN* Hume declared that causal reasoning is 'nothing but a wonderful and unintelligible instinct in our souls' (*THN* 1.3.16.9). Cf. *EHU* 12.7, 16, in addition to the two quotations above from 5.8 and 9.6.

[35] The terms 'reasoning' and 'reasonings' appear 146 times in *EHU*. Relatively few uses manifest a scepticism about the type of reasoning under discussion.

Hume provides both psychological and epistemological analyses of reasoning. In his psychological explanations the categories 'experience', 'habit', 'custom', 'imagination', and 'instinct' have a significant role in explaining reasoning. However, Hume does not suggest that reasoning is to be analysed solely in terms of psychological categories such as custom and instinct. Reasoning may be instinctual (a *psychological* condition) and still be either justified or unjustified (an *epistemological* status). All reasoning is instinctual, but only some reasoning will satisfy additional criteria of justification.

Hume accepts the justifiability of some forms of 'reasoning concerning matters of fact' (4.4, 14; 5.3; 7.29; 9.1; 10.3; 12.17, 21, 34), an epistemological rather than psychological thesis. He also maintains that instincts 'may be fallacious and deceitful' (12.22). Instinct-generated beliefs and past reasonings both stand to be corrected by further reasoning, which may require 'great attention, accuracy, and subtilty' (n. 20).

8.4. Scepticism with Regard to the Senses (Section 12.6–16)

In Section 12 Hume examines scepticism about the senses.[36] He begins his treatment with the following paragraph:

I need not insist upon the more trite topics, employed by the sceptics in all ages, against the evidence of *sense*; such as those which are derived from the imperfection and fallaciousness of our organs, on numberless occasions; the crooked appearance of an oar in water; the various aspects of objects, according to their different distances; the double images which arise from the pressing one eye; with many other appearances of a like nature. These sceptical topics, indeed, are only sufficient to prove, that the senses alone are not implicitly to be depended on; but that we must correct their evidence by reason, and by considerations, derived from the nature of the medium, the distance of the object, and the disposition of the organ, in order to render them, within their sphere, the proper *criteria* of truth and falsehood. There are other more profound arguments against the senses, which admit not of so easy a solution. (12.6)

This paragraph is important both for what it dismisses and as a transition to a problem of scepticism that Hume takes very seriously. Hume abruptly dismisses doubts in classical scepticism regarding the untrustworthiness of the senses, because he believes that proper criteria of truth will permit us to overcome worries about untrustworthiness: the oar can

[36] The heading to this section is adapted from *THN* 1.4.2, which is entitled 'Of Scepticism with regard to the Senses'.

be removed from the water, the distant object brought closer, the eye allowed to return to its normal state, etc. These considerations are 'trite', but underlying these examples is the profound problem that all the images or representations that come before the mind—whether distorted or not—are perceptions. Within the space of this one paragraph, Hume transforms classical problems of scepticism about the untrustworthiness of the senses into a set of concerns about whether we are in contact with external objects.

ROOTS IN LOCKE AND BERKELEY (12.9–12, 15–16)

This problem of the status of 'external' objects derives for Hume more from modern than from ancient philosophy. It is rooted in the belief, common in seventeenth- and eighteenth-century philosophy, that the objects and events that we perceive are impressions, not something in the world beyond impressions: 'the slightest philosophy . . . teaches us, that nothing can ever be present to the mind but an image or perception . . . *this house* and *that tree*, are nothing but perceptions in the mind' (12.9).

If we are aware of nothing but perceptions, then we have no basis on which to become acquainted with objects or events external to our minds. Various philosophers before Hume, notably Locke, claimed that we can infer the existence of these objects and events. They believed that external objects and events cause perceptions in us that represent the external object. In a famous exposition Locke maintained that ideas resemble bodies and that we know some of the actual properties of those bodies (size, shape, figure, extension, state of motion, and the like). This theory has been called both representational realism and the causal theory of perception.[37]

George Berkeley sternly criticized Locke's theory. He argued that, when its true commitments are exposed, the theory promotes a complete scepticism about the material world, because what is immediately perceived is only an idea, not the external object. If we know only ideas, we can never know whether ideas resemble the qualities of external objects or not, which leaves us in the grip of scepticism.[38] Hume follows Berkeley's lead in Section 12. He agrees that we have no reason to believe that we can legitimately infer anything about external objects if we experience only perceptions.

---

[37] On the nature of this theory and its implications, see ann. 12.15–16.

[38] Berkeley, *Principles* 1.18–24.

CONCLUSIONS ABOUT THE EXTERNAL WORLD (SECTION 12.8–16)

However, when Berkeley goes on to say that bodies *are* perceptions (that is, bodies are nothing but perceptions), Hume judges this manoeuvre to be indefensible. He considers Berkeley's arguments 'merely sceptical' and says that they *'produce no conviction'* (n. 32). This statement is puzzling, because a reader might have expected Hume to agree with Berkeley that objects are nothing but perceptions. Instead, Hume maintains that we have no access to information about the actual status of objects and events, whatever that status may be; we are only aware of perceptions.

This strategy may amount to nothing more than a philosophical evasion. Hume himself says that a house and tree are 'nothing but perceptions in the mind' (12.9), a conclusion that seems to render his position indistinguishable from Berkeley's. Perhaps the explanation is that Hume wishes to avoid indefensible overstatement. He does not claim more than the evidence allows, and he thinks that metaphysical reflections like Berkeley's do claim more, eventuating in a dogmatic and unwarranted scepticism.[39]

An alternative interpretation of Hume (one that abandons entirely the interpretation that an object is nothing but a perception) is that he accepts an external world of objects and events that cause perceptions in us, but does not believe that perceptions *resemble* the objects or events. If having a perception is an event and all events have causes, then it would appear that perceptions too must be caused. Occasionally Hume seems to presuppose that impressions are caused by the states of the sensory organs. He even seems to assume the existence of sensory organs as transmission media that eventuate in perceptions. In addition, Hume notes that in common life we cannot withhold belief in the existence of an external world of objects.[40]

However, this interpretation of Hume as a realist about external objects is speculative and difficult to ground in the text. Another way to interpret the passages in which Hume seems to assume external objects is through his thesis that we naturally believe in the independent existence of everyday physical objects and events. He maintains that we 'are carried, by a natural instinct or prepossession, to repose faith' in our senses, which lead us, 'without any reasoning, or even almost before the use of reason

---

[39] See *THN* 1.4.2 for additional details about Hume's arguments on these problems.

[40] For defences of such a realist interpretation of Hume, see Wright, *The Sceptical Realism of David Hume*; Wilson, 'Is Hume a Sceptic with regard to the Senses?'; and Strawson, *The Secret Connexion: Causation, Realism, and David Hume.*

... [to] suppose an external universe' (12.7). Thus, we believe in an independent, external world of objects not because we have good arguments for doing so, but because of a natural instinct.

In the *Treatise* Hume offered an elaborate psychological explanation of how human nature leads us to believe that perceptions represent continuously existing objects that are independent of the mind. He argued that the constancy and coherence of items in experience—for example, the fact that an office building remains similar day in and day out—cause us to ascribe a continuous existence to these items independent of our discontinuous perceptions of them. In *EHU* Hume replaces this elaborate explanation in the *Treatise* with the simpler thesis that human nature steers us to believe that we perceive external objects.

Hume maintains that philosophers typically cast doubt on this universally held opinion by distinguishing objects from images and then instructing us that 'the senses are only the inlets, through which these images are conveyed, without being able to produce any immediate intercourse between the mind and the object' (12.9). None the less, 'philosophy finds herself extremely embarrassed' (12.10), because philosophers are unable to justify either the claim that trees and houses are nothing but perceptions in the mind (Berkeley's theory) or the claim that perceptions in the mind are caused by external objects (Locke's theory). Meanwhile, human nature pushes us to believe that we are in direct contact with external objects, despite our inability to discover a relation between perceptions and objects (12.12).

Hume evidently thinks both that there are no sound philosophical arguments to prove the existence of the external world and that an 'instinct of nature' has led us to a system of belief that is 'fallible and even erroneous' (12.10). Experience cannot resolve the problem, because experience cannot transcend perception (12.12). Hume points out that this conclusion leads to a tangle of other problems about the actual properties of so-called external objects. Then, at the end of Part 1, he comes to a major conclusion:

[One] objection to the evidence of sense or to the opinion of external existence consists in this, that such an opinion, if rested on natural instinct, is contrary to reason, and if referred to reason, is contrary to natural instinct, and at the same time carries no rational evidence with it, to convince an impartial enquirer. The second objection goes farther, and represents this opinion as contrary to reason; at least, if it be a principle of reason, that all sensible qualities are in the mind, not in the object. Bereave matter of all its intelligible qualities, both primary and secondary, you in a manner annihilate it, and leave only a certain unknown, inexplicable *something*, as the cause of our perceptions; a notion so imperfect, that no sceptic will think it worth while to contend against it. (12.16)

Philosophical reason corrects the instinct that leads us to believe, falsely, that we have access to the external world, but philosophical reason does so only to find itself overridden in common belief by instinct and without recourse to rational evidence that will convince an 'impartial enquirer'. Any appeal to the cause of perceptions only sinks us deeper in this sceptical quagmire because we have no information about the cause of perceptions. Hume leaves his reader, at the end of his discussion of the external world, with a profound sceptical problem that to this day philosophers have struggled to resolve.

8.5. The Scope of Hume's Scepticism

Hume's sceptical 'solution' to his sceptical doubts, as it might be called, resembles his earlier sceptical doubts and sceptical solution in Sections 4–5, where he maintains that custom controls our natural belief that the future will resemble the past. We encountered a similar strategy in Sections 7–8, where Hume examines our belief in necessary connection. In each case his science of human nature leads him to *explain* why we hold certain beliefs without any corresponding attempt to *justify* those beliefs. Perceptual judgements (about an external world), like inductive judgements about what is universally the case and causal judgements about power and necessary connection, reach beyond the warrant of experience and yet are tenaciously believed.

The precise character of Hume's scepticism is a difficult problem of textual interpretation. However, it can be plausibly argued that Hume limited his scepticism to the following: (1) scepticism about pretensions to certainty in matters of fact (a fallibilism); (2) a philosophical thesis that even the best empirical data and reasoning can in principle turn out to be mistaken (a weak inductive scepticism); (3) scepticism about claims to know the existence of, the real properties of, and relations among external objects (scepticism about the senses and the external world); (4) scepticism about factual conclusions derived from pure reason (a weak scepticism about reason); and (5) scepticism about both natural and revealed religion (religious scepticism). Each of these forms of scepticism is consistent with Hume's ambition to produce a science of human nature, an outcome that makes this interpretation particularly attractive.

None the less, the complexity of Hume's doctrines makes it doubtful that a single viable interpretation of his scepticism will emerge. Perhaps we can say little more, with confidence, than that he shies away from the extreme commitments of Pyrrhonism and Cartesian scepticism, while associating himself with Academic scepticism and central features of Berkeley's discreditation of Locke. But even this conclusion needs at least one qualification. On more than one occasion Hume indicates that no philosophical arguments refute Pyrrhonism; only instinct and the demands of daily life compel its rejection. In this respect he leaves the door open to the philosophical defensibility and serviceability of Pyrrhonian doubt (12.25).

Although Hume has often been interpreted as a philosopher whose vision of reason and knowledge led him to a deep Pyrrhonian scepticism about virtually all truth-claims, this interpretation is difficult to render consistent with *EHU*. Hume does not appear to have been deeply sceptical about a science of human nature or about beliefs that are well grounded in empirical evidence. He always insisted after the *Treatise* that his philosophy is not deeply sceptical, and his presentation of scepticism in *EHU* seems to be an attempt to remain faithful to this commitment while giving scepticism its due.

Supplementary Reading

These suggested readings include information about Hume's philosophical works, his likely sources, and a selection of books and recent articles on pertinent areas of his philosophy. Readers seeking a more comprehensive list of supplementary readings should consult § 7, Specialized Bibliographical Materials, at the end of this list. The literature on Hume is extensive, and the selective record below is largely confined, in its references to secondary literature, to works that treat the topics covered in *EHU*.

1. WRITINGS BY HUME

This first section presents a list of Hume's writings, in chronological order, with the year of first publication (using the author's last title, if a change of title occurred). These works have been published in numerous editions, many still in print. Electronic editions are also available.

EARLY

A Treatise of Human Nature (1739–40)
An Abstract of . . . A Treatise of Human Nature (1740)
Essays: Moral and Political (1741–2)
A Letter from a Gentleman to his Friend in Edinburgh (1745)

MID-LIFE

An Enquiry concerning Human Understanding (1748)
An Enquiry concerning the Principles of Morals (1751)
Essays: Political Discourses (1752)
A Dissertation on the Passions (1757)
The Natural History of Religion (1757)
The History of England (1754–62)

POSTHUMOUS

My Own Life (1777)
Dialogues concerning Natural Religion (1779)
Essays on Suicide and the Immortality of the Soul (1783)

Oxford University Press is currently publishing a critical edition of Hume's philosophical, political, and literary works under the editorship of Tom L. Beauchamp, David Fate Norton, and M. A. Stewart. At present there is no critical or standard edition of Hume's philosophical or historical publications. The closest approximation is the following outdated collection: *The Philosophical*

Supplementary Reading

Works of David Hume, ed. T. H. Green and T. H. Grose, 4 vols. (London: Longmans, 1882–6; fac. Darmstadt: Scientia, 1964; fac. Bristol: Thoemmes, 1996).

In the absence of critical editions, a mixture of editions has been relied upon in the study of Hume's texts. The following chronological list presents (1) original edition titles and bibliographical data, and, as appropriate, (2) modern editions that have earned a reputation as superior in some features to other editions.

'Hume's Early Memoranda, 1729–1740', ed. Ernest C. Mossner, *Journal of the History of Ideas*, 9 (1948), 492–518.

A Treatise of Human Nature: Being an Attempt to Introduce the Experimental Method of Reasoning into Moral Subjects, 3 vols. (London, 1739–40). See *A Treatise of Human Nature*, ed. David Fate Norton and Mary J. Norton (Oxford: Oxford University Press, forthcoming).

An Abstract of a Book lately Published; Entituled, A Treatise of Human Nature, &c. wherein the Chief Argument of that Book is farther Illustrated and Explained (London, 1740). See *A Treatise of Human Nature*, ed. Norton and Norton, above.

Essays Moral and Political, 2 vols. (Edinburgh, 1741–2); *Political Discourses* (Edinburgh, 1752); and part of *Four Dissertations* (London, 1757). See *Essays: Moral, Political, and Literary*, ed. Eugene F. Miller, 2nd edn. (Indianapolis: LibertyClassics, 1987); *Political Essays*, ed. Knud Haakonssen (Cambridge: Cambridge University Press, 1994); and *David Hume: Selected Essays*, ed. Stephen Copley and Andrew Edgar (Oxford: Oxford University Press, 1993).

A Letter from a Gentleman to his Friend in Edinburgh: Containing Some Observations on A Specimen of the Principles concerning Religion and Morality, said to be maintain'd in a Book lately publish'd, Entituled, A Treatise of Human Nature, &c (Edinburgh, 1745). See *A Letter from a Gentleman to his Friend in Edinburgh*, ed. Ernest C. Mossner and John V. Price (Edinburgh, 1745; fac. Edinburgh: University Press, 1967). Only a portion of this work may have been written by Hume.

An Enquiry concerning Human Understanding, first published as *Philosophical Essays concerning Human Understanding* (London, 1748). A critical edition is forthcoming in the Clarendon Hume, ed. Tom L. Beauchamp.

An Enquiry concerning the Principles of Morals (London, 1751). See *An Enquiry concerning the Principles of Morals*, ed. Tom L. Beauchamp (Oxford: Oxford University Press, 1998). One volume is an Oxford Philosophical Texts student edition, and the other volume is the critical edition in the Clarendon Hume.

Four Dissertations (London, 1757). The items in this work were eventually included in *Essays and Treatises on Several Subjects*. See *The Natural History of Religion*, ed. A. Wayne Colver (Oxford: Clarendon Press, 1976); and *A Dissertation on the Passions*, in *The Philosophical Works of David Hume*, ed. Green and Grose, above. *NHR* and *DIS* are forthcoming in a single-volume critical edition in the

Clarendon Hume, ed. Tom L. Beauchamp. For the other two dissertations, see *Essays*, ed. Miller, above.

The History of England, from the Invasion of Julius Caesar to the Revolution in 1688 (London, 1754–62). See *The History of England*, foreword by William B. Todd (Indianapolis: LibertyClassics, 1983–5).

Dialogues concerning Natural Religion (London, 1779). See *Hume's Dialogues concerning Natural Religion*, ed. Norman Kemp Smith (Oxford: Clarendon Press, 1935; 2nd edn., Edinburgh: Nelson, 1947; repr. Indianapolis: Bobbs-Merrill, 1962).

Three electronic collections of Hume's texts are available. The most comprehensive is in both disk and CD-ROM form in the Past Masters series of the Intelex Corporation (Virginia). Hume's *Treatise* and two *Enquiries* were published by Oxford University Press, which uses the outdated, but classic Selby-Bigge editions. Finally, HUMETEXT 1.0, prepared by Tom L. Beauchamp, David Fate Norton, and M. A. Stewart, is available from the Department of Philosophy, Georgetown University. This collection includes Hume's philosophical, political, and literary works, prepared in pure form from eighteenth-century editions.

2. HUME'S LIFE AND CORRESPONDENCE

The following books provide data and scholarly discussion of Hume's life, publishing history, and personal relationships. Except for Mossner, these works are primarily for advanced scholars. Mossner's biography should be used with caution because of occasional historical inaccuracies, but it contains useful information about Hume's life that is not readily available elsewhere. It is, on the whole, the best biography. Greig as well as Klibansky and Mossner are important (though incomplete) collections of Hume's many letters. Burton is outdated in some respects, but remains the only collection of letters to Hume. Numerous additional letters written by Hume have been published since these volumes. A comprehensive edition of the correspondence of Hume is under preparation for the Oxford University Press by David Raynor.

BURTON, JOHN HILL (ed.), *Letters of Eminent Persons Addressed to David Hume* (Edinburgh, 1849; fac. Bristol: Thoemmes, 1989).

HUME, DAVID, *The Letters of David Hume*, ed. J. Y. T. Greig, 2 vols. (Oxford: Clarendon Press, 1932).

——*New Letters of David Hume*, ed. Raymond Klibansky and Ernest C. Mossner (Oxford: Clarendon Press, 1954).

MOSSNER, ERNEST C., *The Life of David Hume*, 2nd edn. (Oxford: Clarendon Press, 1980).

Supplementary Reading

3. SOURCES IN EARLY MODERN PHILOSOPHY PRIOR TO 1748

The following works were available (in some edition) for Hume to read prior to the publication of *EHU* in 1748. In several cases it is known that he read at least some part of these works. All played important roles in the philosophy of the period in which Hume formed his ideas. Books published after *EHU* that were of importance in eighteenth-century philosophy are not included. See also the list of References, which lists the works of other figures in early modern philosophy.

ARNAULD, ANTOINE, and NICOLE, PIERRE, *Logic or the Art of Thinking*, ed. and trans. Jill Vance Buroker (Cambridge: Cambridge University Press, 1996).

BACON, FRANCIS, *The Works of Francis Bacon*, ed. James Spedding, Robert Leslie Ellis, and Douglas Denon Heath, 14 vols. (London, 1857–74; fac. Stuttgart: Frommann, 1961–3).

BAYLE, PIERRE, *The Dictionary Historical and Critical of M^r. Peter Bayle*, ed. and trans. Pierre Desmaizeaux, 2nd edn., 5 vols. (London, 1734–8; fac. New York: Garland, 1984).

BERKELEY, GEORGE, *Three Dialogues between Hylas and Philonous* and *A Treatise concerning the Principles of Human Knowledge*, in vol. 2 of *The Works of George Berkeley, Bishop of Cloyne*, ed. A. A. Luce and T. E. Jessop, 9 vols. (London: Nelson, 1948–57).

BUTLER, JOSEPH, *The Works of Joseph Butler*, ed. W. E. Gladstone, 2 vols. (Oxford: Clarendon Press, 1896).

CLARKE, SAMUEL, *The Works of Samuel Clarke, D.D.*, 4 vols. (London, 1738; fac. New York: Garland, 1978).

CUDWORTH, RALPH, *The True Intellectual System of the Universe*, 2 vols. (London, 1678; fac. New York: Garland, 1978).

DESCARTES, RENÉ, *The Philosophical Writings of Descartes*, ed. and trans. John Cottingham, Robert Stoothoff, and Dugald Murdoch, 3 vols. (Cambridge: Cambridge University Press, 1984–91).

HOBBES, THOMAS, *Leviathan*, ed. Edwin Curley (Indianapolis: Hackett, 1994).

HUTCHESON, FRANCIS, *Collected Works of Francis Hutcheson*, 7 vols., fac. edn. by Bernhard Fabian (Hildesheim: Olms, 1969–71).

LEIBNIZ, GOTTFRIED WILHELM. See the individual works cited in the list of References.

LOCKE, JOHN, *An Essay concerning Human Understanding*, ed. Peter H. Nidditch (Oxford: Clarendon Press, 1975).

MACLAURIN, COLIN, *An Account of Sir Isaac Newton's Philosophical Discoveries* (London, 1748; fac. New York: Johnson, 1968).

MALEBRANCHE, NICOLAS, *The Search after Truth*, ed. and trans. Thomas M. Lennon and Paul J. Olscamp (Columbus: Ohio State University Press, 1980).

SHAFTESBURY, ANTHONY ASHLEY COOPER, THIRD EARL OF, *Characteristics of Men*,

Manners, Opinions, Times, ed. John M. Robertson, 2 vols. in 1 (London, 1900; fac. Indianapolis: Bobbs-Merrill, 1964).

TILLOTSON, JOHN, *The Works of the Most Reverend Doctor John Tillotson*, 9th edn. (Dublin, 1726; 3 vols., London, 1728).

WOLLASTON, WILLIAM, *The Religion of Nature Delineated* (London, 1724; fac. New York: Garland, 1978).

4. GENERAL STUDIES OF HUME

4.1. Introductory Surveys and Studies

The following works contain introductory sections appropriate for students new to Hume's philosophy. Baier, Jones, and MacNabb's encyclopaedia articles are brief, but often creative, introductory guides useful for grasping the larger picture. MacNabb's book is now dated in some respects, but long has been among the clearest and most philosophically sensitive introductions to Hume. Norton (an anthology) and Penelhum (which contains material from Hume's writings) are outstanding guides to Hume and the literature on Hume, at an advanced introductory level. Overall, Norton and Penelhum are the best introductions currently available.

BAIER, ANNETTE, 'David Hume, 1711–1776', in Edward Craig (ed.), *Routledge Encyclopedia of Philosophy* (London: Routledge, 1997).

JONES, PETER, 'Hume', in N. F. Bunnin (ed.), *The Blackwell Companion to Philosophy* (Oxford: Blackwell, 1996).

MACNABB, D. G. C., *David Hume: His Theory of Knowledge and Morality*, 2nd edn. (London: Hutchinson, 1951; repr. Hamden, Conn.: Archon Books, 1966).

——'Hume, David', in Paul Edwards (ed.), *The Encyclopedia of Philosophy* (New York: Macmillan, 1967).

NORTON, DAVID FATE (ed.), *The Cambridge Companion to Hume* (Cambridge: Cambridge University Press, 1993).

PENELHUM, TERENCE, *David Hume: An Introduction to his Philosophical System* (West Lafayette, Ind.: Purdue University Press, 1992).

4.2. Commentaries on the First Enquiry

The following books are readable and at the same time serious interpretations of Hume's *First Enquiry*. Flew explores themes of mind, liberty, and religion; his book enjoyed considerable attention in the 1960s and early 1970s, though it is uneven and occasionally idiosyncratic. Stern's book focuses on the psychological and epistemological objectives of the *Enquiry* (what Hume called 'a mental geography') and is less comprehensive than Flew's. Both are dated in light of contemporary concerns with Hume's text; but they are the only commentaries in book form specifically devoted to *EHU*.

FLEW, ANTONY, *Hume's Philosophy of Belief: A Study of his* First Inquiry (London: Routledge & Kegan Paul, 1961).

STERN, GEORGE, *A Faculty Theory of Knowledge: The Aim and Scope of Hume's* First Enquiry (Lewisburg, Pa.: Bucknell University Press, 1971).

4.3. Advanced Studies

The works listed below are primarily for the advanced student. Kemp Smith's book, which accentuates the influence of Hutcheson on Hume and Hume's naturalism, has been more influential on Hume scholars than any other work in the twentieth century; it is primarily historical and textual, and remains controversial. Students often find it easier to read Kemp Smith's article first. Stroud provides an unusually clear and well-organized work that follows in the path of Kemp Smith's 'naturalistic' interpretation, but adds philosophical reflection that reaches far beyond his primarily historical work. Noxon is the most specialized, as the title indicates. It is a pioneering study of Hume's intentions, his self-conception as a philosopher, and the relationship between his experimental method and other parts of his philosophical programme.

The books by Hendel, Laird, and Passmore are perceptive, scholarly, and readable treatments of Hume's philosophy, though now little read. Hendel gives a sensitive, historical, and sympathetic reading to the text, while Passmore emphasizes various tensions in Hume's treatments of scepticism, the association of ideas, and other subjects. Laird contains outstanding research on Hume's predecessors and on his position in modern philosophy.

The books by Garrett and Johnson are more recent contributions to Hume scholarship. Johnson's book, though a study of the *Treatise* rather than *EHU*, presents a comprehensive interpretation. Garrett's work is a recent monograph with a sustained argument about the meaning of Hume's most famous doctrines and the nature of his contributions. Winkler's lengthy journal article is an influential attempt to show the severe limits of a 'wave' of recent Hume scholarship (see Strawson, *The Secret Connexion*, § 5.7 below; Wilson, 'Is Hume a Sceptic with regard to the Senses?', § 5.12 below; Wright, *The Sceptical Realism of David Hume*, § 5.12 below) that interprets Hume as a causal realist. Box's book is the best study of the stylistic changes initiated by Hume after his conclusion that the *Treatise* had failed.

Box, M. A., *The Suasive Art of David Hume* (Princeton: Princeton University Press, 1990).

GARRETT, DON, *Cognition and Commitment in Hume's Philosophy* (New York: Oxford University Press, 1997).

HENDEL, CHARLES W., *Studies in the Philosophy of David Hume* (Princeton: Princeton University Press, 1925; new edn. Indianapolis: Bobbs-Merrill, 1963; fac. New York: Garland, 1983).

JOHNSON, OLIVER A., *The Mind of David Hume: A Companion to Book I of* A Treatise of Human Nature (Urbana: University of Illinois Press, 1995).

LAIRD, JOHN, *Hume's Philosophy of Human Nature* (London: Methuen, 1932; fac. New York: Garland, 1983).

NOXON, JAMES, *Hume's Philosophical Development* (Oxford: Clarendon Press, 1973).

PASSMORE, JOHN, *Hume's Intentions*, rev. edn. (Cambridge: Cambridge University Press, 1952).

SMITH, NORMAN KEMP, 'The Naturalism of Hume', *Mind*, 14 (1905), 149–73, 335–47.

—— *The Philosophy of David Hume* (London: Macmillan, 1941; fac. New York: St Martin's Press, 1966).

STROUD, BARRY, *Hume* (London: Routledge & Kegan Paul, 1977).

WINKLER, KENNETH, 'The New Hume', *Philosophical Review*, 100 (1992), 541–79.

4.4. Anthologies and Collected Essays

The collections of articles below are all recommended, although the pre-1980s work is occasionally out of date. These anthologies treat a wide range of topics in Hume's philosophy, and none is devoted exclusively to the *First Enquiry*. The Chappell and Norton *et al.* anthologies have been particularly influential; both contain some moderately dated articles. The two anthologies by Stewart (one with Wright) contain particularly valuable recent scholarly work that is advanced and often heavily historical. The journal *Hume Studies* is a vital source of Hume scholarship. It is the only journal exclusively devoted to Hume and is the official journal of the Hume Society, an international association of scholars. The other anthologies listed below are generally of less value than those just mentioned, but each contains worthwhile materials.

See also Norton, *The Cambridge Companion to Hume* (§ 4.1 above).

CHAPPELL, V. C. (ed.), *Hume: A Collection of Critical Essays* (New York: Doubleday, 1966; fac. Notre Dame, Ind.: University of Notre Dame Press, 1974).

HOPE, VINCENT (ed.), *Philosophers of the Scottish Enlightenment* (Edinburgh: Edinburgh University Press, 1984).

Hume Studies (Apr. and Nov.). Available through and published by the Hume Society in printed and electronic forms.

LIVINGSTON, DONALD, and KING, JAMES (eds.), *Hume: A Re-evaluation* (New York: Fordham University Press, 1976).

MORICE, G. P. (ed.), *David Hume: Bicentenary Papers* (Austin: University of Texas Press, 1977).

NORTON, DAVID FATE, CAPALDI, NICHOLAS, and ROBISON, WADE (eds.), *McGill Hume Studies* (San Diego, Calif.: Austin Hill, 1979).

SESONSKE, A., and FLEMING, N. (eds.), *Human Understanding: Studies in the Philosophy of David Hume* (Belmont, Calif.: Wadsworth, 1965).

STEWART, M. A. (ed.), *Studies in the Philosophy of the Scottish Enlightenment* (Oxford: Clarendon Press, 1990).

—— and WRIGHT, JOHN (eds.), *Hume and Hume's Connexions* (Edinburgh: Edinburgh University Press; University Park: Pennsylvania State University Press, 1995).

5. STUDIES OF HUME BY TOPIC

5.1. Empiricism and the Science of Human Nature

The study by Capaldi is a sympathetic and constructive approach to Hume's philosophy, with an anti-sceptical interpretation. Moore's essay is an outstanding treatment of the social and historical background of Hume's science of human nature. Kuypers is also historical, but of a much earlier generation of scholarship; it is informative, but dated. Pears' book is the most probing philosophical analysis, but lacks close connection to the text.

On these topics, see also Noxon, *Hume's Philosophical Development* (§ 4.3 above), esp. pt. 2; Anderson's essay in Livingston and King (eds.), *Hume: A Re-evaluation* (§ 4.4 above); Wright, *The Sceptical Realism of David Hume* (§ 5.12 below), esp. chs. 1, 5; Penelhum, *David Hume: An Introduction to his Philosophical System* (§ 4.1 above), chs. 2–3; Biro and Rosenberg in Norton (ed.), *The Cambridge Companion to Hume* (§ 4.1 above).

CAPALDI, NICHOLAS, *David Hume: The Newtonian Philosopher* (Boston: Twayne, 1975).

KUYPERS, MARY S., *Studies in the Eighteenth Century Background of Hume's Empiricism* (Minneapolis: University of Minnesota Press, 1930; fac. New York: Garland, 1983).

MOORE, JAMES, 'The Social Background of Hume's Science of Human Nature', in Norton *et al.* (eds.), *McGill Hume Studies* (§ 4.4 above).

PEARS, DAVID, *Hume's System* (New York: Oxford University Press, 1990), chs. 1–2.

5.2. Perception, Ideas, and the External World

Price's influential book is astute, though dated and not widely accepted as the correct account. Bennett provides a philosophically aggressive and probing attempt to deal with themes of perception and causation in Hume and his immediate predecessors. O'Shea maintains that Hume is not merely a sceptic who appeals to common-sense belief in the external world, but a philosopher who defends a pragmatically coherent and reflectively satisfying 'system' of belief. Traiger's work is the most up to date and the closest to the text.

See also Garrett, *Cognition and Commitment in Hume's Philosophy* (§ 4.3 above); Waxman, *Hume's Theory of Consciousness* (§ 5.3 below); Hendel, *Studies in the Philosophy of David Hume* (§ 4.3 above); and the entire section on Scepticism (§ 5.12 below).

BENNETT, JONATHAN, *Locke, Berkeley, Hume: Central Themes* (Oxford: Clarendon Press, 1971).

O'SHEA, JAMES R., 'Hume's Reflective Return to the Vulgar', *British Journal for the History of Philosophy*, 4 (1996), 285–315.

PRICE, H. H., *Hume's Theory of the External World* (Oxford: Clarendon Press, 1940).

TRAIGER, SAUL, 'Impressions, Ideas, and Fictions', *Hume Studies*, 13 (1987), 381–99.

—— 'The Ownership of Perceptions: A Study of Hume's Metaphysics', *History of Philosophy Quarterly*, 5 (1988), 41–51.

5.3. *Philosophy of Mind, Passions, and Sentiments*

The works below rely more heavily on Hume's *Treatise* than on his subsequent work, but they are the best materials on these subjects. Árdal's book presents especially valuable material on the second and third books of the *Treatise*; it was influential in the 1970s and 1980s and is still well known among Hume scholars. Baier's book, which highlights the *Treatise's* unity, appears to be headed for a similar reputation. Baier combines textual work with a rich body of philosophical reflection, emphasizing the importance of Hume's account of the sentiments. Her constructive approach contrasts sharply with Waxman's interpretation, which conforms more to the traditional view of Hume as a sceptic than to recent interpretations of Hume as non-sceptical or anti-sceptical. Bricke's book exhibits careful and insightful thinking about many philosophical issues, though oriented more to the philosophy of mind in general than to detailed interpretation of Hume's text. Flage presents an interpretative rather than philosophical account of Hume's philosophy of mind. Heavily oriented to the *Treatise*, it includes a chapter on the *Enquiries* and contains useful textual interpretations for framing the doctrines in *EHU*.

ÁRDAL, PÁLL S., *Passion and Value in Hume's* Treatise (Edinburgh: Edinburgh University Press, 1966).

BAIER, ANNETTE, *A Progress of Sentiments* (Cambridge, Mass.: Harvard University Press, 1991).

BRICKE, JOHN, *Hume's Philosophy of Mind* (Princeton: Princeton University Press, 1980).

FLAGE, DANIEL E., *David Hume's Theory of Mind* (New York: Routledge & Kegan Paul, 1990).

WAXMAN, WAYNE, *Hume's Theory of Consciousness* (Cambridge: Cambridge University Press, 1994).

5.4. *Association of Ideas and Mental Activity*

The scholars listed below have all maintained, in very different ways, that Hume presents a theory of mental activity as well as an account of the association of ideas. Wolff and Beck bring deep interests in the parallels between Hume and Kant to their investigations. Wolff argues that Hume's theory of mental activity carries him beyond the limits of his own theory of association, which does not appear to allow for mental activity. Wilson maintains, in opposition to Wolff, that Hume consistently accounts for mental activity in terms of the laws of association. Wolff and Wilson both struggle with reconciling Newtonian principles of association and a theory of mental faculties. Beck minimizes the traditional notion that Kant and Hume are diametrically opposed. He maintains that Hume anticipated Kant by presenting a structure of mind that is a necessary condition of experience.

See also Passmore, *Hume's Intentions* (§ 4.3 above), ch. 6; Noxon, *Hume's Philosophical Development* (§ 4.3 above), pt. 3; Baier, *A Progress of Sentiments* (§ 5.3 above), ch. 2.

BECK, LEWIS WHITE, 'A Prussian Hume and a Scottish Kant', in Norton *et al.* (eds.), *McGill Hume Studies* (§ 4.4 above).

WILSON, FRED, 'Hume's Theory of Mental Activity', in Norton *et al.* (eds.), *McGill Hume Studies* (§ 4.4 above).

WOLFF, ROBERT PAUL, 'Hume's Theory of Mental Activity', in Chappell (ed.), *Hume: A Collection of Critical Essays* (§ 4.4 above).

5.5. Induction and Inductive Scepticism

Arnold argues for a version of the radical scepticism commonly attributed to Hume, criticizing interpretations (especially Beauchamp and Rosenberg, *Hume and the Problem of Causation*, § 5.7 below) that Hume held a milder scepticism or no scepticism at all. A similar range of issues is covered in the tightly reasoned essay by Millican. Morris offers an extended criticism of Mackie (*The Cement of the Universe*, § 5.7 below) and Stove, as well as a detailed reconstruction of Hume's argument. Arnold, Morris, and Millican provide judicious and readable interpretations that are careful attempts to explicate the text. By contrast, Stove's book is very difficult for introductory students. It is a philosophically rich exploration of Humean themes, but at a distance from Hume's text and with questionable interpretations of Hume's commitments. Passell is one of the few to isolate the arguments in *EHU* for consideration.

See also Beauchamp and Rosenberg, *Hume and the Problem of Causation* (§ 5.7 below), ch. 2; Baier, *A Progress of Sentiments* (§ 4.3 above), ch. 3; Fogelin, *Hume's Skepticism in the* Treatise of Human Nature (§ 5.12 below); Garrett, *Cognition and Commitment in Hume's Philosophy* (§ 4.3 above); Kemp Smith, *The Philosophy of David Hume* (§ 4.3 above), ch. 19; Owen's essay in Stewart and Wright (eds.), *Hume and Hume's Connexions* (§ 4.4 above).

ARNOLD, N. SCOTT, 'Hume's Skepticism about Inductive Inference', *Journal of the History of Philosophy*, 21 (1983), 31–55.

MILLICAN, PETER J. R., 'Hume's Argument concerning Induction: Structure and Interpretation', in Stanley Tweyman (ed.), *David Hume: Critical Assessments*, 6 vols. (London: Routledge, 1994).

MORRIS, WILLIAM EDWARD, 'Hume's Refutation of Inductive Probabilism', in James H. Fetzer (ed.), *Probability and Causality* (Dordrecht: Kluwer, 1988).

PASSELL, DAN, 'Hume's Arguments for his Sceptical Doubts', *Journal of Philosophical Research*, 22 (1997), 409–22.

Stove, David, *Probability and Hume's Inductive Scepticism* (Oxford: Clarendon Press, 1973).

5.6. Belief and Probability

The articles in this section are at an advanced level. Falkenstein argues that Hume's naturalist account of the causes of belief is rich enough to provide for normative assessments of belief and even for the modification of beliefs in light of these assessments. Owen considers whether a person can adjust beliefs by appeal to evidence, given the way beliefs are formed in Hume's system. Loeb likewise considers issues of justified belief. He maintains that for Hume the point of the distinction between reasonable and unreasonable belief is to call attention to circumstances in which thought is susceptible to instability and uneasiness, even though belief has been achieved.

Hacking concentrates on probable inference and provides an excellent introduction to the subject of probability—in Hume and in general. Gower provides a careful and attentive analysis of both the probability of chances and the probability of causes. He argues that interpreters often attribute to Hume views about probability that he did not hold.

Falkenstein, Lorne, 'Naturalism, Normativity, and Scepticism in Hume's Account of Belief', *Hume Studies*, 23 (1997), 29–72.

Gower, Barry, 'Hume on Probability', *British Journal for the Philosophy of Science*, 42 (1991), 1–19.

Hacking, Ian, 'Hume's Species of Probability', *Philosophical Studies*, 33 (1978), 21–37.

Loeb, Louis, 'Instability and Uneasiness in Hume's Theories of Belief and Justification', *British Journal for the History of Philosophy*, 3 (1995), 301–27.

Owen, David, 'Philosophy and the Good Life: Hume's Defence of Probable Reasoning', *Dialogue*, 35 (1996), 485–503.

5.7. Causation and Necessary Connection

Mackie's philosophically rich book has become a respected classic on causation; it centres less on Hume than on the philosophical problems of causation raised by Hume. Beauchamp and Rosenberg present a close textual analysis of the passages on causation, a critique of Mackie's account, and a philosophical defence of Hume's theory of causation. Strawson presents a resourceful interpretation of Hume as a philosopher who assumed the existence of causal powers and natural necessity, but did not assume that we can *know* powers and necessity. The book employs a useful distinction between metaphysical and epistemological interpretations of Hume. Lesher's article is brief and readable; it goes directly to the heart of the controversy about two definitions of 'cause', while presenting a novel interpretation. Garrett presents four different interpretations of Hume's two definitions and argues that Hume regards both definitions as correct.

Of the many articles published on this subject, Lesher and Garrett are particularly insightful and well argued and Garrett contains a useful discussion of the literature on the subject.

See also Garrett, *Cognition and Commitment in Hume's Philosophy* (§ 4.3 above); Robinson and Richards in Chappell (ed.), *Hume: A Collection of Critical Essays* (§ 4.4 above); Baier, *A Progress of Sentiments* (§ 5.3 above), chs. 3–4; Johnson, *The Mind of David Hume* (§ 4.3 above); Winkler, 'The New Hume' (§ 4.3 above).

BEAUCHAMP, TOM L., and ROSENBERG, ALEXANDER, *Hume and the Problem of Causation* (New York: Oxford University Press, 1981).

GARRETT, DON, 'The Representation of Causation and Hume's Two Definitions of "Cause"', *Nous*, 27 (1993), 167–90.

LESHER, JAMES, 'Hume's Analysis of Cause and the "Two Definitions" Dispute', *Journal of the History of Philosophy*, 11 (1973), 387–92.

MACKIE, JOHN L., *The Cement of the Universe* (Oxford: Clarendon Press, 1974).

STRAWSON, GALEN, *The Secret Connexion: Causation, Realism, and David Hume* (Oxford: Clarendon Press, 1989).

5.8. Liberty and Necessity

On the whole, the literature on this topic is less interesting philosophically than is literature on the topics previously listed. It lacks philosophical quality and imaginativeness in interpretation. However, a few studies deserve consideration.

Huxley's study is of historical interest and contains an interesting treatment of liberty and necessity as well as the reasoning of animals. Hobart's once popular article is a well-written defence of a Humean compatibilist position that says little about Hume himself. Russell's book focuses as much on morality as it does on the metaphysics of liberty and necessity. However, Russell does offer an extensive and informed discussion of Hume's compatibilist position, in which he emphasizes that Hume's compatibilism has generally been misunderstood because his naturalism has been overlooked. Russell sees the moral sentiments as more basic to responsibility than freedom. Flew's chapter also treats the compatibilist character of Hume's theory and is one of the best chapters in the book. Vesey provides a readable introduction to Hume's major concepts and ideas, along with philosophical commentary; it deals more with the literature on liberty than the literature on Hume's theory.

See also Garrett, *Cognition and Commitment in Hume's Philosophy* (§ 4.3 above); Kemp Smith, *The Philosophy of David Hume* (§ 4.3 above), ch. 20; Stroud, *Hume* (§ 4.3 above), ch. 7.

FLEW, ANTONY, 'Necessity, Liberty, and the Possibility of a Moral Science', in *David Hume: Philosopher of Moral Science* (Oxford: Blackwell, 1986).

HOBART, R. E., 'Free-Will as Involving Determination and Inconceivable without It', *Mind*, 43 (1934), 1–27.

HUXLEY, T. H., *Hume, with Helps to the Study of Berkeley* (London, 1894).

RUSSELL, PAUL, *Freedom & Moral Sentiment: Hume's Way of Naturalizing Responsibility* (New York: Oxford University Press, 1995).

VESEY, GODFREY, 'Hume on Liberty and Necessity', in Vesey (ed.), *Philosophers Ancient and Modern* (New York: Cambridge University Press, 1986).

5.9. Reason in Animals

The following articles discuss Hume's arguments in *THN* as well as *EHU*. The authors are sometimes more concerned with the moral implications of Hume's view than with his account of reason and causal inference. Arnold, for example, considers reason only when doing so is necessary to explicate Hume's view of the moral differences between the species (but devotes section 4 of his article to reason). Pitson is more broadly concerned with Hume's view of the similarities and differences in the species, but gives pride of place to issues of moral status. Baier offers some far-reaching conclusions about Hume's passages on reason, pride, love, and sympathy in animals. She suggests that, in addition to reason, animals may possess a moral sense in Hume's treatment.

ARNOLD, DENIS G., 'Hume on the Moral Difference between Humans and Other Animals', *History of Philosophy Quarterly*, 12 (1995), 303–16.

BAIER, ANNETTE, 'Knowing our Place in the Animal World', in *Postures of the Mind: Essays on Mind and Morals* (Minneapolis: University of Minnesota Press, 1985).

PITSON, ANTONY E., 'The Nature of Humean Animals', *Hume Studies*, 19 (1993), 301–16.

5.10. Miracles

Levine's book contains the broadest philosophical (as opposed to historical) treatment of the subject. It places the work on miracles in the context of epistemological arguments on induction and necessary connection. Houston's book is a critique of Hume, often motivated more by theological than philosophical concerns. None the less, it is philosophically probing, exegetically strong, and historically well informed—perhaps the best balance of these different emphases found in the literature on Hume and miracles. The book by Swinburne also contains criticisms of Hume. It is an influential treatment of the more general subject of miracles and their justification. Broad's classic article remains one of the most polished works of the many that discuss Hume's treatment of miracles. Some commentators, almost a century later, regard it as the best general philosophical study. It is criticized by Root, who provides an able combination of textual interpretation and philosophical evaluation. The volume edited by Tweyman focuses on historically important responses to Hume from 1751 to 1882; authors of these responses include Thomas Rutherforth, William Adams, Anthony Ellys, Samuel Vince, James Somerville, William Warburton, Joseph Napier, Joseph Wheeler, and Thomas Huxley.

Supplementary Reading

See also Garrett, *Cognition and Commitment in Hume's Philosophy* (§ 4.3 above); Stewart's essay in Stewart and Wright (eds.), *Hume and Hume's Connexions* (§ 4.4 above); Flew, *Hume's Philosophy of Belief* (§ 4.2 above), ch. 8; Yandell, *Hume's 'Inexplicable Mystery'* (§ 5.11 below), ch. 15; Gaskin, *Hume's Philosophy of Religion* (§ 5.11 below), pt. 2.

BROAD, C. D., 'Hume's Theory of the Credibility of Miracles', *Proceedings of the Aristotelian Society*, 17 (1916–17), 77–94.

HOUSTON, J., *Reported Miracles: A Critique of Hume* (Cambridge: Cambridge University Press, 1994).

LEVINE, MICHAEL P., *Hume and the Problem of Miracles* (Dordrecht: Kluwer, 1989).

ROOT, MICHAEL, 'Miracles and the Uniformity of Nature', *American Philosophical Quarterly*, 26 (1989), 333–42.

SWINBURNE, RICHARD, *The Concept of Miracle* (London: Macmillan, 1970).

TWEYMAN, STANLEY (ed.), *Hume on Miracles* (Bristol: Thoemmes, 1996).

5.11. Providence and a Future State

Relatively little has been published on this section of *EHU*, perhaps because so much work has gone into the study of directly related topics in Hume's *Dialogues*. However, each of the works below provides commentary specific to *EHU* 11.

Gaskin's study of Hume's philosophy of religion is a well-structured, innovative work in the field. It remains influential and is considered by many to be the standard introductory work on the topic. Part 1 contains abundant material on the issues in *EHU* 11 (and Part 2 contains a discussion of miracles). Yandell's book, like Gaskin's, is a comprehensive treatment of Hume's philosophy of religion with unusually thorough attention to Hume's *Natural History of Religion*; it is, however, brief on issues raised in *EHU*. Flew offers a convenient and comprehensive collection of Hume's writings on religion that contains a short introduction to both sections of *EHU* that deal with religion. Penelhum's clearly written and judicious survey of Hume's philosophy contains a brief discussion of *EHU* 11 in ch. 8.

See also Penelhum, *David Hume* (§ 4.1 above), ch. 6; Flew, *Hume's Philosophy of Belief* (§ 4.2 above), esp. ch. 9; Norton, *David Hume* (§ 5.12 below), ch. 4. Scholarly material on Hume's *Dialogues* often covers closely related subjects, such as the design argument.

FLEW, ANTONY (ed.), *David Hume: Writings on Religion* (La Salle, Ill.: Open Court, 1992).

GASKIN, J. C. A., *Hume's Philosophy of Religion*, 2nd edn. (London: Macmillan; Atlantic Highlands, NJ: Humanities Press, 1988).

PENELHUM, TERENCE, *Hume* (New York: St Martin's Press, 1975), ch. 8.

YANDELL, KEITH E., *Hume's 'Inexplicable Mystery'* (Philadelphia: Temple University Press, 1990), pt. 2, esp. pp. 309–14.

5.12. Scepticism

Norton's influential and exceptionally clear book provides an erudite account of Hume's intellectual background in the philosophers of the period. He treats Hume as a sceptical metaphysician but non-sceptical moralist. Wright argues that Hume is both a metaphysical sceptic and metaphysical realist—an apparently unlikely combination, but one presented with some historical and textual subtlety. Popkin and Fogelin both argue that Hume is a Pyrrhonian sceptic. Popkin's study is historically interesting, but Fogelin's animated work is the philosophically and textually more subtle of the two. Norton, Fogelin, and Wright all strive for a more balanced interpretation than that found in traditional scholarship on Hume, especially in the dominant theory of Norman Kemp Smith. Fogelin's book stands in sharp contrast to recent anti-sceptical interpretations of Hume. Immerwahr's article is one of the few published that focuses more on *EHU* than the *Treatise*.

See also Beauchamp and Rosenberg, *Hume and the Problem of Causation* (§ 5.7 above); Garrett, *Cognition and Commitment in Hume's Philosophy* (§ 4.3 above); several essays on scepticism in Norton *et al.* (eds.), *McGill Hume Studies* (§ 4.4 above); Arnold, 'Hume's Skepticism about Inductive Inference' (§ 5.5 above); Stove, *Probability and Hume's Inductive Scepticism* (§ 5.5 above); Johnson, *The Mind of David Hume* (§ 4.3 above), pt. 4; Fogelin in Norton (ed.), *The Cambridge Companion to Hume* (§ 4.1 above); Winkler, 'The New Hume' (§ 4.3 above).

FOGELIN, ROBERT J., *Hume's Skepticism in the* Treatise of Human Nature (Boston: Routledge & Kegan Paul, 1985).

IMMERWAHR, JOHN, 'A Skeptic's Progress: Hume's Preference for the *First Enquiry*', in Norton *et al.* (eds.), *McGill Hume Studies* (§ 4.4 above).

NORTON, DAVID FATE, *David Hume: Common-Sense Moralist, Sceptical Metaphysician*, 2nd edn. (Princeton: Princeton University Press, 1984).

—— 'How a Sceptic may Live Scepticism', in J. J. MacIntosh (ed.), *Essays in Honour of Terence Penelhum* (Calgary: University of Calgary Press, 1993).

POPKIN, RICHARD, *The High Road to Pyrrhonism*, ed. Richard A. Watson and James E. Force (San Diego, Calif.: Austin Hill, 1980).

WILSON, FRED, 'Is Hume a Sceptic with regard to the Senses?', *Journal of the History of Philosophy*, 27 (1989), 49–73.

WRIGHT, JOHN P., *The Sceptical Realism of David Hume* (Manchester: Manchester University Press; Minneapolis: University of Minnesota Press, 1983).

6. GENERAL BIBLIOGRAPHICAL MATERIALS

The work of Jessop and Hall and the follow-up articles in *Hume Studies* by Hall and Morris are indispensable bibliographical materials for serious research in the

Hume literature. The *Philosopher's Index* is pivotal for journal research in the literature after 1940.

HALL, ROLAND, *50 Years of Hume Scholarship* (Edinburgh: Edinburgh University Press, 1978).
——and [later] MORRIS, WILLIAM E., 'The Hume Literature for [years]', *Hume Studies*, 4 and various later volumes. Updated frequently; published as a supplement to Hall, *50 Years of Hume Scholarship* (above).
JESSOP, T. E., *A Bibliography of David Hume and of Scottish Philosophy, from Francis Hutcheson to Lord Balfour* (London: Brown, 1938; fac. New York: Garland, 1983).
LINEBACK, RICHARD H. (ed.), *Philosopher's Index* (Bowling Green, Ohio: Philosophy Documentation Center, Bowling Green State University). Issued quarterly in printed edition. Also available in CD-ROM and On-Line versions. Includes bibliographic citations and abstracts from approximately 300 journals.

7. SPECIALIZED BIBLIOGRAPHICAL MATERIALS

The following materials are specialized and of value primarily for scholars and advanced students. Capaldi *et al.* and Yalden-Thomson are general and extensive surveys of the literature of the period. Todd presents details of the earliest editions of Hume's works. Greig and Beynon and Cunningham catalogue and explain a large collection of Hume's correspondence, manuscripts, and other materials once held by the Royal Society of Edinburgh (now held by the National Library of Scotland). The Chuo University publications contain a bibliography of both Hume's lifetime editions and eighteenth-century British publications by other authors.

CAPALDI, NICHOLAS, KING, JAMES, and LIVINGSTON, DONALD, 'The Hume Literature of the 1970s', *Philosophical Topics*, 12 (1981), 167–92.
—————'The Hume Literature of the 1980s', *American Philosophical Quarterly*, 28 (1991), 255–72.
CHUO UNIVERSITY, *David Hume and the Eighteenth Century British Thought: An Annotated Catalogue*, ed. Sadao Ikeda, 2 vols. (Tokyo: Chuo University Library, 1986, 1988).
CUNNINGHAM, IAN C., 'The Arrangement of the Royal Society of Edinburgh's David Hume Collection', *The Bibliotheck*, 15 (1988), 8–22.
GREIG, J. Y. T., and BEYNON, HAROLD, *Calendar of Hume MSS in the Possession of the Royal Society of Edinburgh* (Edinburgh: Royal Society of Edinburgh, 1932; fac. New York: Garland, 1990).
NORTON, DAVID FATE, and NORTON, MARY J., *The David Hume Library* (Edinburgh: Edinburgh Bibliographical Society, 1996).
TODD, W. B., 'David Hume, A Preliminary Bibliography', in Todd (ed.), *Hume*

and the Enlightenment: Essays Presented to Ernest Campbell Mossner (Edinburgh: Edinburgh University Press, 1974).

YALDEN-THOMSON, D. C., 'Recent Work on Hume', *American Philosophical Quarterly*, 20 (1983), 1–22.

The Text Printed in this Edition

An Enquiry concerning Human Understanding was first published in 1748. The last edition seen through the press with Hume's supervision appeared in 1772. This edition is the basis of the text (the copytext) in the present edition. The posthumous edition of 1777, which contained corrections Hume made shortly before his death, has been consulted for evidence of late changes by the author and has almost always been followed for substantive changes (with the exception of a major and unexplained deletion in Section 3 that occurred in the 1777 edition). The methods used in converting the copytext into the definitive or 'critical' text of the present edition and a history of Hume's revisions are provided in the Clarendon Hume, a critical edition that explains editorial policy with regard to the choice of copytext, emendation, and correction of errors, and records all substantive variants.

The sources cited by Hume in his notes have been checked against original sources and corrected whenever Hume or his compositor introduced errors in the citation of items such as page, book, and chapter numbers. Footnotes have been supplemented by the editor to provide more complete information, including precise titles, volumes, books, chapters, sections, and lines. This editorial amplification appears within square brackets to distinguish it from Hume's text.

No editorial intrusions have been allowed in the text itself except for the daggers that indicate where an annotation appears in Part 3 and the marginal numbers for each paragraph.

PART 2
The Text

ADVERTISEMENT[†]

MOST of the principles, and reasonings, contained in this volume, were published in a work in three volumes, called *A Treatise of Human Nature*: A work which the Author had projected before he left College, and which he wrote and published not long after. But not finding it successful, he was sensible of his error in going to the press too early, and he cast the whole anew in the following pieces, where some negligences in his former reasoning and more in the expression, are, he hopes, corrected. Yet several writers, who have honoured the Author's Philosophy with answers, have taken care to direct all their batteries against that juvenile work, which the Author never acknowledged, and have affected to triumph in any advantages, which, they imagined, they had obtained over it: A practice very contrary to all rules of candour and fair-dealing, and a strong instance of those polemical artifices, which a bigotted zeal thinks itself authorised to employ. Henceforth, the Author desires, that the following Pieces may alone be regarded as containing his philosophical sentiments and principles.

AN ENQUIRY CONCERNING
HUMAN UNDERSTANDING

SECTION 1

OF THE DIFFERENT SPECIES OF PHILOSOPHY

1   MORAL philosophy,[†] or the science of human nature,[†] may be treated after two different manners;[†] each of which has its peculiar merit, and may contribute to the entertainment, instruction, and reformation of mankind. The one considers man chiefly as born for action; and as influenced in his measures by taste and sentiment;[†] pursuing one object, and avoiding another, according to the value which these objects seem to possess, and according to the light in which they present themselves. As virtue, of all objects, is allowed to be the most valuable, this species of philosophers paint her in the most amiable colours; borrowing all helps from poetry and eloquence,[†] and treating their subject in an easy and obvious[†] manner, and such as is best fitted to please the imagination, and engage the affections. They select the most striking observations and instances from common life; place opposite characters in a proper contrast; and alluring us into the paths of virtue by the views of glory and happiness, direct our steps in these paths by the soundest precepts and most illustrious examples. They make us *feel* the difference between vice and virtue; they excite and regulate our sentiments; and so they can but bend our hearts to the love of probity and true honour, they think, that they have fully attained the end of all their labours.

2   The other species of philosophers consider man in the light of a reasonable rather than an active being, and endeavour to form his understanding more than cultivate his manners. They regard human nature as a subject of speculation; and with a narrow scrutiny examine it, in order to find those principles, which regulate our understanding, excite our sentiments, and make us approve or blame any particular object, action, or behaviour. They think it a reproach to all literature,[†] that philosophy should not yet have fixed, beyond controversy, the foundation of morals, reasoning, and criticism;[†] and should for ever talk of truth and falsehood, vice and virtue, beauty and deformity, without being able to determine

the source of these distinctions. While they attempt this arduous task, they are deterred by no difficulties; but proceeding from particular instances to general principles, they still push on their enquiries to principles more general, and rest not satisfied till they arrive at those original principles, by which, in every science,[†] all human curiosity must be bounded. Though their speculations seem abstract, and even unintelligible to common readers, they aim at the approbation of the learned and the wise; and think themselves sufficiently compensated for the labour of their whole lives, if they can discover some hidden truths, which may contribute to the instruction of posterity.

3   It is certain, that the easy and obvious philosophy will always, with the generality of mankind, have the preference above the accurate and abstruse; and by many will be recommended, not only as more agreeable, but more useful than the other. It enters more into common life; SBN 7 moulds the heart and affections; and, by touching those principles which actuate men, reforms their conduct, and brings them nearer to that model of perfection which it describes. On the contrary, the abstruse philosophy, being founded on a turn of mind, which cannot enter into business and action, vanishes when the philosopher leaves the shade, and comes into open day; nor can its principles easily retain any influence over our conduct and behaviour. The feelings of our heart, the agitation of our passions, the vehemence of our affections, dissipate all its conclusions, and reduce the profound philosopher to a mere plebeian.[†]

4   This also must be confessed, that the most durable, as well as justest fame, has been acquired by the easy philosophy, and that abstract reasoners seem hitherto to have enjoyed only a momentary reputation, from the caprice or ignorance of their own age, but have not been able to support their renown with more equitable posterity. It is easy for a profound philosopher to commit a mistake in his subtile reasonings; and one mistake is the necessary parent of another, while he pushes on his consequences, and is not deterred from embracing any conclusion, by its unusual appearance, or its contradiction to popular opinion. But a philosopher, who purposes only to represent the common sense of mankind in more beautiful and more engaging colours, if by accident he falls into error, goes no farther; but renewing his appeal to common sense, and the natural sentiments of the mind, returns into the right path, and secures himself from any dangerous illusions. The fame of CICERO[†] flourishes at present; but that of ARISTOTLE[†] is utterly decayed. LA BRUYERE[†] passes the seas, and still maintains his reputation: But the glory of MALEBRANCHE[†]

is confined to his own nation, and to his own age. And ADDISON,[†] perhaps, will be read with pleasure, when LOCKE[†] shall be entirely forgotten.

5   The mere philosopher is a character, which is commonly but little   *SBN 8* acceptable in the world, as being supposed to contribute nothing either to the advantage or pleasure of society; while he lives remote from communication with mankind, and is wrapped up in principles and notions equally remote from their comprehension. On the other hand, the mere ignorant is still more despised; nor is any thing deemed a surer sign of an illiberal genius in an age and nation where the sciences[†] flourish, than to be entirely destitute of all relish for those noble entertainments. The most perfect character is supposed to lie between those extremes; retaining an equal ability and taste for books, company, and business; preserving in conversation that discernment and delicacy which arise from polite letters;[†] and in business, that probity and accuracy which are the natural result of a just philosophy. In order to diffuse and cultivate so accomplished a character, nothing can be more useful than compositions of the easy style and manner, which draw not too much from life, require no deep application or retreat to be comprehended, and send back the student among mankind full of noble sentiments and wise precepts, applicable to every exigence of human life. By means of such compositions, virtue becomes amiable, science agreeable, company instructive, and retirement entertaining.

6   Man is a reasonable being; and as such, receives from science his proper food and nourishment: But so narrow are the bounds of human understanding, that little satisfaction can be hoped for in this particular, either from the extent or security of his acquisitions. Man is a sociable, no less than a reasonable being: But neither can he always enjoy company agreeable and amusing, or preserve the proper relish for them. Man is also an active being; and from that disposition, as well as from the various necessities of human life, must submit to business and occupation: But the   *SBN 9* mind requires some relaxation, and cannot always support its bent to care and industry. It seems, then, that nature has pointed out a mixed kind of life as most suitable to human race, and secretly admonished them to allow none of these biasses to *draw* too much, so as to incapacitate them for other occupations and entertainments. Indulge your passion for science, says she, but let your science be human, and such as may have a direct reference to action and society. Abstruse thought and profound researches I prohibit, and will severely punish, by the pensive melancholy which they introduce, by the endless uncertainty in which they involve you, and by the cold reception which your pretended discoveries will meet

with, when communicated. Be a philosopher; but, amidst all your philosophy, be still a man.

7   Were the generality of mankind contented to prefer the easy philosophy to the abstract and profound, without throwing any blame or contempt on the latter, it might not be improper, perhaps, to comply with this general opinion, and allow every man to enjoy, without opposition, his own taste and sentiment. But as the matter is often carried farther, even to the absolute rejecting of all profound reasonings, or what is commonly called *metaphysics*,[†] we shall now proceed to consider what can reasonably be pleaded in their behalf.

8   We may begin with observing, that one considerable advantage, which results from the accurate and abstract philosophy, is, its subserviency to the easy and humane; which, without the former, can never attain a sufficient degree of exactness in its sentiments, precepts, or reasonings. All polite letters are nothing but pictures of human life in various attitudes and situations; and inspire us with different sentiments, of praise or blame, admiration or ridicule, according to the qualities of the object, which they set before us. An artist[†] must be better qualified to succeed in this undertaking, who, besides a delicate taste and a quick apprehension, possesses an accurate knowledge of the internal fabric, the operations of the understanding, the workings of the passions, and the various species of sentiment which discriminate vice and virtue. How painful soever this inward search or enquiry may appear, it becomes, in some measure, requisite to those, who would describe with success the obvious and outward appearances of life and manners. The anatomist presents to the eye the most hideous and disagreeable objects; but his science is useful to the painter[†] in delineating even a VENUS or an HELEN.[†] While the latter employs all the richest colours of his art, and gives his figures the most graceful and engaging airs; he must still carry his attention to the inward structure of the human body, the position of the muscles, the fabric of the bones, and the use and figure of every part or organ. Accuracy is, in every case, advantageous to beauty, and just reasoning to delicate sentiment. In vain would we exalt the one by depreciating the other.

SBN

9   Besides, we may observe, in every art or profession, even those which most concern life or action, that a spirit of accuracy, however acquired, carries all of them nearer their perfection, and renders them more subservient to the interests of society. And though a philosopher may live remote from business, the genius of philosophy,[†] if carefully cultivated by several, must gradually diffuse itself throughout the whole society,

and bestow a similar correctness on every art and calling. The politician will acquire greater foresight and subtilty, in the subdividing and balancing of power; the lawyer more method and finer principles in his reasonings; and the general more regularity in his discipline, and more caution in his plans and operations. The stability of modern governments above the ancient, and the accuracy of modern philosophy, have improved, and probably will still improve, by similar gradations.

10   Were there no advantage to be reaped from these studies, beyond the   *SBN 11* gratification of an innocent curiosity, yet ought not even this to be despised; as being one accession to those few safe and harmless pleasures, which are bestowed on human race. The sweetest and most inoffensive path of life leads through the avenues of science and learning; and whoever can either remove any obstructions in this way, or open up any new prospect, ought so far to be esteemed a benefactor to mankind. And though these researches may appear painful and fatiguing, it is with some minds as with some bodies, which, being endowed with vigorous and florid health, require severe exercise, and reap a pleasure from what, to the generality of mankind, may seem burdensome and laborious. Obscurity, indeed, is painful to the mind as well as to the eye; but to bring light from obscurity, by whatever labour, must needs be delightful and rejoicing.

11   But this obscurity in the profound and abstract philosophy, is objected to, not only as painful and fatiguing, but as the inevitable source of uncertainty and error. Here indeed lies the justest and most plausible objection against a considerable part of metaphysics, that they are not properly a science; but arise either from the fruitless efforts of human vanity, which would penetrate into subjects utterly inaccessible to the understanding, or from the craft of popular superstitions,[†] which, being unable to defend themselves on fair ground, raise these intangling brambles to cover and protect their weakness. Chaced from the open country, these robbers fly into the forest, and lie in wait to break in upon every unguarded avenue of the mind, and overwhelm it with religious fears and prejudices. The stoutest antagonist, if he remit his watch a moment, is oppressed. And many, through cowardice and folly, open the gates to the enemies, and willingly receive them with reverence and submission, as their legal sovereigns.

12   But is this a sufficient reason, why philosophers should desist from such   *SBN 12* researches, and leave superstition still in possession of her retreat? Is it not proper to draw an opposite conclusion, and perceive the necessity of carrying the war into the most secret recesses of the enemy? In vain do

we hope, that men, from frequent disappointment, will at last abandon such airy sciences, and discover the proper province of human reason. For, besides that many persons find too sensible an interest in perpetually recalling such topics; besides this, I say, the motive of blind despair can never reasonably have place in the sciences; since, however unsuccessful former attempts may have proved, there is still room to hope, that the industry, good fortune, or improved sagacity of succeeding generations may reach discoveries unknown to former ages. Each adventurous genius will still leap at the arduous prize, and find himself stimulated, rather than discouraged, by the failures of his predecessors; while he hopes that the glory of atchieving so hard an adventure is reserved for him alone. The only method of freeing learning, at once, from these abstruse questions, is to enquire seriously into the nature of human understanding, and show, from an exact analysis of its powers and capacity, that it is by no means fitted for such remote and abstruse subjects. We must submit to this fatigue, in order to live at ease ever after: And must cultivate true metaphysics with some care, in order to destroy the false and adulterate. Indolence, which, to some persons, affords a safeguard against this deceitful philosophy, is, with others, overbalanced by curiosity; and despair, which, at some moments, prevails, may give place afterwards to sanguine hopes and expectations. Accurate and just reasoning is the only catholic remedy,[†] fitted for all persons and all dispositions; and is alone able to subvert that abstruse philosophy and metaphysical jargon, which, being mixed up with popular superstition, renders it in a manner impenetrable to careless reasoners, and gives it the air of science and wisdom.   SBN 1

13   Besides this advantage of rejecting, after deliberate enquiry, the most uncertain and disagreeable part of learning, there are many positive advantages, which result from an accurate scrutiny into the powers and faculties of human nature. It is remarkable concerning the operations of the mind, that, though most intimately present to us, yet, whenever they become the object of reflection, they seem involved in obscurity; nor can the eye readily find those lines and boundaries, which discriminate and distinguish them. The objects are too fine to remain long in the same aspect or situation; and must be apprehended in an instant, by a superior penetration, derived from nature, and improved by habit and reflection. It becomes, therefore, no inconsiderable part of science barely to know the different operations of the mind, to separate them from each other, to class them under their proper heads, and to correct all that seeming disorder, in which they lie involved, when made the object of reflection

i.e. – universal

and enquiry. This task of ordering and distinguishing, which has no merit, when performed with regard to external bodies, the objects of our senses, rises in its value, when directed towards the operations of the mind, in proportion to the difficulty and labour, which we meet with in performing it. And if we can go no farther than this mental geography, or delineation of the distinct parts and powers of the mind, it is at least a satisfaction to go so far; and the more obvious this science may appear (and it is by no means obvious) the more contemptible still must the ignorance of it be esteemed, in all pretenders to learning and philosophy.

14   Nor can there remain any suspicion, that this science is uncertain and chimerical;† unless we should entertain such a scepticism as is entirely subversive of all speculation, and even action. It cannot be doubted, that the mind is endowed with several powers and faculties, that these powers *SBN 14* are distinct from each other, that what is really distinct to the immediate perception may be distinguished by reflection; and consequently, that there is a truth and falsehood in all propositions on this subject, and a truth and falsehood, which lie not beyond the compass of human understanding.† There are many obvious distinctions of this kind, such as those between the will and understanding, the imagination and passions, which fall within the comprehension of every human creature; and the finer and more philosophical distinctions are no less real and certain, though more difficult to be comprehended. Some instances, especially late ones, of success† in these enquiries, may give us a juster notion of the certainty and solidity of this branch of learning. And shall we esteem it worthy the labour of a philosopher to give us a true system of the planets, and adjust the position and order of those remote bodies; while we affect to overlook those, who, with so much success, delineate the parts† of the mind, in which we are so intimately concerned?

15   But may we not hope, that philosophy, if cultivated with care, and encouraged by the attention of the public, may carry its researches still farther, and discover, at least in some degree, the secret springs and principles, by which the human mind is actuated in its operations? Astronomers had long contented themselves with proving, from the phænomena,† the true motions, order, and magnitude of the heavenly bodies: Till a philosopher, at last, arose,† who seems, from the happiest reasoning, to have also determined the laws and forces, by which the revolutions of the planets are governed and directed. The like has been performed with regard to other parts of nature. And there is no reason to despair of equal success in our enquiries concerning the mental powers and œconomy, if prosecuted with equal capacity and caution. It is

probable, that one operation and principle of the mind depends on SBN 1 another; which, again, may be resolved into one more general and universal: And how far these researches may possibly be carried, it will be difficult for us, before, or even after, a careful trial, exactly to determine. This is certain, that attempts of this kind are every day made even by those who philosophize the most negligently: And nothing can be more requisite than to enter upon the enterprize with thorough care and attention; that, if it lie within the compass of human understanding, it may at last be happily atchieved; if not, it may, however, be rejected with some confidence and security. This last conclusion, surely, is not desirable; nor ought it to be embraced too rashly. For how much must we diminish from the beauty and value of this species of philosophy, upon such a supposition? Moralists have hitherto been accustomed, when they considered the vast multitude and diversity of those actions that excite our approbation or dislike, to search for some common principle, on which this variety of sentiments might depend. And though they have sometimes carried the matter too far, by their passion for some one general principle; it must, however, be confessed, that they are excusable in expecting to find some general principles, into which all the vices and virtues were justly to be resolved. The like has been the endeavour of critics, logicians, and even politicians:[†] Nor have their attempts been wholly unsuccessful; though perhaps longer time, greater accuracy, and more ardent application may bring these sciences still nearer their perfection. To throw up at once all pretensions of this kind may justly be deemed more rash, precipitate, and dogmatical, than even the boldest and most affirmative philosophy, that has ever attempted to impose its crude dictates and principles on mankind.

16   What though these reasonings concerning human nature seem abstract, and of difficult comprehension? This affords no presumption SBN 1 of their falsehood. On the contrary, it seems impossible, that what has hitherto escaped so many wise and profound philosophers can be very obvious and easy. And whatever pains these researches may cost us, we may think ourselves sufficiently rewarded, not only in point of profit but of pleasure, if, by that means, we can make any addition to our stock of knowledge, in subjects of such unspeakable importance.

17   But as, after all, the abstractedness of these speculations is no recommendation, but rather a disadvantage to them, and as this difficulty may perhaps be surmounted by care and art, and the avoiding of all unnecessary detail, we have, in the following enquiry, attempted to throw some light upon subjects, from which uncertainty has hitherto deterred the

wise, and obscurity the ignorant. Happy, if we can unite the boundaries of the different species of philosophy, by reconciling profound enquiry with clearness, and truth with novelty! And still more happy, if, reasoning in this easy manner, we can undermine the foundations of an abstruse philosophy, which seems to have hitherto served only as a shelter to superstition, and a cover to absurdity and error!

SECTION 2

OF THE ORIGIN OF IDEAS

1 EVERY one will readily allow, that there is a considerable difference between the perceptions of the mind,[†] when a man feels the pain of excessive heat, or the pleasure of moderate warmth, and when he afterwards recalls to his memory this sensation, or anticipates it by his imagination. These faculties may mimic or copy the perceptions of the senses; but they never can entirely reach the force and vivacity of the original sentiment. The utmost we say of them, even when they operate with greatest vigour, is, that they represent their object in so lively a manner, that we could *almost* say we feel or see it: But, except the mind be disordered by disease or madness,[†] they never can arrive at such a pitch of vivacity, as to render these perceptions altogether undistinguishable. All the colours of poetry, however splendid, can never paint natural objects in such a manner as to make the description be taken for a real landscape. The most lively thought is still inferior to the dullest sensation.

2 We may observe a like distinction to run through all the other perceptions of the mind. A man, in a fit of anger, is actuated in a very different manner from one who only thinks of that emotion. If you tell me, that any person is in love, I easily understand your meaning, and form a just conception of his situation; but never can mistake that conception for the real disorders and agitations of the passion. When we reflect on our past sentiments and affections, our thought is a faithful mirror, and copies its objects truly; but the colours which it employs are faint and dull, in comparison of those in which our original perceptions were clothed. It requires no nice discernment or metaphysical head to mark the distinction between them.

3 Here therefore we may divide all the perceptions of the mind into two classes or species, which are distinguished by their different degrees of force and vivacity. The less forcible and lively are commonly denominated THOUGHTS or IDEAS. The other species want a name in our language, and in most others; I suppose, because it was not requisite for any, but philosophical purposes, to rank them under a general term or appellation. Let

us, therefore, use a little freedom, and call them IMPRESSIONS; employing that word in a sense somewhat different from the usual.[†] By the term *impression*, then, I mean all our more lively perceptions, when we hear, or see, or feel, or love, or hate, or desire, or will. And impressions are distinguished from ideas, which are the less lively perceptions, of which we are conscious, when we reflect on any of those sensations or movements above-mentioned.

4   Nothing, at first view, may seem more unbounded than the thought of man, which not only escapes all human power and authority, but is not even restrained within the limits of nature and reality. To form monsters, and join incongruous shapes and appearances, costs the imagination no more trouble than to conceive the most natural and familiar objects. And while the body is confined to one planet, along which it creeps with pain and difficulty; the thought can in an instant transport us into the most distant regions of the universe; or even beyond the universe, into the unbounded chaos, where nature is supposed to lie in total confusion. What never was seen, or heard of, may yet be conceived; nor is any thing beyond the power of thought, except what implies an absolute contradiction.[†]

5   But though our thought seems to possess this unbounded liberty, we *SBN 19* shall find, upon a nearer examination, that it is really confined within very narrow limits, and that all this creative power of the mind amounts to no more than the faculty of compounding, transposing, augmenting, or diminishing the materials afforded us by the senses and experience. When we think of a golden mountain, we only join two consistent ideas, *gold*, and *mountain*, with which we were formerly acquainted. A virtuous horse we can conceive; because, from our own feeling, we can conceive virtue; and this we may unite to the figure and shape of a horse, which is an animal familiar to us. In short, all the materials of thinking are derived either from our outward or inward sentiment: The mixture and composition of these belongs alone to the mind and will. Or, to express myself in philosophical language, all our ideas or more feeble perceptions are copies of our impressions or more lively ones.

6   To prove this, the two following arguments will, I hope, be sufficient. *First*, When we analyze our thoughts or ideas, however compounded or sublime, we always find, that they resolve themselves into such simple ideas as were copied from a precedent feeling or sentiment. Even those ideas, which, at first view, seem the most wide of this origin, are found, upon a nearer scrutiny, to be derived from it. The idea of God, as meaning *an infinitely intelligent, wise, and good Being*, arises from reflecting on the

operations of our own mind, and augmenting, without limit, those qualities of goodness and wisdom. We may prosecute this enquiry to what length we please; where we shall always find, that every idea which we examine is copied from a similar impression. Those who would assert, that this position is not universally true nor without exception, have only one, and that an easy method of refuting it; by producing that idea, which, in their opinion, is not derived from this source. It will then be incumbent on us, if we would maintain our doctrine, to produce the impression or lively perception, which corresponds to it. *SBN 20*

7   *Secondly*, If it happen, from a defect of the organ, that a man is not susceptible of any species of sensation,† we always find, that he is as little susceptible of the correspondent ideas. A blind man can form no notion of colours; a deaf man of sounds. Restore either of them that sense, in which he is deficient; by opening this new inlet for his sensations, you also open an inlet for the ideas; and he finds no difficulty in conceiving these objects. The case is the same, if the object, proper for exciting any sensation, has never been applied to the organ. A LAPLANDER† or NEGROE has no notion of the relish of wine.† And though there are few or no instances of a like deficiency in the mind, where a person has never felt or is wholly incapable of a sentiment or passion, that belongs to his species; yet we find the same observation to take place in a less degree. A man of mild manners can form no idea of inveterate revenge or cruelty; nor can a selfish heart easily conceive the heights of friendship and generosity. It is readily allowed, that other beings may possess many senses, of which we can have no conception; because the ideas of them have never been introduced to us, in the only manner, by which an idea can have access to the mind, to wit, by the actual feeling and sensation.

8   There is, however, one contradictory phænomenon, which may prove, that it is not absolutely impossible for ideas to arise, independent of their correspondent impressions. I believe it will readily be allowed, that the several distinct ideas of colour, which enter by the eye, or those of sound, which are conveyed by the ear, are really different from each other; though, at the same time, resembling. Now if this be true of different colours, it must be no less so of the different shades of the same colour; and each shade produces a distinct idea, independent of the rest. For if *SBN 21* this should be denied, it is possible, by the continual gradation of shades, to run a colour insensibly into what is most remote from it; and if you will not allow any of the means to be different, you cannot, without absurdity, deny the extremes to be the same. Suppose, therefore, a person to have enjoyed his sight for thirty years, and to have become perfectly

acquainted with colours of all kinds, except one particular shade of blue,[†] for instance, which it never has been his fortune to meet with. Let all the different shades of that colour, except that single one, be placed before him, descending gradually from the deepest to the lightest; it is plain, that he will perceive a blank, where that shade is wanting, and will be sensible, that there is a greater distance in that place between the contiguous colours than in any other. Now I ask, whether it be possible for him, from his own imagination, to supply this deficiency, and raise up to himself the idea of that particular shade, though it had never been conveyed to him by his senses? I believe there are few but will be of opinion that he can: And this may serve as a proof, that the simple ideas are not always, in every instance, derived from the correspondent impressions; though this instance is so singular, that it is scarcely worth our observing, and does not merit, that for it alone we should alter our general maxim.[†]

9   Here, therefore, is a proposition, which not only seems, in itself, simple and intelligible; but, if a proper use were made of it, might render every dispute equally intelligible, and banish all that jargon, which has so long taken possession of metaphysical reasonings,[†] and drawn disgrace upon them. All ideas, especially abstract ones, are naturally faint and obscure: The mind has but a slender hold of them: They are apt to be confounded with other resembling ideas; and when we have often employed any term, *SBN 22* though without a distinct meaning, we are apt to imagine it has a determinate idea, annexed to it. On the contrary, all impressions, that is, all sensations, either outward or inward, are strong and vivid: The limits between them are more exactly determined: Nor is it easy to fall into any error or mistake with regard to them. When we entertain, therefore, any suspicion, that a philosophical term is employed without any meaning or idea[†] (as is but too frequent), we need but enquire, *from what impression is that supposed idea derived?* And if it be impossible to assign any, this will serve to confirm our suspicion. By bringing ideas into so clear a light, we may reasonably hope to remove all dispute, which may arise, concerning their nature and reality.[1]

---

[1] It is probable, that no more was meant by those, who denied innate ideas,[†] than that all *SBN 22* ideas were copies of our impressions; though it must be confessed, that the terms, which they employed, were not chosen with such caution, nor so exactly defined, as to prevent all mistakes about their doctrine. For what is meant by *innate*? If innate be equivalent to natural, then all the perceptions and ideas of the mind must be allowed to be innate or natural, in whatever sense we take the latter word, whether in opposition to what is uncommon, artificial, or miraculous. If by *innate* be meant, *cotemporary to our birth*, the dispute seems to be frivo-

lous; nor is it worth while to enquire at what time thinking begins, whether before, at, or after our birth. Again, the word *idea*, seems to be commonly taken in a very loose sense, by Locke and others; as standing for any of our perceptions, our sensations and passions, as well as thoughts. [John Locke, *An Essay concerning Human Understanding*, bk. 1.] Now in this sense, I should desire to know, what can be meant by asserting, that self-love, or resentment of injuries, or the passion between the sexes is not innate?

But admitting these terms, *impressions* and *ideas*, in the sense above explained, and understanding by *innate*, what is original or copied from no precedent perception, then may we assert, that all our impressions are innate, and our ideas not innate.

To be ingenuous, I must own it to be my opinion, that Locke was betrayed into this question by the schoolmen,[†] who, making use of undefined terms, draw out their disputes to a tedious length, without ever touching the point in question. A like ambiguity and circumlocution seem to run through that philosopher's reasonings on this as well as most other subjects.

SECTION 3

OF THE ASSOCIATION OF IDEAS[†]

1   IT is evident, that there is a principle of connexion between the different thoughts or ideas of the mind, and that, in their appearance to the memory or imagination, they introduce each other with a certain degree of method and regularity. In our more serious thinking or discourse, this is so observable, that any particular thought, which breaks in upon the regular tract or chain of ideas, is immediately remarked and rejected. And even in our wildest and most wandering reveries, nay in our very dreams,[†] we shall find, if we reflect, that the imagination ran not altogether at adventures,[†] but that there was still a connexion upheld among the different ideas, which succeeded each other. Were the loosest and freest conversation to be transcribed, there would immediately be observed something, which connected it in all its transitions. Or where this is wanting, the person, who broke the thread of discourse, might still inform you, that there had secretly revolved in his mind a succession of thought, which had gradually led him from the subject of conversation. Among different languages, even where we cannot suspect the least connexion or communication, it is found, that the words, expressive of ideas, the most compounded, do yet nearly correspond to each other: A certain proof, that the simple ideas, comprehended in the compound ones, were bound together by some universal principle, which had an equal influence on all mankind.

2   Though it be too obvious to escape observation, that different ideas are connected together; I do not find, that any philosopher has attempted to enumerate or class all the principles[†] of association; a subject, however, that seems worthy of curiosity. To me, there appear to be only three principles[†] of connexion among ideas, namely, _Resemblance, Contiguity_ in time or place, and _Cause_ or _Effect_.

3   That these principles serve to connect ideas will not, I believe, be much doubted. A picture naturally leads our thoughts to the original:[2] The mention of one apartment in a building naturally introduces an enquiry

---

[2]   Resemblance.

or discourse concerning the others:[3] And if we think of a wound, we can scarcely forbear reflecting on the pain which follows it.[4] But that this enumeration is compleat, and that there are no other principles of association, except these, may be difficult to prove to the satisfaction of the reader, or even to a man's own satisfaction. All we can do, in such cases, is to run over several instances, and examine carefully the principle, which binds the different thoughts to each other, never stopping till we render the principle as general as possible. The more instances we examine, and the more care we employ, the more assurance shall we acquire, that the enumeration, which we form from the whole, is compleat and entire.* [Instead of entering into a detail of this kind, which would lead into many useless subtilties, we shall consider some of the effects of this connexion upon the passions and imagination;[†] where we may open a field of speculation more entertaining, and perhaps more instructive, than the other.

4   As man is a reasonable being, and is continually in pursuit of happiness, which he hopes to attain by the gratification of some passion or affection, he seldom acts or speaks or thinks without a purpose and intention. He has still some object in view; and however improper the means may sometimes be, which he chooses for the attainment of his end, he never loses view of an end; nor will he so much as throw away his thoughts or reflections, where he hopes not to reap some satisfaction from them.

5   In all compositions of genius,[†] therefore, it is requisite, that the writer have some plan or object; and though he may be hurried from this plan by the vehemence of thought, as in an ode, or drop it carelessly, as in an epistle or essay, there must appear some aim or intention, in his first setting out, if not in the composition of the whole work. A production without a design would resemble more the ravings of a madman, than the sober efforts of genius and learning.

6   As this rule admits of no exception, it follows, that, in narrative compositions, the events or actions, which the writer relates, must be connected together, by some bond or tye: They must be related to each other in the imagination, and form a kind of *Unity*,[†] which may bring them under one plan or view, and which may be the object or end of the writer in his first undertaking.

7   This connecting principle among the several events, which form the subject of a poem or history, may be very different, according to the different designs of the poet or historian. Ovɪᴅ[†] has formed his plan upon

---

[3] Contiguity.   [4] Cause and Effect.

* The remainder of this section did not appear in the 1777 edition. The material did appear in all editions from 1748 to 1772. Ed.

the connecting principle of resemblance. Every fabulous transformation, produced by the miraculous power of the gods, falls within the compass of his work. There needs but this one circumstance in any event to bring it under his original plan or intention.

8   An annalist or historian, who should undertake to write the history of Europe during any century, would be influenced by the connexion of contiguity in time and place. All events, which happen in that portion of space and period of time, are comprehended in his design, though in other respects different and unconnected. They have still a species of unity, amidst all their diversity.

9   But the most usual species of connexion among the different events, which enter into any narrative composition, is that of cause and effect; while the historian traces the series of actions according to their natural order, remounts to their secret springs and principles, and delineates their most remote consequences. He chooses for his subject a certain portion of that great chain of events, which compose the history of mankind: Each link in this chain he endeavours to touch in his narration: Sometimes unavoidable ignorance renders all his attempts fruitless: Sometimes, he supplies by conjecture, what is wanting in knowledge: And always, he is sensible, that the more unbroken the chain is, which he presents to his reader, the more perfect is his production. He sees, that the knowledge of causes is not only the most satisfactory; this relation or connexion being the strongest of all others; but also the most instructive; since it is by this knowledge alone, we are enabled to controul events, and govern futurity.[†]

10   Here therefore we may attain some notion of that *Unity* of *Action*, about which all critics,[†] after Aristotle, have talked so much: Perhaps, to little purpose, while they directed not their taste or sentiment by the accuracy of philosophy.[†] It appears, that, in all productions, as well as in the epic and tragic, there is a certain unity required, and that, on no occasion, can our thoughts be allowed to run at adventures, if we would produce a work, which will give any lasting entertainment to mankind. It appears also, that even a biographer, who should write the life of Achilles, would connect the events, by showing their mutual dependence and relation, as much as a poet, who should make the anger of that hero, the subject of his narration.[5] Not only in any limited portion of life, a

---

[5] Contrary to Aristotle,[†] Μῦθος δ'ἐστὶν εἷς, οὐχ, ὥσπερ τινὲς οἴονται, ἐὰν περὶ ἕνα ᾖ. πολλὰ γὰρ καὶ ἄπειρα τῷ γένει συμβαίνει, ἐξ ὧν ἐνίων οὐδέν ἐστιν ἕν. οὕτω δὲ καὶ πράξεις ἑνὸς πολλαί εἰσιν, ἐξ ὧν μία οὐδεμία γίνεται πρᾶξις, &c. Κεφ. η'. [Aristotle, *Poetics* 1451ᵃ15–19.]

man's actions have a dependence on each other, but also during the whole period of his duration, from the cradle to the grave; nor is it possible to strike off one link, however minute, in this regular chain, without affecting the whole series of events, which follow. The unity of action, therefore, which is to be found in biography or history, differs from that of epic poetry, not in kind, but in degree. In epic poetry,[†] the connexion among the events is more close and sensible: The narration is not carried on through such a length of time: And the actors hasten to some remarkable period, which satisfies the curiosity of the reader. This conduct of the epic poet depends on that particular situation of the *Imagination* and of the *Passions*, which is supposed in that production. The imagination, both of writer and reader, is more enlivened, and the passions more enflamed than in history, biography, or any species of narration, which confine themselves to strict truth and reality. Let us consider the effect of these two circumstances, an enlivened imagination and enflamed passion; circumstances, which belong to poetry, especially the epic kind, above any other species of composition: And let us examine the reason, why they require a stricter and closer unity in the fable.

11   *First*, All poetry, being a species of painting,[†] brings us nearer to the objects than any other species of narration, throws a stronger light upon them, and delineates more distinctly those minute circumstances, which, though to the historian they seem superfluous, serve mightily to enliven the imagery, and gratify the fancy. If it be not necessary, as in the *Iliad*,[†] to inform us each time the hero buckles his shoes, and ties his garters, it will be requisite, perhaps, to enter into a greater detail than in the *Henriade*;[†] where the events are run over with such rapidity, that we scarcely have leisure to become acquainted with the scene or action. Were a poet, therefore, to comprehend in his subject, any great compass of time or series of events, and trace up the death of HECTOR to its remote causes, in the rape of HELEN, or the judgment of PARIS, he must draw out his poem to an immeasurable length, in order to fill this large canvas with just painting and imagery. The reader's imagination, enflamed with such a series of poetical descriptions, and his passions, agitated by a continual sympathy with the actors, must flag long before the period of the narration, and must sink into lassitude and disgust, from the repeated violence of the same movements.

12   *Secondly*, That an epic poet must not trace the causes[†] to any great distance, will farther appear, if we consider another reason, which is drawn from a property of the passions still more remarkable and singular. It is evident, that, in a just composition, all the affections, excited by the dif-

ferent events, described and represented, add mutual force to each other; and that, while the heroes are all engaged in one common scene, and each action is strongly connected with the whole, the concern is continually awake, and the passions make an easy transition from one object to another. The strong connexion of the events, as it facilitates the passage of the thought or imagination from one to another, facilitates also the transfusion of the passions, and preserves the affections still in the same channel and direction. Our sympathy and concern for EVE prepares the way for a like sympathy with ADAM: The affection is preserved almost entire in the transition; and the mind seizes immediately the new object as strongly related to that which formerly engaged its attention. But were the poet to make a total digression from his subject, and introduce a new actor, nowise connected with the personages, the imagination, feeling a breach in the transition, would enter coldly into the new scene; would kindle by slow degrees; and in returning to the main subject of the poem, would pass, as it were, upon foreign ground, and have its concern to excite anew, in order to take part with the principal actors. The same inconvenience follows in a less degree; where the poet traces his events to too great a distance, and binds together actions, which, though not entirely disjoined, have not so strong a connexion as is requisite to forward the transition of the passions. Hence arises the artifice of the oblique narration, employed in the *Odyssey* and *Æneid*;[†] where the hero is introduced, at first, near the period of his designs, and afterwards shows us, as it were in perspective, the more distant events and causes. By this means, the reader's curiosity is immediately excited: The events follow with rapidity, and in a very close connexion: And the concern is preserved alive, and, by means of the near relation of the objects, continually encreases, from the beginning to the end of the narration.

13   The same rule takes place in dramatic poetry; nor is it ever permitted, in a regular composition, to introduce an actor, who has no connexion, or but a small one, with the principal personages of the fable. The spectator's concern must not be diverted by any scenes disjoined and separated from the rest. This breaks the course of the passions, and prevents that communication of the several emotions, by which one scene adds force to another, and transfuses the pity and terror, which it excites, upon each succeeding scene, till the whole produces that rapidity of movement, which is peculiar to the theatre. How must it extinguish this warmth of affection, to be entertained, on a sudden, with a new action and new personages, nowise related to the former; to find so sensible a breach or vacuity in the course of the passions, by means of this breach in the

connexion of ideas; and instead of carrying the sympathy of one scene into the following, to be obliged, every moment, to excite a new concern, and take part in a new scene of action?

14   To return to the comparison of history and epic poetry, we may conclude, from the foregoing reasonings, that, as a certain unity is requisite in all productions, it cannot be wanting in history more than in any other; that, in history, the connexion among the several events, which unites them into one body, is the relation of cause and effect, the same which takes place in epic poetry; and that, in the latter composition, this connexion is only required to be closer and more sensible, on account of the lively imagination and strong passions, which must be touched by the poet in his narration. The PELOPONNESIAN war[†] is a proper subject for history, the siege of ATHENS[†] for an epic poem, and the death of ALCIBIADES[†] for a tragedy.

15   As the difference, therefore, between history and epic poetry consists only in the degrees of connexion, which bind together those several events, of which their subject is composed, it will be difficult, if not impossible, by words, to determine exactly the bounds, which separate them from each other. That is a matter of taste more than of reasoning; and perhaps, this unity may often be discovered in a subject, where, at first view, and from an abstract consideration, we should least expect to find it.

16   It is evident, that HOMER, in the course of his narration, exceeds the first proposition of his subject; and that the anger of ACHILLES, which caused the death of HECTOR, is not the same with that which produced so many ills to the GREEKS. But the strong connexion between these two movements, the quick transition from one to another, the contrast[6] between the effects of concord and discord among the princes, and the natural curiosity which we have to see ACHILLES in action, after so long a repose; all these causes carry on the reader, and produce a sufficient unity in the subject.

17   It may be objected to MILTON,[†] that he has traced up his causes to too great a distance, and that the rebellion of the angels produces the fall of man by a train of events, which is both very long and very casual. Not to mention, that the creation of the world, which he has related at length, is no more the cause of that catastrophe, than of the battle of PHARSALIA,[†]

---

[6] Contrast or contrariety is a connexion among ideas, which may, perhaps, be considered as a mixture of causation and resemblance. Where two objects are contrary, the one destroys the other, i.e. is the cause of its annihilation, and the idea of the annihilation of an object implies the idea of its former existence.

or any other event, that has ever happened. But if we consider, on the other hand, that all these events, the rebellion of the angels, the creation of the world, and the fall of man, *resemble* each other, in being miraculous[†] and out of the common course of nature; that they are supposed to be *contiguous* in time; and that being detached from all other events, and being the only original facts, which revelation discovers, they strike the eye at once, and naturally recall each other to the thought or imagination: If we consider all these circumstances, I say, we shall find, that these parts of the action have a sufficient unity to make them be comprehended in one fable or narration. To which we may add, that the rebellion of the angels and the fall of man have a peculiar resemblance, as being counterparts to each other, and presenting to the reader the same moral, of obedience to our Creator.

18   These loose hints I have thrown together, in order to excite the curiosity of philosophers, and beget a suspicion at least, if not a full persuasion, that this subject is very copious, and that many operations of the human mind depend on the connexion or association of ideas, which is here explained. Particularly, the sympathy between the passions and imagination will, perhaps, appear remarkable; while we observe that the affections, excited by one object, pass easily to another object connected with it; but transfuse themselves with difficulty, or not at all, along different objects, which have no manner of connexion together. By introducing, into any composition, personages and actions, foreign to each other,[†] an injudicious author loses that communication of emotions, by which alone he can interest the heart, and raise the passions to their proper height and period. The full explication of this principle and all its consequences would lead us into reasonings too profound and too copious for this enquiry. It is sufficient, at present, to have established this conclusion, that the three connecting principles of all ideas are the relations of *Resemblance, Contiguity,* and *Causation.*]

SCEPTICAL DOUBTS CONCERNING THE OPERATIONS OF THE UNDERSTANDING†

PART 1

1 ALL the objects of human reason or enquiry may naturally be divided into two kinds, to wit, *Relations of Ideas* and *Matters of Fact*.† Of the first kind are the sciences of Geometry, Algebra, and Arithmetic; and in short, every affirmation, which is either intuitively or demonstratively certain. *That the square of the hypothenuse is equal to the square of the two sides*, is a proposition, which expresses a relation between these figures. *That three times five is equal to the half of thirty*, expresses a relation between these numbers. Propositions of this kind are discoverable by the mere operation of thought, without dependence on what is any where existent in the universe. Though there never were a circle or triangle in nature, the truths, demonstrated by EUCLID,† would for ever retain their certainty and evidence.

2 Matters of fact, which are the second objects of human reason, are not ascertained in the same manner; nor is our evidence of their truth, however great, of a like nature with the foregoing. The contrary of every matter of fact is still possible;† because it can never imply a contradiction, and is conceived by the mind with the same facility and distinctness, as if ever so conformable to reality. *That the sun will not rise* *to-morrow* is no less intelligible a proposition, and implies no more contradiction, than the affirmation, *that it will rise*. We should in vain, therefore, attempt to demonstrate its falsehood. Were it demonstratively false, it would imply a contradiction, and could never be distinctly conceived by the mind.

3 It may, therefore, be a subject worthy of curiosity, to enquire what is the nature of that evidence, which assures us of any real existence and matter of fact, beyond the present testimony of our senses, or the records of our memory. This part of philosophy, it is observable, has been little

cultivated, either by the ancients or moderns;[†] and therefore our doubts and errors, in the prosecution of so important an enquiry, may be the more excusable; while we march through such difficult paths, without any guide or direction. They may even prove useful, by exciting curiosity, and destroying that implicit faith[†] and security, which is the bane of all reasoning and free enquiry. The discovery of defects in the common philosophy, if any such there be, will not, I presume, be a discouragement, but rather an incitement, as is usual, to attempt something more full and satisfactory, than has yet been proposed to the public.

4   All reasonings concerning matter of fact seem to be founded on the relation of *Cause* and *Effect*.[†] By means of that relation alone we can go beyond the evidence of our memory and senses. If you were to ask a man, why he believes any matter of fact, which is absent; for instance, that his friend is in the country, or in FRANCE; he would give you a reason; and this reason would be some other fact; as a letter received from him, or the knowledge of his former resolutions and promises. A man, finding a watch or any other machine in a desert island, would conclude, that there had once been men in that island. All our reasonings concerning fact are of the same nature. And here it is constantly supposed, that there   *SBN 27* is a connexion between the present fact and that which is inferred from it. Were there nothing to bind them together, the inference would be entirely precarious.[†] The hearing of an articulate voice and rational discourse in the dark assures us of the presence of some person: Why? Because these are the effects of the human make and fabric, and closely connected with it. If we anatomize all the other reasonings of this nature, we shall find, that they are founded on the relation of cause and effect, and that this relation is either near or remote, direct or collateral. Heat and light are collateral effects of fire, and the one effect may justly be inferred from the other.

5   If we would satisfy ourselves, therefore, concerning the nature of that evidence, which assures us of matters of fact, we must enquire how we arrive at the knowledge of cause and effect.

6   I shall venture to affirm, as a general proposition, which admits of no exception, that the knowledge of this relation is not, in any instance, attained by reasonings *a priori*;[†] but arises entirely from experience, when we find, that any particular objects are constantly conjoined with each other. Let an object be presented to a man of ever so strong natural reason and abilities; if that object be entirely new to him, he will not be able, by the most accurate examination of its sensible qualities,[†] to discover any of its causes or effects. ADAM,[†] though his rational faculties be supposed,

109

at the very first, entirely perfect, could not have inferred from the fluidity and transparency of water, that it would suffocate him, or from the light and warmth of fire, that it would consume him. No object ever discovers, by the qualities which appear to the senses, either the causes, which produced it, or the effects, which will arise from it; nor can our reason, unassisted by experience, ever draw any inference concerning real existence and matter of fact.

7   This proposition, *that causes and effects are discoverable, not by reason, but by experience,* will readily be admitted with regard to such objects, as we remember to have once been altogether unknown to us; since we must be conscious of the utter inability, which we then lay under, of foretelling, what would arise from them. Present two smooth pieces of marble[†] to a man, who has no tincture of natural philosophy;[†] he will never discover, that they will adhere together, in such a manner as to require great force to separate them in a direct line, while they make so small a resistance to a lateral pressure. Such events, as bear little analogy to the common course of nature, are also readily confessed to be known only by experience; nor does any man imagine that the explosion of gunpowder, or the attraction of a loadstone,[†] could ever be discovered by arguments *a priori*. In like manner, when an effect is supposed to depend upon an intricate machinery or secret structure of parts,[†] we make no difficulty in attributing all our knowledge of it to experience. Who will assert, that he can give the ultimate reason, why milk or bread is proper nourishment for a man, not for a lion or a tyger?

8   But the same truth may not appear, at first sight, to have the same evidence with regard to events, which have become familiar to us from our first appearance in the world, which bear a close analogy to the whole course of nature, and which are supposed to depend on the simple qualities of objects, without any secret structure of parts. We are apt to imagine, that we could discover these effects by the mere operation of our reason, without experience. We fancy, that were we brought, on a sudden, into this world, we could at first have inferred, that one billiard-ball would communicate motion to another upon impulse;[†] and that we needed not to have waited for the event, in order to pronounce with certainty concerning it. Such is the influence of custom,[†] that, where it is strongest, it not only covers our natural ignorance, but even conceals itself, and seems not to take place, merely because it is found in the highest degree.

9   But to convince us, that all the laws of nature, and all the operations of bodies without exception, are known only by experience, the follow-

ing reflections may, perhaps, suffice. Were any object presented to us, and were we required to pronounce concerning the effect, which will result from it, without consulting past observation; after what manner, I beseech you, must the mind proceed in this operation? It must invent or imagine some event, which it ascribes to the object as its effect; and it is plain that this invention must be entirely arbitrary. The mind can never possibly find the effect in the supposed cause, by the most accurate scrutiny and examination. For the effect is totally different from the cause, and consequently can never be discovered in it. Motion in the second billiard-ball is a quite distinct event from motion in the first; nor is there any thing in the one to suggest the smallest hint of the other. A stone or piece of metal raised into the air, and left without any support, immediately falls: But to consider the matter *a priori*, is there any thing we discover in this situation, which can beget the idea of a downward, rather than an upward, or any other motion, in the stone or metal?

10 And as the first imagination or invention of a particular effect, in all natural operations, is arbitrary, where we consult not experience; so must we also esteem the supposed tye or connexion between the cause and effect, which binds them together, and renders it impossible, that any other effect could result from the operation of that cause. When I see, for instance, a billiard-ball moving in a straight line towards another; even suppose motion in the second ball should by accident be suggested to me, as the result of their contact or impulse; may I not conceive, that a hundred different events might as well follow from that cause? May not both these balls remain at absolute rest? May not the first ball return in *SBN 30* a straight line, or leap off from the second in any line or direction? All these suppositions are consistent and conceivable. Why then should we give the preference to one, which is no more consistent or conceivable than the rest? All our reasonings *a priori* will never be able to show us any foundation for this preference.

11 In a word, then, every effect is a distinct event from its cause. It could not, therefore, be discovered in the cause, and the first invention or conception of it, *a priori*, must be entirely arbitrary. And even after it is suggested, the conjunction of it with the cause must appear equally arbitrary; since there are always many other effects, which, to reason, must seem fully as consistent and natural. In vain, therefore, should we pretend to determine any single event, or infer any cause or effect, without the assistance of observation and experience.

12 Hence we may discover the reason, why no philosopher, who is rational and modest, has ever pretended to assign the ultimate cause[†] of any

natural operation, or to show distinctly the action of that power, which produces any single effect in the universe. It is confessed, that the utmost effort of human reason is, to reduce the principles, productive of natural phænomena, to a greater simplicity,[†] and to resolve the many particular effects into a few general causes, by means of reasonings from analogy, experience, and observation. But as to the causes of these general causes,[†] we should in vain attempt their discovery; nor shall we ever be able to satisfy ourselves, by any particular explication of them. These ultimate springs and principles are totally shut up from human curiosity and enquiry. Elasticity, gravity, cohesion of parts, communication of motion by impulse;[†] these are probably the ultimate causes and principles[†] which we shall ever discover in nature; and we may esteem ourselves sufficiently happy, if, by accurate enquiry and reasoning, we can trace up the particular phænomena to, or near to, these general principles. The most SBN 3 perfect philosophy of the natural kind only staves off our ignorance a little longer: As perhaps the most perfect philosophy of the moral or metaphysical kind serves only to discover larger portions of our ignorance. Thus the observation of human blindness and weakness is the result of all philosophy, and meets us, at every turn, in spite of our endeavours to elude or avoid it.

13   Nor is geometry, when taken into the assistance of natural philosophy, ever able to remedy this defect, or lead us into the knowledge of ultimate causes, by all that accuracy of reasoning, for which it is so justly celebrated. Every part of mixed mathematics[†] proceeds upon the supposition, that certain laws are established by nature in her operations; and abstract reasonings are employed, either to assist experience in the discovery of these laws, or to determine their influence in particular instances, where it depends upon any precise degree of distance and quantity. Thus, it is a law of motion, discovered by experience, that the moment or force of any body in motion is in the compound ratio or proportion of its solid contents and its velocity; and consequently, that a small force may remove the greatest obstacle or raise the greatest weight, if, by any contrivance or machinery, we can encrease the velocity of that force, so as to make it an overmatch for its antagonist. Geometry assists us in the application of this law, by giving us the just dimensions of all the parts and figures, which can enter into any species of machine; but still the discovery of the law[†] itself is owing merely to experience, and all the abstract reasonings in the world could never lead us one step towards the knowledge of it. When we reason *a priori*, and consider merely any object or cause, as it appears to the mind, independent of all observation, it never

could suggest to us the notion of any distinct object, such as its effect; much less, show us the inseparable and inviolable connexion between them. A man must be very sagacious, who could discover by reasoning, *SBN 32* that crystal is the effect of heat, and ice of cold, without being previously acquainted with the operations of these qualities.

PART 2

14   But we have not, as yet, attained any tolerable satisfaction with regard to the question first proposed. Each solution still gives rise to a new question as difficult as the foregoing, and leads us on to farther enquiries. When it is asked, *What is the nature of all our reasonings concerning matter of fact?*[†] the proper answer seems to be, that they are founded on the relation of cause and effect. When again it is asked, *What is the foundation of all our reasonings and conclusions concerning that relation?* it may be replied in one word, EXPERIENCE. But if we still carry on our sifting humour, and ask, *What is the foundation of all conclusions from experience?* this implies a new question, which may be of more difficult solution and explication. Philosophers, that give themselves airs of superior wisdom and sufficiency, have a hard task, when they encounter persons of inquisitive dispositions, who push them from every corner, to which they retreat, and who are sure at last to bring them to some dangerous dilemma. The best expedient to prevent this confusion, is to be modest in our pretensions; and even to discover the difficulty ourselves before it is objected to us. By this means, we may make a kind of merit of our very ignorance.

15   I shall content myself, in this section, with an easy task, and shall pretend only to give a negative answer to the question here proposed. I say then, that, even after we have experience of the operations of cause and effect, our conclusions from that experience are *not* founded on reasoning, or any process of the understanding. This answer we must endeavour, both to explain and to defend.

16   It must certainly be allowed, that nature has kept us at a great distance from all her secrets, and has afforded us only the knowledge of a few *SBN 33* superficial qualities of objects; while she conceals from us those powers and principles, on which the influence of these objects entirely depends. Our senses inform us of the colour, weight, and consistence of bread; but neither sense nor reason can ever inform us of those qualities, which fit it for the nourishment and support of a human body. Sight or feeling conveys an idea of the actual motion of bodies; but as to that wonderful

force or power, which would carry on a moving body for ever in a continued change of place, and which bodies never lose but by communicating it to others; of this we cannot form the most distant conception. But notwithstanding this ignorance of natural powers[7] and principles, we always presume, when we see like sensible qualities, that they have like secret powers,[†] and expect, that effects, similar to those, which we have experienced, will follow from them. If a body of like colour and consistence with that bread, which we have formerly eat, be presented to us, we make no scruple of repeating the experiment, and foresee, with certainty, like nourishment and support. Now this is a process of the mind or thought, of which I would willingly know the foundation. It is allowed on all hands, that there is no known connexion between the sensible qualities and the secret powers; and consequently, that the mind is not led to form such a conclusion concerning their constant and regular conjunction, by any thing which it knows of their nature. As to past *Experience*, it can be allowed to give *direct* and *certain* information of those precise objects only, and that precise period of time, which fell under its cognizance: But why this experience should be extended to future times, and to other objects, which, for aught we know, may be only in appearance SBN 3 similar; this is the main question on which I would insist. The bread, which I formerly eat, nourished me; that is, a body of such sensible qualities, was, at that time, endowed with such secret powers: But does it follow, that other bread must also nourish me at another time, and that like sensible qualities must always be attended with like secret powers? The consequence seems nowise necessary. At least, it must be acknowledged, that there is here a consequence drawn by the mind; that there is a certain step taken; a process of thought, and an inference, which wants to be explained. These two propositions are far from being the same, *I have found that such an object has always been attended with such an effect*, and *I foresee, that other objects, which are, in appearance, similar, will be attended with similar effects*. I shall allow, if you please, that the one proposition may justly be inferred from the other: I know in fact, that it always is inferred. But if you insist, that the inference is made by a chain of reasoning, I desire you to produce that reasoning. The connexion between these propositions is not intuitive. There is required a medium,[†] which may enable the mind to draw such an inference, if indeed it be drawn by reasoning and argument. What that medium is, I must confess, passes

---

[7] The word, *power*, is here used in a loose and popular sense. The more accurate explica- SBN 3 tion of it would give additional evidence to this argument. See Section 7.

my comprehension; and it is incumbent on those to produce it, who assert, that it really exists, and is the origin of all our conclusions concerning matter of fact.

17   This negative argument must certainly, in process of time, become altogether convincing, if many penetrating and able philosophers shall turn their enquiries this way; and no one be ever able to discover any connecting proposition or intermediate step, which supports the understanding in this conclusion. But as the question is yet new, every reader may not trust so far to his own penetration, as to conclude, because an argument escapes his enquiry, that therefore it does not really exist. For this reason it may be requisite to venture upon a more difficult task; and   *SBN 35* enumerating all the branches of human knowledge, endeavour to show, that none of them can afford such an argument.

18   All reasonings may be divided into two kinds,[†] namely, demonstrative reasoning, or that concerning relations of ideas, and moral reasoning, or that concerning matter of fact and existence. That there are no demonstrative arguments in the case, seems evident; since it implies no contradiction,[†] that the course of nature may change, and that an object, seemingly like those which we have experienced, may be attended with different or contrary effects. May I not clearly and distinctly conceive, that a body, falling from the clouds, and which, in all other respects, resembles snow, has yet the taste of salt or feeling of fire? Is there any more intelligible proposition than to affirm, that all the trees will flourish in DECEMBER and JANUARY, and decay in MAY and JUNE? Now whatever is intelligible, and can be distinctly conceived, implies no contradiction, and can never be proved false by any demonstrative argument or abstract reasoning *a priori*.

19   If we be, therefore, engaged by arguments to put trust in past experience, and make it the standard of our future judgment, these arguments must be probable only,[†] or such as regard matter of fact and real existence, according to the division above-mentioned. But that there is no argument of this kind, must appear, if our explication of that species of reasoning be admitted as solid and satisfactory. We have said, that all arguments concerning existence are founded on the relation of cause and effect; that our knowledge of that relation is derived entirely from experience; and that all our experimental conclusions[†] proceed upon the supposition, that the future will be conformable to the past. To endeavour, therefore, the proof of this last supposition by probable arguments, or arguments regarding existence, must be evidently going in a circle, and   *SBN 36* taking that for granted, which is the very point in question.

20   In reality, all arguments from experience are founded on the similarity, which we discover among natural objects, and by which we are induced to expect effects similar to those, which we have found to follow from such objects. And though none but a fool or madman will ever pretend to dispute the authority of experience, or to reject that great guide of human life;[†] it may surely be allowed a philosopher to have so much curiosity at least, as to examine the principle of human nature, which gives this mighty authority to experience, and makes us draw advantage from that similarity, which nature has placed among different objects. From causes, which appear *similar*, we expect similar effects. This is the sum of all our experimental conclusions. Now it seems evident, that, if this conclusion were formed by reason, it would be as perfect at first, and upon one instance, as after ever so long a course of experience. But the case is far otherwise. Nothing so like as eggs; yet no one, on account of this appearing similarity, expects the same taste and relish[†] in all of them. It is only after a long course of uniform experiments in any kind, that we attain a firm reliance and security with regard to a particular event. Now where is that process of reasoning, which, from one instance,[†] draws a conclusion, so different from that which it infers from a hundred instances, that are nowise different from that single one? This question I propose as much for the sake of information, as with an intention of raising difficulties. I cannot find, I cannot imagine any such reasoning. But I keep my mind still open to instruction, if any one will vouchsafe to bestow it on me.

21   Should it be said, that, from a number of uniform experiments, we *infer* a connexion between the sensible qualities and the secret powers; this, I must confess, seems the same difficulty, couched in different terms. SBN The question still recurs, On what process of argument this *inference* is founded? Where is the medium, the interposing ideas, which join propositions so very wide of each other? It is confessed, that the colour, consistence, and other sensible qualities of bread appear not, of themselves, to have any connexion with the secret powers of nourishment and support. For otherwise we could infer these secret powers from the first appearance of these sensible qualities, without the aid of experience; contrary to the sentiment of all philosophers, and contrary to plain matter of fact. Here then is our natural state of ignorance with regard to the powers and influence of all objects. How is this remedied by experience? It only shows us a number of uniform effects, resulting from certain objects, and teaches us, that those particular objects, at that particular time, were endowed with such powers and forces. When a new object,

endowed with similar sensible qualities, is produced, we expect similar powers and forces, and look for a like effect. From a body of like colour and consistence with bread, we expect like nourishment and support. But this surely is a step or progress of the mind, which wants to be explained. When a man says, *I have found, in all past instances, such sensible qualities conjoined with such secret powers*: And when he says, *similar sensible qualities will always be conjoined with similar secret powers*; he is not guilty of a tautology, nor are these propositions in any respect the same. You say that the one proposition is an inference from the other. But you must confess, that the inference is not intuitive; neither is it demonstrative:[†] Of what nature is it then? To say it is experimental, is begging the question. For all inferences from experience suppose, as their foundation, that the future will resemble the past, and that similar powers will be conjoined with similar sensible qualities. If there be any suspicion, that the course of nature may change, and that the past may be no rule for the future, *SBN 38* all experience becomes useless, and can give rise to no inference or conclusion. It is impossible, therefore, that any arguments from experience can prove[†] this resemblance of the past to the future; since all these arguments are founded on the supposition of that resemblance. Let the course of things be allowed hitherto ever so regular; that alone, without some new argument or inference, proves not, that, for the future, it will continue so. In vain do you pretend to have learned the nature of bodies from your past experience. Their secret nature, and consequently, all their effects and influence, may change, without any change in their sensible qualities. This happens sometimes, and with regard to some objects: Why may it not happen always, and with regard to all objects? What logic, what process of argument secures you against this supposition? My practice, you say, refutes my doubts. But you mistake the purport of my question. As an agent, I am quite satisfied in the point; but as a philosopher, who has some share of curiosity, I will not say scepticism, I want to learn the foundation of this inference. No reading, no enquiry has yet been able to remove my difficulty, or give me satisfaction in a matter of such importance. Can I do better than propose the difficulty to the public, even though, perhaps, I have small hopes of obtaining a solution? We shall at least, by this means, be sensible of our ignorance, if we do not augment our knowledge.

22   I must confess, that a man is guilty of unpardonable arrogance, who concludes, because an argument has escaped his own investigation, that therefore it does not really exist. I must also confess, that, though all the learned, for several ages, should have employed themselves in fruitless

search upon any subject, it may still, perhaps, be rash to conclude positively, that the subject must, therefore, pass all human comprehension. Even though we examine all the sources of our knowledge, and conclude   *SBN 3* them unfit for such a subject, there may still remain a suspicion, that the enumeration is not compleat, or the examination not accurate. But with regard to the present subject, there are some considerations, which seem to remove all this accusation of arrogance or suspicion of mistake.

23   It is certain, that the most ignorant and stupid peasants, nay infants, nay even brute beasts, improve by experience, and learn the qualities of natural objects, by observing the effects, which result from them. When a child has felt the sensation of pain from touching the flame of a candle, he will be careful not to put his hand near any candle; but will expect a similar effect from a cause, which is similar in its sensible qualities and appearance. If you assert, therefore, that the understanding of the child is led into this conclusion by any process of argument or ratiocination, I may justly require you to produce that argument; nor have you any pretence to refuse so equitable a demand. You cannot say, that the argument is abstruse, and may possibly escape your enquiry; since you confess, that it is obvious to the capacity of a mere infant. If you hesitate, therefore, a moment, or if, after reflection, you produce any intricate or profound argument, you, in a manner, give up the question, and confess, that it is not reasoning which engages us to suppose the past resembling the future, and to expect similar effects from causes, which are, to appearance, similar. This is the proposition which I intended to enforce in the present section. If I be right, I pretend not to have made any mighty discovery. And if I be wrong, I must acknowledge myself to be indeed a very backward scholar; since I cannot now discover an argument, which, it seems, was perfectly familiar to me, long before I was out of my cradle.

SECTION 5

SCEPTICAL SOLUTION

OF THESE DOUBTS

PART 1

1   THE passion for philosophy, like that for religion, seems liable to this inconvenience, that, though it aims at the correction of our manners, and extirpation of our vices, it may only serve, by imprudent management, to foster a predominant inclination, and push the mind, with more determined resolution, towards that side, which already *draws* too much, by the biass and propensity of the natural temper. It is certain, that, while we aspire to the magnanimous firmness of the philosophic sage,† and endeavour to confine our pleasures altogether within our own minds, we may, at last, render our philosophy like that of EPICTETUS, and other STOICS,† only a more refined system of selfishness,† and reason ourselves out of all virtue, as well as social enjoyment. While we study with attention the vanity of human life, and turn all our thoughts towards the empty and transitory nature of riches and honours, we are, perhaps, all the while, flattering our natural indolence, which, hating the bustle of the world, and drudgery of business, seeks a pretence of reason, to give itself a full and uncontrouled indulgence. There is, however, one species of philosophy, which seems little liable to this inconvenience, and that because it strikes in with no disorderly passion of the human mind, nor can mingle itself with any natural affection or propensity; and that is the ACADEMIC or SCEPTICAL philosophy.† The ACADEMICS always talk of doubt and suspence of judgment, of danger in hasty determinations, of confining to very narrow bounds the enquiries of the understanding, and of renouncing all speculations which lie not within the limits of common life and practice. Nothing, therefore, can be more contrary than such a philosophy to the supine indolence of the mind, its rash arrogance, its lofty pretensions, and its superstitious credulity. Every passion is mortified by it, except the love of truth; and that passion never is, nor can be carried to too high a degree. It is surprizing, therefore, that this philosophy, which,

in almost every instance, must be harmless and innocent, should be the subject of so much groundless reproach and obloquy.[†] But, perhaps, the very circumstance, which renders it so innocent, is what chiefly exposes it to the public hatred and resentment. By flattering no irregular passion, it gains few partizans: By opposing so many vices and follies, it raises to itself abundance of enemies, who stigmatize it as libertine, profane, and irreligious.

2   Nor need we fear, that this philosophy, while it endeavours to limit our enquiries to common life, should ever undermine the reasonings of common life, and carry its doubts so far as to destroy all action, as well as speculation. Nature will always maintain her rights, and prevail in the end over any abstract reasoning whatsoever. Though we should conclude, for instance, as in the foregoing section, that, in all reasonings from experience, there is a step taken by the mind, which is not supported by any argument or process of the understanding; there is no danger, that these reasonings, on which almost all knowledge depends, will ever be affected by such a discovery. If the mind be not engaged by argument to make this step, it must be induced by some other principle of equal weight and authority;[†] and that principle will preserve its influence as long as human nature remains the same. What that principle is, may well be worth the   SBN 4 pains of enquiry.

3   Suppose a person, though endowed with the strongest faculties of reason and reflection, to be brought on a sudden into this world;[†] he would, indeed, immediately observe a continual succession of objects, and one event following another; but he would not be able to discover any thing farther. He would not, at first, by any reasoning, be able to reach the idea of cause and effect; since the particular powers, by which all natural operations are performed, never appear to the senses; nor is it reasonable to conclude, merely because one event, in one instance, precedes another, that therefore the one is the cause, the other the effect. Their conjunction may be arbitrary and casual. There may be no reason to infer the existence of one from the appearance of the other. And in a word, such a person, without more experience, could never employ his conjecture or reasoning concerning any matter of fact, or be assured of any thing beyond what was immediately present to his memory and senses.

4   Suppose again, that he has acquired more experience, and has lived so long in the world as to have observed similar objects or events to be constantly conjoined together; what is the consequence of this experience? He immediately infers the existence of one object from the appearance

of the other. Yet he has not, by all his experience, acquired any idea or knowledge of the secret power, by which the one object produces the other; nor is it, by any process of reasoning, he is engaged to draw this inference. But still he finds himself determined to draw it: And though he should be convinced, that his understanding has no part in the operation, he would nevertheless continue in the same course of thinking. There is some other principle, which determines him to form such a conclusion.

5   This principle is CUSTOM or HABIT. For wherever the repetition of any   *SBN 43* particular act or operation produces a propensity to renew the same act or operation, without being impelled by any reasoning or process of the understanding; we always say, that this propensity is the effect of *Custom*. By employing that word, we pretend not to have given the ultimate reason of such a propensity. We only point out a principle of human nature, which is universally acknowledged, and which is well known by its effects. Perhaps, we can push our enquiries no farther, or pretend to give the cause of this cause; but must rest contented with it as the ultimate principle, which we can assign, of all our conclusions from experience. It is sufficient satisfaction, that we can go so far; without repining at the narrowness of our faculties, because they will carry us no farther. And it is certain we here advance a very intelligible proposition at least, if not a true one, when we assert, that, after the constant conjunction[†] of two objects, heat and flame, for instance, weight and solidity, we are determined by custom alone to expect the one from the appearance of the other. This hypothesis seems even the only one, which explains the difficulty, why we draw, from a thousand instances, an inference, which we are not able to draw from one instance, that is, in no respect, different from them. Reason is incapable of any such variation. The conclusions, which it draws from considering one circle, are the same which it would form upon surveying all the circles in the universe. But no man, having seen only one body move after being impelled by another, could infer, that every other body will move after a like impulse. All inferences from experience, therefore, are effects of custom, not of reasoning.[8]

---

[8] Nothing is more usual than for writers, even on *moral, political*, or *physical* subjects, to   *SBN 43* distinguish between *reason* and *experience*, and to suppose, that these species of argumentation are entirely different from each other. The former are taken for the mere result of our   *SBN 44* intellectual faculties, which, by considering *a priori* the nature of things, and examining the effects, that must follow from their operation, establish particular principles of science and philosophy. The latter are supposed to be derived entirely from sense and observation, by which we learn what has actually resulted from the operation of particular objects, and are thence able to infer, what will, for the future, result from them. Thus, for instance, the

6   Custom, then, is the great guide of human life. It is that principle alone, SBN 4 which renders our experience useful to us, and makes us expect, for the future, a similar train of events with those which have appeared in the past. Without the influence of custom, we should be entirely igno- SBN 4 rant of every matter of fact, beyond what is immediately present to the memory and senses. We should never know how to adjust means to ends,

limitations and restraints of civil government, and a legal constitution, may be defended, either from *reason*, which, reflecting on the great frailty and corruption of human nature, teaches, that no man can safely be trusted with unlimited authority; or from *experience* and history, which inform us of the enormous abuses, that ambition, in every age and country, has been found to make of so imprudent a confidence.

The same distinction between reason and experience is maintained in all our deliberations concerning the conduct of life; while the experienced statesman, general, physician, or merchant is trusted and followed; and the unpractised novice, with whatever natural talents endowed, neglected, and despised. Though it be allowed, that reason may form very plausible conjectures with regard to the consequences of such a particular conduct in such particular circumstances; it is still supposed imperfect, without the assistance of experience, which is alone able to give stability and certainty to the maxims, derived from study and reflection.

But notwithstanding that this distinction be thus universally received, both in the active and speculative scenes of life, I shall not scruple to pronounce, that it is, at bottom, erroneous, or at least, superficial.

If we examine those arguments, which, in any of the sciences above-mentioned, are supposed to be the mere effects of reasoning and reflection, they will be found to terminate, at last, in some general principle or conclusion, for which we can assign no reason but observation and experience. The only difference between them and those maxims, which are vulgarly esteemed the result of pure experience, is, that the former cannot be established without some process of thought, and some reflection on what we have observed, in order to distinguish its circumstances, and trace its consequences: Whereas in the latter, the experienced event is exactly and fully similar to that which we infer as the result of any particular situation. The history of a Tiberius or a Nero† makes us dread a like tyranny, were our monarchs freed from the restraints of laws and senates: But the observation of any fraud or cruelty in SBN 4 private life is sufficient, with the aid of a little thought, to give us the same apprehension; while it serves as an instance of the general corruption of human nature, and shows us the danger which we must incur by reposing an entire confidence in mankind. In both cases, it is experience which is ultimately the foundation of our inference and conclusion.

There is no man so young and unexperienced, as not to have formed, from observation, many general and just maxims concerning human affairs and the conduct of life; but it must be confessed, that, when a man comes to put these in practice, he will be extremely liable to error, till time and farther experience both enlarge these maxims, and teach him their proper use and application. In every situation or incident, there are many particular and seemingly minute circumstances, which the man of greatest talents is, at first, apt to overlook, though on them the justness of his conclusions, and consequently the prudence of his conduct, entirely depend. Not to mention, that, to a young beginner, the general observations and maxims occur not always on the proper occasions, nor can be immediately applied with due calmness and distinction. The truth is, an unexperienced reasoner could be no reasoner at all, were he absolutely unexperienced; and when we assign that character to any one, we mean it only in a comparative sense, and suppose him possessed of experience, in a smaller and more imperfect degree.

or to employ our natural powers in the production of any effect. There would be an end at once of all action, as well as of the chief part of speculation.

7   But here it may be proper to remark, that though our conclusions from experience carry us beyond our memory and senses, and assure us of matters of fact, which happened in the most distant places and most remote ages; yet some fact must always be present to the senses or memory, from which we may first proceed in drawing these conclusions. A man, who should find in a desert country the remains of pompous buildings,[†] would conclude, that the country had, in ancient times, been cultivated by civilized inhabitants; but did nothing of this nature occur to him, he could never form such an inference. We learn the events of   *SBN 46* former ages from history; but then we must peruse the volumes, in which this instruction is contained, and thence carry up our inferences from one testimony to another, till we arrive at the eye-witnesses and spectators of these distant events. In a word, if we proceed not upon some fact, present to the memory or senses, our reasonings would be merely hypothetical; and however the particular links might be connected with each other, the whole chain of inferences would have nothing to support it, nor could we ever, by its means, arrive at the knowledge of any real existence. If I ask, why you believe any particular matter of fact, which you relate, you must tell me some reason; and this reason will be some other fact, connected with it. But as you cannot proceed after this manner, *in infinitum*, you must at last terminate in some fact, which is present to your memory or senses; or must allow that your belief is entirely without foundation.

8   What then is the conclusion of the whole matter? A simple one; though, it must be confessed, pretty remote from the common theories of philosophy. All belief of matter of fact or real existence is derived merely from some object, present to the memory or senses, and a customary conjunction between that and some other object. Or in other words; having found, in many instances, that any two kinds of objects, flame and heat, snow and cold, have always been conjoined together; if flame or snow be presented anew to the senses, the mind is carried by custom to expect heat or cold, and to *believe*, that such a quality does exist, and will discover itself upon a nearer approach. This belief is the necessary result of placing the mind in such circumstances. It is an operation of the soul,[†] when we are so situated, as unavoidable as to feel the passion of love, when we receive benefits; or hatred, when we meet with injuries. All these operations are a species of natural instincts,[†] which no   *SBN 47*

reasoning or process of the thought and understanding is able, either to produce, or to prevent.

9   At this point, it would be very allowable for us to stop our philosophical researches. In most questions, we can never make a single step farther; and in all questions, we must terminate here at last, after our most restless and curious enquiries. But still our curiosity will be pardonable, perhaps commendable, if it carry us on to still farther researches, and make us examine more accurately the nature of this *belief*, and of the *customary conjunction*, whence it is derived. By this means we may meet with some explications and analogies, that will give satisfaction; at least to such as love the abstract sciences, and can be entertained with speculations, which, however accurate, may still retain a degree of doubt and uncertainty. As to readers of a different taste;[†] the remaining part of this section is not calculated for them, and the following enquiries may well be understood, though it be neglected.

PART 2[†]

10   Nothing is more free than the imagination of man; and though it cannot exceed that original stock of ideas, furnished by the internal and external senses, it has unlimited power of mixing, compounding, separating, and dividing these ideas, in all the varieties of fiction and vision. It can feign a train of events, with all the appearance of reality, ascribe to them a particular time and place, conceive them as existent, and paint them out to itself with every circumstance, that belongs to any historical fact, which it believes with the greatest certainty. Wherein, therefore, consists the difference between such a fiction and belief?[†] It lies not merely in any peculiar idea, which is annexed to such a conception as commands our assent, and which is wanting to every known fiction. For as the mind has authority over all its ideas, it could voluntarily annex this particular idea   *SBN 48* to any fiction, and consequently be able to believe whatever it pleases; contrary to what we find by daily experience. We can, in our conception, join the head of a man to the body of a horse; but it is not in our power to believe, that such an animal has ever really existed.

11   It follows, therefore, that the difference between *fiction* and *belief* lies in some sentiment or feeling, which is annexed to the latter, not to the former, and which depends not on the will, nor can be commanded at pleasure. It must be excited by nature, like all other sentiments; and must

arise from the particular situation, in which the mind is placed at any particular juncture. Whenever any object is presented to the memory or senses, it immediately, by the force of custom, carries the imagination to conceive that object, which is usually conjoined to it; and this conception is attended with a feeling or sentiment, different from the loose reveries of the fancy. In this consists the whole nature of belief. For as there is no matter of fact which we believe so firmly, that we cannot conceive the contrary, there would be no difference between the conception assented to, and that which is rejected, were it not for some sentiment, which distinguishes the one from the other. If I see a billiard-ball moving towards another, on a smooth table, I can easily conceive it to stop upon contact. This conception implies no contradiction; but still it feels very differently from that conception, by which I represent to myself the impulse, and the communication of motion from one ball to another.

12   Were we to attempt a *definition* of this sentiment,[†] we should, perhaps, find it a very difficult, if not an impossible task; in the same manner as if we should endeavour to define the feeling of cold or passion of anger, to a creature who never had any experience of these sentiments. *Belief* is the true and proper name of this feeling; and no one is ever at a loss to know the meaning of that term; because every man is every moment conscious of the sentiment represented by it. It may not, however, be improper to attempt a *description* of this sentiment; in hopes we may, by that means, arrive at some analogies, which may afford a more perfect explication of it. I say then, that belief is nothing but a more vivid, lively, forcible, firm, steady conception of an object, than what the imagination alone is ever able to attain. This variety of terms, which may seem so unphilosophical, is intended only to express that act of the mind, which renders realities, or what is taken for such, more present to us than fictions, causes them to weigh more in the thought, and gives them a superior influence on the passions and imagination. Provided we agree about the thing, it is needless to dispute about the terms. The imagination has the command over all its ideas, and can join and mix and vary them, in all the ways possible. It may conceive fictitious objects with all the circumstances of place and time. It may set them, in a manner, before our eyes, in their true colours, just as they might have existed. But as it is impossible, that this faculty of imagination can ever, of itself, reach belief, it is evident, that belief consists not in the peculiar nature or order of ideas, but in the *manner* of their conception, and in their *feeling* to the mind. I confess, that it is impossible perfectly to explain this feeling or manner of conception. We may make use of words, which express something near it. But its true

SBN 49

and proper name, as we observed before, is *belief*; which is a term, that every one sufficiently understands in common life. And in philosophy, we can go no farther than assert, that *belief* is something felt by the mind, which distinguishes the ideas of the judgment from the fictions of the imagination. It gives them more weight and influence; makes them appear of greater importance; enforces them in the mind; and renders SBN 5 them the governing principle of our actions. I hear at present, for instance, a person's voice, with whom I am acquainted; and the sound comes as from the next room. This impression of my senses immediately conveys my thought to the person, together with all the surrounding objects. I paint them out to myself as existing at present, with the same qualities and relations, of which I formerly knew them possessed. These ideas take faster hold of my mind, than ideas of an enchanted castle. They are very different to the feeling, and have a much greater influence of every kind, either to give pleasure or pain, joy or sorrow.

13 Let us, then, take in the whole compass of this doctrine, and allow, that the sentiment of belief is nothing but a conception more intense and steady than what attends the mere fictions of the imagination, and that this *manner* of conception arises from a customary conjunction of the object with something present to the memory or senses: I believe that it will not be difficult, upon these suppositions, to find other operations of the mind analogous to it, and to trace up these phænomena to principles still more general.

14 We have already observed, that nature has established connexions among particular ideas, and that no sooner one idea occurs to our thoughts than it introduces its correlative, and carries our attention towards it, by a gentle and insensible movement. These principles of connexion or association we have reduced to three, namely, *Resemblance, Contiguity*, and *Causation*; which are the only bonds, that unite our thoughts together, and beget that regular train of reflection or discourse, which, in a greater or less degree, takes place among all mankind. Now here arises a question, on which the solution of the present difficulty will depend. Does it happen, in all these relations, that, when one of the objects is presented to the senses or memory, the mind is not only carried SBN 5 to the conception of the correlative, but reaches a steadier and stronger conception of it than what otherwise it would have been able to attain? This seems to be the case with that belief, which arises from the relation of cause and effect. And if the case be the same with the other relations or principles of association, this may be established as a general law, which takes place in all the operations of the mind.

5. *Sceptical Solution of these Doubts*

15 We may, therefore, observe, as the first experiment to our present purpose,[†] that, upon the appearance of the picture of an absent friend, our idea of him is evidently enlivened by the *resemblance*, and that every passion, which that idea occasions, whether of joy or sorrow, acquires new force and vigour. In producing this effect, there concur both a relation and a present impression. Where the picture bears him no resemblance, or at least was not intended for him, it never so much as conveys our thought to him: And where it is absent, as well as the person; though the mind may pass from the thought of the one to that of the other; it feels its idea to be rather weakened than enlivened by that transition. We take a pleasure in viewing the picture of a friend, when it is set before us; but when it is removed, rather choose to consider him directly, than by reflection in an image, which is equally distant and obscure.

16 The ceremonies of the ROMAN CATHOLIC religion may be considered as instances of the same nature. The devotees of that superstition usually plead in excuse for the mummeries,[†] with which they are upbraided, that they feel the good effect of those external motions, and postures, and actions, in enlivening their devotion and quickening their fervour, which otherwise would decay, if directed entirely to distant and immaterial objects.[†] We shadow out[†] the objects of our faith, say they, in sensible types and images, and render them more present to us by the immedi- *SBN 52* ate presence of these types, than it is possible for us to do, merely by an intellectual view and contemplation. Sensible objects have always a greater influence on the fancy than any other; and this influence they readily convey to those ideas, to which they are related, and which they resemble. I shall only infer from these practices, and this reasoning, that the effect of resemblance in enlivening the ideas is very common; and as in every case a resemblance and a present impression must concur,[†] we are abundantly supplied with experiments to prove the reality of the foregoing principle.[†]

17 We may add force to these experiments by others of a different kind, in considering the effects of *contiguity* as well as of *resemblance*. It is certain, that distance diminishes the force of every idea, and that, upon our approach to any object; though it does not discover itself to our senses; it operates upon the mind with an influence, which imitates an immediate impression. The thinking on any object readily transports the mind to what is contiguous; but it is only the actual presence of an object, that transports it with a superior vivacity. When I am a few miles from home, whatever relates to it touches me more nearly than when I am two hundred leagues distant; though even at that distance the reflecting on

127

any thing in the neighbourhood of my friends or family naturally produces an idea of them. But as in this latter case, both the objects of the mind are ideas; notwithstanding there is an easy transition between them; that transition alone is not able to give a superior vivacity to any of the ideas, for want of some immediate impression.[9]

18 No one can doubt but causation has the same influence as the other two relations of resemblance and contiguity. Superstitious people are fond of the relicts† of saints and holy men, for the same reason, that they seek after types or images, in order to enliven their devotion, and give them a more intimate and strong conception of those exemplary lives, which they desire to imitate. Now it is evident, that one of the best relicts, which a devotee could procure, would be the handywork of a saint; and if his cloaths and furniture are ever to be considered in this light, it is because they were once at his disposal, and were moved and affected by him; in which respect they are to be considered as imperfect effects, and as connected with him by a shorter chain of consequences than any of those, by which we learn the reality of his existence.

19 Suppose, that the son of a friend, who had been long dead or absent, were presented to us; it is evident, that this object would instantly revive its correlative idea, and recall to our thoughts all past intimacies and familiarities, in more lively colours than they would otherwise have appeared to us. This is another phænomenon, which seems to prove the principle above-mentioned.

20 We may observe, that, in these phænomena, the belief of the correlative object is always presupposed; without which the relation could have no effect. The influence of the picture supposes, that we *believe* our friend to have once existed. Contiguity to home can never excite our ideas of home, unless we *believe* that it really exists. Now I assert, that this belief, where it reaches beyond the memory or senses, is of a similar nature, and arises from similar causes, with the transition of thought and

[9] "Naturane nobis, inquit, datum dicam, an errore quodam, ut, cum ea loca videamus, in quibus memoria dignos viros acceperimus multum esse versatos, magis moveamur, quam siquando eorum ipsorum aut facta audiamus aut scriptum aliquod legamus? Velut ego nunc moveor. Venit enim mihi PLATONIS in mentem, quem accepimus primum hic disputare solitum: Cujus etiam illi hortuli propinqui non memoriam solum mihi afferunt, sed ipsum videntur in conspectu meo hic ponere. Hic SPEUSIPPUS, hic XENOCRATES, hic ejus auditor POLEMO; cujus ipsa illa sessio fuit, quam videmus. Equidem etiam curiam nostram, HOSTILIAM dico, non hanc novam, quae mihi minor esse videtur postquam est major, solebam intuens, SCIPIONEM, CATONEM, LÆLIUM, nostrum vero in primis avum cogitare. Tanta vis admonitionis inest in locis; ut non sine causa ex his memoriae ducta sit disciplina." CICERO, de finibus.† lib. 5. [Cicero, *De finibus bonorum et malorum* 5.1.2.]

128

vivacity of conception here explained. When I throw a piece of dry wood into a fire, my mind is immediately carried to conceive, that it augments, not extinguishes the flame. This transition of thought from the cause to the effect proceeds not from reason. It derives its origin altogether from custom and experience. And as it first begins from an object, present to the senses, it renders the idea or conception of flame more strong and lively than any loose, floating reverie of the imagination. That idea arises immediately. The thought moves instantly towards it, and conveys to it all that force of conception, which is derived from the impression present to the senses. When a sword is levelled at my breast, does not the idea of wound and pain strike me more strongly, than when a glass of wine is presented to me, even though by accident this idea should occur after the appearance of the latter object? But what is there in this whole matter to cause such a strong conception, except only a present object and a customary transition to the idea of another object, which we have been accustomed to conjoin with the former? This is the whole operation of the mind,[†] in all our conclusions concerning matter of fact and existence; and it is a satisfaction to find some analogies, by which it may be explained. The transition from a present object does in all cases give strength and solidity to the related idea.

21   Here, then, is a kind of pre-established harmony[†] between the course of nature and the succession of our ideas; and though the powers and forces, by which the former is governed, be wholly unknown to us; yet our thoughts and conceptions have still, we find, gone on in the same train with the other works of nature. Custom is that principle, by which *SBN 55* this correspondence has been effected; so necessary to the subsistence of our species, and the regulation of our conduct, in every circumstance and occurrence of human life. Had not the presence of an object instantly excited the idea of those objects, commonly conjoined with it, all our knowledge must have been limited to the narrow sphere of our memory and senses; and we should never have been able to adjust means to ends, or employ our natural powers, either to the producing of good, or avoiding of evil. Those, who delight in the discovery and contemplation of *final causes*,[†] have here ample subject to employ their wonder and admiration.

22   I shall add, for a further confirmation of the foregoing theory, that, as this operation of the mind, by which we infer like effects from like causes, and *vice versa*, is so essential to the subsistence of all human creatures, it is not probable, that it could be trusted to the fallacious deductions of our reason,[†] which is slow in its operations; appears not, in any degree,

during the first years of infancy; and at best is, in every age and period of human life, extremely liable to error and mistake. It is more conformable to the ordinary wisdom of nature to secure so necessary an act of the mind, by some instinct or mechanical tendency, which may be infallible in its operations, may discover itself at the first appearance of life and thought, and may be independent of all the laboured deductions of the understanding. As nature has taught us the use of our limbs, without giving us the knowledge of the muscles and nerves, by which they are actuated; so has she implanted in us an instinct, which carries forward the thought in a correspondent course to that which she has established among external objects; though we are ignorant of those powers and forces, on which this regular course and succession of objects totally depends.

SECTION 6

OF PROBABILITY[10†]

1 THOUGH there be no such thing as *Chance*† in the world; our ignorance of the real cause of any event has the same influence on the understanding, and begets a like species of belief or opinion.

2 There is certainly a probability, which arises from a superiority of chances† on any side; and according as this superiority encreases, and surpasses the opposite chances, the probability receives a proportionable encrease, and begets still a higher degree of belief or assent to that side, in which we discover the superiority. If a dye were marked with one figure or number of spots on four sides, and with another figure or number of spots on the two remaining sides, it would be more probable, that the former would turn up than the latter; though if it had a thousand sides marked in the same manner, and only one side different, the probability would be much higher, and our belief or expectation of the event more steady and secure. This process of the thought or reasoning† may seem trivial and obvious; but to those who consider it more narrowly, it may, perhaps, afford matter for curious speculation.

3 It seems evident, that, when the mind looks forward to discover the event, which may result from the throw of such a dye, it considers the turning up of each particular side† as alike probable; and this is the very nature of chance, to render all the particular events, comprehended in it, entirely equal. But finding a greater number of sides† concur in the one event than in the other, the mind is carried more frequently to that event, and meets it oftener, in revolving the various possibilities or chances, on which the ultimate result depends. This concurrence of several views in one particular event begets immediately, by an inexplicable contrivance of nature, the sentiment of belief, and gives that event the advantage over its antagonist,† which is supported by a smaller number of views, and

---

[10] Mr. LOCKE divides all arguments into demonstrative and probable. [John Locke, *An Essay* *concerning Human Understanding* 4.15.] In this view, we must say, that it is only probable all men must die, or that the sun will rise to-morrow.† But to conform our language more to common use, we ought to divide arguments into *demonstrations*, *proofs*, and *probabilities*.† By *proofs* meaning such arguments from experience as leave no room for doubt or opposition.

recurs less frequently to the mind. If we allow, that belief is nothing but a firmer and stronger conception of an object than what attends the mere fictions of the imagination, this operation may, perhaps, in some measure, be accounted for. The concurrence of these several views or glimpses imprints the idea more strongly on the imagination; gives it superior force and vigour; renders its influence on the passions and affections more sensible; and in a word, begets that reliance or security, which constitutes the nature of belief and opinion.[†]

4   The case is the same with the probability of causes, as with that of chance. There are some causes, which are entirely uniform and constant in producing a particular effect; and no instance has ever yet been found of any failure or irregularity in their operation. Fire has always burned, and water suffocated every human creature: The production of motion by impulse and gravity is an universal law,[†] which has hitherto admitted of no exception. But there are other causes, which have been found more irregular and uncertain; nor has rhubarb always proved a purge, or opium a soporific[†] to every one, who has taken these medicines. It is true, when any cause fails of producing its usual effect, philosophers ascribe not this to any irregularity in nature; but suppose, that some secret causes, in the particular structure of parts, have prevented the operation. Our reasonings, however, and conclusions concerning the event are the same as if this principle had no place. Being determined by custom to transfer the past to the future, in all our inferences; where the past has been entirely regular and uniform, we expect the event with the greatest assurance, and leave no room for any contrary supposition. But where different effects have been found to follow from causes, which are to *appearance* exactly similar, all these various effects must occur to the mind in transferring the past to the future, and enter into our consideration, when we determine the probability of the event. Though we give the preference to that which has been found most usual, and believe that this effect will exist, we must not overlook the other effects, but must assign to each of them a particular weight and authority, in proportion as we have found it to be more or less frequent. It is more probable, in almost every country of EUROPE, that there will be frost sometime in JANUARY, than that the weather will continue open[†] throughout that whole month; though this probability varies according to the different climates, and approaches to a certainty[†] in the more northern kingdoms. Here then it seems evident, that, when we transfer the past to the future, in order to determine the effect, which will result from any cause, we transfer all the different events, in the same proportion as they have appeared in the past, and conceive

SBN 58

one to have existed a hundred times, for instance, another ten times, and another once. As a great number of views do here concur in one event, they fortify and confirm it to the imagination, beget that sentiment which we call *belief*, and give its object the preference above the contrary event, which is not supported by an equal number of experiments, and recurs SBN 59 not so frequently to the thought in transferring the past to the future. Let any one try to account for this operation of the mind upon any of the received systems of philosophy, and he will be sensible of the difficulty. For my part, I shall think it sufficient, if the present hints excite the curiosity of philosophers, and make them sensible how defective all common theories[†] are, in treating of such curious and such sublime subjects.

SECTION 7

OF THE IDEA OF NECESSARY
CONNEXION†

PART 1

1　THE great advantage of the mathematical sciences above the moral consists in this, that the ideas of the former, being sensible, are always clear and determinate,† the smallest distinction between them is immediately perceptible, and the same terms are still expressive of the same ideas, without ambiguity or variation. An oval is never mistaken for a circle, nor an hyperbola for an ellipsis. The isosceles and scalenum† are distinguished by boundaries more exact than vice and virtue, right and wrong. If any term be defined in geometry, the mind readily, of itself, substitutes, on all occasions, the definition for the term defined: Or even when no definition is employed, the object itself may be presented to the senses, and by that means be steadily and clearly apprehended. But the finer sentiments of the mind, the operations of the understanding, the various agitations of the passions, though really in themselves distinct, easily escape us, when surveyed by reflection; nor is it in our power to recall the original object, as often as we have occasion to contemplate it. Ambiguity, by this means, is gradually introduced into our reasonings: Similar objects are readily taken to be the same: And the conclusion becomes at last very wide of the premises.

2　One may safely, however, affirm, that, if we consider these sciences in a proper light, their advantages and disadvantages nearly compensate each other, and reduce both of them to a state of equality. If the mind, with greater facility, retains the ideas of geometry clear and determinate, it must carry on a much longer and more intricate chain of reasoning, and compare ideas much wider of each other, in order to reach the abstruser truths of that science. And if moral ideas are apt, without extreme care, to fall into obscurity and confusion, the inferences are always much shorter in these disquisitions, and the intermediate steps, which lead to the conclusion, much fewer than in the sciences which treat of quantity and number. In reality, there is scarcely a proposition in EUCLID[†] so simple, as not to consist of more parts, than are to be found in any moral reasoning which runs not into chimera and conceit.[†] Where we trace the principles of the human mind through a few steps, we may be very well satisfied with our progress; considering how soon nature throws a bar to[†] all our enquiries concerning causes, and reduces us to an acknowledgment of our ignorance. The chief obstacle, therefore, to our improvement in the moral or metaphysical sciences is the obscurity of the ideas, and ambiguity of the terms. The principal difficulty in the mathematics is the length of inferences and compass of thought, requisite to the forming of any conclusion. And, perhaps, our progress in natural philosophy is chiefly retarded by the want of proper experiments and phænomena, which are often discovered by chance, and cannot always be found, when requisite, even by the most diligent and prudent enquiry. As moral philosophy seems hitherto to have received less improvement than either geometry or physics,[†] we may conclude, that, if there be any difference in this respect among these sciences, the difficulties, which obstruct the progress of the former, require superior care and capacity to be surmounted.

3   There are no ideas, which occur in metaphysics, more obscure and uncertain, than those of *power, force, energy,* or *necessary connexion,* of which it is every moment necessary for us to treat in all our disquisitions. We shall, therefore, endeavour, in this section, to fix, if possible, the precise meaning of these terms, and thereby remove some part of that obscurity, which is so much complained of in this species of philosophy.

4   It seems a proposition, which will not admit of much dispute, that all our ideas are nothing but copies of our impressions, or, in other words, that it is impossible for us to *think* of any thing, which we have not antecedently *felt,* either by our external or internal senses. I have endeavoured[11] to explain and prove this proposition, and have expressed my hopes, that, by a proper application of it, men may reach a greater clearness and precision in philosophical reasonings, than what they have hitherto been able to attain. Complex ideas may, perhaps, be well known by definition, which is nothing but an enumeration of those parts or simple ideas,[†] that compose them. But when we have pushed up definitions to the most simple ideas, and find still some ambiguity and obscurity; what resource are we then possessed of? By what invention can we throw light upon these ideas, and render them altogether precise

SBN 62

---

[11] Section 2.

SBN 62

and determinate to our intellectual view? Produce the impressions or original sentiments, from which the ideas are copied. These impressions are all strong and sensible. They admit not of ambiguity. They are not only placed in a full light themselves, but may throw light on their correspondent ideas, which lie in obscurity. And by this means, we may, perhaps, attain a new microscope or species of optics, by which, in the moral sciences, the most minute, and most simple ideas may be so enlarged as to fall readily under our apprehension, and be equally known with the grossest and most sensible ideas, that can be the object of our enquiry.

5   To be fully acquainted, therefore, with the idea of power or necessary   *SBN* 6.
connexion, let us examine its impression; and in order to find the impression with greater certainty, let us search for it in all the sources, from which it may possibly be derived.

6   When we look about us towards external objects, and consider the operation of causes, we are never able, in a single instance, to discover any power or necessary connexion; any quality, which binds the effect to the cause, and renders the one an infallible consequence of the other. We only find, that the one does actually, in fact, follow the other. The impulse of one billiard-ball is attended with motion in the second. This is the whole that appears to the *outward* senses. The mind feels no sentiment or *inward* impression[†] from this succession of objects: Consequently, there is not, in any single, particular instance of cause and effect, any thing which can suggest the idea of power or necessary connexion.

7   From the first appearance of an object, we never can conjecture what effect will result from it. But were the power or energy of any cause discoverable by the mind, we could foresee the effect, even without experience; and might, at first, pronounce with certainty concerning it, by the mere dint of thought and reasoning.

8   In reality, there is no part of matter, that does ever, by its sensible qualities, discover any power or energy, or give us ground to imagine, that it could produce any thing, or be followed by any other object, which we could denominate its effect. Solidity, extension, motion; these qualities are all compleat in themselves, and never point out any other event which may result from them. The scenes of the universe are continually shifting, and one object follows another in an uninterrupted succession; but the power or force, which actuates the whole machine, is entirely concealed from us,[†] and never discovers itself in any of the sensible qualities   *SBN* 6·
of body. We know, that, in fact, heat is a constant attendant of flame; but what is the connexion between them, we have no room so much as to

conjecture or imagine. It is impossible, therefore, that the idea of power can be derived from the contemplation of bodies, in single instances of their operation; because no bodies ever discover any power,[†] which can be the original of this idea.[12]

9   Since, therefore, external objects, as they appear to the senses, give us no idea of power or necessary connexion, by their operation in particular instances, let us see, whether this idea be derived from reflection on the operations of our own minds, and be copied from any internal impression. It may be said, that we are every moment conscious of internal power;[†] while we feel, that, by the simple command of our will, we can move the organs of our body, or direct the faculties of our mind. An act of volition produces motion in our limbs, or raises a new idea in our imagination. This influence of the will we know by consciousness. Hence we acquire the idea of power or energy; and are certain, that we ourselves and all other intelligent beings are possessed of power. This idea, then, is an idea of reflection,[†] since it arises from reflecting on the operations of our own mind, and on the command which is exercised by will, both over the organs of the body and faculties of the soul.

10   We shall proceed to examine this pretension; and first with regard to the influence of volition over the organs of the body. This influence, we may observe, is a fact, which, like all other natural events, can be known only by experience, and can never be foreseen from any apparent energy or power in the cause, which connects it with the effect, and renders the *SBN 65* one an infallible consequence of the other. The motion of our body follows upon the command of our will. Of this we are every moment conscious. But the means, by which this is effected; the energy, by which the will performs so extraordinary an operation; of this we are so far from being immediately conscious, that it must for ever escape our most diligent enquiry.

11   For *first*, is there any principle in all nature more mysterious than the union of soul with body; by which a supposed spiritual substance acquires such an influence over a material one,[†] that the most refined thought is able to actuate the grossest matter? Were we empowered, by a secret wish, to remove mountains, or controul the planets in their orbit; this

---

[12] Mr. Locke, in his chapter of power,[†] says, that, finding from experience, that there are *SBN 64* several new productions in matter, and concluding that there must somewhere be a power capable of producing them, we arrive at last by this reasoning at the idea of power. [John Locke, *An Essay concerning Human Understanding* 2.21.] But no reasoning can ever give us a new, original, simple idea; as this philosopher himself confesses. This, therefore, can never be the origin of that idea.

extensive authority would not be more extraordinary, nor more beyond our comprehension. But if by consciousness we perceived any power or energy in the will, we must know this power; we must know its con-nexion with the effect; we must know the secret union of soul and body, and the nature of both these substances; by which the one is able to operate, in so many instances, upon the other.

12   *Secondly*, We are not able to move all the organs of the body with a like authority; though we cannot assign any reason besides experience, for so remarkable a difference between one and the other. Why has the will an influence over the tongue and fingers, not over the heart or liver? This question would never embarrass us, were we conscious of a power in the former case, not in the latter. We should then perceive, indepen-dent of experience, why the authority of will over the organs of the body is circumscribed within such particular limits. Being in that case fully acquainted with the power or force, by which it operates, we should also know, why its influence reaches precisely to such boundaries, and no farther.

13   A man, suddenly struck with a palsy[†] in the leg or arm, or who had ‎ ‎ *SBN 66* newly lost those members, frequently endeavours, at first, to move them, and employ them in their usual offices. Here he is as much conscious of power to command such limbs, as a man in perfect health is conscious of power to actuate any member which remains in its natural state and condition. But consciousness never deceives.[†] Consequently, neither in the one case nor in the other, are we ever conscious of any power. We learn the influence of our will from experience alone. And experience only teaches us, how one event constantly follows another; without instructing us in the secret connexion, which binds them together, and renders them inseparable.

14   *Thirdly*, We learn from anatomy, that the immediate object of power in voluntary motion, is not the member itself which is moved, but certain muscles, and nerves, and animal spirits,[†] and, perhaps, something still more minute and more unknown, through which the motion is succes-sively propagated, ere it reach the member itself whose motion is the immediate object of volition. Can there be a more certain proof, that the power, by which this whole operation is performed, so far from being directly and fully known by an inward sentiment or consciousness, is, to the last degree, mysterious and unintelligible? Here the mind wills a certain event: Immediately another event, unknown to ourselves, and totally different from the one intended, is produced: This event produces another, equally unknown: Till at last, through a long succession, the

desired event is produced. But if the original power were felt, it must be known: Were it known, its effect must also be known; since all power is relative to its effect. And *vice versa*, if the effect be not known, the power cannot be known nor felt. How indeed can we be conscious of a power to move our limbs, when we have no such power; but only that to move certain animal spirits, which, though they produce at last the motion of our limbs, yet operate in such a manner as is wholly beyond our comprehension? SBN 67

15 We may, therefore, conclude from the whole, I hope, without any temerity, though with assurance; that our idea of power is not copied from any sentiment or consciousness of power within ourselves, when we give rise to animal motion, or apply our limbs to their proper use and office. That their motion follows the command of the will is a matter of common experience, like other natural events: But the power or energy by which this is effected, like that in other natural events, is unknown and inconceivable.[13]

16 Shall we then assert, that we are conscious of a power or energy in our own minds, when, by an act or command of our will, we raise up a new idea, fix the mind to the contemplation of it, turn it on all sides, and at last dismiss it for some other idea, when we think that we have surveyed it with sufficient accuracy? I believe the same arguments will prove, that even this command of the will gives us no real idea of force or energy.

17 *First*, It must be allowed, that, when we know a power, we know that very circumstance in the cause, by which it is enabled to produce the effect: For these are supposed to be synonimous. We must, therefore, know both the cause and effect, and the relation between them. But do we pretend to be acquainted with the nature of the human soul and the nature of an idea, or the aptitude of the one to produce the other? This is a real creation; a production of something out of nothing: Which SBN 68

---

[13] It may be pretended, that the resistance which we meet with in bodies, obliging us fre- SBN 67 quently to exert our force, and call up all our power, this gives us the idea of force and power. It is this *nisus*[†] or strong endeavour, of which we are conscious, that is the original impression from which this idea is copied. But, *first*, we attribute power to a vast number of objects, where we never can suppose this resistance or exertion of force to take place; to the Supreme Being, who never meets with any resistance; to the mind in its command over its ideas and limbs, in common thinking and motion, where the effect follows immediately upon the will, without any exertion or summoning up of force; to inanimate matter, which is not capable of this sentiment. *Secondly*, This sentiment of an endeavour to overcome resistance has no known connexion with any event: What follows it, we know by experience; but could not know it *a priori*. It must, however, be confessed, that the animal *nisus*, which we experience, though it can afford no accurate precise idea of power, enters very much into that vulgar, inaccurate idea,[†] which is formed of it.

implies a power so great, that it may seem, at first sight, beyond the reach of any being, less than infinite. At least it must be owned, that such a power is not felt, nor known, nor even conceivable by the mind. We only feel the event, namely, the existence of an idea, consequent to a command of the will: But the manner, in which this operation is performed; the power, by which it is produced; is entirely beyond our comprehension.

18   *Secondly,* The command of the mind over itself is limited, as well as its command over the body; and these limits are not known by reason, or any acquaintance with the nature of cause and effect; but only by experience and observation, as in all other natural events and in the operation of external objects. Our authority over our sentiments and passions is much weaker than that over our ideas; and even the latter authority is circumscribed within very narrow boundaries. Will any one pretend to assign the ultimate reason of these boundaries, or show why the power is deficient in one case and not in another.

19   *Thirdly,* This self-command is very different at different times. A man in health possesses more of it, than one languishing with sickness. We are more master of our thoughts in the morning than in the evening: Fasting, than after a full meal. Can we give any reason for these variations, except experience? Where then is the power, of which we pretend to be conscious? Is there not here, either in a spiritual or material substance, or both, some secret mechanism or structure of parts, upon which the effect depends, and which, being entirely unknown to us, renders the SBN 69 power or energy of the will equally unknown and incomprehensible?

20   Volition is surely an act of the mind, with which we are sufficiently acquainted. Reflect upon it. Consider it on all sides. Do you find any thing in it like this creative power, by which it raises from nothing a new idea, and with a kind of FIAT, imitates the omnipotence of its Maker, if I may be allowed so to speak, who called forth into existence all the various scenes of nature? So far from being conscious of this energy in the will, it requires as certain experience, as that of which we are possessed, to convince us, that such extraordinary effects do ever result from a simple act of volition.

21   The generality of mankind never find any difficulty in accounting for the more common and familiar operations of nature; such as the descent of heavy bodies, the growth of plants, the generation of animals, or the nourishment of bodies by food: But suppose, that, in all these cases, they perceive the very force or energy of the cause, by which it is connected with its effect, and is for ever infallible in its operation. They acquire, by long habit, such a turn of mind, that, upon the appearance of the cause, they immediately expect with assurance its usual attendant, and hardly

conceive it possible, that any other event could result from it. It is only on the discovery of extraordinary phænomena, such as earthquakes, pestilence, and prodigies of any kind, that they find themselves at a loss to assign a proper cause, and to explain the manner, in which the effect is produced by it. It is usual for men, in such difficulties, to have recourse to some invisible intelligent principle,[14][†] as the immediate cause of that event, which surprizes them, and which, they think, cannot be accounted for from the common powers of nature. But philosophers,[†] who carry their scrutiny a little farther, immediately perceive, that, even in the most *SBN 70* familiar events, the energy of the cause is as unintelligible as in the most unusual, and that we only learn by experience the frequent CONJUNCTION of objects, without being ever able to comprehend any thing like CON-NEXION between them. Here then, many philosophers think themselves obliged by reason to have recourse, on all occasions, to the same principle, which the vulgar never appeal to but in cases, that appear miraculous and supernatural. They acknowledge mind and intelligence to be, not only the ultimate and original cause of all things, but the immediate and sole cause of every event,[†] which appears in nature. They pretend, that those objects, which are commonly denominated *causes*, are in reality nothing but *occasions*;[†] and that the true and direct principle of every effect is not any power or force in nature, but a volition of the Supreme Being, who wills, that such particular objects should, for ever, be conjoined with each other. Instead of saying, that one billiard-ball moves another, by a force, which it has derived from the author of nature; it is the Deity himself, they say, who, by a particular volition, moves the second ball, being determined to this operation by the impulse of the first ball; in consequence of those general laws, which he has laid down to himself in the government of the universe. But philosophers, advancing still in their enquiries, discover, that, as we are totally ignorant of the power, on which depends the mutual operation of bodies, we are no less ignorant of that power, on which depends the operation of mind on body, or of body on mind; nor are we able, either from our senses or consciousness, to assign the ultimate principle in one case, more than in the other. The same ignorance, therefore, reduces them to the same conclusion. They assert, that the Deity is the immediate cause of the union between soul and body; and that they are not the organs of sense, which, being agitated by external objects, produce sensations in the mind; but that it is a particular *SBN 71* volition of our omnipotent Maker, which excites such a sensation,[†] in

---

[14] Θεὸς ἀπὸ μηχανῆς. *SBN 69*

consequence of such a motion in the organ. In like manner, it is not any energy in the will, that produces local motion in our members: It is God himself, who is pleased to second our will,[†] in itself impotent, and to command that motion, which we erroneously attribute to our own power and efficacy. Nor do philosophers stop at this conclusion. They sometimes extend the same inference to the mind itself, in its internal operations. Our mental vision or conception of ideas is nothing but a revelation made to us by our Maker.[†] When we voluntarily turn our thoughts to any object, and raise up its image in the fancy; it is not the will which creates that idea: It is the universal Creator, who discovers it to the mind, and renders it present to us.

22   Thus, according to these philosophers, every thing is full of God. Not content with the principle, that nothing exists but by his will, that nothing possesses any power but by his concession: They rob nature, and all created beings, of every power, in order to render their dependence on the Deity still more sensible and immediate. They consider not, that, by this theory, they diminish, instead of magnifying, the grandeur of those attributes, which they affect so much to celebrate. It argues surely more power in the Deity to delegate a certain degree of power to inferior creatures, than to produce every thing by his own immediate volition. It argues more wisdom to contrive at first the fabric of the world with such perfect foresight, that, of itself, and by its proper operation, it may serve all the purposes of providence, than if the great Creator were obliged every moment to adjust its parts, and animate by his breath all the wheels of that stupendous machine.[†]

23   But if we would have a more philosophical confutation of this theory, perhaps the two following reflections may suffice.

24   *First*, It seems to me, that this theory of the universal energy and operation of the Supreme Being,[†] is too bold ever to carry conviction with it to a man, sufficiently apprized of the weakness of human reason, and the narrow limits, to which it is confined in all its operations. Though the chain of arguments, which conduct to it, were ever so logical, there must arise a strong suspicion, if not an absolute assurance, that it has carried us quite beyond the reach of our faculties,[†] when it leads to conclusions so extraordinary, and so remote from common life and experience. We are got into fairy land, long ere we have reached the last steps of our theory; and *there* we have no reason to trust our common methods of argument, or to think that our usual analogies and probabilities have any authority. Our line is too short to fathom such immense abysses. And however we may flatter ourselves, that we are guided, in every step which

SBN 72

we take, by a kind of verisimilitude and experience; we may be assured, that this fancied experience has no authority, when we thus apply it to subjects, that lie entirely out of the sphere of experience. But on this we shall have occasion to touch afterwards.[15]

25   *Secondly*, I cannot perceive any force in the arguments, on which this theory is founded. We are ignorant, it is true, of the manner in which bodies operate on each other: Their force or energy is entirely incomprehensible: But are we not equally ignorant of the manner or force by which a mind, even the supreme mind, operates either on itself or on body? Whence, I beseech you, do we acquire any idea of it? We have no sentiment or consciousness of this power in ourselves. We have no idea of the Supreme Being but what we learn from reflection on our own faculties. Were our ignorance, therefore, a good reason for rejecting any thing, we should be led into that principle of denying all energy in the Supreme Being as much as in the grossest matter. We surely comprehend as little the operations of one as of the other. Is it more difficult to conceive, that motion may arise from impulse, than that it may arise from volition? All we know is our profound ignorance[†] in both cases.[16]   SBN 73

PART 2

26   But to hasten to a conclusion of this argument, which is already drawn out to too great a length: We have sought in vain for an idea of power

---

[15] Section 12.   SBN 72

[16] I need not examine at length the *vis inertiæ*[†] which is so much talked of in the new philosophy,[†] and which is ascribed to matter. We find by experience, that a body at rest or in motion continues for ever in its present state, till put from it by some new cause; and that a body impelled takes as much motion from the impelling body as it acquires itself. These are facts. When we call this a *vis inertiæ*, we only mark these facts, without pretending to have any idea of the inert power; in the same manner as, when we talk of gravity, we mean certain effects, without comprehending that active power. It was never the meaning of Sir Isaac Newton to rob second causes[†] of all force or energy; though some of his followers have endeavoured to establish that theory upon his authority. On the contrary, that great philosopher had recourse to an etherial active fluid[†] to explain his universal attraction; though he was so cautious and modest as to allow, that it was a mere hypothesis, not to be insisted on, without more experiments. I must confess, that there is something in the fate of opinions a little extraordinary. Des Cartes insinuated[†] that doctrine of the universal and sole efficacy of the Deity, without insisting on it. Malebranche and other Cartesians made it the foundation of all their philosophy. It had, however, no authority in England. Locke, Clarke, and Cudworth,[†] never so much as take notice of it, but suppose all along, that matter has a real, though subordinate and derived power. By what means has it become so prevalent among our modern metaphysicians?[†]   SBN 73

or necessary connexion, in all the sources from which we could suppose it to be derived. It appears, that, in single instances of the operation of bodies, we never can, by our utmost scrutiny, discover any thing but one event following another; without being able to comprehend any force or power, by which the cause operates, or any connexion between it and its *SBN 74* supposed effect. The same difficulty occurs in contemplating the operations of mind on body; where we observe the motion of the latter to follow upon the volition of the former; but are not able to observe or conceive the tye, which binds together the motion and volition, or the energy by which the mind produces this effect. The authority of the will over its own faculties and ideas is not a whit more comprehensible: So that, upon the whole, there appears not, throughout all nature, any one instance of connexion, which is conceivable by us. All events seem entirely loose and separate. One event follows another; but we never can observe any tye between them. They seem *conjoined*, but never *connected*. And as we can have no idea of any thing, which never appeared to our outward sense or inward sentiment, the necessary conclusion *seems* to be, that we have no idea of connexion or power at all, and that these words are absolutely without any meaning, when employed either in philosophical reasonings, or common life.

27 But there still remains one method of avoiding this conclusion, and one source which we have not yet examined. When any natural object or event is presented, it is impossible for us, by any sagacity or penetration, to discover, or even conjecture, without experience, what event will result from it, or to carry our foresight beyond that object, which is immediately present to the memory and senses. Even after one instance or experiment, where we have observed a particular event to follow upon another, we are not entitled to form a general rule, or foretel what will happen in like cases; it being justly esteemed an unpardonable temerity to judge of the whole course of nature from one single experiment, however accurate or certain. But when one particular species of event has always, in all instances, been conjoined with another, we make no longer any scruple of foretelling one upon the appearance of the other, *SBN 7.* and of employing that reasoning, which can alone assure us of any matter of fact or existence. We then call the one object, *Cause*; the other, *Effect*. We suppose, that there is some connexion between them; some power in the one, by which it infallibly produces the other, and operates with the greatest certainty and strongest necessity.

28 It appears, then, that this idea of a necessary connexion among events arises from a number of similar instances, which occur, of the constant

conjunction of these events; nor can that idea ever be suggested by any one of these instances, surveyed in all possible lights and positions. But there is nothing in a number of instances, different from every single instance, which is supposed to be exactly similar; except only, that after a repetition of similar instances, the mind is carried by habit, upon the appearance of one event, to expect its usual attendant, and to believe, that it will exist. This connexion, therefore, which we *feel* in the mind, this customary transition† of the imagination from one object to its usual attendant, is the sentiment or impression, from which we form the idea of power or necessary connexion. Nothing farther is in the case. Contemplate the subject on all sides; you will never find any other origin of that idea. This is the sole difference between one instance, from which we can never receive the idea of connexion, and a number of similar instances, by which it is suggested. The first time a man saw the communication of motion by impulse, as by the shock of two billiard-balls, he could not pronounce that the one event was *connected*; but only that it was *conjoined* with the other. After he has observed several instances of this nature, he then pronounces them to be *connected*. What alteration has happened to give rise to this new idea of *connexion*? Nothing but that he now *feels* these events to be *connected* in his imagination, and can readily foretel the existence of one from the appearance of the other. When we say, therefore, that one object is connected with another, we mean only, that they have acquired a connexion in our thought, and give rise to this inference, by which they become proofs of each other's existence: A conclusion, which is somewhat extraordinary; but which seems founded on sufficient evidence. Nor will its evidence be weakened by any general diffidence of the understanding, or sceptical suspicion concerning every conclusion, which is new and extraordinary. No conclusions can be more agreeable to scepticism than such as make discoveries concerning the weakness and narrow limits of human reason and capacity.

SBN 76

29 And what stronger instance can be produced of the surprizing ignorance and weakness of the understanding, than the present? For surely, if there be any relation among objects, which it imports to us to know perfectly, it is that of cause and effect. On this are founded all our reasonings concerning matter of fact or existence. By means of it alone we attain any assurance concerning objects, which are removed from the present testimony of our memory and senses. The only immediate utility of all sciences, is to teach us, how to controul and regulate future events by their causes. Our thoughts and enquiries are, therefore, every moment, employed about this relation. Yet so imperfect are the ideas which we

form concerning it, that it is impossible to give any just definition of *cause*, except what is drawn from something extraneous and foreign to it. Similar objects are always conjoined with similar. Of this we have experience. Suitably to this experience, therefore, we may define a cause[†] to be *an object, followed by another, and where all the objects, similar to the first, are followed by objects similar to the second.* Or in other words, *where, if the first object had not been, the second never had existed.* The appearance of a cause always conveys the mind, by a customary transition, to the idea of the   SBN 7 effect. Of this also we have experience. We may, therefore, suitably to this experience, form another definition of *cause*; and call it, *an object followed by another, and whose appearance always conveys the thought to that other.* But though both these definitions be drawn from circumstances foreign to the cause, we cannot remedy this inconvenience, or attain any more perfect definition, which may point out that circumstance in the cause, which gives it a connexion with its effect. We have no idea of this connexion; nor even any distinct notion what it is we desire to know, when we endeavour at a conception of it. We say, for instance, that the vibration of this string is the cause of this particular sound. But what do we mean by that affirmation? We either mean, *that this vibration is followed by this sound, and that all similar vibrations have been followed by similar sounds*: Or, *that this vibration is followed by this sound, and that upon the appearance of one, the mind anticipates the senses, and forms immediately an idea of the other.* We may consider the relation of cause and effect in either of these two lights; but beyond these, we have no idea of it.[17]

---

[17] According to these explications and definitions, the idea of *power* is relative as much as   SBN 7 that of *cause*; and both have a reference to an effect, or some other event constantly conjoined with the former. When we consider the *unknown* circumstance of an object, by which the degree or quantity of its effect is fixed and determined, we call that its power: And accordingly, it is allowed by all philosophers, that the effect is the measure of the power. But if they had any idea of power, as it is in itself, why could not they measure it in itself? The dispute whether the force of a body[†] in motion be as its velocity, or the square of its velocity; this dispute, I say, needed not be decided by comparing its effects in equal or unequal times; but by a direct mensuration[†] and comparison.

As to the frequent use of the words, *force, power, energy, &c.* which every where occur in common conversation, as well as in philosophy; that is no proof, that we are acquainted, in any instance, with the connecting principle between cause and effect, or can account ultimately for the production of one thing by another. These words, as commonly used, have   SBN 7 very loose meanings annexed to them; and their ideas are very uncertain and confused. No animal can put external bodies in motion without the sentiment of a *nisus* or endeavour; and every animal has a sentiment or feeling from the stroke or blow of an external object, that is in motion. These sensations, which are merely animal, and from which we can *a priori* draw no inference, we are apt to transfer to inanimate objects, and to suppose, that they have some such feelings, whenever they transfer or receive motion. With regard to energies, which are

7. The Idea of Necessary Connexion

30   To recapitulate, therefore, the reasonings of this section: Every idea is copied from some preceding impression or sentiment; and where we cannot find any impression, we may be certain that there is no idea. In all single instances of the operation of bodies or minds, there is nothing that produces any impression, nor consequently can suggest any idea, of power or necessary connexion. But when many uniform instances appear, and the same object is always followed by the same event; we then begin to entertain the notion of cause and connexion. We then *feel* a new sentiment or impression, to wit, a customary connexion in the thought or imagination between one object and its usual attendant; and this sentiment is the original of that idea which we seek for. For as this idea arises from a number of similar instances, and not from any single instance; it must arise from that circumstance, in which the number of instances differ from every individual instance. But this customary connexion or transition of the imagination is the only circumstance, in which they differ. In every other particular they are alike. The first instance which we saw of motion, communicated by the shock of two billiard-balls (to return to this obvious illustration) is exactly similar to any instance that may, at present, occur to us; except only, that we could not, at first, *infer* one event from the other; which we are enabled to do at present, after so long a course of uniform experience. I know not, whether the reader will readily apprehend this reasoning. I am afraid, that, should I multiply words about it, or throw it into a greater variety of lights, it would only become more obscure and intricate. In all abstract reasonings, there is one point of view, which, if we can happily hit, we shall go farther towards illustrating the subject, than by all the eloquence and copious expression in the world. This point of view we should endeavour to reach, and reserve the flowers of rhetoric for subjects which are more adapted to them.

exerted, without our annexing to them any idea of communicated motion, we consider only the constant experienced conjunction of the events; and as we *feel* a customary connexion between the ideas, we transfer that feeling to the objects; as nothing is more usual than to apply to external bodies every internal sensation,[†] which they occasion.

SECTION 8

OF LIBERTY AND NECESSITY†

PART 1

1   I T might reasonably be expected, in questions, which have been canvassed and disputed with great eagerness, since the first origin of science and philosophy, that the meaning of all the terms, at least, should have been agreed upon among the disputants; and our enquiries, in the course of two thousand years, been able to pass from words to the true and real subject of the controversy. For how easy may it seem to give exact definitions of the terms employed in reasoning, and make these definitions, not the mere sound of words, the object of future scrutiny and examination? But if we consider the matter more narrowly, we shall be apt to draw a quite opposite conclusion. From this circumstance alone, that a controversy has been long kept on foot, and remains still undecided, we may presume, that there is some ambiguity in the expression, and that the disputants affix different ideas to the terms employed in the controversy. For as the faculties of the mind are supposed to be naturally alike in every individual; otherwise nothing could be more fruitless than to reason or dispute together; it were impossible, if men affix the same ideas to their terms, that they could so long form different opinions of the same subject; especially when they communicate their views, and each party turn themselves on all sides, in search of arguments, which may give them the victory over their antagonists. It is true; if men attempt the discussion of questions, which lie entirely beyond the reach of human capacity, such as those concerning the origin of worlds, or the œconomy of the intellectual system or region of spirits, they may long beat the air in their fruitless contests, and never arrive at any determinate conclusion. But if the question regard any subject of common life and experience; nothing, one would think, could preserve the dispute so long undecided, but some ambiguous expressions, which keep the antagonists still at a distance, and hinder them from grappling with each other.

2   This has been the case in the long disputed question† concerning liberty and necessity; and to so remarkable a degree, that, if I be not much mis-

taken, we shall find, that all mankind, both learned and ignorant, have always been of the same opinion[†] with regard to this subject, and that a few intelligible definitions would immediately have put an end to the whole controversy. I own, that this dispute has been so much canvassed on all hands, and has led philosophers into such a labyrinth of obscure sophistry, that it is no wonder, if a sensible reader indulge his ease so far as to turn a deaf ear to the proposal of such a question, from which he can expect neither instruction nor entertainment. But the state of the argument here proposed may, perhaps, serve to renew his attention; as it has more novelty, promises at least some decision of the controversy, and will not much disturb his ease by any intricate or obscure reasoning.

3   I hope, therefore, to make it appear, that all men have ever agreed in the doctrines both of necessity and of liberty, according to any reasonable sense, which can be put on these terms; and that the whole controversy has hitherto turned merely upon words.[†] We shall begin with examining the doctrine of necessity.

4   It is universally allowed, that matter,[†] in all its operations, is actuated by a necessary force, and that every natural effect is so precisely determined by the energy of its cause, that no other effect, in such particular circumstances, could possibly have resulted from it. The degree and direction of every motion is, by the laws of nature, prescribed with such exactness, that a living creature may as soon arise from the shock of two bodies, as motion, in any other degree or direction than what is actually produced by it. Would we, therefore, form a just and precise idea of *necessity*, we must consider whence that idea arises, when we apply it to the operation of bodies.   SBN 82

5   It seems evident, that, if all the scenes of nature were continually shifted in such a manner, that no two events bore any resemblance to each other, but every object was entirely new, without any similitude to whatever had been seen before, we should never, in that case, have attained the least idea of necessity, or of a connexion among these objects. We might say, upon such a supposition, that one object or event has followed another; not that one was produced by the other. The relation of cause and effect must be utterly unknown[†] to mankind. Inference and reasoning concerning the operations of nature would, from that moment, be at an end; and the memory and senses remain the only canals, by which the knowledge of any real existence could possibly have access to the mind. Our idea, therefore, of necessity and causation arises entirely from the uniformity, observable in the operations of nature; where similar objects are constantly conjoined together, and the mind is determined by

custom to infer the one from the appearance of the other. These two circumstances form the whole of that necessity, which we ascribe to matter. Beyond the constant *conjunction* of similar objects, and the consequent *inference* from one to the other, we have no notion of any necessity, or connexion.

6   If it appear, therefore, that all mankind have ever allowed, without any   SBN 83
doubt or hesitation, that these two circumstances take place in the voluntary actions of men, and in the operations of the mind; it must follow, that all mankind have ever agreed in the doctrine of necessity,[†] and that they have hitherto disputed, merely for not understanding each other.

7   As to the first circumstance, the constant and regular conjunction of similar events; we may possibly satisfy ourselves by the following considerations. It is universally acknowledged, that there is a great uniformity among the actions of men,[†] in all nations and ages, and that human nature remains still the same, in its principles and operations. The same motives always produce the same actions: The same events follow from the same causes. Ambition, avarice, self-love, vanity, friendship, generosity, public spirit; these passions, mixed in various degrees, and distributed through society, have been, from the beginning of the world, and still are, the source of all the actions and enterprizes, which have ever been observed among mankind. Would you know the sentiments, inclinations, and course of life of the GREEKS and ROMANS? Study well the temper and actions of the FRENCH and ENGLISH:[†] You cannot be much mistaken in transferring to the former *most* of the observations, which you have made with regard to the latter. Mankind are so much the same, in all times and places, that history informs us of nothing new or strange in this particular. Its chief use is only to discover the constant and universal principles of human nature, by showing men in all varieties of circumstances and situations, and furnishing us with materials, from which we may form our observations, and become acquainted with the regular springs of human action and behaviour. These records of wars, intrigues, factions, and revolutions, are so many collections of experiments, by which the politician or moral philosopher fixes the principles of his science; in the   SBN 84
same manner as the physician or natural philosopher becomes acquainted with the nature of plants, minerals, and other external objects, by the experiments, which he forms concerning them. Nor are the earth, water, and other elements, examined by ARISTOTLE, and HIPPOCRATES, more like to those, which at present lie under our observation, than the men, described by POLYBIUS and TACITUS,[†] are to those who now govern the world.

8. *Of Liberty and Necessity*

8 Should a traveller, returning from a far country,[†] bring us an account of men, wholly different from any, with whom we were ever acquainted; men, who were entirely divested of avarice, ambition, or revenge; who knew no pleasure but friendship, generosity, and public spirit; we should immediately, from these circumstances, detect the falsehood, and prove him a liar, with the same certainty as if he had stuffed his narration with stories of centaurs and dragons, miracles and prodigies. And if we would explode any forgery in history, we cannot make use of a more convincing argument, than to prove, that the actions, ascribed to any person, are directly contrary to the course of nature, and that no human motives, in such circumstances, could ever induce him to such a conduct. The veracity of Quintus Curtius is as much to be suspected, when he describes the supernatural courage of Alexander,[†] by which he was hurried on singly to attack multitudes, as when he describes his supernatural force and activity, by which he was able to resist them. So readily and universally do we acknowledge a uniformity in human motives and actions[†] as well as in the operations of body.

9 Hence likewise the benefit of that experience, acquired by long life and a variety of business and company, in order to instruct us in the principles of human nature, and regulate our future conduct, as well as speculation. By means of this guide, we mount up to the knowledge of men's inclinations and motives, from their actions, expressions, and even *SBN 85* gestures; and again, descend to the interpretation of their actions from our knowledge of their motives and inclinations. The general observations, treasured up by a course of experience, give us the clue of human nature, and teach us to unravel all its intricacies. Pretexts and appearances no longer deceive us. Public declarations pass for the specious colouring of a cause. And though virtue and honour be allowed their proper weight and authority, that perfect disinterestedness, so often pretended to, is never expected in multitudes and parties; seldom in their leaders; and scarcely even in individuals of any rank or station. But were there no uniformity in human actions, and were every experiment, which we could form of this kind, irregular and anomalous, it were impossible to collect any general observations concerning mankind; and no experience, however accurately digested by reflection, would ever serve to any purpose. Why is the aged husbandman more skilful in his calling than the young beginner, but because there is a certain uniformity in the operation of the sun, rain, and earth, towards the production of vegetables; and experience teaches the old practitioner the rules, by which this operation is governed and directed?

10   We must not, however, expect, that this uniformity of human actions should be carried to such a length, as that all men, in the same circumstances, will always act precisely in the same manner, without making any allowance for the diversity of characters, prejudices, and opinions. Such a uniformity in every particular, is found in no part of nature. On the contrary, from observing the variety of conduct in different men, we are enabled to form a greater variety of maxims, which still suppose a degree of uniformity and regularity.

11   Are the manners of men different in different ages and countries? We
learn thence the great force of custom and education, which mould the human mind from its infancy, and form it into a fixed and established character. Is the behaviour and conduct of the one sex very unlike that of the other? It is thence we become acquainted with the different characters, which nature has impressed upon the sexes, and which she preserves with constancy and regularity. Are the actions of the same person much diversified in the different periods of his life, from infancy to old age? This affords room for many general observations concerning the gradual change of our sentiments and inclinations, and the different maxims, which prevail in the different ages of human creatures. Even the characters, which are peculiar to each individual, have a uniformity in their influence; otherwise our acquaintance with the persons, and our observation of their conduct, could never teach us their dispositions, or serve to direct our behaviour with regard to them.

12   I grant it possible to find some actions, which seem to have no regular connexion with any known motives, and are exceptions to all the measures of conduct, which have ever been established for the government of men. But if we would willingly know, what judgment should be formed of such irregular and extraordinary actions; we may consider the sentiments, commonly entertained with regard to those irregular events, which appear in the course of nature, and the operations of external objects. All causes are not conjoined to their usual effects, with like uniformity. An artificer, who handles only dead matter,[†] may be disappointed of his aim, as well as the politician, who directs the conduct of sensible and intelligent agents.

13   The vulgar, who take things according to their first appearance,[†] attribute the uncertainty of events to such an uncertainty in the causes as makes the latter often fail of their usual influence; though they meet with no impediment in their operation. But philosophers, observing, that, almost in every part of nature, there is contained a vast variety of springs
and principles, which are hid, by reason of their minuteness or remote-

ness, find, that it is at least possible the contrariety of events may not proceed from any contingency in the cause, but from the secret operation of contrary causes. This possibility is converted into certainty by farther observation; when they remark, that, upon an exact scrutiny, a contrariety of effects always betrays a contrariety of causes, and proceeds from their mutual opposition. A peasant can give no better reason for the stopping of any clock or watch than to say that it does not commonly go right: But an artist easily perceives, that the same force in the spring or pendulum has always the same influence on the wheels; but fails of its usual effect, perhaps by reason of a grain of dust, which puts a stop to the whole movement. From the observation of several parallel instances, philosophers form a maxim, that the connexion between all causes and effects is equally necessary, and that its seeming uncertainty in some instances proceeds from the secret opposition of contrary causes.

14   Thus for instance, in the human body, when the usual symptoms of health or sickness disappoint our expectation; when medicines operate not with their wonted powers;[†] when irregular events follow from any particular cause; the philosopher and physician are not surprized at the matter, nor are ever tempted to deny, in general, the necessity and uniformity of those principles, by which the animal œconomy[†] is conducted. They know, that a human body is a mighty complicated machine: That many secret powers lurk in it, which are altogether beyond our comprehension: That to us it must often appear very uncertain in its operations: And that therefore the irregular events, which outwardly discover themselves, can be no proof, that the laws of nature are not observed with the greatest regularity in its internal operations and government.

15   The philosopher, if he be consistent, must apply the same reasoning   *SBN 88* to the actions and volitions of intelligent agents. The most irregular and unexpected resolutions of men may frequently be accounted for by those, who know every particular circumstance of their character and situation. A person of an obliging disposition[†] gives a peevish answer: But he has the toothake, or has not dined. A stupid fellow discovers an uncommon alacrity in his carriage:[†] But he has met with a sudden piece of good fortune. Or even when an action, as sometimes happens, cannot be particularly accounted for, either by the person himself or by others; we know, in general, that the characters of men are, to a certain degree, inconstant and irregular. This is, in a manner, the constant character of human nature; though it be applicable, in a more particular manner, to some persons, who have no fixed rule for their conduct, but proceed in a continued course of caprice and inconstancy. The internal principles

and motives may operate in a uniform manner, notwithstanding these seeming irregularities; in the same manner as the winds, rain, clouds, and other variations of the weather are supposed to be governed by steady principles; though not easily discoverable by human sagacity and enquiry.

16   Thus it appears, not only that the conjunction between motives and voluntary actions is as regular and uniform, as that between the cause and effect in any part of nature; but also that this regular conjunction has been universally acknowledged among mankind, and has never been the subject of dispute, either in philosophy or common life. Now, as it is from past experience, that we draw all inferences concerning the future, and as we conclude, that objects will always be conjoined together, which we find to have always been conjoined; it may seem superfluous to prove, that this experienced uniformity in human actions is a source, whence we draw *inferences* concerning them. But in order to throw the argument   SBN 8 into a greater variety of lights, we shall also insist, though briefly, on this latter topic.

17   The mutual dependence of men is so great, in all societies, that scarce any human action is entirely compleat in itself, or is performed without some reference to the actions of others, which are requisite to make it answer fully the intention of the agent. The poorest artificer, who labours alone, expects at least the protection of the magistrate, to ensure him the enjoyment of the fruits of his labour. He also expects, that, when he carries his goods to market, and offers them at a reasonable price, he shall find purchasers; and shall be able, by the money he acquires, to engage others to supply him with those commodities, which are requisite for his subsistence. In proportion as men extend their dealings, and render their intercourse with others more complicated, they always comprehend, in their schemes of life, a greater variety of voluntary actions, which they expect, from the proper motives, to co-operate with their own. In all these conclusions, they take their measures from past experience, in the same manner as in their reasonings concerning external objects; and firmly believe, that men, as well as all the elements, are to continue, in their operations, the same, that they have ever found them. A manufacturer reckons upon the labour of his servants, for the execution of any work, as much as upon the tools, which he employs, and would be equally sur-prized, were his expectations disappointed. In short, this experimental inference and reasoning concerning the actions of others enters so much into human life, that no man, while awake, is ever a moment without employing it. Have we not reason, therefore, to affirm, that all mankind

have always agreed in the doctrine of necessity, according to the foregoing definition and explication of it?

18   Nor have philosophers ever entertained a different opinion from the people in this particular. For not to mention, that almost every action of their life supposes that opinion; there are even few of the speculative parts   *SBN 90* of learning, to which it is not essential. What would become of *history*, had we not a dependence on the veracity of the historian, according to the experience, which we have had of mankind? How could *politics* be a science,[†] if laws and forms of government had not a uniform influence upon society? Where would be the foundation of *morals*, if particular characters had no certain or determinate power to produce particular sentiments, and if these sentiments had no constant operation on actions? And with what pretence could we employ our *criticism* upon any poet or polite author, if we could not pronounce the conduct and sentiments of his actors, either natural or unnatural, to such characters, and in such circumstances? It seems almost impossible, therefore, to engage, either in science or action of any kind, without acknowledging the doctrine of necessity, and this *inference* from motives to voluntary actions;[†] from characters to conduct.

19   And indeed, when we consider how aptly *natural* and *moral* evidence[†] link together, and form only one chain of argument, we shall make no scruple to allow, that they are of the same nature, and derived from the same principles. A prisoner, who has neither money nor interest, discovers the impossibility of his escape, as well when he considers the obstinacy of the gaoler, as the walls and bars, with which he is surrounded; and, in all attempts for his freedom, chooses rather to work upon the stone and iron of the one, than upon the inflexible nature of the other. The same prisoner, when conducted to the scaffold, foresees his death as certainly from the constancy and fidelity of his guards, as from the operation of the ax or wheel.[†] His mind runs along a certain train of ideas: The refusal of the soldiers to consent to his escape; the action of the executioner; the separation of the head and body; bleeding, convulsive motions, and death. Here is a connected chain of natural causes and voluntary actions; but the mind feels no difference[†] between them, in passing from one link   *SBN 91* to another: Nor is less certain of the future event than if it were connected with the objects present to the memory or senses, by a train of causes, cemented together by what we are pleased to call a *physical* necessity.[†] The same experienced union has the same effect on the mind, whether the united objects be motives, volition, and actions; or figure

and motion. We may change the names of things; but their nature and their operation on the understanding never change.

20   Were a man, whom I know to be honest and opulent, and with whom I live in intimate friendship, to come into my house, where I am surrounded with my servants, I rest assured, that he is not to stab me before he leaves it, in order to rob me of my silver standish; and I no more suspect this event, than the falling of the house itself, which is new, and solidly built and founded.—*But he may have been seized with a sudden and unknown frenzy.*—So may a sudden earthquake arise, and shake and tumble my house about my ears. I shall therefore change the suppositions. I shall say, that I know with certainty, that he is not to put his hand into the fire, and hold it there, till it be consumed: And this event, I think I can foretel with the same assurance, as that, if he throw himself out at the window, and meet with no obstruction, he will not remain a moment suspended in the air. No suspicion of an unknown frenzy can give the least possibility to the former event, which is so contrary to all the known principles of human nature. A man who at noon leaves his purse full of gold on the pavement at Charing Cross,† may as well expect that it will fly away like a feather, as that he will find it untouched an hour after. Above one half of human reasonings contain inferences of a similar nature, attended with more or less degrees of certainty, proportioned to our experience of the usual conduct of mankind in such particular situations.

21   I have frequently considered, what could possibly be the reason, why SBN 9 all mankind, though they have ever, without hesitation, acknowledged the doctrine of necessity, in their whole practice and reasoning, have yet discovered such a reluctance to acknowledge it in words, and have rather shown a propensity, in all ages, to profess the contrary opinion. The matter, I think, may be accounted for, after the following manner. If we examine the operations of body, and the production of effects from their causes, we shall find, that all our faculties can never carry us farther in our knowledge of this relation, than barely to observe, that particular objects are *constantly conjoined* together, and that the mind is carried, by a *customary transition*, from the appearance of one to the belief of the other. But though this conclusion concerning human ignorance be the result of the strictest scrutiny of this subject, men still entertain a strong propensity to believe, that they penetrate farther into the powers of nature,† and perceive something like a necessary connexion between the cause and the effect. When again they turn their reflections towards the operations of their own minds, and *feel* no such connexion of the motive

and the action; they are thence apt to suppose, that there is a difference between the effects, which result from material force, and those which arise from thought and intelligence. But being once convinced, that we know nothing farther of causation of any kind, than merely the *constant conjunction* of objects, and the consequent *inference* of the mind from one to another, and finding, that these two circumstances are universally allowed to have place in voluntary actions; we may be more easily led to own the same necessity common to all causes. And though this reasoning may contradict the systems of many philosophers,[†] in ascribing necessity to the determinations of the will,[†] we shall find, upon reflection, that they dissent from it in words only, not in their real sentiment. Necessity, according to the sense, in which it is here taken, has never yet been rejected,[†] nor can ever, I think, be rejected by any philosopher. It may only, perhaps, be pretended, that the mind can perceive, in the operations of matter, some farther connexion between the cause and effect; and a connexion that has not place in the voluntary actions of intelligent beings. Now whether it be so or not, can only appear upon examination; and it is incumbent on these philosophers to make good their assertion, by defining or describing that necessity, and pointing it out to us in the operations of material causes. SBN 93

22   It would seem, indeed, that men begin at the wrong end of this question concerning liberty and necessity, when they enter upon it by examining the faculties of the soul, the influence of the understanding, and the operations of the will. Let them first discuss a more simple question, namely, the operations of body and of brute unintelligent matter; and try whether they can there form any idea of causation and necessity, except that of a constant conjunction of objects, and subsequent inference of the mind from one to another. If these circumstances form, in reality, the whole of that necessity, which we conceive in matter, and if these circumstances be also universally acknowledged to take place in the operations of the mind, the dispute is at an end; at least, must be owned to be thenceforth merely verbal.[†] But as long as we will rashly suppose, that we have some farther idea of necessity and causation in the operations of external objects; at the same time, that we can find nothing farther, in the voluntary actions of the mind; there is no possibility of bringing the question to any determinate issue, while we proceed upon so erroneous a supposition. The only method of undeceiving us, is, to mount up higher; to examine the narrow extent of science when applied to material causes; and to convince ourselves, that all we know of them, is, the constant conjunction and inference above-mentioned. We may,

perhaps, find, that it is with difficulty we are induced to fix such narrow SBN 9 limits to human understanding: But we can afterwards find no difficulty, when we come to apply this doctrine to the actions of the will. For as it is evident, that these have a regular conjunction with motives and circumstances and characters, and as we always draw inferences from one to the other, we must be obliged to acknowledge in words, that necessity, which we have already avowed, in every deliberation of our lives, and in every step of our conduct and behaviour.[18]

23   But to proceed in this reconciling project[†] with regard to the question SBN 9 of liberty and necessity; the most contentious question, of metaphysics, the most contentious science; it will not require many words to prove, that all mankind have ever agreed in the doctrine of liberty as well as in that of necessity, and that the whole dispute, in this respect also, has been hitherto merely verbal. For what is meant by *liberty*, when applied to voluntary actions? We cannot surely mean, that actions have so little connexion with motives, inclinations, and circumstances, that one does not follow with a certain degree of uniformity from the other, and that one

---

[18] The prevalence of the doctrine of liberty may be accounted for, from another cause, SBN 9 *viz.* a false sensation or seeming experience which we have, or may have, of liberty or indifference,[†] in many of our actions. The necessity of any action, whether of matter or of mind, is not, properly speaking, a quality in the agent, but in any thinking or intelligent being, who may consider the action; and it consists chiefly in the determination of his thoughts to infer the existence of that action from some preceding objects; as liberty, when opposed to necessity, is nothing but the want of that determination, and a certain looseness or indifference, which we feel, in passing, or not passing, from the idea of one object to that of any succeeding one. Now we may observe, that, though, in *reflecting* on human actions, we seldom feel such a looseness or indifference, but are commonly able to infer them with considerable certainty from their motives, and from the dispositions of the agent; yet it frequently happens, that, in *performing* the actions themselves, we are sensible of something like it: And as all resembling objects are readily taken for each other, this has been employed as a demonstrative and even intuitive proof of human liberty. We feel, that our actions are subject to our will, on most occasions; and imagine we feel, that the will itself is subject to nothing,[†] because, when by a denial of it we are provoked to try, we feel, that it moves easily every way, and produces an image of itself, (or a *Velleïty*,[†] as it is called in the schools) even on that side, on which it did not settle. This image, or faint motion, we persuade ourselves, could, at that time, have been compleated into the thing itself; because, should that be denied, we find, upon a second trial, that, at present, it can. We consider not, that the fantastical desire of showing liberty, is here the motive of our actions. And it seems certain, that, however we may imagine we feel a liberty within ourselves, a spectator can commonly infer our actions from our motives and character; and even where he cannot, he concludes in general, that he might, were he perfectly acquainted with every circumstance of our situation and temper, and the most secret springs of our complexion[†] and disposition. Now this is the very essence of necessity, according to the foregoing doctrine.

affords no inference by which we can conclude the existence of the other. For these are plain and acknowledged matters of fact. By *liberty*, then, we can only mean *a power of acting or not acting, according to the determinations of the will*; that is, if we choose to remain at rest, we may; if we choose to move, we also may. Now this hypothetical liberty[†] is universally allowed to belong to every one, who is not a prisoner and in chains. Here then is no subject of dispute.

24   Whatever definition we may give of *liberty*, we should be careful to observe two requisite circumstances; *first*, that it be consistent with plain matter of fact; *secondly*, that it be consistent with itself. If we observe these circumstances, and render our definition intelligible, I am persuaded that all mankind will be found of one opinion with regard to it.

25   It is universally allowed, that nothing exists without a cause of its existence, and that *chance*, when strictly examined, is a mere negative word,[†] and means not any real power, which has, any where, a being in nature. But it is pretended, that some causes are necessary, some not necessary. Here then is the advantage of definitions. Let any one *define* a cause, without comprehending, as a part of the definition, a *necessary connexion* with its effect; and let him show distinctly the origin of the idea, expressed   SBN 96 by the definition; and I shall readily give up the whole controversy. But if the foregoing explication of the matter be received, this must be absolutely impracticable. Had not objects a regular conjunction with each other, we should never have entertained any notion of cause and effect; and this regular conjunction produces that inference of the understanding, which is the only connexion, that we can have any comprehension of. Whoever attempts a definition of *cause*, exclusive of these circumstances, will be obliged, either to employ unintelligible terms, or such as are synonimous to the term, which he endeavours to define.[19] And if the definition above-mentioned be admitted; liberty, when opposed to necessity, not to constraint, is the same thing with chance; which is universally allowed to have no existence.

---

[19] Thus, if a cause be defined, *that which produces any thing*; it is easy to observe, that *producing* is synonimous to *causing*. In like manner, if a cause be defined, *that by which any thing exists*; this is liable to the same objection. For what is meant by these words, *by which*? Had it been said, that a cause is *that* after which *any thing constantly exists*; we should have understood the terms. For this is, indeed, all we know of the matter. And this constancy forms the very essence of necessity, nor have we any other idea of it.   SBN 96

PART 2

26 There is no method of reasoning more common, and yet none more blameable, than, in philosophical disputes, to endeavour the refutation of any hypothesis, by a pretence of its dangerous consequences to religion[†] and morality. When any opinion leads to absurdities, it is certainly false; but it is not certain that an opinion is false, because it is of dangerous consequence. Such topics, therefore, ought entirely to be forborne; as serving nothing to the discovery of truth, but only to make the person of an antagonist odious. This I observe in general, without pretending to draw any advantage from it. I frankly submit to an examination of this *SBN 9* kind, and shall venture to affirm, that the doctrines, both of necessity and of liberty, as above explained, are not only consistent with morality, but are absolutely essential to its support.

27 *Necessity* may be defined two ways, conformably to the two definitions of *cause*,[†] of which it makes an essential part. It consists either in the constant conjunction of like objects, or in the inference of the understanding from one object to another. Now necessity, in both these senses, (which, indeed, are, at bottom, the same) has universally, though tacitly, in the schools,[†] in the pulpit, and in common life, been allowed to belong to the will of man;[†] and no one has ever pretended to deny, that we can draw inferences concerning human actions, and that those inferences are founded on the experienced union of like actions, with like motives, inclinations, and circumstances. The only particular, in which any one can differ, is, that either, perhaps, he will refuse to give the name of *necessity* to this property of human actions: But as long as the meaning is understood, I hope the word can do no harm: Or that he will maintain it possible to discover something farther in the operations of matter. But this, it must be acknowledged, can be of no consequence to morality or religion, whatever it may be to natural philosophy or metaphysics. We may here be mistaken in asserting, that there is no idea of any other necessity or connexion in the actions of body: But surely we ascribe nothing to the actions of the mind, but what every one does, and must readily allow of. We change no circumstance in the received orthodox system[†] with regard to the will, but only in that with regard to material objects and causes. Nothing therefore can be more innocent, at least, than this doctrine.

28 All laws being founded on rewards and punishments, it is supposed as a fundamental principle, that these motives have a regular and uniform *SBN 9* influence on the mind, and both produce the good and prevent the evil actions. We may give to this influence what name we please; but as it

is usually conjoined with the action, it must be esteemed a *cause*, and be looked upon as an instance of that necessity, which we would here establish.

29   The only proper object of hatred or vengeance, is a person or creature, endowed with thought and consciousness; and when any criminal or injurious actions excite that passion, it is only by their relation to the person, or connexion with him. Actions are, by their very nature, temporary and perishing; and where they proceed not from some *cause* in the character and disposition of the person who performed them, they can neither redound to his honour, if good; nor infamy, if evil. The actions themselves may be blameable; they may be contrary to all the rules of morality and religion: But the person is not answerable for them;[†] and as they proceeded from nothing in him, that is durable and constant, and leave nothing of that nature behind them, it is impossible he can, upon their account, become the object of punishment or vengeance. According to the principle, therefore, which denies necessity, and consequently causes, a man is as pure and untainted, after having committed the most horrid crime, as at the first moment of his birth, nor is his character any wise concerned in his actions; since they are not derived from it, and the wickedness of the one can never be used as a proof of the depravity of the other.

30   Men are not blamed for such actions, as they perform ignorantly and casually, whatever may be the consequences. Why? but because the principles of these actions are only momentary, and terminate in them alone. Men are less blamed for such actions as they perform hastily and unpremeditately, than for such as proceed from deliberation. For what reason? but because a hasty temper, though a constant cause or principle in the mind, operates only by intervals, and infects not the whole character. Again, repentance wipes off every crime, if attended with a reformation of life and manners. How is this to be accounted for? but by asserting, that actions render a person criminal, merely as they are proofs of criminal principles in the mind; and when, by an alteration of these principles, they cease to be just proofs, they likewise cease to be criminal. But, except upon the doctrine of necessity, they never were just proofs, and consequently never were criminal. *SBN 99*

31   It will be equally easy to prove, and from the same arguments, that *liberty*, according to that definition above-mentioned, in which all men agree, is also essential to morality, and that no human actions, where it is wanting, are susceptible of any moral qualities, or can be the objects either of approbation or dislike. For as actions are objects of our moral

161

sentiment, so far only as they are indications of the internal character, passions, and affections; it is impossible that they can give rise either to praise or blame, where they proceed not from these principles, but are derived altogether from external violence.

32   I pretend not to have obviated or removed all objections to this theory, with regard to necessity and liberty. I can foresee other objections, derived from topics, which have not here been treated of. It may be said, for instance, that, if voluntary actions be subjected to the same laws of necessity with the operations of matter, there is a continued chain of necessary causes, pre-ordained and pre-determined, reaching from the original cause of all, to every single volition of every human creature. No contingency any where in the universe; no indifference; no liberty. While we act, we are, at the same time, acted upon. The ultimate Author of all our volitions is the Creator of the world, who first bestowed motion on this immense machine, and placed all beings in that particular position, whence every subsequent event, by an inevitable necessity, must result.   SBN 1 Human actions, therefore, either can have no moral turpitude at all, as proceeding from so good a cause; or if they have any turpitude, they must involve our Creator in the same guilt, while he is acknowledged to be their ultimate cause and author. For as a man, who fired a mine, is answerable for all the consequences, whether the train[†] he employed be long or short; so wherever a continued chain of necessary causes is fixed,[†] that Being, either finite or infinite, who produces the first, is likewise the author of all the rest, and must both bear the blame and acquire the praise, which belong to them. Our clear and unalterable ideas of morality establish this rule, upon unquestionable reasons, when we examine the consequences of any human action; and these reasons must still have greater force, when applied to the volitions and intentions of a Being, infinitely wise and powerful. Ignorance or impotence may be pleaded for so limited a creature as man; but those imperfections have no place in our Creator. He foresaw, he ordained, he intended all those actions of men, which we so rashly pronounce criminal. And we must therefore conclude, either that they are not criminal, or that the Deity, not man, is accountable for them. But as either of these positions is absurd and impious, it follows, that the doctrine, from which they are deduced, cannot possibly be true, as being liable to all the same objections. An absurd consequence, if necessary, proves the original doctrine to be absurd; in the same manner as criminal actions render criminal the original cause, if the connexion between them be necessary and inevitable.

33   This objection consists of two parts, which we shall examine sepa-

rately; *first*, that, if human actions can be traced up, by a necessary chain, to the Deity, they can never be criminal; on account of the infinite perfection of that Being, from whom they are derived, and who can intend nothing but what is altogether good and laudable. Or, *secondly*, if they be criminal, we must retract the attribute of perfection, which we ascribe to the Deity, and must acknowledge him to be the ultimate author of guilt and moral turpitude in all his creatures. *SBN 101*

34   The answer to the first objection seems obvious and convincing. There are many philosophers, who, after an exact scrutiny of all the phænomena of nature, conclude, that the WHOLE, considered as one system, is, in every period of its existence, ordered with perfect benevolence; and that the utmost possible happiness will, in the end, result to all created beings, without any mixture of positive or absolute ill and misery. Every physical ill, say they, makes an essential part of this benevolent system, and could not possibly be removed, even by the Deity himself, considered as a wise agent, without giving entrance to greater ill, or excluding greater good, which will result from it. From this theory, some philosophers, and the ancient STOICS[†] among the rest, derived a topic of consolation under all afflictions, while they taught their pupils, that those ills, under which they laboured, were, in reality, goods to the universe; and that to an enlarged view, which could comprehend the whole system of nature, every event became an object of joy and exultation. But though this topic be specious and sublime, it was soon found in practice weak and ineffectual. You would surely more irritate, than appease a man, lying under the racking pains of the gout, by preaching up to him the rectitude of those general laws, which produced the malignant humours[†] in his body, and led them through the proper canals, to the sinews and nerves, where they now excite such acute torments. These enlarged views may, for a moment, please the imagination of a speculative man, who is placed in ease and security; but neither can they dwell with constancy on his mind, even though undisturbed by the emotions of pain or passion; much less *SBN 102* can they maintain their ground, when attacked by such powerful antagonists. The affections take a narrower and more natural survey of their object; and by an œconomy, more suitable to the infirmity of human minds, regard alone the beings around us, and are actuated by such events as appear good or ill to the private system.

35   The case is the same with *moral* as with *physical* ill. It cannot reasonably be supposed, that those remote considerations,[†] which are found of so little efficacy with regard to one, will have a more powerful influence with regard to the other. The mind of man is so formed by nature, that,

upon the appearance of certain characters, dispositions, and actions, it immediately feels the sentiment of approbation or blame;[†] nor are there any emotions more essential to its frame and constitution. The characters, which engage our approbation, are chiefly such as contribute to the peace and security of human society; as the characters, which excite blame, are chiefly such as tend to public detriment and disturbance: Whence it may reasonably be presumed, that the moral sentiments arise, either mediately or immediately, from a reflection on these opposite interests. What though philosophical meditations establish a different opinion or conjecture; that every thing is right with regard to the WHOLE, and that the qualities, which disturb society, are, in the main, as beneficial, and are as suitable to the primary intention of nature, as those which more directly promote its happiness and welfare? Are such remote and uncertain speculations[†] able to counterbalance the sentiments, which arise from the natural and immediate view of the objects? A man, who is robbed of a considerable sum; does he find his vexation for the loss any wise diminished by these sublime reflections? Why then should his moral resentment against the crime be supposed incompatible with them? Or why should not the acknowledgment of a real distinction between vice and virtue be reconcileable to all speculative systems of philosophy, as well as that of a real distinction between personal beauty and deformity? Both these distinctions are founded in the natural sentiments of the human mind: And these sentiments are not to be controuled or altered by any philosophical theory or speculation whatsoever. | *SBN 10*

36   The *second* objection admits not of so easy and satisfactory an answer; nor is it possible to explain distinctly, how the Deity can be the mediate cause[†] of all the actions of men, without being the author of sin and moral turpitude. These are mysteries, which mere natural and unassisted reason is very unfit to handle; and whatever system she embraces, she must find herself involved in inextricable difficulties, and even contradictions, at every step which she takes with regard to such subjects. To reconcile the indifference and contingency of human actions with prescience; or to defend absolute decrees, and yet free the Deity from being the author of sin, has been found hitherto to exceed all the power of philosophy. Happy, if she be thence sensible of her temerity, when she pries into these sublime mysteries; and leaving a scene so full of obscurities and perplexities, return, with suitable modesty, to her true and proper province, the examination of common life; where she will find difficulties enow to employ her enquiries, without launching into so boundless an ocean of doubt, uncertainty, and contradiction!

SECTION 9

OF THE REASON OF ANIMALS†

1 ALL our reasonings concerning matter of fact are founded on a species of ANALOGY,† which leads us to expect from any cause the same events, which we have observed to result from similar causes. Where the causes are entirely similar, the analogy is perfect, and the inference, drawn from it, is regarded as certain and conclusive: Nor does any man ever entertain a doubt, where he sees a piece of iron, that it will have weight and cohesion of parts;† as in all other instances, which have ever fallen under his observation. But where the objects have not so exact a similarity, the analogy is less perfect, and the inference is less conclusive; though still it has some force, in proportion to the degree of similarity and resemblance. The anatomical observations, formed upon one animal, are, by this species of reasoning, extended to all animals; and it is certain, that when the circulation of the blood, for instance, is clearly proved to have place in one creature, as a frog, or fish,† it forms a strong presumption, that the same principle has place in all. These analogical observations may be carried farther, even to this science, of which we are now treating; and any theory, by which we explain the operations of the understanding, or the origin and connexion of the passions† in man, will acquire additional authority, if we find, that the same theory is requisite to explain the same phænomena in all other animals. We shall make trial of this, with regard to the hypothesis, by which, we have, in the foregoing discourse, endeav- oured to account for all experimental reasonings; and it is hoped, that this new point of view will serve to confirm all our former observations.

2 *First*, It seems evident, that animals, as well as men, learn many things from experience, and infer, that the same events will always follow from the same causes. By this principle they become acquainted with the more obvious properties of external objects, and gradually, from their birth, treasure up a knowledge of the nature of fire, water, earth, stones, heights, depths, &c. and of the effects, which result from their operation. The ignorance and inexperience of the young are here plainly distinguishable from the cunning and sagacity of the old, who have learned, by long observation, to avoid what hurt them, and to pursue what gave ease or

pleasure. A horse, that has been accustomed to the field, becomes acquainted with the proper height, which he can leap, and will never attempt what exceeds his force and ability. An old greyhound will trust the more fatiguing part of the chace to the younger, and will place himself so as to meet the hare in her doubles;[†] nor are the conjectures, which he forms on this occasion, founded in any thing but his observation and experience.

3   This is still more evident from the effects of discipline and education on animals, who, by the proper application of rewards and punishments, may be taught any course of action, the most contrary to their natural instincts and propensities. Is it not experience, which renders a dog apprehensive of pain, when you menace him, or lift up the whip to beat him? Is it not even experience, which makes him answer to his name, and infer, from such an arbitrary sound, that you mean him rather than any of his fellows, and intend to call him, when you pronounce it in a certain manner, and with a certain tone and accent?

4   In all these cases, we may observe, that the animal infers some fact   SBN 1 beyond what immediately strikes his senses; and that this inference is altogether founded on past experience, while the creature expects from the present object the same consequences, which it has always found in its observation to result from similar objects.

5   *Secondly*, It is impossible, that this inference of the animal can be founded on any process of argument or reasoning, by which he concludes, that like events must follow like objects, and that the course of nature will always be regular in its operations. For if there be in reality any arguments of this nature, they surely lie too abstruse for the observation of such imperfect understandings; since it may well employ the utmost care and attention of a philosophic genius to discover and observe them. Animals, therefore, are not guided in these inferences by reasoning:[†] Neither are children: Neither are the generality of mankind, in their ordinary actions and conclusions: Neither are philosophers themselves, who, in all the active parts of life, are, in the main, the same with the vulgar, and are governed by the same maxims. Nature must have provided some other principle, of more ready, and more general use and application; nor can an operation of such immense consequence in life, as that of inferring effects from causes, be trusted to the uncertain process of reasoning and argumentation. Were this doubtful with regard to men, it seems to admit of no question with regard to the brute creation; and the conclusion being once firmly established in the one, we have a strong presumption, from all the rules of analogy, that it ought to be universally

admitted, without any exception or reserve. It is custom alone, which engages animals, from every object, that strikes their senses, to infer its usual attendant, and carries their imagination, from the appearance of the one, to conceive the other, in that particular manner, which we denominate *belief*. No other explication can be given of this operation, in all the higher, as well as lower classes of sensitive beings, which fall under our notice and observation.[20] SBN 107

6   But though animals learn many parts of their knowledge from obser- SBN 108 vation, there are also many parts of it, which they derive from the original hand of nature; which much exceed the share of capacity they possess on ordinary occasions; and in which they improve, little or nothing, by the longest practice and experience. These we denominate *instincts*,[†] and

---

[20] Since all reasoning concerning facts or causes is derived merely from custom, it may be SBN 107 asked how it happens, that men so much surpass animals in reasoning, and one man so much surpasses another? Has not the same custom the same influence on all?

We shall here endeavour briefly to explain the great difference in human understandings: After which the reason of the difference between men and animals will easily be comprehended.

1. When we have lived any time, and have been accustomed to the uniformity of nature, we acquire a general habit, by which we always transfer the known to the unknown, and conceive the latter to resemble the former. By means of this general habitual principle, we regard even one experiment as the foundation of reasoning, and expect a similar event with some degree of certainty, where the experiment has been made accurately, and free from all foreign circumstances. It is therefore considered as a matter of great importance to observe the consequences of things; and as one man may very much surpass another in attention and memory and observation, this will make a very great difference in their reasoning.

2. Where there is a complication of causes to produce any effect, one mind may be much larger than another, and better able to comprehend the whole system of objects, and to infer justly their consequences.

3. One man is able to carry on a chain of consequences to a greater length than another.

4. Few men can think long without running into a confusion of ideas, and mistaking one for another; and there are various degrees of this infirmity.

5. The circumstance, on which the effect depends, is frequently involved in other circumstances, which are foreign and extrinsic. The separation of it often requires great attention, accuracy, and subtilty.

6. The forming of general maxims from particular observation is a very nice operation; and nothing is more usual, from haste or a narrowness of mind, which sees not on all sides, than to commit mistakes in this particular.

7. When we reason from analogies, the man, who has the greater experience or the greater promptitude of suggesting analogies, will be the better reasoner.

8. Biasses from prejudice, education, passion, party, *&c.* hang more upon one mind than another.

9. After we have acquired a confidence in human testimony, books and conversation enlarge much more the sphere of one man's experience and thought than those of another.

It would be easy to discover many other circumstances that make a difference in the understandings of men.

are so apt to admire, as something very extraordinary, and inexplicable by all the disquisitions of human understanding. But our wonder will, perhaps, cease or diminish; when we consider, that the experimental reasoning[†] itself, which we possess in common with beasts, and on which the whole conduct of life depends, is nothing but a species of instinct[†] or mechanical power,[†] that acts in us unknown to ourselves; and in its chief operations, is not directed by any such relations or comparisons of ideas, as are the proper objects of our intellectual faculties. Though the instinct be different, yet still it is an instinct, which teaches a man to avoid the fire; as much as that, which teaches a bird, with such exactness, the art of incubation, and the whole œconomy and order of its nursery.[†]

SECTION 10
OF MIRACLES

PART 1

1   THERE is, in Dr. TILLOTSON's writings,[†] an argument against the *real presence*,[†] which is as concise, and elegant, and strong as any argument can
possibly be supposed against a doctrine, so little worthy of a serious refutation. It is acknowledged on all hands, says that learned prelate, that the
authority, either of the scripture or of tradition, is founded merely in the
testimony of the apostles, who were eye-witnesses to those miracles of
our Saviour, by which he proved his divine mission. Our evidence, then,
for the truth of the CHRISTIAN religion is less than the evidence for the
truth of our senses; because, even in the first authors of our religion, it
was no greater; and it is evident it must diminish in passing from them
to their disciples; nor can any one rest such confidence in their testimony,
as in the immediate object of his senses. But a weaker evidence can never
destroy a stronger; and therefore, were the doctrine of the real presence
ever so clearly revealed in scripture, it were directly contrary to the rules
of just reasoning to give our assent to it. It contradicts sense, though both
the scripture and tradition, on which it is supposed to be built, carry not
such evidence with them as sense; when they are considered merely as
external evidences, and are not brought home to every one's breast, by
the immediate operation of the Holy Spirit.

2   Nothing is so convenient as a decisive argument of this kind, which
must at least *silence* the most arrogant bigotry and superstition, and free
us from their impertinent solicitations. I flatter myself, that I have discovered an argument of a like nature, which, if just, will, with the wise
and learned, be an everlasting check to all kinds of superstitious delusion, and consequently, will be useful as long as the world endures. For
so long, I presume, will the accounts of miracles and prodigies be found
in all history, sacred and profane.

3   Though experience be our only guide in reasoning concerning matters
of fact; it must be acknowledged, that this guide is not altogether infallible, but in some cases is apt to lead us into errors. One, who, in our

climate, should expect better weather in any week of JUNE than in one of DECEMBER, would reason justly, and conformably to experience; but it is certain, that he may happen, in the event, to find himself mistaken. However, we may observe, that, in such a case, he would have no cause to complain of experience; because it commonly informs us before-hand of the uncertainty, by that contrariety of events, which we may learn from a diligent observation. All effects follow not with like certainty from their supposed causes. Some events are found, in all countries and all ages, to have been constantly conjoined together: Others are found to have been more variable, and sometimes to disappoint our expectations; so that, in our reasonings concerning matter of fact, there are all imaginable degrees of assurance, from the highest certainty to the lowest species of moral evidence.[†]

4   A wise man, therefore, proportions his belief to the evidence. In such conclusions as are founded on an infallible experience, he expects the event with the last degree of assurance, and regards his past experience as a full *proof* of the future existence of that event. In other cases, he proceeds with more caution: He weighs the opposite experiments: He considers which side is supported by the greater number of experiments: To that side he inclines, with doubt and hesitation; and when at last he fixes his judgment, the evidence exceeds not what we properly call *probability*. All probability, then, supposes an opposition of experiments and observations; where the one side is found to overbalance the other, and to produce a degree of evidence,[†] proportioned to the superiority. A hundred instances or experiments on one side, and fifty on another, afford a doubtful expectation of any event; though a hundred uniform experiments, with only one that is contradictory, reasonably beget a pretty strong degree of assurance. In all cases, we must balance the opposite experiments, where they are opposite, and deduct the smaller number from the greater, in order to know the exact force of the superior evidence. *SBN 1*

5   To apply these principles to a particular instance; we may observe, that there is no species of reasoning more common, more useful, and even necessary to human life, than that which is derived from the testimony of men, and the reports of eye-witnesses and spectators. This species of reasoning, perhaps, one may deny to be founded on the relation of cause and effect. I shall not dispute about a word. It will be sufficient to observe, that our assurance in any argument of this kind is derived from no other principle than our observation of the veracity of human testimony, and of the usual conformity of facts to the reports of witnesses. It being a general maxim, that no objects have any discoverable connexion together,

and that all the inferences, which we can draw from one to another, are founded merely on our experience of their constant and regular conjunction; it is evident, that we ought not to make an exception to this maxim in favour of human testimony, whose connexion with any event seems, in itself, as little necessary as any other. Were not the memory *SBN 112* tenacious to a certain degree; had not men commonly an inclination to truth and a principle of probity; were they not sensible to shame, when detected in a falsehood: Were not these, I say, discovered by *experience* to be qualities, inherent in human nature, we should never repose the least confidence in human testimony. A man delirious, or noted for falsehood and villany, has no manner of authority with us.

6   And as the evidence, derived from witnesses and human testimony,[†] is founded on past experience, so it varies with the experience, and is regarded either as a *proof* or a *probability*, according as the conjunction between any particular kind of report and any kind of object has been found to be constant or variable. There are a number of circumstances to be taken into consideration in all judgments of this kind; and the ultimate standard, by which we determine all disputes, that may arise concerning them, is always derived from experience and observation. Where this experience is not entirely uniform on any side, it is attended with an unavoidable contrariety in our judgments, and with the same opposition and mutual destruction of argument as in every other kind of evidence. We frequently hesitate concerning the reports of others. We balance the opposite circumstances, which cause any doubt or uncertainty; and when we discover a superiority on any side, we incline to it; but still with a diminution of assurance, in proportion to the force of its antagonist.

7   This contrariety of evidence, in the present case, may be derived from several different causes; from the opposition of contrary testimony; from the character or number of the witnesses; from the manner of their delivering their testimony; or from the union of all these circumstances. We entertain a suspicion concerning any matter of fact, when the witnesses contradict each other; when they are but few, or of a doubtful character; when they have an interest in what they affirm; when they deliver their *SBN 113* testimony with hesitation, or on the contrary, with too violent asseverations. There are many other particulars of the same kind, which may diminish or destroy the force of any argument, derived from human testimony.

8   Suppose, for instance, that the fact, which the testimony endeavours to establish, partakes of the extraordinary and the marvellous;[†] in that case, the evidence, resulting from the testimony, admits of a diminution,

171

greater or less, in proportion as the fact is more or less unusual. The reason, why we place any credit in witnesses and historians, is not derived from any *connexion*, which we perceive *a priori*, between testimony and reality, but because we are accustomed to find a conformity between them. But when the fact attested is such a one as has seldom fallen under our observation, here is a contest of two opposite experiences; of which the one destroys the other, as far as its force goes, and the superior can only operate on the mind by the force, which remains. The very same principle of experience, which gives us a certain degree of assurance in the testimony of witnesses, gives us also, in this case, another degree of assurance against the fact, which they endeavour to establish; from which contradiction there necessarily arises a counterpoise, and mutual destruction of belief and authority.

9   *I should not believe such a story were it told me by* CATO;[†] was a proverbial saying in ROME, even during the lifetime of that philosophical patriot.[21] The incredibility of a fact, it was allowed, might invalidate so great an authority.

10   The INDIAN prince,[†] who refused to believe the first relations concerning the effects of frost, reasoned justly; and it naturally required very strong testimony to engage his assent to facts, that arose from a state of nature, with which he was unacquainted, and which bore so little analogy to   *SBN 11* those events, of which he had had constant and uniform experience. Though they were not contrary to his experience, they were not conformable to it.[22]

11   But in order to encrease the probability against the testimony of witnesses, let us suppose, that the fact, which they affirm, instead of being

---

[21]   PLUTARCH. in vita CATONIS. [Plutarch, *Lives*, 'Cato the Younger' 19.4.768B–C.]   *SBN 11*

[22]   No INDIAN, it is evident, could have experience that water did not freeze in cold climates.   *SBN 11* This is placing nature in a situation quite unknown to him; and it is impossible for him to tell *a priori* what will result from it. It is making a new experiment, the consequence of which is always uncertain. One may sometimes conjecture from analogy what will follow; but still this is but conjecture. And it must be confessed, that, in the present case of freezing, the event follows contrary to the rules of analogy, and is such as a rational INDIAN would not look for. The operations of cold upon water are not gradual, according to the degrees of cold; but whenever it comes to the freezing point, the water passes in a moment, from the utmost liquidity to perfect hardness. Such an event, therefore, may be denominated *extraordinary*, and requires a pretty strong testimony, to render it credible to people in a warm climate: But still it is not *miraculous*, nor contrary to uniform experience of the course of nature in cases where all the circumstances are the same. The inhabitants of SUMATRA have always seen water fluid in their own climate, and the freezing of their rivers ought to be deemed a prodigy: But they never saw water in MUSCOVY[†] during the winter; and therefore they cannot reasonably be positive what would there be the consequence.

only marvellous, is really miraculous; and suppose also, that the testimony, considered apart and in itself, amounts to an entire proof; in that case, there is proof against proof, of which the strongest must prevail, but still with a diminution of its force, in proportion to that of its antagonist.

12   A miracle is a violation of the laws of nature;[†] and as a firm and unalterable experience has established these laws, the proof against a miracle, from the very nature of the fact, is as entire as any argument from experience can possibly be imagined. Why is it more than probable, that all men must die; that lead cannot, of itself, remain suspended in the air; that fire consumes wood, and is extinguished by water; unless it be, that these events are found agreeable to the laws of nature, and there is *SBN 115* required a violation of these laws, or in other words, a miracle to prevent them? Nothing is esteemed a miracle, if it ever happen in the common course of nature. It is no miracle that a man, seemingly in good health, should die on a sudden; because such a kind of death, though more unusual than any other, has yet been frequently observed to happen. But it is a miracle, that a dead man should come to life; because that has never been observed, in any age or country. There must, therefore, be a uniform experience against every miraculous event, otherwise the event would not merit that appellation. And as a uniform experience amounts to a proof, there is here a direct and full *proof*, from the nature of the fact, against the existence of any miracle; nor can such a proof be destroyed, or the miracle rendered credible, but by an opposite proof, which is superior.[23†]

13   The plain consequence is (and it is a general maxim worthy of our

---

[23] Sometimes an event may not, *in itself*, *seem* to be contrary to the laws of nature, and *SBN 115* yet, if it were real, it might, by reason of some circumstances, be denominated a miracle; because, in *fact*, it is contrary to these laws. Thus if a person, claiming a divine authority, should command a sick person to be well, a healthful man to fall down dead, the clouds to pour rain, the winds to blow, in short, should order many natural events, which immediately follow upon his command; these might justly be esteemed miracles, because they are really, in this case, contrary to the laws of nature. For if any suspicion remain, that the event and command concurred by accident, there is no miracle and no transgression of the laws of nature. If this suspicion be removed, there is evidently a miracle, and a transgression of these laws; because nothing can be more contrary to nature than that the voice or command of a man should have such an influence. A miracle may be accurately defined, *a transgression of a law of nature by a particular volition of the Deity, or by the interposition of some invisible agent*. A miracle may either be discoverable by men or not. This alters not its nature and essence. The raising of a house or ship into the air is a visible miracle. The raising of a feather, when the wind wants ever so little of a force requisite for that purpose, is as real a miracle, though not so sensible with regard to us.

attention), "That no testimony is sufficient to establish a miracle, unless
the testimony be of such a kind, that its falsehood would be more miraculous, than the fact, which it endeavours to establish: And even in that
case, there is a mutual destruction of arguments, and the superior only
gives us an assurance suitable to that degree of force, which remains,
after deducting the inferior." When any one tells me, that he saw a dead
man restored to life, I immediately consider with myself, whether it be
more probable, that this person should either deceive or be deceived, or
that the fact, which he relates, should really have happened. I weigh the
one miracle against the other; and according to the superiority, which I
discover, I pronounce my decision, and always reject the greater miracle.
If the falsehood of his testimony would be more miraculous, than the
event which he relates; then, and not till then, can he pretend to command
my belief or opinion.

PART 2

14 In the foregoing reasoning we have supposed, that the testimony, upon
which a miracle is founded, may possibly amount to an entire proof, and
that the falsehood of that testimony would be a real prodigy: But it is
easy to show, that we have been a great deal too liberal in our concession, and that there never was a miraculous event established on so full
an evidence.

15   For *first*, there is not to be found, in all history, any miracle attested by
a sufficient number of men, of such unquestioned good sense, education, and learning, as to secure us against all delusion in themselves; of
such undoubted integrity, as to place them beyond all suspicion of any
design to deceive others; of such credit and reputation in the eyes of
mankind, as to have a great deal to lose in case of their being detected
in any falsehood; and at the same time, attesting facts, performed in such
a public manner, and in so celebrated a part of the world, as to render
the detection unavoidable: All which circumstances are requisite to give
us a full assurance in the testimony of men.

16   *Secondly*, We may observe in human nature a principle, which, if strictly
examined, will be found to diminish extremely the assurance, which we
might, from human testimony, have, in any kind of prodigy. The maxim,
by which we commonly conduct ourselves in our reasonings, is, that the
objects, of which we have no experience, resemble those, of which we

have; that what we have found to be most usual is always most probable; and that where there is an opposition of arguments, we ought to give the preference to such as are founded on the greatest number of past observations. But though, in proceeding by this rule, we readily reject any fact which is unusual and incredible in an ordinary degree; yet in advancing farther, the mind observes not always the same rule; but when any thing is affirmed utterly absurd and miraculous, it rather the more readily admits of such a fact, upon account of that very circumstance, which ought to destroy all its authority. The passion of *surprize* and *wonder*, arising from miracles, being an agreeable emotion, gives a sensible tendency towards the belief of those events, from which it is derived. And this goes so far, that even those who cannot enjoy this pleasure immediately, nor can believe those miraculous events, of which they are informed, yet love to partake of the satisfaction at second-hand or by rebound, and place a pride and delight in exciting the admiration of others.

17   With what greediness are the miraculous accounts of travellers received, their descriptions of sea and land monsters, their relations of wonderful adventures, strange men, and uncouth manners? But if the spirit of religion join itself to the love of wonder, there is an end of common sense; and human testimony, in these circumstances, loses all pretensions to authority. A religionist may be an enthusiast, and imagine he sees what has no reality: He may know his narrative to be false, and *SBN 118* yet persevere in it, with the best intentions in the world, for the sake of promoting so holy a cause: Or even where this delusion has no place, vanity, excited by so strong a temptation, operates on him more powerfully than on the rest of mankind in any other circumstances; and self-interest with equal force. His auditors[†] may not have, and commonly have not, sufficient judgment to canvass his evidence: What judgment they have, they renounce by principle, in these sublime and mysterious subjects: Or if they were ever so willing to employ it, passion and a heated imagination disturb the regularity of its operations. Their credulity[†] encreases his impudence: And his impudence overpowers their credulity.

18   Eloquence,[†] when at its highest pitch, leaves little room for reason or reflection; but addressing itself entirely to the fancy or the affections, captivates the willing hearers, and subdues their understanding. Happily, this pitch it seldom attains. But what a Tully or a Demosthenes could scarcely effect over a Roman or Athenian audience, every *Capuchin*,[†] every itinerant or stationary teacher can perform over the generality of mankind, and in a higher degree, by touching such gross and vulgar passions.[†]

19   The many instances of forged miracles, and prophecies, and super-

175

natural events, which, in all ages, have either been detected[†] by contrary evidence, or which detect themselves by their absurdity, prove sufficiently the strong propensity of mankind to the extraordinary and the marvellous, and ought reasonably to beget a suspicion against all relations of this kind. This is our natural way of thinking, even with regard to the most common and most credible events. For instance: There is no kind of report, which rises so easily, and spreads so quickly, especially in country places and provincial towns, as those concerning marriages; insomuch that two young persons of equal condition never see each other SBN 1: twice, but the whole neighbourhood immediately join them together. The pleasure of telling a piece of news so interesting, of propagating it, and of being the first reporters of it, spreads the intelligence. And this is so well known, that no man of sense gives attention to these reports, till he find them confirmed by some greater evidence. Do not the same passions, and others still stronger, incline the generality of mankind to believe and report, with the greatest vehemence and assurance, all religious miracles?

20   *Thirdly,* It forms a strong presumption against all supernatural and miraculous relations, that they are observed chiefly to abound among ignorant and barbarous nations; or if a civilized people has ever given admission to any of them, that people will be found to have received them from ignorant and barbarous ancestors, who transmitted them with that inviolable sanction and authority, which always attend received opinions. When we peruse the first histories of all nations, we are apt to imagine ourselves transported into some new world; where the whole frame of nature is disjointed, and every element performs its operations in a different manner, from what it does at present. Battles, revolutions, pestilence, famine, and death, are never the effects of those natural causes, which we experience. Prodigies, omens, oracles, judgments, quite obscure the few natural events, that are intermingled with them. But as the former grow thinner every page, in proportion as we advance nearer the enlightened ages, we soon learn, that there is nothing mysterious or supernatural in the case, but that all proceeds from the usual propensity of mankind towards the marvellous, and that, though this inclination may at intervals receive a check from sense and learning, it can never be thoroughly extirpated from human nature.

21   *It is strange,* a judicious reader is apt to say, upon the perusal of these wonderful historians,[†] *that such prodigious events never happen in our days.* SBN 1. But it is nothing strange, I hope, that men should lie in all ages. You must surely have seen instances enow of that frailty. You have yourself heard

many such marvellous relations started, which, being treated with scorn by all the wise and judicious, have at last been abandoned even by the vulgar. Be assured, that those renowned lies, which have spread and flourished to such a monstrous height, arose from like beginnings; but being sown in a more proper soil, shot up at last into prodigies almost equal to those which they relate.

22   It was a wise policy in that false prophet, ALEXANDER, who, though now forgotten, was once so famous, to lay the first scene of his impostures in PAPHLAGONIA, where, as LUCIAN tells us,[†] the people were extremely ignorant and stupid, and ready to swallow even the grossest delusion. People at a distance, who are weak enough to think the matter at all worth enquiry, have no opportunity of receiving better information. The stories come magnified to them by a hundred circumstances. Fools are industrious in propagating the imposture; while the wise and learned are contented, in general, to deride its absurdity, without informing themselves of the particular facts, by which it may be distinctly refuted. And thus the impostor above-mentioned was enabled to proceed, from his ignorant PAPHLAGONIANS, to the enlisting of votaries,[†] even among the GRECIAN philosophers, and men of the most eminent rank and distinction in ROME: Nay, could engage the attention of that sage emperor MARCUS AURELIUS;[†] so far as to make him trust the success of a military expedition to his delusive prophecies.

23   The advantages are so great, of starting an imposture among an ignorant people, that, even though the delusion should be too gross to impose on the generality of them (*which, though seldom, is sometimes the case*) it has a much better chance for succeeding in remote countries, than if the first scene had been laid in a city renowned for arts and knowledge. The *SBN 121* most ignorant and barbarous of these barbarians carry the report abroad. None of their countrymen have a large correspondence, or sufficient credit and authority to contradict and beat down the delusion. Men's inclination to the marvellous has full opportunity to display itself. And thus a story, which is universally exploded in the place where it was first started, shall pass for certain at a thousand miles distance. But had ALEXANDER fixed his residence at ATHENS, the philosophers of that renowned mart of learning had immediately spread, throughout the whole ROMAN empire, their sense of the matter; which, being supported by so great authority, and displayed by all the force of reason and eloquence, had entirely opened the eyes of mankind. It is true; LUCIAN, passing by chance through PAPHLAGONIA, had an opportunity of performing this good office. But, though much to be wished, it does not always happen, that every

ALEXANDER meets with a LUCIAN, ready to expose and detect his impostures.

24   I may add as a *fourth* reason, which diminishes the authority of prodigies, that there is no testimony for any, even those which have not been expressly detected, that is not opposed by an infinite number of witnesses; so that not only the miracle destroys the credit of the testimony, but the testimony destroys itself. To make this the better understood, let us consider, that, in matters of religion, whatever is different is contrary; and that it is impossible the religions of ancient ROME, of TURKEY, of SIAM, and of CHINA should, all of them, be established on any solid foundation. Every miracle, therefore, pretended to have been wrought in any of these religions (and all of them abound in miracles), as its direct scope is to establish the particular system to which it is attributed; so has it the same force, though more indirectly, to overthrow every other system. In destroying a rival system,[†] it likewise destroys the credit of those miracles, on which that system was established; so that all the prodigies of   *SBN 1* different religions are to be regarded as contrary facts, and the evidences of these prodigies, whether weak or strong, as opposite to each other. According to this method of reasoning, when we believe any miracle of MAHOMET or his successors, we have for our warrant the testimony of a few barbarous ARABIANS:[†] And on the other hand, we are to regard the authority of TITUS LIVIUS,[†] PLUTARCH, TACITUS, and, in short, of all the authors and witnesses, GRECIAN, CHINESE, and ROMAN CATHOLIC, who have related any miracle in their particular religion; I say, we are to regard their testimony in the same light as if they had mentioned that MAHOMETAN miracle, and had in express terms contradicted it, with the same certainty as they have for the miracle they relate. This argument may appear over subtile and refined; but is not in reality different from the reasoning of a judge, who supposes, that the credit of two witnesses, maintaining a crime against any one, is destroyed by the testimony of two others, who affirm him to have been two hundred leagues distant, at the same instant when the crime is said to have been committed.

25   One of the best attested miracles in all profane history, is that which TACITUS reports of VESPASIAN, who cured a blind man in ALEXANDRIA, by means of his spittle, and a lame man by the mere touch of his foot; in obedience to a vision of the god SERAPIS, who had enjoined them to have recourse to the emperor, for these miraculous cures. The story may be seen in that fine historian;[24] where every circumstance seems to add

---

[24] Hist. lib. 4. cap. 81. SUETONIUS gives nearly the same account, in vita VESP. [Tacitus, *His-*   *SBN 1* *tories* 4.81. Suetonius, *Lives of the Caesars* 8, 'Vespasian' 7.2-3.]

weight to the testimony, and might be displayed at large[†] with all the force of argument and eloquence, if any one were now concerned to enforce the evidence of that exploded and idolatrous superstition. The gravity, solidity, age, and probity of so great an emperor, who, through the whole course of his life, conversed in a familiar manner with his friends and courtiers, and never affected those extraordinary airs of divinity assumed by ALEXANDER and DEMETRIUS.[†] The historian, a cotemporary writer, noted for candour and veracity, and withal, the greatest and most penetrating genius, perhaps, of all antiquity; and so free from any tendency to credulity, that he even lies under the contrary imputation, of atheism and profaneness: The persons, from whose authority he related the miracle, of established character for judgment and veracity, as we may well presume; eye-witnesses of the fact, and confirming their testimony, after the FLAVIAN family was despoiled of the empire, and could no longer give any reward, as the price of a lie. "Utrumque, qui interfuere, nunc quoque memorant, postquam nullum mendacio pretium."[†] To which if we add the public nature of the facts, as related, it will appear, that no evidence can well be supposed stronger for so gross and so palpable a falsehood. *SBN 123*

26   There is also a memorable story related by Cardinal DE RETZ,[†] which may well deserve our consideration. When that intriguing politician fled into SPAIN, to avoid the persecution of his enemies, he passed through SARAGOSSA, the capital of ARRAGON, where he was shown, in the cathedral, a man, who had served seven years as a door-keeper, and was well known to every body in town, that had ever paid his devotions at that church. He had been seen, for so long a time, wanting a leg; but recovered that limb by the rubbing of holy oil upon the stump; and the cardinal assures us that he saw him with two legs. This miracle was vouched by all the canons of the church;[†] and the whole company in town were appealed to for a confirmation of the fact; whom the cardinal found, by their zealous devotion, to be thorough believers of the miracle. Here the relater was also cotemporary to the supposed prodigy, of an incredulous and libertine character, as well as of great genius; the miracle of so *singular* a nature as could scarcely admit of a counterfeit, and the witnesses very numerous, and all of them, in a manner, spectators of the fact, to which they gave their testimony. And what adds mightily to the force of the evidence, and may double our surprize on this occasion, is, that the cardinal himself, who relates the story, seems not to give any credit to it, and consequently cannot be suspected of any concurrence in the holy fraud. He considered justly, that it was not requisite, in order to reject a *SBN 124*

fact of this nature, to be able accurately to disprove the testimony, and to trace its falsehood, through all the circumstances of knavery and credulity which produced it. He knew, that, as this was commonly altogether impossible at any small distance of time and place; so was it extremely difficult, even where one was immediately present, by reason of the bigotry, ignorance, cunning, and roguery of a great part of mankind. He therefore concluded, like a just reasoner, that such an evidence carried falsehood upon the very face of it, and that a miracle, supported by any human testimony, was more properly a subject of derision than of argument.

27   There surely never was a greater number of miracles ascribed to one person than those, which were lately said to have been wrought in FRANCE upon the tomb of Abbé PARIS, the famous JANSENIST,† with whose sanctity the people were so long deluded. The curing of the sick, giving hearing to the deaf, and sight to the blind, were every where talked of as the usual effects of that holy sepulchre.† But what is more extraordinary; many of the miracles were immediately proved upon the spot, before judges of unquestioned integrity, attested by witnesses of credit and distinction, in a learned age, and on the most eminent theatre that is now in the world. Nor is this all: A relation of them was published and dispersed every where; nor were the JESUITS, though a learned body, supported by the civil magistrate, and determined enemies to those opinions, in whose favour the miracles were said to have been wrought, ever able distinctly to refute or detect them.[25] Where shall we find such a number

SBN 1

---

[25] This book was writ by Mons. MONTGERON,† counsellor or judge of the parliament of PARIS, a man of figure and character, who was also a martyr to the cause,† and is now said to be somewhere in a dungeon on account of his book. [Louis Basile Carré de Montgeron, *La Verité des miracles operés par l'intercession de M. de Pâris, demontrée contre M. l'archevêque de Sens.*]

There is another book in three volumes (called *Recueil des Miracles de l'Abbé* PARIS)† giving an account of many of these miracles, and accompanied with prefatory discourses, which are very well written. [*Recueil des miracles operés au tombeau de M. de Paris Diacre. . . .* Published with: *Second recueil des miracles operés par l'intercession de M. de Paris*; *Réflexions sur les miracles operés au tombeau de M. de Paris*; and *Acte passé pardevant notaires, contenant plusieurs pièces au sujet du miracle operé en la personne de Mademoiselle Hardouin.*] There runs, however, through the whole of these a ridiculous comparison between the miracles of our Saviour and those of the Abbé; wherein it is asserted, that the evidence for the latter is equal to that for the former: As if the testimony of men could ever be put in the balance with that of God himself, who conducted the pen of the inspired writers. If these writers, indeed, were to be considered merely as human testimony, the FRENCH author is very moderate in his comparison; since he might, with some appearance of reason, pretend, that the JANSENIST miracles much surpass the other in evidence and authority. The following circumstances are drawn from authentic papers, inserted in the above-mentioned book.

SBN 3

of circumstances, agreeing to the corroboration of one fact? And what have we to oppose to such a cloud of witnesses, but the absolute impossibility or miraculous nature of the events, which they relate? And this surely, in the eyes of all reasonable people, will alone be regarded as a sufficient refutation.

Many of the miracles of Abbé Paris were proved immediately by witnesses before the officiality or bishop's court at Paris, under the eye of Cardinal Noailles,[†] whose character for integrity and capacity was never contested even by his enemies.

His successor in the archbishopric[†] was an enemy to the Jansenists, and for that reason promoted to the see by the court. Yet 22 rectors or *curés* of Paris, with infinite earnestness, press him to examine those miracles, which they assert to be known to the whole world, and undisputably certain: But he wisely forbore.

The Molinist party[†] had tried to discredit these miracles in one instance, that of Mademoiselle Le Franc.[†] But, besides that their proceedings were in many respects the most irregular in the world, particularly in citing only a few of the Jansenist witnesses, whom they tampered with: Besides this, I say, they soon found themselves overwhelmed by a cloud of new witnesses, one hundred and twenty in number, most of them persons of credit and substance in Paris, who gave oath for the miracle. This was accompanied with a solemn and earnest appeal to the parliament. But the parliament were forbid by authority to meddle in the affair. It was at last observed, that where men are heated by zeal and enthusiasm, there is no degree of human testimony so strong as may not be procured for the greatest absurdity: And those who will be so silly as to examine the affair by that medium, and seek particular flaws in the testimony, are almost sure to be confounded. It must be a miserable imposture, indeed, that does not prevail in that contest. *SBN 345*

All who have been in France about that time have heard of the reputation of Mons. Herault,[†] the *Lieutenant de Police*, whose vigilance, penetration, activity, and extensive intelligence have been much talked of. This magistrate, who by the nature of his office is almost absolute, was invested with full powers, on purpose to suppress or discredit these miracles; and he frequently seized immediately, and examined the witnesses and subjects of them: But never could reach any thing satisfactory against them.

In the case of Mademoiselle Thibault he sent the famous de Sylva[†] to examine her; whose evidence is very curious. The physician declares, that it was impossible she could have been so ill as was proved by witnesses; because it was impossible she could, in so short a time, have recovered so perfectly as he found her. He reasoned, like a man of sense, from natural causes; but the opposite party told him, that the whole was a miracle, and that his evidence was the very best proof of it.

The Molinists were in a sad dilemma. They durst not assert the absolute insufficiency of human evidence, to prove a miracle. They were obliged to say, that these miracles were wrought by witchcraft and the devil. But they were told, that this was the resource of the Jews of old.

No Jansenist was ever embarrassed to account for the cessation of the miracles, when the church-yard was shut up by the king's edict. It was the touch of the tomb, which produced these extraordinary effects; and when no one could approach the tomb, no effects could be expected. God, indeed, could have thrown down the walls in a moment; but he is master of his own graces and works, and it belongs not to us to account for them. He did not throw down the walls of every city like those of Jericho, on the sounding of the rams horns,[†] nor break up the prison of every apostle,[†] like that of St. Paul. *SBN 346*

No less a man, than the Duc de Chatillon,[†] a duke and peer of France, of the highest

28   Is the consequence just, because some human testimony has the utmost force and authority in some cases, when it relates the battle of PHILIPPI or PHARSALIA[†] for instance; that therefore all kinds of testimony must, in all cases, have equal force and authority? Suppose that the CÆSAREAN and POMPEIAN factions had, each of them, claimed the victory in these battles, and that the historians of each party had uniformly ascribed the advantage to their own side; how could mankind, at this distance, have been able to determine between them? The contrariety is equally strong between the miracles related by HERODOTUS or PLUTARCH,[†] and those delivered by MARIANA, BEDE,[†] or any monkish historian.

29   The wise lend a very academic faith to every report which favours the passion of the reporter; whether it magnifies his country, his family, or himself, or in any other way strikes in with his natural inclinations and propensities. But what greater temptation than to appear a missionary, a prophet, an ambassador from heaven? Who would not encounter many dangers and difficulties, in order to attain so sublime a character? Or if, by the help of vanity and a heated imagination, a man has first made a convert of himself, and entered seriously into the delusion; who ever scru-

rank and family, gives evidence of a miraculous cure, performed upon a servant of his, who had lived several years in his house with a visible and palpable infirmity.

I shall conclude with observing, that no clergy are more celebrated for strictness of life and manners than the secular clergy of FRANCE, particularly the rectors or curés of PARIS, who bear testimony to these impostures.

The learning, genius, and probity of the gentlemen, and the austerity of the nuns of PORT-ROYAL,[†] have been much celebrated all over EUROPE. Yet they all give evidence for a miracle, wrought on the niece of the famous PASCAL,[†] whose sanctity of life, as well as extraordinary capacity, is well known. The famous RACINE gives an account of this miracle in his famous history of PORT-ROYAL, and fortifies it with all the proofs, which a multitude of nuns, priests, physicians, and men of the world, all of them of undoubted credit, could bestow upon it. [Jean Racine, *Abrégé de l'histoire de Port-Royal*.] Several men of letters, particularly the bishop of TOURNAY,[†] thought this miracle so certain, as to employ it in the refutation of atheists and free-thinkers.[†] The queen-regent of FRANCE,[†] who was extremely prejudiced against the PORT-ROYAL, sent her own physician to examine the miracle, who returned an absolute convert. In short, the supernatural cure was so incontestable, that it saved, for a time, that famous monastery from the ruin with which it was threatened by the JESUITS. Had it been a cheat, it had certainly been detected by such sagacious and powerful antagonists, and must have hastened the ruin of the contrivers. Our divines, who can build up a formidable castle from such despicable materials; what a prodigious fabric could they have reared from these and many other circumstances, which I have not mentioned! How often would the great names of PASCAL, RACINE, ARNAULD, NICOLE, have resounded in our ears! But if they be wise, they had better adopt the miracle, as being more worth, a thousand times, than all the rest of their collection. Besides, it may serve very much to their purpose. For that miracle was really performed by the touch of an authentic holy prickle of the holy thorn, which composed the holy crown, which, &c.

ples to make use of pious frauds,[†] in support of so holy and meritorious a cause?

30   The smallest spark may here kindle into the greatest flame; because *SBN 126* the materials are always prepared for it. The *avidum genus auricularum*,[26†] the gazing populace, receive greedily, without examination, whatever sooths superstition, and promotes wonder.

31   How many stories of this nature have, in all ages, been detected and exploded in their infancy? How many more have been celebrated for a time, and have afterwards sunk into neglect and oblivion? Where such reports, therefore, fly about, the solution of the phænomenon is obvious; and we judge in conformity to regular experience and observation, when we account for it by the known and natural principles of credulity and delusion. And shall we, rather than have a recourse to so natural a solution, allow of a miraculous violation of the most established laws of nature?

32   I need not mention the difficulty of detecting a falsehood in any private or even public history, at the place, where it is said to happen; much more when the scene is removed to ever so small a distance. Even a court of judicature,[†] with all the authority, accuracy, and judgment, which they can employ, find themselves often at a loss to distinguish between truth and falsehood in the most recent actions. But the matter never comes to any issue, if trusted to the common method of altercation and debate and flying rumours; especially when men's passions have taken part on either side.

33   In the infancy of new religions, the wise and learned commonly esteem the matter too inconsiderable to deserve their attention or regard. And when afterwards they would willingly detect the cheat,[†] in order to undeceive the deluded multitude, the season is now past, and the records and witnesses, which might clear up the matter, have perished beyond recovery.

34   No means of detection remain, but those which must be drawn from *SBN 127* the very testimony itself of the reporters: And these, though always sufficient with the judicious and knowing, are commonly too fine to fall under the comprehension of the vulgar.

35   Upon the whole, then, it appears, that no testimony for any kind of miracle has ever amounted to a probability, much less to a proof; and that, even supposing it amounted to a proof, it would be opposed by another proof; derived from the very nature of the fact, which it would

---

[26] LUCRET. [Lucretius, *De rerum natura* 4.594 (598 in older editions).] *SBN 126*

endeavour to establish. It is experience only, which gives authority to human testimony; and it is the same experience, which assures us of the laws of nature. When, therefore, these two kinds of experience are contrary, we have nothing to do but subtract the one from the other,[†] and embrace an opinion, either on one side or the other, with that assurance which arises from the remainder. But according to the principle here explained, this subtraction, with regard to all popular religions, amounts to an entire annihilation; and therefore we may establish it as a maxim, that no human testimony can have such force as to prove a miracle, and make it a just foundation for any such system of religion.

36   I beg the limitations here made may be remarked, when I say, that a miracle can never be proved, so as to be the foundation of a system of religion. For I own, that otherwise, there may possibly be miracles, or violations of the usual course of nature, of such a kind as to admit of proof from human testimony; though, perhaps, it will be impossible to find any such in all the records of history. Thus, suppose, all authors, in all languages, agree, that, from the first of JANUARY 1600, there was a total darkness over the whole earth for eight days: Suppose that the tradition of this extraordinary event is still strong and lively among the people: That all travellers, who return from foreign countries, bring us accounts of the same tradition, without the least variation or contradiction: It is *SBN 1* evident, that our present philosophers, instead of doubting the fact, ought to receive it as certain, and ought to search for the causes whence it might be derived. The decay, corruption, and dissolution of nature, is an event rendered probable by so many analogies, that any phænomenon, which seems to have a tendency towards that catastrophe, comes within the reach of human testimony, if that testimony be very extensive and uniform.

37   But suppose, that all the historians, who treat of ENGLAND, should agree, that, on the first of JANUARY 1600, Queen ELIZABETH died; that both before and after her death she was seen by her physicians and the whole court, as is usual with persons of her rank; that her successor was acknowledged and proclaimed by the parliament; and that, after being interred a month, she again appeared, resumed the throne, and governed ENGLAND for three years: I must confess that I should be surprized at the concurrence of so many odd circumstances, but should not have the least inclination to believe so miraculous an event. I should not doubt of her pretended death, and of those other public circumstances that followed it: I should only assert it to have been pretended, and that it neither was, nor possibly could be real. You would in vain object to me the difficulty,

and almost impossibility of deceiving the world in an affair of such consequence; the wisdom and solid judgment of that renowned queen; with the little or no advantage which she could reap from so poor an artifice: All this might astonish me; but I would still reply, that the knavery and folly of men are such common phænomena, that I should rather believe the most extraordinary events to arise from their concurrence, than admit of so signal a violation of the laws of nature.

38   But should this miracle be ascribed to any new system of religion; men, in all ages, have been so much imposed on by ridiculous stories of *SBN 129* that kind, that this very circumstance would be a full proof of a cheat, and sufficient, with all men of sense, not only to make them reject the fact, but even reject it without farther examination. Though the Being, to whom the miracle is ascribed, be, in this case, Almighty, it does not, upon that account, become a whit more probable; since it is impossible for us to know the attributes or actions of such a Being, otherwise than from the experience which we have of his productions, in the usual course of nature. This still reduces us to past observation, and obliges us to compare the instances of the violations of truth in the testimony of men with those of the violation of the laws of nature by miracles, in order to judge which of them is most likely and probable. As the violations of truth are more common in the testimony concerning religious miracles, than in that concerning any other matter of fact; this must diminish very much the authority of the former testimony, and make us form a general resolution, never to lend any attention to it, with whatever specious pretence it may be covered.

39   Lord BACON seems to have embraced the same principles of reasoning. "We ought," says he, "to make a collection or particular history of all monsters and prodigious births or productions, and in a word of every thing new, rare, and extraordinary in nature. But this must be done with the most severe scrutiny, lest we depart from truth. Above all, every relation must be considered as suspicious, which depends in any degree upon religion, as the prodigies of LIVY:[†] And no less so, every thing that is to be found in the writers of natural magic or alchimy,[†] or such authors, who seem, all of them, to have an unconquerable appetite for falsehood and fable."[27]

40   I am the better pleased with the method of reasoning here delivered, as I think it may serve to confound those dangerous friends or disguised *SBN 130* enemies to the CHRISTIAN religion, who have undertaken to defend it by

---

[27] Nov. Org. lib. 2. aph. 29. [Francis Bacon, *Novum organum* 2.29.]   *SBN 129*

the principles of human reason. Our most holy religion[†] is founded on *Faith*, not on reason;[†] and it is a sure method of exposing it to put it to such a trial as it is, by no means, fitted to endure. To make this more evident, let us examine those miracles, related in scripture; and not to lose ourselves in too wide a field, let us confine ourselves to such as we find in the *Pentateuch*,[†] which we shall examine, according to the principles of these pretended CHRISTIANS, not as the word or testimony of God himself, but as the production of a mere human writer and historian.[†] Here then we are first to consider a book, presented to us by a barbarous and ignorant people, written in an age when they were still more barbarous, and in all probability long after the facts which it relates, corroborated by no concurring testimony, and resembling those fabulous accounts, which every nation gives of its origin. Upon reading this book, we find it full of prodigies and miracles. It gives an account of a state of the world and of human nature entirely different from the present: Of our fall from that state: Of the age of man, extended to near a thousand years: Of the destruction of the world by a deluge: Of the arbitrary choice of one people, as the favourites of heaven; and that people the countrymen of the author: Of their deliverance from bondage by prodigies the most astonishing imaginable: I desire any one to lay his hand upon his heart, and after serious consideration declare, whether he thinks that the falsehood of such a book, supported by such a testimony, would be more extraordinary and miraculous than all the miracles it relates; which is, however, necessary to make it be received, according to the measures of probability above established.

41   What we have said of miracles may be applied, without any variation, to prophecies;[†] and indeed, all prophecies are real miracles,[†] and as such only, can be admitted as proofs of any revelation. If it did not exceed the capacity of human nature to foretel future events, it would be absurd to employ any prophecy as an argument for a divine mission or authority from heaven. So that, upon the whole, we may conclude, that the CHRISTIAN religion not only was at first attended with miracles, but even at this day[†] cannot be believed by any reasonable person without one. Mere reason is insufficient to convince us of its veracity: And whoever is moved by *Faith* to assent to it, is conscious of a continued miracle in his own person, which subverts all the principles of his understanding, and gives him a determination to believe what is most contrary to custom and experience.

SBN

SECTION 11

OF A PARTICULAR PROVIDENCE†
AND OF A FUTURE STATE†

1   I was lately engaged in conversation with a friend who loves sceptical paradoxes; where, though he advanced many principles, of which I can by no means approve, yet as they seem to be curious, and to bear some relation to the chain of reasoning carried on throughout this enquiry, I shall here copy them from my memory as accurately as I can, in order to submit them to the judgment of the reader.

2   Our conversation began with my admiring the singular good fortune of philosophy, which, as it requires entire liberty above all other privileges, and chiefly flourishes from the free opposition of sentiments and argumentation, received its first birth in an age and country† of freedom and toleration, and was never cramped, even in its most extravagant principles, by any creeds, confessions, or penal statutes. For, except the banishment of PROTAGORAS,† and the death of SOCRATES,† which last event proceeded partly from other motives, there are scarcely any instances to be met with, in ancient history, of this bigotted jealousy, with which the present age is so much infested. EPICURUS lived at ATHENS to an advanced age, in peace and tranquillity: EPICUREANS[28]† were even admitted to receive the sacerdotal character,† and to officiate at the altar, in the most sacred rites of the established religion: And the public encouragement[29] of pensions and salaries was afforded equally, by the wisest of all the ROMAN emperors,[30] to the professors of every sect of philosophy.† How requisite such kind of treatment was to philosophy, in her early youth, will easily be conceived, if we reflect, that, even at present, when she may be supposed more hardy and robust, she bears with much difficulty the inclemency of the seasons, and those harsh winds of calumny and persecution, which blow upon her.

3   You admire, says my friend, as the singular good fortune of

---

[28] LUCIAN. συμπ. ἢ Λαπίθαι. [Lucian, *The Drinking Party, or Lapithae* 9.]
[29] LUCIAN. εὐνοῦχος. [Lucian, *The Eunuch* 3, 8.]
[30] Id. & DIO. [Lucian, *The Eunuch* 3; Dio Cassius, *Roman History* 72.31.3.]

philosophy, what seems to result from the natural course of things, and to be unavoidable in every age and nation. This pertinacious bigotry, of which you complain, as so fatal to philosophy, is really her offspring,[†] who, after allying with superstition, separates himself entirely from the interest of his parent, and becomes her most inveterate enemy and persecutor. Speculative dogmas of religion, the present occasions of such furious dispute, could not possibly be conceived or admitted in the early ages of the world; when mankind, being wholly illiterate, formed an idea of religion more suitable to their weak apprehension, and composed their sacred tenets of such tales chiefly as were the objects of traditional belief, more than of argument or disputation. After the first alarm, therefore, was over, which arose from the new paradoxes and principles of the philosophers; these teachers seem ever after, during the ages of antiquity, to have lived in great harmony with the established superstition, and to have made a fair partition of mankind between them; the former claiming all the learned and wise, the latter possessing all the vulgar and illiterate.

4   It seems then, say I, that you leave politics entirely out of the question, and never suppose, that a wise magistrate can justly be jealous of certain tenets of philosophy, such as those of EPICURUS,[†] which, denying a divine existence, and consequently a providence and a future state, seem to loosen, in a great measure, the ties of morality,[†] and may be supposed, for that reason, pernicious to the peace of civil society.   SBN *

5   I know, replied he, that in fact these persecutions never, in any age, proceeded from calm reason, or from experience of the pernicious consequences of philosophy; but arose entirely from passion and prejudice. But what if I should advance farther, and assert, that, if EPICURUS had been accused before the people, by any of the *sycophants* or informers of those days, he could easily have defended his cause, and proved his principles of philosophy to be as salutary as those of his adversaries, who endeavoured, with such zeal, to expose him to the public hatred and jealousy?

6   I wish, said I, you would try your eloquence upon so extraordinary a topic, and make a speech for EPICURUS, which might satisfy, not the mob of ATHENS, if you will allow that ancient and polite city to have contained any mob, but the more philosophical part of his audience, such as might be supposed capable of comprehending his arguments.

7   The matter would not be difficult, upon such conditions, replied he: And if you please, I shall suppose myself EPICURUS for a moment, and make you stand for the ATHENIAN people, and shall deliver you such an

harangue as will fill all the urn with white beans, and leave not a black one[†] to gratify the malice of my adversaries.

8   Very well: Pray proceed upon these suppositions.

9   I come hither, O ye ATHENIANS, to justify in your assembly what I maintained in my school, and I find myself impeached by furious antagonists, instead of reasoning with calm and dispassionate enquirers. Your deliberations, which of right should be directed to questions of public good, and the interest of the commonwealth, are diverted to the disquisitions of speculative philosophy; and these magnificent, but perhaps fruitless enquiries, take place of your more familiar but more useful occupations. *SBN 135* But so far as in me lies, I will prevent this abuse. We shall not here dispute concerning the origin and government of worlds. We shall only enquire how far such questions concern the public interest. And if I can persuade you, that they are entirely indifferent to the peace of society and security of government, I hope that you will presently send us back to our schools, there to examine, at leisure, the question, the most sublime, but, at the same time, the most speculative of all philosophy.

10   The religious philosophers,[†] not satisfied with the tradition of your forefathers, and doctrine of your priests (in which I willingly acquiesce), indulge a rash curiosity, in trying how far they can establish religion upon the principles of reason; and they thereby excite, instead of satisfying, the doubts, which naturally arise from a diligent and scrutinous enquiry. They paint, in the most magnificent colours, the order, beauty, and wise arrangement of the universe;[†] and then ask, if such a glorious display of intelligence could proceed from the fortuitous concourse of atoms,[†] or if chance could produce what the greatest genius can never sufficiently admire. I shall not examine the justness of this argument.[†] I shall allow it to be as solid as my antagonists and accusers can desire. It is sufficient, if I can prove, from this very reasoning, that the question is entirely speculative, and that, when, in my philosophical disquisitions, I deny a providence and a future state,[†] I undermine not the foundations of society, but advance principles, which they themselves, upon their own topics, if they argue consistently, must allow to be solid and satisfactory.

11   You then, who are my accusers, have acknowledged, that the chief or sole argument for a divine existence (which I never questioned) is derived from the order of nature; where there appear such marks of intelligence and design, that you think it extravagant to assign for its cause, either chance, or the blind and unguided force of matter.[†] You allow, that this is an argument drawn from effects to causes.[†] From the order of the work, *SBN 136* you infer, that there must have been project and forethought in the

workman. If you cannot make out this point, you allow, that your conclusion fails; and you pretend not to establish the conclusion in a greater latitude than the phænomena of nature will justify. These are your concessions. I desire you to mark the consequences.

12 When we infer any particular cause from an effect, we must proportion the one to the other, and can never be allowed to ascribe to the cause any qualities, but what are exactly sufficient to produce the effect. A body of ten ounces raised in any scale may serve as a proof, that the counterbalancing weight exceeds ten ounces; but can never afford a reason that it exceeds a hundred. If the cause, assigned for any effect, be not sufficient to produce it, we must either reject that cause, or add to it such qualities as will give it a just proportion to the effect. But if we ascribe to it farther qualities, or affirm it capable of producing other effects, we can only indulge the licence of conjecture,[†] and arbitrarily suppose the existence of qualities and energies, without reason or authority.

13 The same rule holds, whether the cause assigned be brute unconscious matter, or a rational intelligent being. If the cause be known only by the effect, we never ought to ascribe to it any qualities, beyond what are precisely requisite to produce the effect: Nor can we, by any rules of just reasoning, return back from the cause, and infer other effects from it, beyond those by which alone it is known to us. No one, merely from the sight of one of ZEUXIS's pictures,[†] could know, that he was also a statuary or architect, and was an artist no less skilful in stone and marble than in colours. The talents and taste, displayed in the particular work before us; these we may safely conclude the workman to be possessed of. The cause must be proportioned to the effect; and if we exactly and precisely SBN ▮ proportion it, we shall never find in it any qualities, that point farther, or afford an inference concerning any other design or performance. Such qualities must be somewhat beyond what is merely requisite for producing the effect, which we examine.

14 Allowing, therefore, the gods to be the authors of the existence or order of the universe; it follows, that they possess that precise degree of power, intelligence, and benevolence, which appears in their workmanship; but nothing farther can ever be proved, except we call in the assistance of exaggeration and flattery to supply the defects of argument and reasoning. So far as the traces of any attributes, at present, appear, so far may we conclude these attributes to exist. The supposition of farther attributes is mere hypothesis; much more the supposition, that, in distant regions of space or periods of time, there has been, or will be, a more magnificent display of these attributes, and a scheme of administration

more suitable to such imaginary virtues. We can never be allowed to mount up from the universe, the effect, to JUPITER,[†] the cause; and then descend downwards, to infer any new effect from that cause; as if the present effects alone were not entirely worthy of the glorious attributes, which we ascribe to that deity. The knowledge of the cause being derived solely from the effect, they must be exactly adjusted to each other; and the one can never refer to any thing farther, or be the foundation of any new inference and conclusion.

15   You find certain phænomena in nature. You seek a cause or author. You imagine that you have found him. You afterwards become so enamoured of this offspring of your brain, that you imagine it impossible, but he must produce something greater and more perfect than the present scene of things, which is so full of ill and disorder. You forget, that this superlative intelligence and benevolence are entirely imaginary, or, at least, without any foundation in reason; and that you have no ground to   *SBN 138* ascribe to him any qualities, but what you see he has actually exerted and displayed in his productions. Let your gods, therefore, O philosophers, be suited to the present appearances of nature: And presume not to alter these appearances by arbitrary suppositions, in order to suit them to the attributes, which you so fondly ascribe to your deities.

16   When priests and poets, supported by your authority, O ATHENIANS, talk of a golden or silver age,[†] which preceded the present state of vice and misery, I hear them with attention and with reverence. But when philosophers, who pretend to neglect authority, and to cultivate reason, hold the same discourse, I pay them not, I own, the same obsequious submission and pious deference. I ask; who carried them into the celestial regions, who admitted them into the councils of the gods, who opened to them the book of fate, that they thus rashly affirm, that their deities have executed, or will execute, any purpose beyond what has actually appeared? If they tell me, that they have mounted on the steps or by the gradual ascent of reason, and by drawing inferences from effects to causes, I still insist, that they have aided the ascent of reason by the wings of imagination; otherwise they could not thus change their manner of inference, and argue from causes to effects; presuming, that a more perfect production than the present world would be more suitable to such perfect beings as the gods, and forgetting that they have no reason to ascribe to these celestial beings any perfection or any attribute, but what can be found in the present world.

17   Hence all the fruitless industry to account for the ill appearances of nature, and save the honour of the gods; while we must acknowledge the

reality of that evil and disorder, with which the world so much abounds. The obstinate and intractable qualities of matter,[†] we are told, or the observance of general laws, or some such reason, is the sole cause, which controuled the power and benevolence of JUPITER, and obliged him to create mankind and every sensible creature so imperfect and so unhappy. These attributes, then, are, it seems, before-hand, taken for granted, in their greatest latitude. And upon that supposition, I own, that such conjectures may, perhaps, be admitted as plausible solutions of the ill phænomena. But still I ask; Why take these attributes for granted, or why ascribe to the cause any qualities but what actually appear in the effect?[†] Why torture your brain to justify the course of nature upon suppositions, which, for aught you know, may be entirely imaginary, and of which there are to be found no traces in the course of nature?

18   The religious hypothesis, therefore, must be considered only as a particular method of accounting for the visible phænomena of the universe: But no just reasoner will ever presume to infer from it any single fact, and alter or add to the phænomena, in any single particular. If you think, that the appearances of things prove such causes, it is allowable for you to draw an inference concerning the existence of these causes. In such complicated and sublime subjects, every one should be indulged in the liberty of conjecture and argument. But here you ought to rest. If you come backward, and arguing from your inferred causes, conclude, that any other fact has existed, or will exist, in the course of nature, which may serve as a fuller display of particular attributes; I must admonish you, that you have departed from the method of reasoning, attached to the present subject, and have certainly added something to the attributes of the cause, beyond what appears in the effect; otherwise you could never, with tolerable sense or propriety, add any thing to the effect, in order to render it more worthy of the cause.

19   Where, then, is the odiousness of that doctrine, which I teach in my school, or rather, which I examine in my gardens?[†] Or what do you find in this whole question, wherein the security of good morals, or the peace and order of society is in the least concerned?

20   I deny a providence, you say, and supreme governor of the world, who guides the course of events, and punishes the vicious with infamy and disappointment, and rewards the virtuous with honour and success, in all their undertakings. But surely, I deny not the course itself of events, which lies open to every one's enquiry and examination. I acknowledge, that, in the present order of things, virtue is attended with more peace of mind than vice, and meets with a more favourable reception from the

world. I am sensible, that, according to the past experience of mankind, friendship is the chief joy of human life, and moderation the only source of tranquillity and happiness. I never balance between the virtuous and the vicious course of life; but am sensible, that, to a well disposed mind, every advantage is on the side of the former. And what can you say more, allowing all your suppositions and reasonings? You tell me, indeed, that this disposition of things proceeds from intelligence and design. But whatever it proceeds from, the disposition itself, on which depends our happiness or misery, and consequently our conduct and deportment in life, is still the same. It is still open for me, as well as you, to regulate my behaviour, by my experience of past events. And if you affirm, that, while a divine providence is allowed, and a supreme distributive justice in the universe, I ought to expect some more particular reward of the good, and punishment of the bad, beyond the ordinary course of events; I here find the same fallacy, which I have before endeavoured to detect. You persist in imagining, that, if we grant that divine existence, for which you so earnestly contend, you may safely infer consequences from it, and add something to the experienced order of nature, by arguing from the attri- *SBN 141* butes which you ascribe to your gods. You seem not to remember, that all your reasonings on this subject can only be drawn from effects to causes; and that every argument, deduced from causes to effects, must of necessity be a gross sophism; since it is impossible for you to know any thing of the cause, but what you have antecedently, not inferred, but discovered to the full, in the effect.

21   But what must a philosopher think of those vain reasoners, who, instead of regarding the present scene of things as the sole object of their contemplation, so far reverse the whole course of nature, as to render this life merely a passage† to something farther; a porch, which leads to a greater, and vastly different building; a prologue, which serves only to introduce the piece, and give it more grace and propriety? Whence, do you think, can such philosophers derive their idea of the gods? From their own conceit and imagination surely. For if they derived it from the present phænomena, it would never point to any thing farther, but must be exactly adjusted to them. That the divinity may *possibly* be endowed with attributes, which we have never seen exerted;† may be governed by principles of action, which we cannot discover to be satisfied: All this will freely be allowed. But still this is mere *possibility* and hypothesis. We never can have reason to *infer* any attributes, or any principles of action in him, but so far as we know them to have been exerted and satisfied.

22   *Are there any marks of a distributive justice in the world?* If you answer in

the affirmative, I conclude, that, since justice here exerts itself, it is satisfied. If you reply in the negative, I conclude, that you have then no reason to ascribe justice, in our sense of it, to the gods. If you hold a medium between affirmation and negation, by saying, that the justice of the gods, at present, exerts itself in part, but not in its full extent; I answer, that you have no reason to give it any particular extent, but only so far as you see it, *at present*, exert itself.[†]   *SBN 1-*

23   Thus I bring the dispute, O ATHENIANS, to a short issue with my antagonists. The course of nature lies open to my contemplation as well as to theirs. The experienced train of events is the great standard, by which we all regulate our conduct. Nothing else can be appealed to in the field, or in the senate.[†] Nothing else ought ever to be heard of in the school, or in the closet.[†] In vain would our limited understanding break through those boundaries, which are too narrow for our fond imagination. While we argue from the course of nature, and infer a particular intelligent cause, which first bestowed, and still preserves order in the universe, we embrace a principle, which is both uncertain and useless. It is uncertain; because the subject lies entirely beyond the reach of human experience. It is useless; because our knowledge of this cause being derived entirely from the course of nature, we can never, according to the rules of just reasoning, return back from the cause with any new inference, or making additions to the common and experienced course of nature, establish any new principles of conduct and behaviour.

24   I observe (said I, finding he had finished his harangue) that you neglect not the artifice of the demagogues of old; and as you were pleased to make me stand for the people, you insinuate yourself into my favour by embracing those principles, to which, you know, I have always expressed a particular attachment. But allowing you to make experience (as indeed I think you ought) the only standard of our judgment concerning this, and all other questions of fact; I doubt not but, from the very same experience, to which you appeal, it may be possible to refute this reasoning,   *SBN 1* which you have put into the mouth of EPICURUS. If you saw, for instance, a half-finished building, surrounded with heaps of brick and stone and mortar, and all the instruments of masonry; could you not *infer* from the effect, that it was a work of design and contrivance? And could you not return again, from this inferred cause, to infer new additions to the effect, and conclude, that the building would soon be finished, and receive all the further improvements, which art[†] could bestow upon it? If you saw upon the sea-shore the print of one human foot, you would conclude, that a man had passed that way, and that he had also left the traces of the

other foot, though effaced by the rolling of the sands or inundation of the waters. Why then do you refuse to admit the same method of reasoning with regard to the order of nature? Consider the world and the present life only as an imperfect building, from which you can infer a superior intelligence; and arguing from that superior intelligence, which can leave nothing imperfect; why may you not infer a more finished scheme or plan, which will receive its completion in some distant point of space or time? Are not these methods of reasoning exactly similar? And under what pretence can you embrace the one, while you reject the other?

25   The infinite difference of the subjects, replied he, is a sufficient foundation for this difference in my conclusions. In works of *human* art and contrivance, it is allowable to advance from the effect to the cause, and returning back from the cause, to form new inferences concerning the effect, and examine the alterations, which it has probably undergone, or may still undergo. But what is the foundation of this method of reasoning? Plainly this; that man is a being, whom we know by experience, whose motives and designs we are acquainted with, and whose projects and inclinations have a certain connexion and coherence, according to the laws which nature has established for the government of such a creature. When, therefore, we find, that any work has proceeded from the skill and industry of man; as we are otherwise acquainted with the nature of the animal, we can draw a hundred inferences concerning what may be expected from him; and these inferences will all be founded in experience and observation. But did we know man only from the single work or production which we examine, it were impossible for us to argue in this manner; because our knowledge of all the qualities, which we ascribe to him, being in that case derived from the production, it is impossible they could point to any thing farther, or be the foundation of any new inference. The print of a foot in the sand can only prove, when considered alone, that there was some figure adapted to it, by which it was produced: But the print of a human foot proves likewise, from our other experience, that there was probably another foot, which also left its impression, though effaced by time or other accidents. Here we mount from the effect to the cause; and descending again from the cause, infer alterations in the effect; but this is not a continuation of the same simple chain of reasoning. We comprehend in this case a hundred other experiences and observations, concerning the *usual* figure and members of that species of animal, without which this method of argument must be considered as fallacious and sophistical.

SBN 144

26   The case is not the same with our reasonings from the works of nature. The Deity is known to us only by his productions, and is a single being in the universe, not comprehended under any species or genus, from whose experienced attributes or qualities, we can, by analogy,[†] infer any attribute or quality in him. As the universe shows wisdom and goodness, we infer wisdom and goodness. As it shows a particular degree of these perfections, we infer a particular degree of them, precisely adapted to the *SBN 1* effect which we examine. But farther attributes or farther degrees of the same attributes, we can never be authorized to infer or suppose, by any rules of just reasoning. Now, without some such licence of supposition, it is impossible for us to argue from the cause, or infer any alteration in the effect, beyond what has immediately fallen under our observation. Greater good produced by this Being must still prove a greater degree of goodness: A more impartial distribution of rewards and punishments must proceed from a greater regard to justice and equity. Every supposed addition to the works of nature makes an addition to the attributes of the Author of nature; and consequently, being entirely unsupported by any reason or argument, can never be admitted but as mere conjecture and hypothesis.[31]

27   The great source of our mistake[†] in this subject, and of the unbounded licence of conjecture, which we indulge, is, that we tacitly consider ourselves, as in the place of the Supreme Being, and conclude, that he will, on every occasion, observe the same conduct, which we ourselves, in his *SBN 1* situation, would have embraced as reasonable and eligible. But, besides that the ordinary course of nature may convince us, that almost every thing is regulated by principles and maxims very different from ours; besides this, I say, it must evidently appear contrary to all rules of analogy to reason, from the intentions and projects of men, to those of a Being

---

[31] In general, it may, I think, be established as a maxim, that where any cause is known *SBN 1* only by its particular effects, it must be impossible to infer any new effects from that cause; since the qualities, which are requisite to produce these new effects along with the former, must either be different, or superior, or of more extensive operation, than those which simply produced the effect, whence alone the cause is supposed to be known to us. We can never, therefore, have any reason to suppose the existence of these qualities. To say, that the new effects proceed only from a continuation of the same energy, which is already known from the first effects, will not remove the difficulty. For even granting this to be the case, (which can seldom be supposed) the very continuation and exertion of a like energy, (for it is impossible it can be absolutely the same) I say, this exertion of a like energy, in a different period of space and time, is a very arbitrary supposition, and what there cannot possibly be any traces of in the effects, from which all our knowledge of the cause is originally derived. Let the *inferred* cause be exactly proportioned (as it should be) to the known effect; and it is impossible that it can possess any qualities, from which new or different effects can be *inferred*.

so different, and so much superior. In human nature, there is a certain experienced coherence of designs and inclinations; so that when, from any fact, we have discovered one intention of any man, it may often be reasonable, from experience, to infer another, and draw a long chain of conclusions concerning his past or future conduct. But this method of reasoning can never have place with regard to a Being, so remote and incomprehensible, who bears much less analogy to any other being in the universe than the sun to a waxen taper, and who discovers himself only by some faint traces or outlines, beyond which we have no authority to ascribe to him any attribute or perfection. What we imagine to be a superior perfection may really be a defect. Or were it ever so much a perfection, the ascribing of it to the Supreme Being, where it appears not to have been really exerted, to the full, in his works, savours more of flattery and panegyric, than of just reasoning and sound philosophy. All the philosophy, therefore, in the world, and all the religion, which is nothing but a species of philosophy, will never be able to carry us beyond the usual course of experience, or give us measures of conduct and behaviour different from those which are furnished by reflections on common life. No new fact can ever be inferred from the religious hypothesis; no event foreseen or foretold; no reward or punishment expected or dreaded, beyond what is already known by practice and observation. So that my apology† for EPICURUS will still appear solid and satisfactory; nor have the   *SBN 147* political interests of society any connexion with the philosophical disputes concerning metaphysics and religion.†

28   There is still one circumstance, replied I, which you seem to have overlooked. Though I should allow your premises, I must deny your conclusion. You conclude, that religious doctrines and reasonings *can* have no influence on life, because they *ought* to have no influence; never considering, that men reason not in the same manner you do, but draw many consequences from the belief of a divine Existence, and suppose that the Deity will inflict punishments on vice, and bestow rewards on virtue,† beyond what appear in the ordinary course of nature. Whether this reasoning of theirs be just or not, is no matter. Its influence on their life and conduct must still be the same. And those, who attempt to disabuse them of such prejudices, may, for aught I know, be good reasoners, but I cannot allow them to be good citizens† and politicians; since they free men from one restraint upon their passions, and make the infringement of the laws of society, in one respect, more easy and secure.

29   After all, I may, perhaps, agree to your general conclusion in favour of liberty, though upon different premises from those, on which you endeav-

our to found it. I think, that the state ought to tolerate every principle[†] of philosophy; nor is there an instance, that any government has suffered in its political interests by such indulgence. There is no enthusiasm among philosophers;[†] their doctrines are not very alluring to the people; and no restraint can be put upon their reasonings, but what must be of dangerous consequence to the sciences, and even to the state, by paving the way for persecution and oppression in points, where the generality of mankind are more deeply interested and concerned.

30   But there occurs to me (continued I) with regard to your main topic,   SBN 14 a difficulty, which I shall just propose to you, without insisting on it; lest it lead into reasonings of too nice and delicate a nature. In a word, I much doubt whether it be possible for a cause to be known only by its effect (as you have all along supposed) or to be of so singular and particular a nature as to have no parallel[†] and no similarity with any other cause or object, that has ever fallen under our observation. It is only when two *species* of objects are found to be constantly conjoined, that we can infer the one from the other; and were an effect presented, which was entirely singular, and could not be comprehended under any known *species*, I do not see, that we could form any conjecture or inference at all concerning its cause. If experience and observation and analogy be, indeed, the only guides which we can reasonably follow in inferences of this nature; both the effect and cause must bear a similarity and resemblance to other effects and causes, which we know, and which we have found, in many instances, to be conjoined with each other. I leave it to your own reflection to pursue the consequences of this principle. I shall just observe, that, as the antagonists of EPICURUS always suppose the universe, an effect quite singular and unparalleled, to be the proof of a Deity, a cause no less singular and unparalleled; your reasonings, upon that supposition, seem, at least, to merit our attention. There is, I own, some difficulty, how we can ever return from the cause to the effect,[†] and, reasoning from our ideas of the former, infer any alteration on the latter, or any addition to it.

SECTION 12

OF THE ACADEMICAL OR SCEPTICAL PHILOSOPHY†

PART 1

1 THERE is not a greater number of philosophical reasonings, displayed upon any subject, than those, which prove the existence of a Deity, and refute the fallacies of *Atheists*;† and yet the most religious philosophers still dispute whether any man can be so blinded as to be a speculative atheist. How shall we reconcile these contradictions? The knights-errant, who wandered about to clear the world of dragons and giants, never entertained the least doubt with regard to the existence of these monsters.

2 The *Sceptic* is another enemy of religion,† who naturally provokes the indignation of all divines and graver philosophers; though it is certain, that no man ever met with any such absurd creature, or conversed with a man, who had no opinion or principle concerning any subject, either of action or speculation. This begets a very natural question; What is meant by a sceptic? And how far it is possible to push these philosophical principles of doubt and uncertainty?

3 There is a species of scepticism, *antecedent*† to all study and philosophy, which is much inculcated by DES CARTES and others, as a sovereign preservative against error and precipitate judgment. It recommends an universal doubt, not only of all our former opinions and principles, but also of our very faculties; of whose veracity, say they, we must assure SBN 150 ourselves, by a chain of reasoning, deduced from some original principle, which cannot possibly be fallacious or deceitful. But neither is there any such original principle, which has a prerogative above others, that are self-evident and convincing: Or if there were, could we advance a step beyond it, but by the use of those very faculties, of which we are supposed to be already diffident. The CARTESIAN doubt,† therefore, were it ever possible to be attained by any human creature (as it plainly is not) would be entirely incurable; and no reasoning could ever bring us to a state of assurance and conviction upon any subject.

4   It must, however, be confessed, that this species of scepticism, when more moderate,† may be understood in a very reasonable sense, and is a necessary preparative to the study of philosophy, by preserving a proper impartiality in our judgments, and weaning our mind from all those prejudices, which we may have imbibed from education† or rash opinion. To begin with clear and self-evident principles, to advance by timorous and sure steps, to review frequently our conclusions, and examine accurately all their consequences; though by these means we shall make both a slow and a short progress in our systems; are the only methods, by which we can ever hope to reach truth, and attain a proper stability and certainty in our determinations.

5   There is another species of scepticism, *consequent*† to science and enquiry, when men are supposed to have discovered, either the absolute fallaciousness of their mental faculties, or their unfitness to reach any fixed determination in all those curious subjects of speculation, about which they are commonly employed. Even our very senses are brought into dispute, by a certain species of philosophers; and the maxims of common life are subjected to the same doubt as the most profound principles or conclusions of metaphysics and theology. As these paradoxical tenets (if they may be called tenets) are to be met with in some philoso-   SBN 1 phers, and the refutation of them in several, they naturally excite our curiosity, and make us enquire into the arguments, on which they may be founded.

6   I need not insist upon the more trite topics, employed by the sceptics in all ages, against the evidence of *sense*; such as those which are derived from the imperfection and fallaciousness of our organs, on numberless occasions; the crooked appearance of an oar in water; the various aspects of objects, according to their different distances; the double images which arise from the pressing one eye;† with many other appearances of a like nature. These sceptical topics, indeed, are only sufficient to prove, that the senses alone are not implicitly to be depended on; but that we must correct their evidence by reason, and by considerations, derived from the nature of the medium, the distance of the object, and the disposition of the organ, in order to render them, within their sphere, the proper *criteria* of truth and falsehood. There are other more profound arguments against the senses, which admit not of so easy a solution.

7   It seems evident, that men are carried, by a natural instinct or prepossession, to repose faith in their senses; and that, without any reasoning, or even almost before the use of reason, we always suppose an external universe, which depends not on our perception, but would exist,

though we and every sensible creature were absent or annihilated. Even the animal creation are governed by a like opinion, and preserve this belief of external objects, in all their thoughts, designs, and actions.

8 It seems also evident, that, when men follow this blind and powerful instinct of nature, they always suppose the very images, presented by the senses, to be the external objects, and never entertain any suspicion, that the one are nothing but representations of the other. This very table, which we see white, and which we feel hard, is believed to exist, inde- *SBN 152* pendent of our perception, and to be something external to our mind, which perceives it. Our presence bestows not being on it: Our absence does not annihilate it. It preserves its existence uniform and entire, independent of the situation of intelligent beings, who perceive or contemplate it.

9 But this universal and primary opinion of all men is soon destroyed by the slightest philosophy,[†] which teaches us, that nothing can ever be present to the mind but an image or perception, and that the senses are only the inlets, through which these images are conveyed, without being able to produce any immediate intercourse between the mind and the object. The table, which we see, seems to diminish, as we remove farther from it: But the real table, which exists independent of us, suffers no alteration: It was, therefore, nothing but its image, which was present to the mind. These are the obvious dictates of reason; and no man, who reflects, ever doubted, that the existences, which we consider, when we say, *this house* and *that tree*, are nothing but perceptions in the mind, and fleeting copies or representations of other existences, which remain uniform and independent.

10 So far, then, are we necessitated by reasoning to contradict or depart from the primary instincts of nature, and to embrace a new system with regard to the evidence of our senses. But here philosophy finds herself extremely embarrassed, when she would justify this new system, and obviate the cavils[†] and objections of the sceptics. She can no longer plead the infallible and irresistible instinct of nature: For that led us to a quite different system, which is acknowledged fallible and even erroneous. And to justify this pretended philosophical system, by a chain of clear and convincing argument, or even any appearance of argument, exceeds the power of all human capacity.

11 By what argument can it be proved, that the perceptions of the mind *SBN 153* must be caused by external objects,[†] entirely different from them, though resembling them (if that be possible) and could not arise either from the energy of the mind itself, or from the suggestion of some invisible and

unknown spirit, or from some other cause still more unknown to us? It is acknowledged, that, in fact, many of these perceptions arise not from any thing external, as in dreams, madness, and other diseases. And nothing can be more inexplicable than the manner, in which body should so operate upon mind as ever to convey an image of itself to a substance, supposed of so different, and even contrary a nature.

12   It is a question of fact, whether the perceptions of the senses be produced by external objects, resembling them: How shall this question be determined? By experience surely; as all other questions of a like nature. But here experience is, and must be entirely silent. The mind has never any thing present to it but the perceptions, and cannot possibly reach any experience of their connexion with objects. The supposition of such a connexion is, therefore, without any foundation in reasoning.

13   To have recourse to the veracity of the Supreme Being,[†] in order to prove the veracity of our senses, is surely making a very unexpected circuit. If his veracity were at all concerned in this matter, our senses would be entirely infallible; because it is not possible that he can ever deceive. Not to mention, that, if the external world be once called in question, we shall be at a loss to find arguments, by which we may prove the existence of that Being or any of his attributes.

14   This is a topic, therefore, in which the profounder and more philosophical sceptics will always triumph, when they endeavour to introduce an universal doubt into all subjects of human knowledge and enquiry. Do you follow the instincts and propensities of nature, may they say, in assenting to the veracity of sense? But these lead you to believe, that the SBN 1 very perception or sensible image is the external object. Do you disclaim this principle, in order to embrace a more rational opinion, that the perceptions are only representations of something external? You here depart from your natural propensities and more obvious sentiments; and yet are not able to satisfy your reason, which can never find any convincing argument from experience to prove, that the perceptions are connected with any external objects.

15   There is another sceptical topic of a like nature, derived from the most profound philosophy; which might merit our attention, were it requisite to dive so deep, in order to discover arguments and reasonings, which can so little serve to any serious purpose. It is universally allowed by modern enquirers,[†] that all the sensible qualities of objects, such as hard, soft, hot, cold, white, black, &c. are merely secondary, and exist not in the objects themselves, but are perceptions of the mind, without any external archetype[†] or model, which they represent. If this be allowed, with regard to

secondary qualities, it must also follow, with regard to the supposed primary qualities of extension and solidity;[†] nor can the latter be any more entitled to that denomination than the former. The idea of extension is entirely acquired from the senses of sight and feeling; and if all the qualities, perceived by the senses, be in the mind, not in the object, the same conclusion must reach the idea of extension, which is wholly dependent on the sensible ideas or the ideas of secondary qualities. Nothing can save us from this conclusion, but the asserting, that the ideas of those primary qualities are attained by *Abstraction*; an opinion, which, if we examine it accurately, we shall find to be unintelligible, and even absurd.[†] An extension, that is neither tangible nor visible, cannot possibly be conceived: And a tangible or visible extension, which is neither $SBN\ 155$ hard nor soft, black nor white, is equally beyond the reach of human conception. Let any man try to conceive a triangle in general, which is neither *Isosceles* nor *Scalenum*, nor has any particular length or proportion of sides; and he will soon perceive the absurdity of all the scholastic notions[†] with regard to abstraction and general ideas.[32]

16 Thus the first philosophical objection to the evidence of sense or to the opinion of external existence consists in this, that such an opinion, if rested on natural instinct, is contrary to reason, and if referred to reason, is contrary to natural instinct, and at the same time carries no rational evidence with it, to convince an impartial enquirer. The second objection goes farther, and represents this opinion as contrary to reason; at least, if it be a principle of reason, that all sensible qualities are in the mind, not in the object. Bereave matter of all its intelligible qualities, both primary and secondary, you in a manner annihilate it, and leave only a certain unknown, inexplicable *something*, as the cause of our perceptions; a notion so imperfect, that no sceptic will think it worth while to contend against it.[†]

---

[32] This argument is drawn from Dr. BERKELEY;[†] and indeed most of the writings of that $SBN\ 155$ very ingenious author form the best lessons of scepticism, which are to be found either among the ancient or modern philosophers, BAYLE[†] not excepted. He professes, however, in his title-page (and undoubtedly with great truth) to have composed his book against the sceptics[†] as well as against the atheists and free-thinkers. [George Berkeley, *A Treatise Concerning the Principles of Human Knowledge. Wherein the Chief Causes of Error and Difficulty in the Sciences, with the Grounds of Scepticism, Atheism, and Irreligion, are inquired into. To which are added Three Dialogues Between Hylas and Philonous, In Opposition to Scepticks and Atheists.*] But that all his arguments, though otherwise intended, are, in reality, merely sceptical,[†] appears from this, *that they admit of no answer and produce no conviction.* Their only effect is to cause that momentary amazement and irresolution and confusion, which is the result of scepticism.

PART 2

17 It may seem a very extravagant attempt of the sceptics to destroy *reason*[†]
by argument and ratiocination; yet is this the grand scope of all their
enquiries and disputes. They endeavour to find objections, both to our   <small>SBN 15</small>
abstract reasonings, and to those which regard matter of fact and exis-
tence.

18   The chief objection against all *abstract* reasonings is derived from the
ideas of space and time; ideas, which, in common life and to a careless
view, are very clear and intelligible, but when they pass through the
scrutiny of the profound sciences (and they are the chief object of these
sciences) afford principles, which seem full of absurdity and contradiction. No priestly *dogmas*, invented on purpose to tame and subdue the
rebellious reason of mankind, ever shocked common sense more than
the doctrine of the infinite divisibility[†] of extension, with its consequences; as they are pompously displayed by all geometricians and metaphysicians, with a kind of triumph and exultation. A real quantity,
infinitely less than any finite quantity, containing quantities infinitely less
than itself, and so on, *in infinitum*; this is an edifice so bold and prodigious, that it is too weighty for any pretended demonstration to support,
because it shocks the clearest and most natural principles of human
reason.[33] But what renders the matter more extraordinary, is, that these
seemingly absurd opinions are supported by a chain of reasoning, the
clearest and most natural; nor is it possible for us to allow the premises
without admitting the consequences. Nothing can be more convincing
and satisfactory than all the conclusions concerning the properties of   <small>SBN 15</small>
circles and triangles; and yet, when these are once received, how can we
deny, that the angle of contact between a circle and its tangent is infinitely
less than any rectilineal angle, that as you may encrease the diameter of
the circle *in infinitum*, this angle of contact becomes still less, even *in
infinitum*, and that the angle of contact between other curves and their
tangents may be infinitely less than those between any circle and its

---

[33] Whatever disputes there may be about mathematical points,[†] we must allow that there   <small>SBN 15</small>
are physical points; that is, parts of extension, which cannot be divided or lessened, either by
the eye or imagination. These images, then, which are present to the fancy or senses, are
absolutely indivisible, and consequently must be allowed by mathematicians to be infinitely
less than any real part of extension; and yet nothing appears more certain to reason, than
that an infinite number of them composes an infinite extension. How much more an infinite
number of those infinitely small parts of extension, which are still supposed infinitely
divisible.

tangent, and so on, *in infinitum?* The demonstration of these principles seems as unexceptionable as that which proves the three angles of a triangle to be equal to two right ones, though the latter opinion be natural and easy, and the former big with contradiction and absurdity. Reason here seems to be thrown into a kind of amazement and suspence, which, without the suggestions of any sceptic, gives her a diffidence of herself, and of the ground on which she treads. She sees a full light, which illuminates certain places; but that light borders upon the most profound darkness. And between these she is so dazzled and confounded, that she scarcely can pronounce with certainty and assurance concerning any one object.

19   The absurdity of these bold determinations of the abstract sciences seems to become, if possible, still more palpable with regard to time than extension. An infinite number of real parts of time, passing in succession,[†] and exhausted one after another, appears so evident a contradiction, that no man, one should think, whose judgment is not corrupted, instead of being improved, by the sciences, would ever be able to admit of it.

20   Yet still reason must remain restless and unquiet, even with regard to that scepticism, to which she is driven by these seeming absurdities and contradictions. How any clear, distinct idea can contain circumstances, contradictory to itself, or to any other clear, distinct idea, is absolutely incomprehensible; and is, perhaps, as absurd as any proposition, which   *SBN 158* can be formed. So that nothing can be more sceptical, or more full of doubt and hesitation, than this scepticism itself, which arises from some of the paradoxical conclusions of geometry or the science of quantity.[34]

21   The sceptical objections to *moral* evidence, or to the reasonings con-

---

[34] It seems to me not impossible to avoid these absurdities and contradictions, if it be   *SBN 158* admitted, that there is no such thing as abstract or general ideas,[†] properly speaking; but that all general ideas are, in reality, particular ones, attached to a general term, which recalls, upon occasion, other particular ones, that resemble, in certain circumstances, the idea, present to the mind. Thus when the term *horse*, is pronounced, we immediately figure to ourselves the idea of a black or a white animal, of a particular size or figure: But as that term is also usually applied to animals of other colours, figures, and sizes, these ideas, though not actually present to the imagination, are easily recalled; and our reasoning and conclusion proceed in the same way, as if they were actually present. If this be admitted (as seems reasonable) it follows that all the ideas of quantity, upon which mathematicians reason, are nothing but particular, and such as are suggested by the senses and imagination, and consequently, cannot be infinitely divisible. It is sufficient to have dropped this hint at present, without prosecuting it any farther. It certainly concerns all lovers of science not to expose themselves to the ridicule and contempt of the ignorant by their conclusions; and this seems the readiest solution of these difficulties.

cerning matter of fact, are either *popular* or *philosophical.*[†] The popular objections are derived from the natural weakness of human understanding; the contradictory opinions, which have been entertained in different ages and nations; the variations of our judgment in sickness and health, youth and old age, prosperity and adversity; the perpetual contradiction of each particular man's opinions and sentiments; with many other topics of that kind. It is needless to insist farther on this head. These objections are but weak. For as, in common life, we reason every moment concerning fact and existence, and cannot possibly subsist, without continually employing this species of argument, any popular objections, derived from thence, must be insufficient to destroy that evidence. The great subverter of PYRRHONISM[†] or the excessive principles of scepticism, is action, and employment, and the occupations of common life. These principles may flourish and triumph in the schools; where it is, indeed, difficult, if not impossible, to refute them. But as soon as they leave the shade, and by the presence of the real objects, which actuate our passions and sentiments, are put in opposition to the more powerful principles of our nature, they vanish like smoke, and leave the most determined sceptic in the same condition as other mortals.[†] SBN 1

22 The sceptic, therefore, had better keep within his proper sphere, and display those *philosophical* objections, which arise from more profound researches.[†] Here he seems to have ample matter of triumph; while he justly insists, that all our evidence for any matter of fact, which lies beyond the testimony of sense or memory, is derived entirely from the relation of cause and effect; that we have no other idea of this relation than that of two objects, which have been frequently *conjoined* together; that we have no argument to convince us, that objects, which have, in our experience, been frequently conjoined, will likewise, in other instances, be conjoined in the same manner; and that nothing leads us to this inference but custom or a certain instinct of our nature; which it is indeed difficult to resist, but which, like other instincts, may be fallacious and deceitful. While the sceptic insists upon these topics, he shows his force, or rather, indeed, his own and our weakness; and seems, for the time at least, to destroy all assurance and conviction. These arguments might be displayed at greater length, if any durable good or benefit to society could ever be expected to result from them.

23 For here is the chief and most confounding objection to *excessive* scepticism,[†] that no durable good can ever result from it; while it remains in its full force and vigour. We need only ask such a sceptic, *What his meaning is? And what he proposes by all these curious researches?* He is immediately at SBN 16

a loss, and knows not what to answer. A Copernican or Ptolemaic,[†] who supports each his different system of astronomy, may hope to produce a conviction, which will remain constant and durable, with his audience. A Stoic or Epicurean[†] displays principles, which may not only be durable, but which have an effect on conduct and behaviour. But a Pyrrhonian cannot expect, that his philosophy will have any constant influence on the mind: Or if it had, that its influence would be beneficial to society. On the contrary, he must acknowledge, if he will acknowledge any thing, that all human life must perish, were his principles universally and steadily to prevail. All discourse, all action would immediately cease; and men remain in a total lethargy, till the necessities of nature, unsatisfied, put an end to their miserable existence. It is true; so fatal an event is very little to be dreaded. Nature is always too strong for principle. And though a Pyrrhonian may throw himself or others into a momentary amazement and confusion by his profound reasonings; the first and most trivial event in life will put to flight all his doubts and scruples, and leave him the same, in every point of action and speculation, with the philosophers of every other sect, or with those who never concerned themselves in any philosophical researches. When he awakes from his dream, he will be the first to join in the laugh against himself, and to confess, that all his objections are mere amusement, and can have no other tendency than to show the whimsical condition of mankind, who must act and reason and believe; though they are not able, by their most diligent enquiry, to satisfy themselves concerning the foundation of these operations, or to remove the objections, which may be raised against them.

PART 3

SBN 161

24 There is, indeed, a more *mitigated* scepticism, or Academical philosophy, which may be both durable and useful, and which may, in part, be the result of this Pyrrhonism,[†] or *excessive* scepticism, when its undistinguished doubts are, in some measure, corrected by common sense and reflection. The greater part of mankind are naturally apt to be affirmative and dogmatical in their opinions; and while they see objects only on one side, and have no idea of any counterpoising argument, they throw themselves precipitately into the principles, to which they are inclined; nor have they any indulgence for those who entertain opposite sentiments. To hesitate or balance perplexes their understanding, checks their passion,

and suspends their action. They are, therefore, impatient till they escape from a state, which to them is so uneasy; and they think, that they can never remove themselves far enough from it, by the violence of their affirmations and obstinacy of their belief. But could such dogmatical reasoners become sensible of the strange infirmities of human understanding, even in its most perfect state, and when most accurate and cautious in its determinations; such a reflection would naturally inspire them with more modesty and reserve, and diminish their fond opinion of themselves, and their prejudice against antagonists. The illiterate may reflect on the disposition of the learned, who, amidst all the advantages of study and reflection, are commonly still diffident in their determinations: And if any of the learned be inclined, from their natural temper, to haughtiness and obstinacy, a small tincture of PYRRHONISM might abate their pride, by showing them, that the few advantages, which they may have attained over their fellows, are but inconsiderable, if compared with the universal perplexity and confusion, which is inherent in human nature. In general, there is a degree of doubt, and caution, and modesty, which, in all kinds of scrutiny and decision, ought for ever to accompany a just reasoner. SBN 1

25   Another species of *mitigated* scepticism, which may be of advantage to mankind, and which may be the natural result of the PYRRHONIAN doubts and scruples, is the limitation of our enquiries to such subjects as are best adapted to the narrow capacity of human understanding. The *imagination* of man is naturally sublime, delighted with whatever is remote and extraordinary, and running, without controul, into the most distant parts of space and time, in order to avoid the objects, which custom has rendered too familiar to it. A correct *Judgment* observes a contrary method, and avoiding all distant and high enquiries, confines itself to common life,† and to such subjects as fall under daily practice and experience; leaving the more sublime topics to the embellishment of poets and orators, or to the arts of priests and politicians. To bring us to so salutary a determination, nothing can be more serviceable, than to be once thoroughly convinced of the force of the PYRRHONIAN doubt,† and of the impossibility, that any thing, but the strong power of natural instinct, could free us from it. Those who have a propensity to philosophy, will still continue their researches; because they reflect, that, besides the immediate pleasure, attending such an occupation, philosophical decisions are nothing but the reflections of common life, methodized and corrected. But they will never be tempted to go beyond common life, so

long as they consider the imperfection of those faculties which they employ, their narrow reach, and their inaccurate operations. While we cannot give a satisfactory reason, why we believe, after a thousand experiments, that a stone will fall, or fire burn; can we ever satisfy ourselves concerning any determination, which we may form, with regard to the origin of worlds, and the situation of nature, from, and to eternity?

26   This narrow limitation, indeed, of our enquiries, is, in every respect, *SBN 163* so reasonable, that it suffices to make the slightest examination into the natural powers of the human mind, and to compare them with their objects, in order to recommend it to us. We shall then find what are the proper subjects of science and enquiry.

27   It seems to me, that the only objects of the abstract sciences or of demonstration are quantity and number, and that all attempts to extend this more perfect species of knowledge beyond these bounds are mere sophistry and illusion.[†] As the component parts of quantity and number are entirely similar, their relations become intricate and involved; and nothing can be more curious, as well as useful, than to trace, by a variety of mediums, their equality or inequality, through their different appearances. But as all other ideas are clearly distinct and different from each other, we can never advance farther, by our utmost scrutiny, than to observe this diversity, and, by an obvious reflection, pronounce one thing not to be another. Or if there be any difficulty in these decisions, it proceeds entirely from the undeterminate meaning of words, which is corrected by juster definitions. That *the square of the hypothenuse is equal to the squares of the other two sides,*[†] cannot be known, let the terms be ever so exactly defined, without a train of reasoning and enquiry. But to convince us of this proposition, *that where there is no property, there can be no injustice*, it is only necessary to define the terms, and explain injustice to be a violation of property. This proposition is, indeed, nothing but a more imperfect definition.[†] It is the same case with all those pretended syllogistical reasonings, which may be found in every other branch of learning, except the sciences of quantity and number; and these may safely, I think, be pronounced the only proper objects of knowledge and demonstration.

28   All other enquiries of men regard only matter of fact and existence; *SBN 164* and these are evidently incapable of demonstration. Whatever *is* may *not be*. No negation of a fact can involve a contradiction.[†] The non-existence of any being, without exception, is as clear and distinct an idea as its existence. The proposition, which affirms it not to be, however false, is no

less conceivable and intelligible, than that which affirms it to be. The case is different with the sciences, properly so called.[†] Every proposition, which is not true, is there confused and unintelligible. That the cube root of 64 is equal to the half of 10, is a false proposition, and can never be distinctly conceived. But that CÆSAR, or the angel GABRIEL, or any being never existed, may be a false proposition, but still is perfectly conceivable, and implies no contradiction.

29   The existence, therefore, of any being can only be proved by arguments from its cause or its effect; and these arguments are founded entirely on experience. If we reason *a priori*, any thing may appear able to produce any thing. The falling of a pebble may, for aught we know, extinguish the sun; or the wish of a man controul the planets in their orbits. It is only experience, which teaches us the nature and bounds of cause and effect, and enables us to infer the existence of one object from that of another.[35] Such is the foundation of moral reasoning, which forms the greater part of human knowledge, and is the source of all human action and behaviour.

30   Moral reasonings are either concerning particular or general facts. All deliberations in life regard the former; as also all disquisitions in history, chronology, geography, and astronomy.

31   The sciences, which treat of general facts, are politics, natural philos-   SBN 1 ophy, physic, chymistry, *&c.* where the qualities, causes, and effects of a whole species of objects are enquired into.

32   Divinity or Theology, as it proves the existence of a Deity, and the immortality of souls, is composed partly of reasonings concerning particular, partly concerning general facts. It has a foundation in *reason*, so far as it is supported by experience. But its best and most solid foundation is *faith* and divine revelation.[†]

33   Morals and criticism are not so properly objects of the understanding as of taste and sentiment.[†] Beauty, whether moral or natural, is felt, more properly than perceived. Or if we reason concerning it, and endeavour to fix its standard, we regard a new fact, to wit, the general taste of mankind, or some such fact, which may be the object of reasoning and enquiry.

---

[35] That impious maxim of the ancient philosophy, *Ex nihilo, nihil fit,*[†] by which the creation   SBN 1 of matter was excluded, ceases to be a maxim, according to this philosophy. Not only the will of the Supreme Being may create matter; but, for aught we know *a priori*, the will of any other being might create it, or any other cause, that the most whimsical imagination can assign.

34   When we run over libraries, persuaded of these principles, what havoc must we make? If we take in our hand any volume; of divinity or school metaphysics,[†] for instance; let us ask, *Does it contain any abstract reasoning concerning quantity or number?* No. *Does it contain any experimental reasoning concerning matter of fact and existence?* No. Commit it then to the flames: For it can contain nothing but sophistry and illusion.

PART 3

Supplementary Material

Annotations to the *Enquiry*

Scope of the Annotations

Each annotation is introduced by paragraph numbers or footnote numbers in the text. Each serves at least one of the following eight purposes.

1. *Definition.* A number of potentially confusing terms are handled in the Glossary. However, context-sensitive meanings are often treated in the annotations.

2. *Translation.* Translations are provided for all French, Latin, and Greek quotations supplied by Hume.

3. *Interpretation.* Interpretations are presented of difficult terms, phrases, sentences, and passages. If a relevant explanation is provided in the Editor's Introduction ('Ed. Intro.'), reference is made to that source.

4. *Summarization.* A summary of the main arguments and conclusions in each section is provided at the beginning of the annotations for that section.

5. *Completion of a self-reference.* A few annotations identify a passage in *EHU* to which Hume is referring (a cross-reference), even when he does not provide an explicit section reference.

6. *Information on passages in named authors.* A few annotations explain the context or content of a work that Hume identifies or to which he alludes. These reports are needed whenever Hume's surrounding sentences assume more than the reader could be expected to know.

7. *Identification of passages in unnamed authors.* Several annotations identify Hume's allusions to unnamed authors. Full names and titles are sometimes found only in the reference list.

8. *Identification of the intellectual background.* A few annotations discuss Hume's possible sources of information, especially where a passage suggests an author known to have been read by Hume. Editorial mention of sources is selective and serves more as a pointer than a comprehensive or definitive discussion of the intellectual background.

References to other works by Hume usually include paragraph numbers, rather than page numbers in specific editions. *'Letters'* refers exclusively to the two-volume Greig edition of Hume's letters. All materials cited in the Annotations are listed in the References.

Translations

All Greek and Latin words or passages presented by Hume are translated by M. A. Stewart. All French words or passages presented by Hume are translated by Tom L. Beauchamp.

ADVERTISEMENT

Hume had written this Advertisement (meaning *notification*) by 26 October 1775, when he sent it to his London printer, William Strahan (1715–85). In saying he 'never acknowledged' his *Treatise*, Hume is alluding to the fact that he published the book anonymously. 'Contained in this volume' and 'the following pieces' are references to the contents of his collected works, entitled *Essays and Treatises on Several Subjects*. *EHU* appeared as the first treatise in this volume. The 'several writers' include the Scottish philosophers Thomas Reid (1710–96) and James Beattie (1735–1803), as Hume declares in his correspondence (*Letters*, 2: 301).

SECTION 1

The science of human nature pursued throughout *EHU* is introduced in this section. Hume thinks that philosophers often engage in fruitless debate because they lack a scientific method to study the human mind. Philosophy needs an experimental method shaped by the successful methods used in astronomy and the physical sciences. This science of the mind must rely on experience and careful observation to delineate the mind's distinct powers and faculties. In particular, the functions and limits of human understanding and reasoning (a 'mental geography') must be ascertained. Only in this way can we hope to correct mistakes that are as old as philosophy itself.

Two species of philosophy need to be distinguished. Philosophy in the 'easy and obvious manner' engages, excites, and regulates sentiments of approval and blame. It shapes the conduct and affections of people. The other species is more theoretical. It enters into 'a narrow scrutiny [of human nature] . . . in order to find those principles, which regulate our understanding, excite our sentiments, and make us approve or blame any particular object, action, or behaviour' (1.2). With a distanced admiration for good philosophers of the former species, Hume's primary identification is with good philosophers of the latter species. However, in the final sentence of Section 1 he indicates that he hopes to retain the best of both species: 'Happy, if we can unite the boundaries of the different species of philosophy, by reconciling profound enquiry with clearness' (1.17).

Hume seeks to couple the practical interest and accessible style of the first species with the deeper substance of the second. By examining the human understanding he hopes to show which subjects can be meaningfully studied. The resultant philosophy will not be easy and obvious, but it also will not be so abstract and speculative that it cannot be confirmed in experience. More speculative theories, often filled with abstruse metaphysical jargon, fail to delineate the proper scope and limits of human understanding. Once this scope has been delineated, philosophy will be placed on a new scientific foundation.

1 Moral **philosophy**] The word 'moral' is often used in *EHU* in a broader sense than is now commonplace. 'Moral philosophy' referred in Hume's day to everything from a theory of manners to a theory of ethics to a theory of mind and action. When Hume speaks of 'moral philosophy', 'moral reasoning', and the 'moral sciences', he is referring to the full range of topics concerned with mind and spirit, as well as conduct and character. Perception, conception, reasoning, taste, and judgement are all within its scope.

science of human nature] Hume proposes that moral philosophy employ the experimental method used in natural philosophy, making it too an experimental science. (See Ed. Intro., §3.) This science was the stated objective of *THN*, where Hume declared it 'the only Solid foundation for the other sciences' (Introduction, esp. pars. 6–7). Hume's objective is to study human nature systematically, especially the nature and limits of human understanding and various other faculties and functions of the mind.

two different manners] These two 'different species of philosophy' are discussed in the summary of Section 1 immediately above.

taste and sentiment] Taste is a properly cultivated faculty of mind that equips a person to reach good judgements about what is appropriate, excellent, beautiful, and the like. Sentiment is an inner sensing, feeling, or emotion—for example, anger, approval, disgust, sympathy, and compassion. The term 'sentiment' is also used, like 'taste', to refer to opinion and judgement. Hume does not sharply distinguish sensing, judging, believing, and the like. However, he does believe that factual statements are true or false and can be disputed by appeal to empirical evidence, whereas matters of taste are not true, false, or disputable on a factual basis.

eloquence] The principles of eloquence—the art of speaking well—were closely studied during Hume's period. Hume's essay 'Of Eloquence' contains his most detailed statement. This essay mentions the achievements of Demosthenes (4th c. BC) and Cicero (1st c. BC) and the analyses of the subject in Quintilian and Longinus.

easy and obvious] In *THN* (Introduction 3; 3.1.1.1) Hume said that his philosophy is abstruse and not 'easy and obvious'. He does not mean that his philosophy is unclear or hard for an attentive reader to follow. Today we might say that his philosophy is abstract and theoretical, by contrast to practical and easy to follow. See also *EHU* 1.3, 16.

2 **literature**] literary culture and learning.

criticism] literary and related forms of criticism of the arts; science (or art) of judging discourse and writing. See ann. 1.15, 'Moralists . . . critics, logicians . . . politicians'.

science] Science is theoretical and independent of its applications, by contrast to art. Hume regards morals, politics, logic, and criticism as sciences related to the study of human nature. See 1.5 and 1.15.

3 **plebeian**] a member of the common people, deriving from the Roman class division of plebs (plebeians or commoners) and patricians. A 'mere plebeian' has no special knowledge or refinement.

4 CICERO] Roman orator, politician, and philosopher Cicero was an influential writer in Hume's time; his letters were engaging and his orations powerful, even if loosely constructed.

ARISTOTLE] The influence of Athenian philosopher Aristotle (4th c. BC) had waned under the force of criticism levelled from the Renaissance through the early 18th century.

LA BRUYERE] French author Jean de La Bruyère (1645–96) was a prose stylist, satirist, and moralist whose appeals were often to the sentiments and contained comic and ironic touches. He concentrated on contemporary moral problems such as the widespread social abuses of the French court.

MALEBRANCHE] French priest and philosopher Nicolas Malebranche (1638–1715) was trained in Aristotelianism and became immersed in Cartesian philosophy and its reconciliation to Church doctrine. Although some readers commend his elegant and careful style, others find his meticulous reasoning difficult.

ADDISON] English essayist Joseph Addison (1672–1719) wrote in a popular and orderly style, often using modest forms of ridicule and satire. Some commentators maintain that his style elevated the essay to new levels of excellence in organization, simplicity, and precision.

4 LOCKE] English philosopher John Locke (1632–1704) wrote his major philosophical works in an abstract and studied, although generally clear and precise, style. His *Essay concerning Human Understanding* is a good example, and one well known to Hume.

5 **the sciences**] According to *THN* Introduction 4–5, these sciences included mathematics, natural philosophy, natural religion, logic, morals, criticism, and politics.

polite letters] literature exhibiting refined taste and quality of style. In his *History of England* (vol. 6, ch. 71) Hume lists poetry, eloquence, and history as among the 'branches of polite letters'. Polite authors (Addison being an example) often reinforced the standards of cultured society in matters of taste, manners, morals, and religion.

7 **profound reasonings . . . *metaphysics***] 'Metaphysics' in general refers to inquiry that explores the ultimate nature of reality. Hume is concerned with a metaphysics of the mind. The 'profound reasonings' are those done by metaphysicians, especially in describing the functions of human understanding and explaining human thought. Hume will, upon considering what can be 'pleaded in their behalf', defend these reasonings as far as they deserve to be defended.

8 **artist**] a person proficient in the learned disciplines (the arts).

anatomist . . . painter] Hume presented himself in correspondence with Irish philosopher Francis Hutcheson (1696–1746) as an 'anatomist' in moral philosophy, not a 'painter' (*Letters*, 1: 32–3). His goal was to present an anatomy or dissection of human nature that amounted to a science, rather than to commend virtue or paint broad theories.

VENUS **or an** HELEN] Venus is the Roman goddess of love. Regarding Helen, see also ann. 3.11, '*Iliad*'.

9 **genius of philosophy**] The *genius* (special capacity or disposition) of philosophy is the way it is spread by general learning throughout educated society, having an effect on reasoning and perspective at many levels.

11 **superstitions**] Popular superstitions are common religious beliefs and practices, especially unreflective traditional doctrines—for example, popular observances, forms of sacrifice, and ascetic practices. The paradigm in the case of a supernatural religion is Roman Catholicism. See Hume's essay 'Of Superstition and Enthusiasm'.

12 **catholic remedy**] universally applicable way of alleviating or eliminating the effects of poorly controlled metaphysical speculation.

14 **chimerical**] imaginary; fanciful; visionary—and without ground of truth. Hume wants to explain as much about human nature as can be explained scientifically, confining his conclusions to what experience warrants so as not to produce conclusions that are chimerical.

compass of human understanding] Locke introduced the last chapter in his *Essay* 4.21 by citing 'All that can fall within the compass of Humane Understanding'. For both Locke and Hume, the term 'compass' refers to the 'scope and reach' of human understanding.

late ones, of success] In the Introduction to *THN*, and again in his *Abstract*, Hume mentions Locke, Hutcheson, English philosopher and politician Lord Shaftesbury (Anthony Ashley Cooper, 1671–1713), physician and philosopher Bernard Mandeville (*c*.1670–1733), and Anglican bishop and philosopher Joseph Butler (1692–1752) as among 'some late philosophers in *England*, who have begun to put the science of man on a new footing' by using an experimental method. An oblique reference is also made to philosopher and politician Francis Bacon (1561–1626) as the father of experimental natural philosophy.

delineate the parts] The first two editions of *EHU* (1748 and 1750) contained at this point an additional note in which Hume acknowledged the influence of Hutcheson and expressed an indebtedness to Butler's *Sermons*.

15 **Astronomers . . . phænomena**] Hume frequently uses the word 'phænomenon', which in natural philosophy means any appearance, effect, or operation of a natural body. More generally, it means any appearance or effect present to the mind or any observed operation of the mind.

philosopher . . . arose] The reference is to English astronomer and natural philosopher Isaac Newton (1642–1727), who gave a law-governed explanation of the physical universe, including the motions of comets, planets, the moon, and even of the tides of the sea. (The word 'philosopher' here includes a person who engages in such scientific inquiry.) Newton used the term 'phænomena' in *Mathematical Principles*, book 3 (in the second and later editions) to refer to the observed planetary movements.

Moralists . . . critics, logicians . . . politicians] See ann. 1.2, 'science'. Hume viewed many writers in moral philosophy (possibly including himself, in *THN*) as having serious shortcomings in their analyses of unifying principles. 'Politicians' are those skilled in governing a political state by maintaining public safety, order, and peace, as well as instituting a policy of good morals. 'Logicians' are those who teach how to reason correctly. See ann. 1.2, 'criticism'.

SECTION 2

Hume establishes the elements of the human mind in Sections 2–3. His analysis emphasizes the nature and origin of ideas—as the title of Section 2 indicates.

The basic elements of the mind are *perceptions*. Mental activities such as thinking, sensing, preferring, and believing do not occur in the absence of perceptions. Perceptions are of two types: *impressions* and *ideas*. Impressions are the materials first presented to the mind from which ideas are copied. To sense a dog is to have an *impression*. To remember this same dog or to envision it through an artist's sketch involves having an idea of the dog. All ideas have their origins in impressions.

Both impressions and ideas are either *simple* (not further divisible) or *complex* (combinations divisible into simple perceptions). Every simple idea derives from a prior impression, but complex ideas can be created at will by the imagination. There are no *innate* ideas of any kind in the mind, although there are innate capacities or functions of the mind, such as the imagination, memory, and reason. (For additional discussion of Section 2, see Ed. Intro., §4.1–3.)

1 **perceptions of the mind**] See Ed. Intro., §4.1. Perceptions are the items present to the mind when a person is thinking, feeling, perceiving, desiring, etc. In Hume's philosophy 'perception' carries no suggestion of something beyond the perception itself—such as an object being perceived. Hume is introducing a body of terminology that

derives from and refines Locke's. Of special historical importance is Hume's substitution of 'perception' for Locke's 'idea'. (See Locke, *Essay*, Epistle; 1.1.8; 2.1.23; 2.8.8; 4.1.1.)

Section 2 is a significant revision of *THN* 1.1.1–3. In *THN* 1.2.6.7 Hume said that 'nothing is ever really present with the mind but its perceptions or impressions and ideas, and that external objects become known to us only by those perceptions they occasion'.

1 **disease or madness**] Hume's statement that exceptions to his criteria are found when the mind is disordered raises questions about a possible inadequacy in the criteria: these disordered perceptions seem to have a different and unexplained status. See, similarly, problems introduced by his comment on 'one particular shade of blue' at *EHU* 2.8. On both problems, see Ed. Intro., §4.1–3.

3 **different from the usual**] Hume is defining 'impression' so that it gains a specific sense suitable to his philosophy. The 'usual' meaning of 'impression' is any strong effect on the mind resulting from the influence of something.

4 **absolute contradiction**] Hume is not asserting that people cannot utter a contradiction, but only that contradictory ideas cannot be coherently formulated or combined. A non-mountainous mountain or four-sided triangle cannot be coherently formulated. The imagination only allows us to combine any string of *non*-contradictory ideas coherently—as the examples of a golden mountain and a virtuous horse indicate. (See Ed. Intro., §4.2–3.)

7 **organ . . . sensation**] Organs of sensation are sensory capacities in the body, such as touch and vision.

LAPLANDER] Lapland is a region of northern Scandinavia above the Arctic Circle that ranges over the Kola Peninsula of north-west Russia. The Laplanders or Lapps inhabited the region. They were traditionally nomadic and often isolated from the activities of other cultures and governments.

no notion of . . . wine] People who have had no exposure to wine have no idea how it tastes, just as 'a blind man can form no notion of colours'. The point of these examples is that a person must have the relevant experience in order for any conception or idea about the world to come before the mind.

8 **particular shade of blue**] See Ed. Intro., §4.2–3 and Hume's nearly identical treatment of the problem in *THN* 1.1.1.10.

general maxim] axiom or fundamental principle. The general maxim that simple ideas are always derived from correspondent impressions was introduced at 2.6. That Hume will not throw away his maxim because he has discovered a single reverse phenomenon is not surprising, considering the method of experimentalism that he follows.

9 **metaphysical reasonings**] Despite his criticisms of certain types of metaphysics, Hume's own reflections in *EHU* would, in his sense, be *metaphysical*—a term he used to cover inquiry into causation, identity, liberty and necessity, God, space and time, etc.

without any meaning or idea] Hume maintains that words lack meaning unless they refer to ideas that are traceable to parent impressions. See Ed. Intro., §4.

n. 1 **innate ideas**] These ideas are inborn concepts that are not the products of experience. Hume denies that ideas arise other than by experience. On the whole, Hume follows Locke's philosophy, in which the human mind has inborn *capacities* for knowledge but no inborn *ideas* (*Essay*, esp. 1.2.1, 5, 8, 14–17, 21–4; 1.3.15–19), although in *Abstract* 6 Hume puts some distance between his views and Locke's on the nature of ideas.

n. 1 **schoolmen**] The schoolmen are scholastic theologians and philosophers of the medieval and early modern periods. See ann. 8.27, 'the schools'.

SECTION 3

The imagination, though free to combine ideas as it sees fit, also typically operates naturally to relate ideas in fixed ways. One type of idea routinely introduces another type of idea. Thus, the imagination is methodical, despite its freedom to combine ideas. Three principles of association (or connection) explain this phenomenon: *resemblance*, *contiguity* (in time or place), and *causation*. These principles arrange ideas in organized patterns, allowing for regularity in the way in which ideas enter and exit the mind.

Once this account of the association of ideas (found in 3.1–3) is in hand, it can be applied to the unity and connectedness found in literary and historical writings. This discussion occurs in Section 3 because assorted types of literary composition acquire their forceful and convincing character by the manner in which the authors of these works employ the principles of association. This application is summarized in Ed. Intro., §4.4.

> **ASSOCIATION OF IDEAS**] A native capacity for associating—so that the awareness of one type of idea naturally fosters an awareness of another idea—was a recurrent topic of interest in Hume's time. Section 3, in its early paragraphs, is a pruning and reshaping of *THN* 1.1.4–6.
>
> 1 **wandering reveries . . . dreams**] daydreaming or imaginative musings. Even under these 'loosest and freest' conditions, regular connections exist among the series of ideas. See Hume's comment at *EHU* 5.10: 'Nothing is more free than the imagination . . .'.
>
> **at adventures**] at random, without design, or by chance.
>
> 2 **class all the principles**] Hume's innovation was to delineate *universal* principles of association. He sought to explain how otherwise loose and disconnected ideas are associated in a regular and predictable manner.
>
> 2–3 **three principles**] These 'three principles of connexion' comprise the framework of principles in Hume's account of the association of ideas. He acknowledges that 'this enumeration' may not seem complete, and he apparently treats his proposal as a scientific hypothesis to be put to the test.
>
> 3–5 **passions and imagination**] Hume now begins to examine the role of principles of association in narrative compositions. Using traditional categories and principles, he argues against attempts to splice different genres or species of literature into a single composition.
>
> 5 **compositions of genius**] Hume believes that principles of association steer the imagination of artists. In *THN* 1.1.7.15 he characterized the associations of the imagination as a form of 'genius'—that is, 'a kind of magical faculty in the soul' that brings together ideas through the principle of resemblance.
>
> 6 **kind of Unity**] See Ed. Intro., §4.4 and ann. 3.10, '*Unity* of Action'. Hume here begins to use traditional theories of unity of action to argue against mixing different types of literature.

7 OVID] The Roman poet Ovid (1st c. BC–1st c. AD) wrote *Metamorphoses*, which recounts legends about transformations or metamorphoses (bodies taking new shapes), from the earliest of times to the age of Julius Caesar (1st c. BC). The work attains narrative continuity, variety in its stories, and unity through the overarching idea of metamorphosis—the feature that makes every account *resemble* the previous and the subsequent account.

9 **govern futurity**] Knowledge of cause and effect allows a person to predict and plan for the future.

10 ***Unity* of *Action*, about which all critics**] apparently a reference to Aristotelian and neoclassical accounts of unity. Hume uses these accounts, together with his three principles of association, to discuss unity in drama, poetry, and history. Unity of time, place, and action have often been distinguished. For a useful general account, see English poet John Dryden (1631–1700), *An Essay of Dramatick Poesie* (*Works*, 17: 16–19, 36–7, 46–7), which contains a number of references.

accuracy of philosophy] presumably a reference to the theory of principles of association.

n. 5 ARISTOTLE] The passage from Aristotle may be translated, 'A plot is not unitary, as some suppose, in virtue of being about one individual. For many, indeed countless, things happen to the individual from which there is no single outcome. Likewise, many are the actions of an individual, out of which no unitary action ensues.'

epic poetry] On unity in an epic and also its connection to tragedy, see Aristotle, *Poetics* 1461^{b}26–1462^{b}15.

11 **species of painting**] Poetry can be a type of painting because Hume has a broad sense of painting as artistic representation in general.

Iliad] Homer (9th–8th c. BC) relates an episode in the Trojan War that reveals the tragic consequences of the wrath of Achilles. Hector leads the Trojans out of battle, but then later kills Achilles' friend Patroclus (bks. 11–17). Achilles avenges the death by killing Hector (bks. 19–24). Hector's death serves as the vengeance of Menelaus for the injury received when Paris escaped with Helen. Though a pawn of the gods, her departure is the precipitating cause of the Trojan War. In Troy she becomes Paris' wife, bearing him several children, all of whom die in infancy. Hume considers this work to conform to his account of principles of association and to have sufficient unity of action.

Henriade] French philosopher and man of letters Voltaire (François Marie Arouet, 1694–1778) wrote *La Henriade*, an epic poem whose hero is Henry of Navarre, later Henri IV of France (1553–1610). The poem treats the siege of Paris, the assassination of Henri III (1551–89), and Henri IV's entry into Paris. Voltaire extols the virtues of Henri IV, France's last tolerant king.

12 **trace the causes**] In a narration one understands the sequence of events by understanding the causes that link the prominent events, which Hume depicts through the model of a causal chain.

oblique narration . . . *Odyssey* and *Æneid*] The use of Homer and Roman poet Virgil (1st c. BC) as models of storytelling was popular when Hume wrote. By 'oblique narration' Hume means the telling of a story, not through the narrator, but through a character in retrospect. In the *Odyssey* the story is framed around Odysseus' struggles to return home after the end of the Trojan War. In Virgil's

Aeneid the divine origins of the Romans are presented through the adventures and struggles of Aeneas in his attempt to reach home after the Trojan War. The action of both the *Odyssey* and the *Aeneid* involves central figures in the midst of their journeys.

Scottish clergyman and rhetorician Hugh Blair (1718–1800), in *Lectures on Rhetoric* 42, provides commentary on this oblique narration in both of these works: 'In the narration of the poet . . . it is not material, whether he relate the whole story in his own character, or introduce some of his personages to relate any part of the action that had passed before the poem opens. Homer follows the one method in his Iliad, and the other in his Odyssey; Virgil has, in this respect, imitated the conduct of the Odyssey'.

Hume and Blair are pairing the *Odyssey* and the *Aeneid* because the works are of similar structure. See also the elaborate account of the unity of action and themes related to these works in English poet and translator Alexander Pope (1688–1744), Preface to the *Iliad* and 'A General View of the Epic Poem and of the *Iliad* and *Odyssey*. Extracted from *Bossu*' (*Twickenham Edition*, 7: 3–25; 9: 3–24); the latter also contains a discussion of the *Aeneid*.

14 PELOPONNESIAN war] The Peloponnesian War between Athens and Sparta (431– 404 BC) was among the most decisive events in ancient history. The Greek historian Thucydides (5th c. BC) maintained that Sparta's fear of Athens' developing power was the primary cause of the war.

siege of ATHENS] The Siege of Athens occurred at the end of the Peloponnesian War. Subjected to a Spartan trap from land and sea, the city had no adequate defence against starvation. Athenians stood firm in heroic defiance, but the starvation increased to intolerable proportions and Athens was forced to accept Sparta's dictation of the terms of surrender. Xenophon, *Hellenica* 2.2; Plutarch, *Lives*, 'Lysander' 13–15; Diodorus Siculus, *The Library of History* 13.107.

death of ALCIBIADES] In his younger years politician and military commander Alcibiades (5th c. BC) was considered among the most talented and promising Athenians. He was superbly educated and blessed with the gifts needed for political success. However, after every major accomplishment Alcibiades suffered a tragic failure. The Persian governor, while under Spartan influence, had him murdered. His death by darts and arrows is graphically described by the biographer Plutarch (1st–2nd c. AD), *Lives*, 'Alcibiades' 39.

17 MILTON] English poet John Milton's (1608–74) *Paradise Lost* deals with the biblical story of creation. The subject of the work is human temptation, disobedience, and the consequent loss of Paradise. Throughout the work, divine providence is a unifying factor in what would otherwise appear to be disconnected events.

battle of PHARSALIA] Pharsala, mentioned also at *EHU* 10.28, was a city near which Julius Caesar conquered Roman military commander Pompey (1st c. BC) in 48 BC. In this battle, called Pharsalia (from the name of the region around the town), Caesar fought on the right wing and Marc Antony (1st c. BC) the left.

miraculous] On the nature of the miraculous, see Section 10 below.

18 foreign to each other] In *THN* 2.2.8.17–18 and *DIS* 4.10–14 Hume briefly discusses problems of foreign elements inappropriately mixed together. See his treatment there of Matthew Prior's *Alma* and *Solomon*.

SECTION 4

In Part 1 Hume observes that two types of statement or proposition need to be distinguished: those of fact and those of relations between ideas. The latter are truths of mathematics and logic (e.g. 'Triangles contain three angles'). These truths are beyond doubt or refutation and are immune to disproof by appeal to experience. They are statements exclusively about our ideas, not about the world. By contrast, statements of fact (e.g. 'The sun will rise tomorrow') are about the world and are known only through experience. These statements are merely probable; even when well confirmed, they could turn out to be false. Thought alone can never tell us whether statements about matters of fact are either true or false. Our knowledge of relations of ideas is not problematic, but whether we *know* matters of fact is an intricate philosophical problem. No matter of fact can be *demonstrated* to be true; and yet we are confident of many factual beliefs such as those gained in immediate experience and those retained in memory. The nature of the evidence that assures us of matters of fact therefore deserves the most careful study, as does the reliability of matter-of-fact claims.

In Part 2 a problem now called the problem of induction is treated: What form of evidence, if any, assures us that a matter-of-fact statement is true, given that the statement cannot be entirely confirmed in experience? All matter-of-fact reasoning is based on the relation of cause and effect and involves inference from experience, not inference directly from reason or the understanding. The assurance we have about factual reasoning comes from this causal relation; we readily infer effects from causes. But what warrants belief in these conclusions? 'What is the foundation of all conclusions from experience?' (4.14). This foundation is not provided by demonstrative reasoning, but it cannot be provided by matter-of-fact reasoning either, because that appeal would beg the question at issue. In the end it seems that factual conclusions are '*not* founded on reasoning, or any process of the understanding' (4.15).

For additional details of Hume's arguments in this section, especially in Part 2, see Ed. Intro., § 5.1–4.

OPERATIONS OF THE UNDERSTANDING] Section 4 and Part 1 of Section 5 form a connected unit of argument. They are parallel in several respects to *THN* 1.3.2, 4. More generally, Sections 4–7 are Hume's considerably revised versions of *THN* 1.3, entitled 'Of Knowledge and Probability'.

1 *Relations of Ideas* and *Matters of Fact*] See Ed. Intro., § 5.1. The distinction between these two types of proposition or object of human reason is found in many philosophers. For instance, Malebranche differentiated relations between ideas and relations between things. Hume and Malebranche (*Search after Truth* 6.1.5) both cite arithmetic, algebra, and geometry as prime examples of disciplines dealing with relations of ideas. EUCLID] See ann. 7.2, 'proposition in EUCLID'.

2 **contrary . . . is still possible**] Hume is making a logical point: in the case of propositions that are necessarily true, their contraries cannot be coherently conceived. By contrast, the contraries of propositions about matters of fact can always be conceived. Both 'The sun will rise tomorrow' and 'The sun will not rise tomorrow' are possibly true and make perfectly good sense, even if only one is in fact true. (Hume is not, of course, supposing that a statement of fact and its opposite can be true simultaneously.)

3 **little cultivated, either by the ancients or moderns**] To say 'little cultivated' is not
to say there were no predecessors. Hume may mean that analysis of induction had
been inadequately treated by philosophers. Among modern philosophers questions
about evidence in general had been prominently discussed by French philosopher
René Descartes (1596–1650) in his *Meditations* and Locke in his *Essay*. Among the
ancients, physician and philosopher Sextus Empiricus (2nd–3rd c. AD) rejected induction on grounds that the particulars omitted in an induction may turn out to render
false any universal formed on the basis of the merely partial evidence (*Outlines of
Pyrrhonism* 2.15).

implicit faith] An implicit faith is a deeply rooted trust in the judgement or authority of faculties, sentiments, or parties.

4 **founded on the relation of *Cause* and *Effect***] See Ed. Intro., §§ 5.2–6.1.

entirely precarious] 'Entirely precarious' here means either without evidence or with
merely a slenderness of evidence that yields small assurance and little security.

6 **reasonings *a priori***] processes of thinking that are independent of experience.

examination of its sensible qualities] Several of Hume's predecessors had observed
that causality is unperceivable, that it is known only by repetition in experience and
experimentation, or that we do not discover necessary connections in experience. See
English philosopher and clergyman Joseph Glanvill (1636–80), *Scepsis Scientifica* 23,
25; Irish bishop and philosopher George Berkeley (1685–1753), *Principles* 1.32, 103,
and *Three Dialogues*, Dials. 1–2; Irish natural philosopher Robert Boyle (1627–91), *The
Christian Virtuoso* (*Works*, 5: 526–8).

ADAM] See the commentary on Adam in Ed. Intro., § 5.3; and cf. *Abstract* 11–14; *DIS*
2.47; *NHR* 1.6; and *THN* 2.1.6.9.

7 **pieces of marble**] This example of two smooth pieces of marble was a widely cited
instance of what Hume here calls adherence—and calls cohesion at 4.12 below. How
to explain the cohesion of physical particles—the cement holding them together—
was a fundamental scientific problem of the late 17th century. Hume's point is that
causal relations that were once unknown can be discovered by experimental investigation; the need for experience is less easy to see in the case of known and familiar
cases of causation (e.g. colliding billiard balls) that have never been puzzling or in
need of some form of discovery.

natural philosophy] When Hume wrote, this term was effectively synonymous with
'natural science' (referring to the scientific study of the properties and powers of
natural entities).

loadstone] A lodestone is a rich iron ore known for its magnetic qualities. In free
position it directs itself to the earth's poles. Early compasses were constructed from
pieces of a lodestone.

secret structure of parts] unintentionally hidden or unknown conditions. Hume
believes that we can know the effects caused by items such as bread or a lodestone,
yet not know what hidden or unknown part of the item is the causal agent. The
observable qualities (colour, shape, smell, and the like) of bread, gunpowder, and the
lodestone may not be causally relevant, and the hidden qualities may alone be relevant. When we penetrate to the hidden qualities, we establish a more fine-grained
causal relationship of the sort Hume describes in Sections 4 and 7.

8 **impulse**] collision or impact—a contact that causes motion. See also *EHU* 4.10, 12;
5.5, 11; 6.4; 7.6, 21, 25.

8 **influence of custom**] The custom mentioned is a psychological habit of the mind, not the custom of a culture. It is universally the case that people become accustomed to one ball causing another ball to move on impact.

12 **ultimate cause**] Philosophers, here including physical scientists, were divided during Hume's period about the nature of causes and forces in nature. Hume is maintaining that cautious reasoners respect the scientific evidence, know the limits of their understanding, and withhold claims about knowledge of deeper causes. See further the discussion of the occasionalists in ann. 7.21–4.

greater simplicity] a reference to the methodological principle known as Ockham's Razor, which asserts that one ought not multiply entities in an explanation beyond those actually needed. That is, one should admit as few principles, causes, or explanations as are needed to explain the phenomenon. In *Dialogues* 5.9 (and cf. *THN* 3.3.1.10) Hume states the principle as follows: 'To multiply causes, without necessity, is indeed contrary to true philosophy'.

general causes] Hume takes the goal of science to be finding these general causes, which are the most general laws of nature. At some point in the process of scientific discovery and explanation, a scientist can go no further in the search for causes than general principles beyond which we cannot reasonably expect to find a more general principle (that is, a more general causal law). See also 'ultimate causes and principles' almost immediately below.

Elasticity, gravity, cohesion . . . impulse] 'Cohesion of parts' of matter refers to the phenomenon of the parts of solid bodies adhering or sticking together; see ann. 4.7, 'pieces of marble'. Scientific work on elasticity, gravity, communication of motion, and cohesion sought such general causes. Isaac Newton was an important source for the scientific concepts and principles mentioned in this passage and the next few paragraphs.

ultimate causes and principles] Hume's idea of an experimental (or experience-based) philosophy was rooted in methods designed to determine nature's ultimate causes and principles in the sense of basic general laws or uniformities. Hume does not think our ignorance so vast that we should not be comfortable with what can be learned by scientific investigation; yet we should avoid the temptation to *speculate* about ultimate causes.

13 **mixed mathematics**] mathematical applications in physical theory, as in mechanics. 'Mixed' contrasts with 'pure'. Newton argued that the principles of mechanics can be presented in a mathematical system, but that statements of the ultimate principles (laws) are based on empirical testing. See the Newtonian explanation of mixed mathematics in Dutch mathematician and philosopher James s'Gravesande (1688–1742), *Mathematical Elements of Natural Philosophy*, Preface (1: ii) and 'An Oration concerning Evidence' (1: xxxix).

discovery of the law] A mathematically expressible statement qualifies as a scientific law only if empirical evidence supports it. Exact mathematical formulations do not ensure the certainty of a physical theory, all parts of which are subject to future correction or disconfirmation.

14 *reasonings concerning matter of fact*] See Ed. Intro., §5.2–5, for an explanation of Hume's famous discussion of the problem of induction.

16 **secret powers**] hidden causes (but not hidden by design). Hume does not mean that the human mind can never discover qualities that presently are not known. Careful

scientific work or new inventions such as the telescope may lead to the discovery. However, as long as these qualities remain hidden, we cannot explain sensible qualities in terms of them.

medium] the middle term or premiss in a syllogism (that is, a valid deductive argument with two premisses and a conclusion), which functions as a ground of proof or inference. 'Hume is a human' is the medium in the following argument: All humans are mortal; Hume is a human; therefore, Hume is mortal. Hume is looking for a medium that will connect what we have experienced and what we can justifiably expect to experience in the future.

18 **two kinds**] See ann. 4.1, '*Relations of Ideas and Matters of Fact*' for this division into these two types of proposition and its implications.

implies no contradiction] See the discussion of propositions in ann. 4.2. We can conceive propositions about matters of fact to be false even when the propositions are true. False propositions about matters of fact imply no contradiction.

19 **probable only**] Compare the arguments by French philosopher and scientist Pierre Gassendi (1592–1655) that it is not possible to demonstrate the universality of propositions arrived at by induction (*Exercises Against the Aristotelians* 2.5.5); see also his views about probability and the criterion of truth (*The Syntagma*, Logic 2.5).

19–20 **experimental conclusions**] 'Experimental' here carries the meaning of based on experience so as to provide a basis for sound (probabilistic) generalization. Experimental philosophy relies on observation and experiment to find correct causal generalizations (see *THN* Introduction 7; 1.3.15.11). Hume uses 'experimental' to include the observational and the experiential.

20 **guide of human life**] Compare Joseph Butler's well-known statement 'Probability is the very guide of life' (*Analogy*, Introduction). Hume's emphasis on natural belief, causal inference, experimentation, and probable evidence as imperfect shows some similarity to Butler's analyses (as well as to Cicero's *De natura deorum* 1.5.12).

same taste and relish] We expect the same taste from eggs when they are prepared in the same way, but different conditions and preparations can give the eggs different tastes; we may not be able to determine that the taste will be different merely by visual inspection of the eggs.

one instance] Hume is arguing that we cannot infer conclusions from a single instance in the same way we can reliably make inferences from a hundred instances. He is only 'open to instruction' in the sense that he is challenging his readers to produce a case in which a person can infer an effect from a cause when the person has never previously had any experience with this type of cause.

21 **intuitive . . . demonstrative**] The intuitive is known immediately to the apprehending mind without inference or reasoning; the demonstrative is a series of intuitive comparisons of ideas so that a conclusion can be established by reason alone. Like Descartes (*Rules for the Direction of the Mind* and *Discourse on the Method* 2) and Locke (*Essay* 4.2.1–14), Hume maintains that experimental methods yield probability, not intuitive or demonstrative certainty or knowledge. See Hume's use of these terms at *EHU* 4.1, 16, 18, 21; n. 10; n. 18; and *THN* 1.3.1.2; 1.3.7.3; 1.3.14.35.

nature may change . . . arguments . . . can prove] Hume means 'prove' in the sense of conclusively demonstrate. Nothing guarantees that the regularities that we have found in nature will not change (and, of course, we might find new information about a type of regularity that alters our understanding of the regularity, as when we modify the formulation of a scientific law).

SECTION 5

Having established in Section 4 that the mind does not reason to its inductive conclusions, the 'principle' of the mind underlying inductive inferences will now be delineated.

In Part 1 it is shown that 'this principle is CUSTOM or HABIT' (5.8). Thus, a psychological explanation of inductive inference provides a sceptical solution to the sceptical doubts raised in Section 4 about inductive inference. Such inference rests entirely on customary associations between causes and effects—not on reason or the understanding. These customary associations arise from the repetition in experience of types of conjoined items— for example, bread and the nutrition that it supplies. This philosophy renders custom 'the great guide of life' (5.6) and a vital feature of human nature.

Part 2 presents an account of the nature of *belief* and concentrates on beliefs that certain effects will follow from certain causes. The many past instances that constitute our experience of a constant conjunction lead us to infer that an effect will occur whenever an associated cause appears. This belief—indeed, all belief—is analysable as a specific type of sentiment or feeling that accompanies the idea that is believed. Unlike the experience of fiction and merely imagined items, belief is a 'vivid, lively, forcible, firm, steady conception of an object' that imagination alone can never achieve (5.12). Belief does not alter the *content* of what is conceived (that is, the idea that accompanies the feeling), only the *way* in which it is conceived. Thus, to have a belief is not only to have an idea, but to have it in a singularly vivid, lively, and forcible manner. (For additional discussion of Section 5, see Ed. Intro., § 5.5–6.)

1 **philosophic sage**] In some ancient philosophical writings the ideal wise person or sage provided a model of virtue, self-sufficiency, autonomy, and happiness. Such views were found among the Stoics and Epicureans. For example, the Roman Stoic philosopher Seneca (1st c. AD) analysed how to better the human condition by introducing forms of tranquillity that elevate a person ('On Tranquillity of Mind' 9.2.4, in *Moral Essays*), and Epicurus of Athens (4th–3rd c. BC, founder of the Epicurean school) recommended an untroubled life free from disturbance as the highest good (*Epicurus Reader*, texts 3.85–7; 4.128–31; 9; 16.53).

EPICTETUS, **and other** STOICS] The Stoic school or Stoa flourished from the third century BC until the second century AD. The Stoics, among them the freed slave Epictetus (1st–2nd c. AD), taught that the primary virtue is to live harmoniously with nature and suggested that the good or wise person remains free of control by the passions and the demands of public life. Much in Epictetus' teaching centred round personal self-examination. See *Discourses* 1.6.

system of selfishness] The reference is to the Stoic preference, esp. in Epictetus, for a focus on cultivation of the self (self-mastery, self-salvation, and the like), as distinct from pleasure and self-indulgence. Epictetus, like Seneca, honoured virtue rather than pleasure. For Epictetus' views, see the previous annotation and *Discourses* 2.11; *Fragments* 14; for Seneca's views, see 'De beneficiis' 4.1–3, in *Moral Essays*, where Seneca criticizes the Epicureans for viewing virtue as the vehicle of pleasure.

ACADEMIC or SCEPTICAL philosophy] 'Academic' is the name of a type of sceptic. (See Ed. Intro., §8.1–2, and ann. Section 12.) Academic sceptics recommended doubt and suspense of judgement in contexts that Hume generally approved. See ann. 12.21–3; see also Cicero, *Academica* 1.12.45; 2.18.59; 2.31–32.99–104; 2.46.141.

groundless reproach and obloquy] Ancient philosophers such as Epictetus (*Discourses* 1.5, 'Against the Academics') and modern philosophers such as Malebranche (*The Search after Truth* 1.20.3; 2.3.5) harshly judged academic sceptics.

2 principle of equal weight and authority] This principle helps to explain the surprising title placed on Section 5: 'Sceptical Solution of these Doubts'. The solution is not to provide an argument that justifies the missing step in causal (inductive) inference, but to describe the features of mind that lead it to behave as it does. At 5.5 Hume reveals that 'This principle is CUSTOM or HABIT'. From one perspective, Hume is denying that inductive inference is a form of reasoning (because it is based on custom or habit rather than reason), but from another perspective he is giving an account of the psychological basis of induction as a form of reasoning.

3 sudden into this world] Compare the example of Adam at 4.6; see further *Abstract* 11–14; *DIS* 2.47; *THN* 2.1.6.9.

5 constant conjunction] Hume provides a more elaborate account of the constant conjunction of events in *THN* (1.1.1.8; 1.3.6.3–4, 8, 11–16; 1.3.11.11; 1.3.12.25; 1.3.14.12, 31–3; 1.3.15.1), where the notion is analysed in terms of repeated and uniform contiguity and succession. In *EHU* uniform succession is emphasized.

n. 8 TIBERIUS or a NERO] The Julio-Claudian emperors began with Tiberius' ascendancy in 14 AD and ended with Nero's death in 68 AD. In *EPM* 5.34 Hume makes a similar comment and invokes the accounts of their intrigues found in the Roman historian and biographer Suetonius (1st–2nd c. AD) and the Roman politician and historian Cornelius Tacitus (1st–2nd c. AD). Both historians describe Nero and Tiberius in highly unfavourable terms.

7 pompous buildings] splendid, grand, magnificent structures.

8 soul] mind. Operations include reason, passion, imagination, etc.

natural instincts] Hume classified these operations of the mind as instincts, whereas other philosophers saw at least some of the same operations as functions of reason. Instinctive behaviour had generally been contrasted with voluntary behaviour and sometimes with thought (so that instinct operates without thought). However, Hume does not exclude either voluntariness or thought, because in his analysis even functions of the mind such as reason have an instinctual basis. See further Section 9 (esp. 9.6) on instinct in animals and humans.

9 abstract sciences . . . different taste] Hume sometimes presents an abstract science as a science such as mathematics, the conclusions of which are derived from reason rather than experience. Here, however, he seems to mean a theoretical and difficult philosophical inquiry. '[R]eaders of a different taste' are presumably those less enamoured of abstract inquiry.

PART 2] This part corresponds in important respects to *THN* 1.3.5–10.

fiction and belief] The content of a fiction may be identical to the content of a belief, yet the way a person experiences them will be very different.

12 *definition* of this sentiment] Belief *is* this sentiment, accompanied by an idea that supplies the content of what is believed (what Hume calls 'realities' in this paragraph).

Hume is here interested in the nature of the sentiment, which he describes but does not define.

15 **present purpose**] Hume uses the fiction–belief distinction in the example involving the picture (in this section) and the example involving religion (in the next section). As noted at *EHU* 5.13, he is exploring 'other operations of the mind analogous to' the distinction between mere fictions and the intensity, weight, and influence of belief. The presence of a picture is weighty and influential by comparison to a mere thought or fiction about the picture.

16 **plead in excuse for the mummeries**] defend certain religious rituals, ceremonies, rites, or performances. Protestants often used the term 'mummeries' derogatorily to suggest ceremonial masquerading. It was associated with superstitious Roman Catholic beliefs and rituals such as transubstantiation, or the belief that the host (the wafer) becomes the body of Christ when consecrated. Hume apparently believes that the mummeries enliven devotion and increase fervour in comparison to distant 'immaterial objects', such as the depictions of God in philosophical and theological writings.

immaterial objects] objects that are incorporeal or abstract.

shadow out] represent by an imperfect image; here, in particular, to use pictures, images, icons, statues, and the like as sensible representations of an object of devotion or worship.

present impression must concur] In each case that Hume has presented to illustrate the effect of resemblance, a resemblance has been combined with a present impression, such as an impression of a picture or an impression of a performance with actors.

foregoing principle] the principle regarding the effects of resemblance.

n. 9 de finibus] While passing an afternoon at the Academy, Piso (a character in Cicero's dialogue) discourses on the power of the setting to intensify emotions and focus thinking. Piso discusses how his ideas of the ancients are enlivened by the Academy itself, thus illustrating how contiguity enlivens ideas. He then offers the following comment quoted by Hume:

> Why are we more affected, asked Piso, when we learn that the places we see were often frequented by famous men than we are when we hear a report of the same men's exploits or read a written account of them? Is it a natural endowment we have, or is it some sort of aberration? I feel the effect now, for example. For I am put in mind of Plato, who we are told was the first to practice disputation here; indeed the adjoining gardens not only bring him back to mind but seem to place the man himself before my eyes. Here is Speusippus, here Xenocrates, and here his follower Polemo: The bench we see over there was Polemo's. In the same way, even when looking at our own senate building—I mean the Hostilia, not the new building, which looks slighter to me since it was enlarged—I used to think of Scipio, Cato, Laelius, and especially my grandfather. So great is the suggestive power of places, that it is no accident that they shape our memory training.

18 **relicts**] relics; items revered because they belonged to a holy person.

20 **operation of the mind**] the function of the mind in a causal inference from an effect to its cause or a cause to its effects. The mind moves from awareness of a presently

experienced object to belief in an expected effect or to belief in a no longer experienced cause of a presently experienced object.

21 **pre-established harmony**] This term came to prominence in philosophy through the 'harmonie préetablie' of German philosopher and mathematician Gottfried Wilhelm Leibniz (1646–1716). Hume names Leibniz (in *Dialogues* 10.6) as the author of a closely related view. Leibniz held that God created every individual atomic unit in the universe so that whatever happens to the atom is the result of its nature (*Leibniz–Arnauld Correspondence*, 23 Mar. 1690). Leibniz applied his deterministic thesis to the mind–body problem: 'The soul follows its own laws, and the body follows its own likewise, and they agree with each other by virtue of the harmony pre-established between all substances' (*Monadology*, n. 78). Leibniz further claimed that the perceptions of the world that occur simultaneously in many different minds were similar not because those perceptions were caused in percipients by objects that they all perceived, but rather because God pre-established the occurrence of these perceptions in them at the same time.

Hume's use of 'pre-established harmony' is witty, but the analogy is not frivolous. Hume is pointing out that we have the ability to form beliefs that correspond to the course of nature; our beliefs about causal sequences are harmonious with causation in nature because of the principle of custom.

final causes] This term derives from Aristotle's account of the four causes (material, final, formal, and efficient), which he developed as an explanation of the types of change that occur in nature (*Physics* 198ª14–ᵇ9; *Metaphysics* 1013ª24–ᵇ28). The final cause is the end towards which some change is directed. As with 'pre-established harmony' (see immediately above), the term 'final cause' can refer to the purposes, ends, goals, or designs found in the universe as a whole. Hume rejects the doctrine of final causes, but many philosophers still accepted it at the time he wrote.

22 **fallacious deductions of our reason**] Hume is pointing out that reason makes mistakes. Given the narrow set of functions that Hume assigns to reason (see Ed. Intro., § 5.1, 3–8), that faculty cannot be the one that infers effects from causes. Hume thinks that we are *habituated* to infer effects from causes.

SECTION 6

Probability is the likelihood that an object or event of a certain type will be followed by another object or event of a different type. Probable reasoning (that is, inductive reasoning) does not amount to a demonstration and is not accompanied by certainty, because there is only a likelihood of the second object or event following the first.

There is no such thing as *chance* in the world, but our ignorance of the real cause of events often suggests chance as the explanation of these events. The better perspective is that some events are more probable than others. Some sequences of events are entirely uniform (and thus highly probable), whereas other sequences are quite irregular (and thus not highly probable). Causes are entirely uniform sequences (constant conjunctions), yet on many occasions an expected effect does not follow from an event that normally causes it. When the expected effect does not follow the event that usually causes it, we inquire into the underlying condition that has prevented the expected effect from occurring in this particular case.

In general, we assign to an event a particular weight or likelihood of bringing about an effect. When a type of event, such as the rolling of dice, has a measurable outcome, we think in terms of the probability of that outcome. For example, we think in terms of the probability of a particular side of a die turning up. Such probabilistic thinking governs much of our thought and action. (For additional discussion of Section 2, see Ed. Intro., § 5.7.)

> PROBABILITY] By 'probability' Hume often means the reasoning from experience discussed in the previous two sections, as contrasted to demonstration. This may explain why Section 6 is positioned prior to Section 7, which continues the themes of causal inference and causation found in Sections 3–5. Section 6 corresponds in important respects to *THN* 1.3.11–13 (see also 1.3.2) and can profitably be read with those sections.
>
> n. 10 **only probable . . . the sun will rise to-morrow**] Hume is not expressing doubt that the sun will rise tomorrow. His point is that there is no demonstrative proof, only a probability, that the sun will rise.
>
> n. 10 ***demonstrations, proofs,*** and ***probabilities***] A demonstration is associated with knowledge (especially mathematical knowledge) and a proof with science (uniform correlations of events ('causes' and 'effects')); merely probable arguments (not-so-uniform correlations), by contrast, yield only opinion or belief. This usage can confuse readers, since 'proofs' are based on probabilities of a special sort, namely those so well confirmed that they cannot be reasonably doubted as expressions of causal relations. Prior to Hume 'probability' had an etymological association with 'proof' that he appears to be attempting to retain without committing himself to the view that all probabilities amount to proofs. *THN* 1.3.11.2 helps explain his usage: Hume there proposes that we 'distinguish human reason into three kinds, viz. *that from knowledge* [rational demonstration or truths of reason], *from proofs* [causal arguments], *and from probabilities* [arguments from mere probability, which are inferior to arguments from universal causation]'. See also *EHU* 10.4 and Ed. Intro., §§ 5.7 and 7.1.
>
> 1 ***Chance***] Chance (the absence of causes; fortuity) was often viewed in philosophy and mathematics as merely the function of human ignorance of real causes; in every so-called chance event causes are actually at work. The ancient contrast between chance and science began to diminish with the rise of accounts of probability, because probabilities could be computed for games of chance, insurance policies, scientific predictions, and the like. The term 'chance' then became associated with unpredictability, luck, fortune, risk, and hazard, rather than with the absence of causes.
>
> 2 **superiority of chances**] When Hume speaks of the 'superiority of chances' he means that, given the available evidence, one event has a greater likelihood of occurrence than another event. Chance and hazard (risking loss in a game of chance) were of interest to mathematicians such as J. Bernoulli (1654–1705) (*Ars conjectandi* 3) and Abraham de Moivre (1667–1754) (*Doctrine of Chances*), who computed a variety of chances in different circumstances with the practical goal of determining where the advantage lies in playing games of chance.
>
> **process of the thought or reasoning**] Hume is discussing quantitative computation and belief based on past frequencies. More generally in his thought, 'probability' is

linked to reasoning, reasonableness, and reasonable belief—a kind of model of common-sense reasonableness that relies on probabilities.

3 **dye . . . particular side**] Numerous works on probability and gaming had used the example of dice to express basic problems and propositions in probability theory. Cf. *THN* 1.3.11.6.

number of sides] on a pair of die.

antagonist] that which is opposite, opposed to, or vies against. In this context one probability successfully vies with another probability, resulting in belief.

nature of belief and opinion] Mere belief, opinion, and probability had often been contrasted with science and knowledge in the history of philosophy.

4 **universal law**] Such a law is causal and known by induction from experience; it there-fore rests on a *proof*, not on a *demonstration*. Newton's law is that gravity is inversely proportional to distance.

purge, or opium a soporific] A purge is a cleansing or scouring medicine, and to purge is to cleanse the body of ill humours. Rhubarb was sometimes used as a purge or medicine to produce evacuations of the bowels. Opium is the juice of the white poppy; it contains morphine and acts as a narcotic. It was sometimes given to patients. Johnson's *Dictionary* ('opium') reports that opium's 'first effect is the making the patient cheerful, as if he had drank moderately of wine; it removes melancholy, excites boldness, and dissipates the dread of danger. . . . It afterward quiets the spirits, eases pain, and disposes to sleep.'

open] clear (and frost-free).

approaches to a certainty] presumably a conclusion based on a causal uniformity (not merely a very high probability). Though 'certainty' is normally not the term one would expect from Hume (as he thinks his experimental method yields probability rather than certainty), this usage makes sense in the light of his distinction between proofs and probabilities.

common theories] 'Received systems' means the leading philosophical theories, which are presumably here the same as 'common theories'. These theories typically treated *knowledge*, but lacked serious treatment of *probability*, which falls short of knowledge. At *Abstract* 4 Hume indicates that the 'common systems' of Locke, Malebranche, and French philosopher-theologians Antoine Arnauld (1612–94) and Pierre Nicole (1625–95) (see *Logic or the Art of Thinking*, Fourth Part, chs. 6–15) all emphasize understanding and demonstration while failing to address questions of 'probabilities, . . . which are our guides even in most of our philosophical specula-tions'. Hume attributes to Leibniz insights about defects in common theories.

SECTION 7

When we say that two causally related objects or events are necessarily connected, what idea of *necessity* is involved? Many philosophers maintain that the necessary connection between cause and effect is a *power* in the cause, but we neither experience such power nor have an outward impression of it. In the absence of an impression of necessary con-nection or power between causally related items, we have no basis for a belief that neces-sity bonds objects or events.

None the less, the idea of necessary connection can be traced to a distinct kind of inward parent impression. This impression is that of the determination of the mind that occurs in inductive inference. This determination of the mind is felt when, after repeated observation of events and their successor events, habit leads us to expect that one type of event will follow the other type. Only when this connection has been established do we make causal inferences. This habit-induced transition from the cause-event to the expected effect-event is something we feel at the time the cause-event occurs. This feeling of determination in the mind *is* the impression of necessary connection. Thus, although we experience no causal necessity in or between causally related events, we do experience a determination of the mind that is the parent impression of the idea of necessary connection.

From this perspective the causal relation can be defined in two ways, depending on whether the definition features a relation among events (a constant conjunction) or a relation in the mind (a necessary connection brought about by awareness of a constant conjunction). (For additional discussion of Section 7, see Ed. Intro., §6.1.)

> OF THE IDEA OF NECESSARY CONNEXION] Section 7 corresponds in important respects to *THN* 1.3.14, which is also entitled 'Of the Idea of Necessary Connexion'.
>
> 1 **clear and determinate**] Hume is presumably following Locke, who regarded the Cartesian language of 'clear and distinct ideas' as unduly difficult to understand. Locke declared that he had *'in most places chose to put determinate or determined, instead of clear and distinct. . . . By determinate, when applied to a simple Idea, I mean that simple appearance, which the Mind has in its view, or perceives in it self* (*Essay*, 'Epistle to the Reader', 13).
>
> **ellipsis . . . scalenum**] An ellipsis is a plain figure—commonly called an oval or an oval figure—that is cut obliquely from the section of a cone, but not parallel to the base (which would be a circle). A scalenum is a scalene triangle, which has sides of unequal length.
>
> 2 **proposition in EUCLID**] The mathematician Euclid (4th–3rd c. BC) wrote a work on geometry that was a standard manual in Hume's era, when geometry was sometimes referred to as 'Euclid'. See the earlier reference to Euclid at 4.1.
>
> **chimera and conceit**] A chimera is a fabrication of the imagination, mere wild fancy or whimsy, or unfounded conception, such as the imagining of a fire-breathing monster with the head of a lion, torso of a goat, and tail of a serpent (the chimera of Greek mythology). A conceit is an imaginative conceiving or fanciful notion.
>
> **throws a bar to**] presents a barrier to, prevents, or obstructs.
>
> **natural philosophy . . . physics**] 'Natural philosophy' was closely associated with 'physics' (see ann. 4.7, 'natural philosophy'). Hume views physics as consisting of systems of natural philosophy that display the nature, powers, motions, and operations of natural bodies.
>
> 4 **simple ideas**] On the nature of simple and complex ideas, see Ed. Intro., §4.2. For the philosophical background of Hume's views on these topics, see Locke, *Essay* 2.2; 2.11.6–7; 2.12; 3.4.6–7.
>
> 6 ***inward* impression**] The *'outward* senses' of vision, touch, hearing, smell, and taste convey no impression of power or necessary connection. Instead, a new inward impression of necessary connection arises in the mind that is not derived from the outward senses; that is, empirical investigation of objects and events will not detect

234

this inner impression. (See Ed. Intro., §6.1.) Locke had acknowledged that we do not observe causal powers through the outward senses, yet was confident that these powers exist, that we can detect them in human agency, and that they are needed to explain causal relations (*Essay*, esp. 4.16.12). Hume is criticizing this theory.

8 **machine . . . concealed from us**] Hume often presents theses about some writers' overambitious claims to know the hidden causes of things. He presumably accepts the idea of a machine in the sense of a system of interacting parts, but not in the sense of a designed system.

discover any power] We never discover powers in bodies, because the notion of power arises only from an internal impression. In ordinary life we project the internal impression onto bodies or events and believe that the power is in these objects. But philosophers appreciate that power is only a subjective property or feeling in the mind, not an objective property in bodies.

n. 12 LOCKE . . . chapter of power] In 'Of Power' Locke writes that: 'The Mind . . . concluding from what it has so constantly observed to have been [the case], that the like Changes will for the future be made, in the same things, by like Agents, and by the like ways . . . and so comes by that *Idea* which we call *Power*' (*Essay* 2.21.1). See the next annotation.

9 **internal power**] For the widespread thesis that the 'operations of our own minds' furnish a basis for 'the idea of power', see Locke, *Essay* 2.1.2–4; 2.7.8; 2.21.1–5; 2.22.2, 10; 2.23.28, 33; 3.6.11; Henry Lee, *Anti-Scepticism; or, Notes upon Each Chapter of Mr. Lock's Essay* 2.19.2–3; Leibniz, *New Essays* 2.21–3; Peter Browne, *The Procedure, Extent, and Limits of Human Understanding*, 387–8. On Locke, cf. ann. above.

idea of reflection] Reflection is the mind's consciousness of its own operations. A detailed account of ideas and impressions of reflection is found in *THN* 1.1.2.1 (see also 2.1.1), but this is his sole reference in *EHU*.

11 **spiritual . . . material one**] This statement of the mind–body problem seems to refer primarily to the dualism of Descartes and his followers, especially Malebranche. Hume here and elsewhere alternates between the language of 'mind' and 'soul'. He maintains that we do not 'know the secret union of soul and body', and do not even know 'the nature of both these substances'. He believes that our experience is limited to the qualities of objects and events and never penetrates to their alleged substance.

13 **palsy**] paralysis (loss of voluntary motion and sense of feeling).

consciousness never deceives] Hume believes that if a perception were present in experience, we would be aware of it and its properties; there are no unconscious perceptions. Consciousness does not deceive in the present case because it never has a perception of power, only an awareness of a constant conjunction. Hume does not deny, however, that we can make erroneous judgements about our perceptions once we think about them; indeed, we may think we have perceived power in an event when we have not.

14 **animal spirits**] nerves. According to some anatomists of Hume's time, the spirit or principle involved in sensation and voluntary motion is accounted for by a nerve fluid (inside nerve-tubes) called animal spirits. This fluid is the material source of nervous transmission in animals and humans.

n. 13 *nisus*] impulse or effort. This idea was developed by Aristotelian philosophers, who held that movement throughout nature derives from the operation of a nisus or principle analogous to desire or endeavour. The nisus drives objects to develop in a specific manner. See also n. 17.

n. 13 **vulgar, inaccurate idea**] 'Vulgar' means common or ordinary, here probably with the connotation of an unsophisticated and inaccurate idea.

21 **invisible intelligent principle**] Hume is referring to appeals to a divine principle, but not necessarily monotheistic appeals. In *NHR* (Introduction, *et passim*), Hume presents the thesis that belief in an 'invisible, intelligent power' has been diffused over people in all nations and ages.

n. 14 Θεὸς ἀπὸ μηχανῆς] This phrase (*deus ex machina* in Latin) means 'god out of a machine'. The expression derives from Hellenic and Roman drama, in which a deity was presented as interceding in human affairs. Playwrights adopted a practice of ending certain dramas by using a mechanical trolley to lower to the stage an actor representing a god who, using superior judgement and commands, solved the problems presented by human situations. The phrase eventually came to refer to an author's use of a contrived or improbable strategy to resolve problems, especially when a supernatural being serves as a mere stopgap that is inadequate to truly resolve a problem.

philosophers] Philosophers who thought that 'the energy of the cause is . . . unintelligible' in the relevant sense include Berkeley and the occasionalists discussed immediately below.

sole cause of every event] In a similar passage in *THN* 1.4.5.31 Hume provides a footnote to 'father *Malebranche* and other *Cartesians*'. His reference there and here is to a group of philosophers influenced by Descartes (once spelled Des Cartes, and hence the term 'Cartesian'), especially the occasionalists, whose most prominent representative was Malebranche. Descartes's philosophy suggests, without concluding, that God is the moving force of bodies, though this moving force is not in the bodies themselves. (See *Principles of Philosophy* 1.21; 2.36, 39, 42; *Objections and Replies*, Fifth Set of Replies [2: 253–5]; Sixth Set of Replies [2: 293–4]). In Malebranche's theory everything takes place because of the intervention of God; no causes other than God exist in nature or in humans. See Malebranche, *The Search after Truth* 6.2.3 and Eluc. 15; French occasionalist philosopher Géraud de Cordemoy (*c*.1620–84), *Six discours*, 'Discours 4—De la première cause du mouvement' (*Œuvres*, 136–40, 143–4, esp. Conclusions 3–4 and Axiom 5); French occasionalist philosopher Louis de La Forge, *Traité de l'esprit de l'homme* 16; and German Cartesian philosopher Johann Clauberg (1622–65), *Opera omnia, Disputationes physicæ* 13, 17–18.

causes . . . **nothing but** *occasions*] Occasionalists maintain that God is the sole cause of motion in bodies and of sensations and voluntary actions. When any object makes contact with any other, the action of God is required at the point of impact, as there is no moving force in bodies. We therefore have no knowledge of causes; we only know that an event occurred *on the occasion of* another event. We call the first item the *cause* and the second the *effect*, but such 'causes' are merely occasions.

excites such a sensation] God produces sensations in the body; external bodies do not cause the sensations.

second our will] The human will is merely the occasion of movement in the body; God causes the movement.

our Maker] Hume is again attributing this view to the occasionalists, who consider God to be the sole cause of the ideas in our mind.

22 **stupendous machine**] To extricate occasionalists (and perhaps other believers in divine providence) from difficulties in their theories, Hume here offers an alternative, namely deism. The deists were late 17th- and early 18th-century figures in France and England who maintained that God contrives the fabric of the world, but does not intervene after Creation.

24 **the Supreme Being**] The reference is again to the occasionalists. Despite his indebtedness to some aspects of their accounts of causation, Hume thinks that the occasionalists' theories take them 'into fairy land'.

reach of our faculties] The reference is again to Malebranche and the occasionalists, who Hume thinks reach beyond experience and evidence. Hume's experimental method does not permit recourse to occult causes.

25 **profound ignorance**] Hume's point is that we are ignorant not only of powers and forces in nature, but of God's powers.

n. 16 **vis inertiæ**] *Vis inertiæ* means force of inertia. It is the natural resistance of a body to a change in its state of motion, or the natural property of a body to retain its state of rest or motion along a straight line. This force explains why a body at rest resists being set in motion, and a body in motion resists changes in direction or speed.

n. 16 **the new philosophy**] The reference is to modern natural philosophy as influenced by developments in science, especially the fruits of Newton. The new philosophy arose in the work of Galileo, Gassendi, Descartes, Hobbes, and Boyle. The philosophy was 'new' as a replacement of prevailing scholastic views.

n. 16 NEWTON . . . **second causes**] Boyle and Newton believed in the reality and efficacy of second causes—that is, material or natural causes, a primary cause being God or that which actuates second causes. Ephraim Chambers (*c*.1680–1740), the encyclopaedist, defines 'second causes' as 'those which derive the power, and faculty of acting, from a first *cause*. Such causes [in the occasionalist philosophy] don't properly act at all; but are acted on: and therefore are improperly called causes: of which kind are all those that we call Natural Causes. . . . second Cause . . . is acted upon by some superior or first Cause, to produce any Effect' (*Cyclopædia*, 'Cause').

'To rob second causes' of any real efficacy means to explain natural causes by reference to something external to them, as Malebranche had done in making God's power responsible for causation.

n. 16 **etherial active fluid**] In writings before the *Principia* Newton appealed to motions and pressures in his account of an ethereal medium of gravitational transmission. In the *Principia* he suspended judgement about both ether and the causal mechanism in gravitation. He argued that gravitational attraction can be explained in terms of a universal mathematical law.

n. 16 DES CARTES **insinuated**] Regarding Descartes's and other Cartesians' hypotheses about the efficacy of the Deity, see ann. 7.21 ff. On the deeper mechanical explanation, see ann. n. 17, 'dispute . . . force of a body'.

n. 16 CLARKE, **and** CUDWORTH] Cambridge philosopher Ralph Cudworth (1617–88) was a significant figure in metaphysical topics of the sort mentioned by Hume, but not a major figure in the scientific controversies discussed in this footnote. Cudworth, Locke, and English philosopher and theologian Samuel Clarke (1675–1729) discussed philosophical issues about whether matter has force, but none adopted occasionalism.

n. 16 **modern metaphysicians**] The modern metaphysicians are supporters of occasionalism either on the Continent or in Britain (subsequent to the time of Locke and Clarke). After the occasionalists Berkeley was the most prominent modern metaphysician not specifically listed. He never had any 'authority in ENGLAND', where his views were universally rejected.

28 **customary transition**] Many modern philosophers prior to Hume maintained that certain properties we believe to be found in objects and events are not really in them (see ann. 12.15, 'primary qualities of extension and solidity'). For example, we believe that coloured and cold objects actually contain these properties, whereas these philosophers thought that we project these properties onto objects and events. Hume is maintaining that the necessity we believe to be in causally related objects and events is merely a mental inference projected outward onto objects and events. Thus, we come to believe these objects to be necessarily connected in somewhat the same way that we believe them to be coloured and cold.

29 **define a cause**] On the nature and importance of these two definitions, see Ed. Intro., § 6.1, final subsection. Hume's gloss on the first definition has puzzled many readers. He says 'in other words' the first definition means '*if the first object had not been, the second never had existed*'. However, his two formulations of the first definition seem more dissimilar than similar in meaning. The first formulation suggests that causes are defined in terms of *sufficient* conditions, the second formulation suggests analysis in terms of *necessary* conditions. Hume's precise message remains a mystery.

n. 17 **dispute . . . force of a body**] The dispute mentioned is between Leibniz (and his followers), on the one hand, and the Cartesians and Newtonians, on the other. Leibniz argued that the force (*vis viva*, or living force) of a body in motion is properly measured by the formula mv^2—that is, the product of mass (m) and velocity (v) squared. Cartesians and Newtonians, including Clarke, defended the simpler formula mv, the product of mass and velocity. These formulae vied for status in mechanics, a dispute sometimes called the '*vis viva* controversy'.

n. 17 **direct mensuration**] Mensuration refers to the act or art of discovering by measurement the properties of bodies. Hume means a direct rather than indirect measurement and examination of 'power, as it is in itself'.

n. 17 **apply to external bodies every internal sensation**] As noted in ann. 7.28, many philosophers held that objects are not truly coloured or cold; such properties are only projected from our minds out onto events or objects. Malebranche mentions the mind's disposition to spread itself onto objects or events by placing on them what it has extracted from itself (*The Search after Truth* 1.12.5; 5.6).

SECTION 8

This section treats freely willed actions. These events are sometimes conceived as free in the sense of independent of the laws of nature, yet all events appear to have causes. If human actions are true expressions of liberty, can they also be caused? Can they be necessitated, that is, determined? This philosophical problem is a struggle over the meaning of the terms 'liberty' and 'necessity'. 'Liberty' means a capacity of acting and forbearing from action, whereas 'necessity' refers to a constant conjunction between a type of cause and a type of effect. Actions are free whenever they flow from a person's own motives and are not constrained by causes that make the person do other than what the person wills to do. Even while free (freely willed), these actions are also determined (necessitated). That is, under the full set of circumstances (including desires and motives), free actions could not have been other than the actions that were performed.

Because these actions are our actions (not those of a divine creator or of impersonal powers in nature), we are responsible for what we do. The conduct is necessitated, yet free. These conclusions are not eccentric and indeed are part of ordinary beliefs about causation and free will. (For additional discussion of Section 8, see Ed. Intro., § 6.2.)

OF LIBERTY AND NECESSITY] Section 8 corresponds in important respects to *THN* 2.3.1–3, the first two sections of which are entitled 'Of Liberty and Necessity'.

2 **long disputed question**] The problem of liberty or free will is ancient, stretching back at least to a discussion in Aristotle's *Nicomachean Ethics* and to the deterministic atomism of Lucretius (see ann. 10.30) and Democritus (5th–4th c. BC). Landmark discussions of freedom and determinism in modern philosophy before Hume appear in English philosopher Thomas Hobbes (1588–1679); Anglican bishop John Bramhall (1594–1663); English theologian and free-thinker Anthony Collins (1676–1729); Dutch philosopher Baruch Spinoza (1632–77); Leibniz; Clarke; and Locke.

same opinion] Hume believes that people do not, in general, doubt that we are both free and determined in the sense he uses these terms. However, these terms are used with different meanings and thus require proper definitions to prevent people from thinking that 'liberty' is incompatible with 'necessity'. See also ann. 8.3 and 8.22.

3 **merely upon words**] The controversy is about the meaning or definition of *terms* such as 'liberty' and 'necessity'—rather than the *nature* of liberty and necessity. Hume often sees such controversies as 'merely verbal'—as he puts it in *EPM* (n. 64 and Appx. 4.2); *THN* 1.4.6.21; and *NHR* 7.1. See *EHU* 8.22–3.

4 **universally allowed, that matter**] Hume is referring to the mechanistic systems of the Cartesians and Newtonians, which are discussed in n. 16 and n. 17. Brief statements of the system Hume apparently most admired can be found in Newton's Preface to the first edition of the *Principia* and in the *Opticks* 3.1. In the *Opticks* Newton announces that he seeks 'to unfold the Mechanism of the World' (369).

5 **utterly unknown**] Under the conditions imagined—namely, that no two events in nature resemble each other—causal relations could never be known and there could be no causal (inductive) inference.

6 **agreed in the doctrine of necessity**] Hume's views often resemble those in Collins; see *A Philosophical Inquiry concerning Human Liberty*, pp. ii, 10–19, 27–9. Collins mentions figures such as Aristotle, Cicero, Locke, Pierre Bayle (1647–1706), Leibniz, and others because of the historical and philosophical importance of their theories of liberty and necessity. Hume's apparent claim that all such people agree in this doctrine was at the time, and still is, highly controversial.

7 **uniformity among the actions of men**] See Ed. Intro., § 6.2, final subsection.

GREEKS . . . ROMANS . . . FRENCH **and** ENGLISH] Hume is not discussing the distinguishing characteristics of these four nationalities. Rather, he is pointing out that 'mankind are so much the same' everywhere in their general motives and actions that we find uniformity: in all nations human actions are similar and are similarly motivated by ambition, self-love, vanity, friendship, generosity, public spirit, and the like. ARISTOTLE . . . HIPPOCRATES . . . POLYBIUS **and** TACITUS] Hume's point is that earth, water, and other elements in physical nature are the same today as they were in ancient times. Similarly, human nature is the same today as when ancient historians wrote about human nature and actions. Aristotle drew on his predecessors for his novel account of basic elements (see *Metaphysics* 983^{b}7–984^{a}11, 986^{b}25–987^{a}19; *Physics* 187^{a}12–188^{a}17). Physician Hippocrates of Cos (5th–4th c. BC) wrote in *Nature of Man* 1 about air, fire, water, and earth as constituents of the human body. Hellenic historian Polybius (2nd c. BC) and Tacitus were keen observers of human actions. Both moved beyond the narration of particular events to what is general or universal in human history. Both writers connected motives with actions, sometimes to explain and sometimes to praise or blame. See Polybius, *Histories* 1.1, 4, 14; 4.8; 8.2, 8; 9.22–3; 16.28; Tacitus, *Annals* 3.55, 65; 6.6, 22.

8 **far country**] Because Hume believes that human nature is universally the same in so far as the same motives produce the same actions, he is convinced that such a traveller's story could not be true. We can 'detect the falsehood' in this story because motives such as 'avarice, ambition, or revenge' are said to be absent, yet we know from experience that they are universally present in human affairs.

QUINTUS CURTIUS . . . ALEXANDER] Quintus Curtius Rufus (1st c. AD), historian of Alexander the Great (4th c. BC), often discussed Alexander's courage. An act of courage so elevated as to be supernatural occurs in *History of Alexander* 9.5, where Alexander is depicted as battling single-handedly and successfully against overwhelming odds, with spears falling on him from all sides, while severely wounded. The text also describes Alexander's act as rash and his avoidance of the spears as partially a matter of luck.

uniformity in human motives and actions] This appears to be a thesis Bramhall is eager to deny in his debate with Hobbes. He argues that 'motives determine not naturally but morally' and without necessitation (*Defence of True Liberty*, 166–9, 206–7).

12 **artificer, who handles only dead matter**] Artists and craftsmen find that their inanimate materials do not always produce expected effects.

13 **vulgar . . . first appearance**] In *THN* 1.3.12.5–6 and 1.4.2.36 (and elsewhere) Hume portrays the vulgar as unphilosophical and unreflective people who judge by first appearances, but he notes that we all in some judgements fall into this class. See also *EHU* 7.21; 9.5; 10.21, 34.

14 **medicines operate not with their wonted powers**] See Hume's examples of this problem at *EHU* 6.4: rhubarb as an inconsistent purge and opium as an inconsistent narcotic.

animal œconomy] 'Œconomy' refers to the organization or internal constitution in the major subdivisions in nature; there is an animal economy, a vegetable economy, etc. Most of the books on animal economy available in the 18th century were on the human œconomy. In his widely read *Cyclopædia* (see 'œconomy'), Chambers defined animal œconomy as 'the first branch of the theory of medicine; or that which explains the parts of the human body, their structure and use; the nature and causes of life and health, and the effects or phænomena arising from them'.

15 **obliging disposition**] an accommodating nature. Such a person ordinarily would not give peevish (cross, irritable) answers, but his exceptional behaviour is explained in this circumstance by his toothache or his being weak from hunger.

stupid fellow . . . alacrity in his carriage] This man of dulled faculties does not ordinarily have a briskness or cheerful readiness in behaviour, but in this instance he has met with a piece of good luck, which accounts for his irregular, unexpected conduct. 'Stupid' here means unresponsive, dull, or apathetic.

18 *politics* **be a science**] See Hume's essay 'That Politics may be Reduced to a Science'. The role of both the constitution and the form of government in determining human conduct in politics is an aspect of his 'scientific' explanation.

inference **from motives to voluntary actions**] Hume is transporting his theory of cause and effect to human conduct and the evaluation of human conduct. He hypothesizes a causal connection between motives and actions, character and sentiments, etc.

19 *natural* **and** *moral* **evidence**] Natural evidence is based on the constant conjunction of objects or events in nature. Moral evidence is based on the constant conjunction of motives and acts. Inferences are made from each type of evidence to support factual claims; evidence in each case rests on constant conjunctions and can amount to what Hume earlier called a *proof.*

wheel] circular instrument of torture on which a person is stretched until disjointed. According to English traveller Thomas Coryate (*c.*1577–1617), 'wheeling' was only used for murderers (*Coryat's Crudities*, 388).

mind feels no difference] In passing from one link in the chain of causes to another, it makes no difference to us whether the link in the chain is a physical condition (the axe meeting the neck, say) or a human motive or action (a soldier's refusal to go into battle, say). A single causal explanation can easily incorporate both physical events and human motives and actions.

physical **necessity**] Physical necessity occurs when a person is determined to do something but lacks all power to act or to prevent it from occurring (see Chambers, *Cyclopædia*, 'necessity'). Hume's point is that we explain events through chains of prior events that can include both voluntary actions and natural causes. The voluntary actions are themselves caused by motives.

20 **Charing Cross**] Charing Cross, a heavily travelled area of London, is sometimes described as the centre of the city because road distances from London are commonly measured from this location. Edward I (1239–1307) erected a cross on this site in 1290.

21 **powers of nature**] Although we experience no more than a constant conjunction between cause and effect, the tendency to believe in a necessary connection between them is so powerful that when we see a particular cause and effect we think that we do experience the necessity. Hume argues that we all tend to believe more than the evidence warrants.

contradict the systems of many philosophers] This thesis and various philosophers whose systems contradict it are discussed in Collins, *A Philosophical Inquiry concerning Human Liberty*, 36–40, 50–2, 74–5. Bramhall is an example of one who insists that the will is a true cause (it determines itself) and not an effect (it is not itself determined); see *Defence of True Liberty*, 11, 13, 228 ff.

determinations of the will] Hume here brings the will into his analysis of liberty (cf. also *EHU* 7.26 and 8.23–7 on the will). In *THN* 2.3 ('Of the Will and Direct Passions') he treats the will not as a mental faculty or power, but as the internal impression felt in knowingly producing bodily or mental changes. 'Will' and 'volition' are apparently close in meaning. His question in *THN* and here is whether volitions are free or determined—or both.

21 **Necessity . . . never yet been rejected**] For Hume 'necessity' in the relevant sense means 'regularity'. He thinks that philosophers generally accept a regular connection between certain motives and certain voluntary actions—for example, motives to help people in need and consequent beneficent actions; these philosophers therefore also believe in necessity.

22 **dispute . . . merely verbal**] a controversy merely about the definition, meaning, or classification of words. See ann. 8.3.

n. 18 **liberty or indifference**] Compare the use of these notions in *THN* 2.3.1.3; 2.3.2.1–2; and *Abstract* 31. See also the explanation by English hymnodist and philosopher Isaac Watts (1674–1748) of the 'liberty of indifference' as the 'power to choose or refuse, to choose one thing or another among several things which are proposed, without any inward or outward restraint, force, or constraining bias or influence'. Watts declared this freedom 'inconsistent with all necessity' as well as with all doctrines of internal causal determination of the will (*Works*, vol. 6, *An Essay on the Freedom of the Will in God and in Creatures* 1.4–5).

n. 18 **will itself is subject to nothing**] Although we often feel that we are free in the sense that we are free to will without any causal conditions controlling our will, there are always causal conditions present at any time we act, at least in the form of motives and dispositions. In order to modify an action different motives or dispositions must be in place.

n. 18 ***Velleïty***] A velleïty is a pure wishing, desiring, or inclination unaccompanied by any attempt to obtain what is fancied. In this manner a mental act occurs without a corresponding act of implementation. Velleïty is to be contrasted with both resolve and volition. A velleïty is felt, but without sufficient conviction and mastery.

n. 18 **complexion**] properties of a person; nature.

23 **this reconciling project**] this attempt to render liberty and necessity compatible.

hypothetical liberty] As long as we are not externally constrained, we can act as we choose. Hypothetically, we can act in *any way* we choose, though in fact conditions will be such that we will act in only one way.

25 ***chance . . . negative word***] The term 'negative' does not have a pejorative connotation as Hume uses it here. It refers to an absence of causal conditions. See ann. 6.1–2 above for further explanations.

26 **dangerous consequences to religion**] It was standard fare in the 18th century to denounce philosophers, especially atheists, because of the presumed threat that their systems posed to religion and morality, which were thought to stand in a close and indissoluble relationship. Hobbes was a favourite target. Many reservations centred on the apparent elimination by those committed to necessity of categories such as praise, blame, punishment, and sin.

27 **two definitions of *cause***] Hume is referring to his two definitions of cause at *EHU* 7.29. See also Ed. Intro., §6.1, final subsection.

the schools] The Aristotelian and Scholastic centres of learning, often abbreviated as 'the schools', were under attack in many writings of the period. See, for example, Locke, *Essay* 3.4.8–10 and 3.10.6–8. Attacks on the substance and method of the schools formed a part of Locke's programme of establishing the limits of human understanding. See also the caustic observations in Hobbes, *Leviathan* 1.5; 2.9; 5.15; 8.27; 12.31; 46.13–30.

will of man] Hume is claiming that it is an ordinary belief that causal necessity (in

the two senses provided) applies to the will of persons no less than to physical events.
received orthodox system] The reference is to philosophical views that the will is itself free of prior causal determination and that human choices create new causal chains (rather than the choices being effects in a longer chain of causation). See Descartes, *Principles of Philosophy* 1.39–42 (1: 205–6) and Bramhall, as cited at 8.21 above. Though he rejects this philosophy, Hume is arguing that his account of the causal connection between motives and actions does not undermine freedom of the will in the only sense in which freedom exists.

29 **not answerable for them**] A person could not be held responsible if the will is totally uncaused—that is, without causal conditions in the person's motive, desires, character, and disposition. Unless these conditions were present, Hume asks, how could the action be attributed to the person rather than to chance? His wider objective seems to be to refute those who deny that the will is caused by showing that they would have to forgo legitimate punishment and the holding of persons responsible for their actions.

32 **train**] trail of explosive gunpowder laid to fire a mine—that is, a subterranean placement of gunpowder. 'Fire' here means ignite or explode the gunpowder.
chain of necessary causes is fixed] Hume is contemplating an objection that might be brought against his views: suppose one were to argue that there is a link of causes reaching from God the Creator to 'every single volition of every human creature'. We would not, on this hypothesis, be responsible for our criminal (wrongful) actions because God would be responsible for them. In the next few paragraphs Hume considers the merits of this objection.

34 **some philosophers . . . ancient STOICS**] These philosophers might include Flemish classicist Justus Lipsius (1547–1606), *Of Constancie* 1.13–15, 18–20. Lipsius was a popular author who embraced these Stoic attitudes and an author elsewhere cited by Hume. Hume's expression 'constancy on his mind' later in this paragraph could be an allusion to Lipsius. Although ancient Stoics and other philosophers cannot be identified with confidence, Seneca's theory and language in 'De providentia' 3.1 and 5.7–8 (in *Moral Essays*) strikingly resemble Hume's formulation. See also Marcus Aurelius (1st c. AD), *Meditations* 10.5–6.
humours] A humour is a fluid or semi-fluid substance found in the body. According to ancient teachings in medicine, four humours govern the body and determine its characteristics: blood, yellow bile, black bile, and phlegm. An imbalance among the humours was thought to cause pain and disease, whereas good health was believed to be dependent upon a proper or proportional balance.

35 **remote considerations**] Hume refers to these speculative, philosophical–theological considerations immediately before and after this passage. The view that the world system is ordered by a perfect benevolence is especially important. Hume is arguing that such remote metaphysical speculation has no impact on people who suffer from what they regard as physical evils or moral evils.
sentiment of approbation or blame] a major theme in Hume's moral philosophy: we approve or disapprove of the actions and characters of other people when their actions promote public utility or disutility.
uncertain speculations] These speculative theories hold that apparently evil and blameworthy events have benign explanations. The reference seems to be to philosophers and theologians who offered a 'theodicy', an account of the compatibility of

evil and divine creation. Hume thinks that their speculations exceed the available evidence.

36 **mediate cause**] a cause that acts through an intermediate agency or condition. In this case the Deity acts indirectly through the conditions of human action to cause those actions.

SECTION 9

If humans have beliefs, learn from experience, form psychological dispositions or habits, and engage in causal inference, why cannot non-human animals do the same? There are obvious analogies between human and non-human qualities: non-human animals perceive, apprehend, learn, deliberate, infer, believe, and the like. Just as humans learn how to reach their goals by experience and inference, so animals exhibit similar capacities. Although non-human animals are not entirely similar to humans, the similarities warrant the attribution of reason in the sense of reasoning from causes to effects and effects to causes. In humans and non-humans alike such experimental reasoning is a species of instinct. (For additional discussion of Section 9, see Ed. Intro., § 5.8.)

REASON OF ANIMALS] Influential background sources for this section include Descartes's theory that animals do not have minds, Locke's *Essay* 2.11.4–7, 10–11, and the *Dictionary* ('Pereira' and 'Rorarius') of French–Dutch philosopher Pierre Bayle (1647–1706). Some issues are ancient, dating at least from the Pythagoreans and, in their first developed form, in the Neoplatonist philosopher Porphyry (3rd–4th c. AD), *On Abstinence from Animal Food*, esp. bk. 3. Hume discusses the nature and extent of reason *and the passions* in animals in three sections of *THN*: 1.3.16 ('Of the Reason of Animals'); 2.1.12 ('Of the Pride and Humility of Animals'); 2.2.12 ('Of the Love and Hatred of Animals').

1 ANALOGY] Hume is explicating his account of causal (or inductive) inference, noting that it rests on analogy. Present causes appear to be like past causes, prompting our expectation of an effect that is analogous to the past effects that we have experienced. Hume will now pursue analogies between humans and non-human animals that are encouraged by 'anatomical observations' and by his consideration of various forms of behaviour and thought.

cohesion of parts] cohesion of the parts of matter. See ann. 4.12, 'Elasticity, gravity, cohesion . . . impulse'.

blood . . . as a frog, or fish] English physician William Harvey (1578–1657) used widely discussed examples of the frog and fish (as well as a variety of other animal species) in his discovery of the way the blood circulates in animal and human bodies (*Motion of the Heart and Blood in Animals* 2–6, 10, 17).

science . . . understanding . . . passions] The science is Hume's theory of human nature. *EHU* is a work on the 'operations of the understanding'. *A Dissertation on the Passions* is a work principally on 'the passions in man'. *THN* 1–2 covers these two topics in that order. Hume contemplates, in the present passage, a possible analogical extension of his theory to explain similar phenomena in animals—presumably doing for the mind what Harvey and other physiologists had done for the body.

2 **doubles**] sharp backward and forward turns of reversal of direction in running—for

example, those of a hunted hare when doubling back. Reasons for the phenomenon (and its abandonment when dogs get near the hare) had been discussed in a well-known book on animal behaviour by English diplomat and writer Kenelme Digby (1603–65), *Treatises*, First Treatise 36, p. 387.

5 **not guided . . . by reasoning**] Hume's denial of demonstrative reasoning and concomitant affirmation of causal 'reasoning' may be his way of incorporating the widely held view that animals are conscious and have capacities of instinct, perception, memory, emotion, and imagination, but lack true rationality. This theory goes back at least to Aristotle (see Sorabji, *Animal Minds and Human Morals*).

6 **we denominate *instincts*]** See ann. 5.8, 'natural instincts' and 9.6, 'nothing but a species of instinct'. Hume concludes Section 5 by discussing how nature has 'implanted in us an instinct, which carries forward the thought'. This instinct underlies human causal reasoning. In this respect humans do not fundamentally differ from non-human animals in kind, whatever the differences of degree may be. Both learn by experience and reason by instinct.

experimental reasoning] reasoning based on experience.

nothing but a species of instinct] Numerous treatises and pamphlets were written in the 17th and 18th centuries on this subject. Discussion both before and after Descartes had focused on whether the beasts are mere machines that lack souls, powers of reason, and the like (see Porphyry, *On Abstinence from Animal Food* 3.10, 25; Bayle, *Dictionary*, 'Rorarius'). Hume is suggesting that much of the debate about animals is misplaced, because animals who reason do so from a mechanical or instinctual power. See ann. 5.8, 'natural instincts' and *EHU* 9.3 on instinct.

mechanical power] capacity that operates automatically. Cf. *THN* 1.3.16.9: 'reason is nothing but a wonderful and unintelligible instinct'.

œconomy . . . of its nursery] organization and management of the bird's dwelling, in which growth and flourishing occur.

SECTION 10

Are there good reasons to believe in miracles? By relying on arguments in prior sections about causal inference, belief, and probability, it can be shown that factual evidence adduced for miracles and testimony in support of miracles are suspect. A 'decisive argument' is adduced in this section that will '*silence* the most arrogant bigotry and superstition' (10.2) by showing that no miracle merits belief.

In Part 1 Hume maintains that careful reasoners who proportion belief to the evidence find little support for miracles. Because miracles are violations of laws of nature, testimony for miracles conflicts with the evidence for the laws, which is extremely good evidence. The reliability of those who report miracles is also in doubt. They are typically motivated by religious interests that produce bias, thus putting their credentials as impartial observers in doubt. On balance the evidence against miracles (the evidence for laws of nature) outweighs the testimony in favour of miracles.

In Part 2 Hume argues that there never has been a miracle established on the basis of adequate testamentary evidence by credible witnesses. Throughout history those who report miracles have lacked the requisite authority. We can envisage a situation in which reports of miracles might be supported by reliable testimony, but such a situation seems never to have existed. Hume also argues that testimony in favour of miracles fails to support the belief structures of particular religions. (For additional discussion of Section 10, see Ed. Intro., §7.1.)

1 **Dr. TILLOTSON's writings**] John Tillotson (1630–94) was an influential Protestant preacher and archbishop of Canterbury. He inveighed against both atheism and Roman Catholicism, insisting on reasoned, non-dogmatic argument in theological inquiry. The argument that Hume attributes to Tillotson most closely resembles the argument in Tillotson's sermon 'The Hazard of being Sav'd in the Church of *Rome*' (Sermon 11, in *Works*).

    real presence] The term 'real presence' refers to that into which the substance of the bread and wine of the sacrament of Holy Communion are allegedly transformed—the actual body and blood of Jesus Christ. The term 'transubstantiation' refers to this doctrine. Roman Catholics have traditionally held that this transformation of substance is not perceptible to the senses and is a *mystery* known only by faith. Their appeal has not been explicitly to a *miracle*, which they regard as an extraordinary event produced by God and perceptible to the senses. Tillotson recognized these distinctions and argued that the idea of conversion in substance is neither a teaching of Christ, nor received by the early Church Fathers, nor passed on by uninterrupted tradition. Moreover, it is shown by experience to be false. See 'A Discourse against Transubstantiation' (Sermon 26, in *Works*).

3 **moral evidence**] factual evidence about human behaviour gained from experience. In *THN* 2.3.1.15 Hume says that moral evidence is 'nothing but a conclusion concerning the actions of men, deriv'd from the consideration of their motives, temper and situation'. In this way moral evidence is contrasted with physical and mathematical evidence. A related notion in some writers is 'moral certainty'. Neither notion was always used with the same meaning by writers of the period. See English scientist John Wilkins (1614–72), *Principles and Duties of Natural Religion* 1.1.1–3; 1.3.1–5; Berkeley, *Alciphron*, Dials. 6–7; Descartes, *Discourse* 4 and *Principles* 206; Leibniz, *New Essays*, Preface and 4.10. See also *THN* 2.3.1.15–17; 2.3.2.8; *Abstract* 33; *EHU* 8.19; 12.21.

4 **degree of evidence**] See ann. n. 10 (Section 6), '*demonstrations, proofs*, and *probabilities*'; also *THN* 1.3.6.4 and 1.3.11.2 on knowledge, probability, and degrees of evidence (especially the contrast between proof and probability). Locke argued that testimony favouring miracles constituted an exception to the general rule that degree of probability and evidence diminishes as the distance from eyewitnesses increases (*Essay* 4.15–16, esp. 4.16.9–14). Hume disagrees.

6 **witnesses and human testimony**] It was widely believed at the time Hume wrote that belief in miracles could be critically evaluated by historical evidence regarding the quantity of witnesses and the quality of their testimony. See Dutch jurist and statesman Hugo Grotius (1583–1645), *Truth of the Christian Religion* 2.6; 3.7; and contributors to theological controversies in England such as English bishop Thomas J. Sherlock (1678–1761), *The Trial of the Witnesses*; Peter Annet, *Answer to the Tryal of the Witnesses*; and John Jackson, *An Address to Deists*.

8 **extraordinary and the marvellous**] In his *History of England* Hume distinguishes the miraculous, the marvellous, and the extraordinary and discusses what circumspect historians will allow. Though good historians reject claims of the miraculous and doubt the marvellous, they can accept extraordinary reports whenever solid

testimony and known facts constitute adequate support (*History*, 2: 398–404).

9 CATO] Plutarch depicts the Stoic Cato the Younger (1st c. BC) as a person of virtue and high repute. According to Plutarch, many people, 'when speaking of matters that were strange and incredible, would say, as though using a proverb, "This is not to be believed even though Cato says it" ' (*Lives*, 'Cato the Younger' 19.4).

10 INDIAN prince] A version of this story appears in Locke, *Essay* 4.15.5. In his narrative a Dutch ambassador relates a story to the king of Siam (Thailand) about frozen water possessing the strength to bear the weight of an elephant. The king is certain the report is a lie. In the Introduction to his *Analogy* (1: 5) Joseph Butler gives a brief account of this story, attributing it to Locke. Hume's version is closer to Butler's restatement.

n. 22 MUSCOVY] the region of Moscow, possibly extended here to include all of Russia.

12 **violation of the laws of nature**] A law of nature is a causal law, that is, any perfectly uniform causal regularity in nature, such as strong winds causing the leaves of trees to move. A miracle violates a law by not conforming to a universal regularity, as when a rushing sea suddenly stops flowing and parts in half. See Ed. Intro., §7.1 for the role of Hume's definition of a miracle and the idea of a violation of a law.

opposite proof, which is superior] This difficult argument and the language in which it is expressed are explained in the Ed. Intro., §§5.7 and 7.1. On the relevant sense of 'proof', see n. 10: 'By *proofs* meaning such arguments from experience as leave no room for doubt or opposition.'

17 **auditors**] those who listen or attend to what is said.

Their credulity] In *THN* 1.3.9.12–15 'credulity' is defined as 'a too easy faith in the testimony of others'.

18 **Eloquence**] See *EHU* 1.1. The art of oratory was widely discussed in the 18th century, and Demosthenes (4th c. BC) was the most widely examined orator. Eloquence was typically viewed as a constructive way of guiding a community by moving the passions. See Hume's essay 'Of Eloquence'.

TULLY . . . DEMOSTHENES . . . *Capuchin*] Tully is Cicero. Known for forcefulness in writing and speaking, he made a reputation as a prosecutor and consul. He and Demosthenes both enjoyed reputations for eloquence. Capuchins are friars of an austere branch of the order of St Francis. They were dedicated missionaries and skilled preachers. Hume apparently believes that they touched common passions more effectively than even the great classical orators.

vulgar passions] English critic and playwright John Dennis (1657–1734) discussed the distinction between 'vulgar passion' (that is, 'ordinary passion') and 'enthusiasm' in both *The Advancement and Reformation of Modern Poetry* 5–6 and *The Grounds of Criticism in Poetry* 4 (*Critical Works*, esp. 1: 215–18, 338–9). He linked 'Religious Subjects' to 'stronger Enthusiasms'. Though guarded about the role of passions in eloquence, religion, and the like, he regarded appeals to vulgar passion as essential in poetry.

19 **forged miracles . . . been detected**] Because of the power of enthusiasm and the problem of forgery, claims of the miraculous had for centuries been placed under clerical and judicial inspection in the Roman Catholic Church. Standards in canon law determined the authenticity of miraculous claims. Few claims of reported miracles withstood this official scrutiny. Those that did were declared authentic miracles and appeared in papal bulls of canonization. On the origins of the practice, see Michael E. Goodich, *Violence and Miracle in the Fourteenth Century*, 4–14.

21 **wonderful historians**] historians whose histories report wonders that are either marvellous or miraculous. Many such 'historians' (here including persons who publish chronicles of events) were discussed before and during Hume's period. An informative list of these writers, and of the 'wise and judicious' who scorned the reports, is found in the text, notes, and index of *A Free Inquiry into the Miraculous Powers* by English clergyman Conyers Middleton (1683–1750).

22 ALEXANDER . . . LUCIAN **tells us**] Hellenic poet and satirist Lucian (2nd c. AD) told how Alexander the False Prophet became celebrated as an oracle. Alexander and a friend perpetrated a hoax to deceive gullible citizens of his home region of Paphlagonia in north Asia Minor, now in Turkey. Their magic trick made it seem that Asclepias, the god of healing, was being born from a goose egg in the figure of a snake with a human head. Alexander then claimed to be holding Asclepias in his hand. According to Lucian the crowd followed Alexander 'full of religious fervour and crazed with expectations' (*Alexander, or the False Prophet* 1–61, esp. 13–14).

enlisting of votaries] Votaries are people under obligations of religious vows. 'Enlisting' is used metaphorically.

MARCUS AURELIUS] As Roman emperor, the Stoic philosopher Marcus Aurelius (2nd c. AD) ruled over Paphlagonia. Most of his reign was spent in warfare. In one battle, according to Lucian, Marcus followed Alexander's prophecy that victory would be assured if two lions and other offerings were cast into the Danube. After Marcus cast the objects into the river, the barbarians vanquished the lions and administered a crushing defeat to the Roman forces. For his part Alexander coyly explained that the oracle had not revealed to whom the victory would go (*Alexander, or the False Prophet* 47–8).

24 **destroying a rival system**] Hume thinks that religious people believe that miracles confirm their particular religious tradition and disconfirm the claims of other traditions. Miracles thus have a tendency to 'overthrow every other system'. From a more impartial viewpoint the appeals of the different traditions cancel each other out and discredit appeals to miracles generally.

MAHOMET . . . **barbarous** ARABIANS] Mahomet or Muhammad (6th–7th c. AD) is the founder and major prophet of Islam. 'Arabians' means Arabs. Hume is repeating a typical European view of the period, namely that Islam is a ruthless, tyrannical, and intolerant religion. Hume presents this view in *NHR* 9.3.

TITUS LIVIUS] Roman historian Livy (1st c. BC–1st c. AD). The nature and degree of scepticism in Livy when he reported on claims of miracles, marvels, and prodigies is a subject of scholarly disagreement. See his *History* 21.62; 24.3.4–8; 26.19.3–10.

25 **at large**] in detail.

ALEXANDER **and** DEMETRIUS] There are indications, though no conclusive evidence, that Macedonian king Alexander the Great (4th c. BC) requested that city-states honour him as a god. Prevailing religious practices permitted the deification of humans, but political power as much as religious conviction is a plausible motive for seeking deification. A possible source of Hume's information is Arrian's *Anabasis of Alexander* 7.23.2. Demetrius I of Macedonia (4th–3rd c. BC) pursued the policy of his father (Antigonus I) to reunite Alexander's empire. He was victorious in Cyprus and the Hellenic city-states. Plutarch reports that the Athenians paid extravagant honours to Demetrius, including the appellation of 'Saviour-god' and an acknowledgement of Demetrius' capacity to deliver oracles (*Lives*, 'Demetrius' 10–13; 24–6).

cured a blind man . . . "Utrumque . . . pretium"] Vespasian (1st c. AD) is the emperor. From 69 to 96 AD the Roman empire was ruled by the Flavian family, which included Vespasian. The miracle is reported in the sources in n. 24, which relate stories of Vespasian's healing of both a blind man and a crippled man. Tacitus (*Histories* 4.81) concludes his account with the Latin cited by Hume ('*Utrumque, qui . . .*'), which may be translated, 'Those who were present recount both incidents even now, when there is nothing to gain from deceit.' Serapis is an Egyptian god worshipped during the time of Ptolemaic Egypt.

26 **Cardinal DE RETZ**] The archbishop of Paris, Cardinal de Retz (1613–79), relates in his *Mémoires* the story of the doorkeeper of the cathedral (*Œuvres*, 974, here translated):

> I was shown a man employed to light the lamps, which are vast in number. I was told that he had been seen, at the door of the church, for seven years with only one leg; whereas I saw him there with two legs. The dean and all the prebends assured me that the whole town had seen it just as they had; and that if I would stay only two days longer, I could speak to more than 20,000 people from the neighbourhood who had seen him, as well as to people from the town. He had recovered his leg, according to what they said, by anointing himself with some oil from his lamps. Every year they celebrate a holiday in honour of this miracle, with an incredible show of people.

De Retz relates this miracle in the context of a travelogue written on a trip through Spain. His comments on the miracle suggest, but do not directly report, the view that Hume attributed to him.

vouched by all the canons of the church] A canon is an ecclesiastical definition, rule, or law approved by a council or other authority—and, in the Roman Catholic Church, approved by the Pope. Several canons specify criteria of authentic miracles, by contrast to fraud, magic, mere enthusiasm, and the like. See ann. 10.19.

27 **PARIS, the famous JANSENIST**] The deacon François de Pâris (1690–1727) was a follower of the doctrinal system of Bishop Cornelius Jansen (1585–1638), a significant figure in the Roman Catholic Church. Jansenism was committed to forms of religious life aligned with early Christian teachings, especially moral austerity. Pâris was known for his devotion to these ideals. Jansenists and Jesuits were often in deep disagreement over religious and political matters.

holy sepulchre] the tomb of Abbé Pâris, where miraculous cures were said to occur. These cures were sometimes accompanied by violent convulsions, allegedly signifying a struggle between life and death for the sick person. Crowds appeared daily at the tomb, with many people falling into trances and convulsions and engaging in acts of religious enthusiasm and ecstasy. These proclaimed miracles were among the most widely examined and witnessed in modern religion, but Jesuits and Protestants alike rejected both the testimonials and the surrounding practices.

n. 25 Mons. MONTGERON] The book by Jansenist defender Louis-Basile Carré de Montgeron (1686–1754) *La Vérité des miracles* provides detailed discussions of several cures, each supported by a body of testimonial evidence and medical documentation. These meticulously prepared 'demonstrations' constituted, in Montgeron's judgement, the primary argument for miraculous cures. (The particular case of Marguerite Thibault is discussed a few entries below.) The book also attempts to show the importance of these miracles and provides responses to the principal objections put forth by critics.

n. 25 **martyr to the cause**] In his zeal for the Jansenist cause Montgeron went unannounced to the court of Louis XV at Versailles on 29 July 1737 to hand-deliver a copy of his work. He found his way to the royal dining-room, offered the copy of his book to the king, and issued a warning that Rome and the Jesuits posed a threat to the king's power. For this act he was later arrested by agents of the lieutenant of police René Hérault (1691–1740; see below), and put in prison.

n. 25 *Recueil . . . l'Abbé* PARIS] The anonymously published *Recueil* is an anthology of investigatory evidence about four of the many miraculous cures allegedly 'performed at the Tomb of the Deacon, Monsieur de Pâris'. On 13 August 1731 twenty-three *curés* (priests) addressed a formal request to the archbishop of Paris to further investigate the cures. The *Recueil* materials were among the documents accompanying this petition, which called for the archbishop to publish and promote them as records of 'true miracles' (*Recueil* 1). Without waiting for a reply, the *curés* had the formal request and *Recueil* published (anonymously). Enraged, the archbishop decided not to reply. On 4 October 1731 twenty-two curés sent another formal request for an investigation of the affair (Kreiser, *Miracles*, 93–6, 131–5).

n. 25 **Cardinal** NOAILLES] Cardinal Louis Antoine Noailles (1651–1729) attempted to prevent the French government's efforts to have Jansenism condemned by clerical authorities in France and Rome. A series of papal condemnations of Jansenism culminated in the papal bull (solemn edict) *Unigenitus* (1713). Noailles and various bishops refused to accept the bull without an explanation from Rome. When Noailles was rebuffed by the papacy, there ensued a major social and political battle, with hundreds of pamphlets and books published by each side.

n. 25 **successor in the archbishopric**] Noailles's successor was Archbishop Vintimille of Aix, who supported the bull *Unigenitus*. Vintimille collaborated with Hérault (see below).

n. 25 **MOLINIST party**] The Spanish Jesuit Luis de Molina (1535–1600) published a major theological system in 1588, subsequently known as Molinism. His work divided Spanish and French theologians: the Jesuits supported his system, while Thomists (followers of St Thomas Aquinas) and Jansenists opposed it. Molinists became active in the political realm, and 'Molinistes' were called a party in France. They were often in conflict with the Jansenists. 'Molinism' was often treated as a virtual synonym for 'Jesuit perspective'.

n. 25 **Mademoiselle** LE FRANC] A significant confrontation occurred over the alleged miraculous cure of Anne Le Franc (also Lefranc). She visited Saint-Médard and offered prayers, requesting a miracle through Abbé Pâris. Within a few days her symptoms were relieved; her blindness, paralysis, and other infirmities allegedly disappeared. Anonymous pro-Jansenists petitioned Archbishop Vintimille to open an investigation into the miracle. Evidence was published. The Jesuits worked to discredit it, and Vintimille sent his own investigators to look into the miracle.

n. 25 **Mons.** HERAULT] The lieutenant of police René Hérault attempted to suppress the supporters of Abbé Pâris and all who opposed the bull *Unigenitus*. His collaboration with Vintimille gave him special authority. Hérault employed undercover informers and sent them throughout Paris in order to intimidate and arrest Jansenists and others.

n. 25 THIBAULT . . . DE SYLVA] Hérault attempted to discredit the cure of Marguerite Thibault, whose 'documented' miraculous healing is presented in both Montgeron's *La Vérité des miracles* and in the Second *Recueil* (see above). News of this miracle spread quickly through Paris, to the dismay of Hérault, who recruited physician Jean-Baptiste Silva (de Sylva) (1682–1742) to examine the case.

n. 25 JERICHO . . . rams horns] a reference to the collapse of the walls of Jericho at the sounding of ram's horn trumpets. These trumpets signalled attacks; the trumpet was also associated with God's judgement of the world. See Josh. 6: 5–20.

n. 25 prison of every apostle] More than one of Jesus' apostles was imprisoned. In the dramatic case of Paul an earthquake shook the prison. See Acts 16: 26.

n. 25 Duc de CHATILLON] The duc de Châtillon is Paul Sigismond de Montmorency (1663–1731). He is identified in the Second *Recueil* (107–16) in the presentation of the miracle of Blaise Neret, an 8-year-old boy paralysed over the entire left side of his body. In July 1731 Neret went to the tomb of the Abbé Pâris and two days later felt pains on his paralysed side. Within two additional days he was cured. The duc saw Neret and became convinced of the authenticity of the miracle.

n. 25 PORT-ROYAL] a central Jansenist monastery near Paris. It exerted an impressive influence on French intellectuals in the late 17th century and represented a challenge to the Jesuit monopoly on education and spiritual doctrine.

n. 25 niece of the famous PASCAL] This 'miracle of the holy thorn' is reported in the *Abrégé de l'histoire de Port-Royal* by dramatist Jean Racine (1639–99), to which Hume refers in this paragraph. Racine explains how Marguerite Périer, niece of French philosopher and Jansenist Blaise Pascal (1623–62), was cured of an apparently incurable problem. She had a painful, inflamed ulcer that penetrated the bony structure around the corner of the left eye. On 24 March 1656 Monsieur de la Potherie, a collector of relics, had brought to the nuns of Port Royal what he claimed to be a thorn from the crown worn by Christ at his crucifixion. One nun was inspired to apply the thorn to Marguerite's afflicted eye. That evening the inflammation disappeared and the pain ceased. This miracle of the holy thorn had many witnesses and was declared a verified miracle by authorities such as Cardinal de Retz and by a physician who had declared the malady incurable. (Racine, *Abrégé*, 77–85.)

n. 25 bishop of TOURNAY] The 'bishop of Tournay', Gilbert de Choiseul du Plessis-Praslin (also Gilbert de Choyseul du Plessy-Praslain, 1613–89), took part in negotiations to restore peace to the Church, then split over Jansenism. These negotiations worked to aggravate both parties, and he was accused of siding with the Jansenists. In his *Abrégé* (77–8) Racine says that the bishop used the story of the miracle of the holy thorn to present a brilliant proof of the truth of religion directed at atheists and free-thinkers. Racine also indicates that this report of the miracle was received with indifference by the majority who knew of it.

n. 25 free-thinkers] 'Free-thinkers' refers to those who weigh the evidence and judge for themselves in matters of religion. Several authors that Hume knew well had employed the term. Bayle's *Dictionary* was widely regarded as a resource for free-thinkers, but the term had been given notoriety by Anthony Collins in *A Discourse of Free-Thinking*, 5 ff. Subsequently the term was applied to deists and sometimes to atheists.

n. 25 queen-regent of FRANCE] This queen regent of France was Anne of Austria (1601–66). When the story of the miracle of the holy thorn circulated widely, an outpouring of religious conviction occurred. The queen regent, a deeply religious woman, was embarrassed by the commotion. She sent her personal physician, M. Félix, to investigate the reports of physicians. He was convinced that a miracle had occurred. Racine maintains that 'the piety of the Queen Mother was touched by the visible protection of God over these nuns' (*Abrégé*, 84–7). However, the queen issued no public statement, thereby avoiding the theological controversy between Jansenists and Jesuits.

28 PHILIPPI or PHARSALIA] Philippi was a town in Macedonia in which the army of Marc Antony defeated Brutus and Cassius in 42 BC. Pharsala or Pharsalus was a city in Thessaly, now northern Greece, near where Julius Caesar conquered Pompey in 48 BC in the battle known as Pharsalia (see ann. 3.17, 'battle of PHARSALIA').

HERODOTUS or PLUTARCH] Marvels prominent in 5th-century Greece appeared in stories of the Persian War related by the historian Herodotus (5th c. BC). Oracles, portents, dreams, omens, miracles, and divinations were used to explain human behaviour and national policies. Oracles that inform and warn were especially prominent. (See e.g. *History* 8.135.) In his *Lives* Plutarch joined sceptical philosophical commentary with historical reports of miraculous events. He mentions divine marvels, signs, and miracles in 'Camillus' 6.1–3; 'Gaius Marcius Coriolanus' 37–8; 'Dion' 24.4–5; 'Themistocles' 30; and 'Brutus' 36–7. In his *Moralia* prophecy occasionally involves divine providence: see 'The Oracles at Delphi'. In 'Dion' the following report appears: 'The water of the sea which washed the base of the acropolis was sweet and potable for a whole day, as all who tasted it could see.'

MARIANA, BEDE] Spanish Jesuit Juan de Mariana (1536–1624) wrote a history, *The General History of Spain*, that reports several miracles. The early English historian now known as the Venerable Bede (7th–8th c. AD) had a reputation for reliability as a reporter of events. In 'The Life and Miracles of Saint Cuthbert' Bede reports numerous miracles, often displaying a simple faith less noticeable in his historical writings. In his best-known work, *Ecclesiastical History of the English Nation*, he occasionally reports miracles and cites authorities or evidence in support of them.

29 **pious frauds**] a widely used expression. In reporting on fantastic stories and miracles, English philosopher William Wollaston (1659–1724) discusses 'frauds pious and impious' in *Religion of Nature Delineated* 3.16 (p. 57). See also the controversy between Anthony Collins (*Discourse of Free-Thinking*, 92–3) and English classical scholar Richard Bentley (1662–1742) (*Remarks upon a Late Discourse of Free-Thinking*, 35–6 (pp. 376 ff.)) on pious and impious frauds in biblical translations.

30 *avidum genus auricularum*] The expression in Latin poet Lucretius (Titus Lucretius Carus, 1st c. BC) is 'humanum genus est avidum nimis auricularum', which means 'the human species is too eager for gossipy ears'. Hume's shortened version, *avidum genus auricularum*, means 'the tribe with an eager ear for gossip'. Lucretius uses the full expression while discussing how miraculous tales are exchanged and spread. Hume applies to a part of the population a phrase which, in its original context, Lucretius applied to all humanity (*De rerum natura* 4.594).

32 **court of judicature**] Judicature is justice (dispensed by legal trial); a court of judicature is a court that interprets the law and oversees the administration of justice.

33 **detect the cheat**] Hume uses the language of 'falsehood' and 'the cheat' to communicate the difficulty of determining whether testimony for miracles is reliable. He

does not suggest that anyone intentionally cheats or tells less than what they believe to be the truth.

35 **subtract the one from the other**] balance the weight of one testimony against that of the other to see where the weight of the testimony falls.

39 BACON . . . LIVY] This passage is Hume's translation of the Latin from the *Novum organum* 2.29. Bacon's reference to the prodigies of Livy is to passages in the latter's *History*.

alchimy] the chemistry of the Middle Ages, the practical aim of which was to turn baser metals into gold (through a magical or miraculous power of transmutation).

40 **most holy religion**] the Christian religion. Hume could assume this understanding on the part of his readers. He need not be taken to mean that Christianity is holier than other religions or even a holy religion.

***Faith*, not on reason**] Theologians and philosophers had articulated the theme of 'faith, not reason' for centuries. To cite two figures mentioned elsewhere in these annotations, Montaigne commented on the *inability* of reason to establish the truths known by faith, whereas Bayle and others found reason *in opposition to* religious faith.

Pentateuch] The first five books of the Hebrew Bible, or the five books of Moses, report numerous miracles, several of which are listed by Hume later in this paragraph.

writer and historian] Prior to Hume prominent writers, including Anglican bishop Edward Stillingfleet (1635–99), had defended the soundness of biblical history. They incorporated accounts of miracles and the history related in the Pentateuch, often using appeals to common sense and historiographical standards. See Stillingfleet, *Origines sacrae* 2.1–4, 7–10.

41 **applied . . . to prophecies**] Like miracles, a large literature existed on prophecies. Stillingfleet, *Origines sacrae* 2.6–10, associated miracles and prophecies, defending both. Relevant connections are made between prophecies and miracles in Spinoza's *Theologico-Political Treatise* 1–3, 6, and Anthony Collins's *Discourse of the Grounds and Reasons of the Christian Religion* 1.6–11—two influential works by free-thinkers.

real miracles] Hume is suggesting that prophecies form one species of miracle and serve as the same kind of 'proof' of a religious tradition. His arguments against miracles therefore hold against prophecies.

at this day] today.

SECTION 11

This section is written as a dialogue between the author and a friend. The dialogue appears to be about the good fortune of ancient philosophy in having remained relatively free of control by political and religious authorities. The question arises whether Epicurus—who denied God's existence and providence, as well as a 'future state' (life after death)—presented a serious threat to political authorities and even to social morality and religion. The friend in the dialogue declares that he could 'make a speech for EPICURUS' to defend his philosophy. In paragraph 9 the dialogue style gives way to a monologue–speech, put in the mouth of Epicurus as an address to Athenians.

'Epicurus' considers whether religious doctrines can be established on the basis of philosophy. He proceeds to raise serious questions about the possibility of a natural or philosophical theology, arguing that such theological reasoning is unduly speculative. The chief argument considered is that which alleges that God's existence can be proved from signs in nature that point to the creation of the universe by a wise and good divine being. This argument is drawn from effects to causes (from the nature of the world to God as its creator).

'Epicurus' points to several weaknesses in this argument, especially those pertaining to causation, analogy, and the justification of evil. These weaknesses are revealed when earlier conclusions reached in *EHU* are applied to this argument. Conclusions about induction and causation are especially pertinent. (For additional discussion of Section 11, see Ed. Intro., §7.2.)

PARTICULAR PROVIDENCE] A *particular* providence is to be contrasted to a *general* providence. Particular providence is God's oversight of and intervention in the affairs of particular individuals; general providence is God's provision for everything through the universal laws of nature.

FUTURE STATE] In the first edition of *EHU* (1748) Hume gave this section the title '*Of the* Practical Consequences *of* Natural Religion', thus indicating that it is concerned with the moral and social import of religion. His change in 1750 to the present title suggests related but different concerns about God's providence. The term 'natural religion' (the project of basing religious principles and doctrines of God on reason and science, by contrast to revelation) did not appear in *EHU* after the 1748 edition, yet Section 11 is arguably on the topic of natural religion and includes subjects addressed in greater depth in Hume's *Dialogues concerning Natural Religion*. Neither of Hume's two titles seems quite to capture what he is attempting in Section 11. He may be disguising his philosophical and religious targets both by his titles and by his transfer of responsibility for the arguments to historical and imaginary characters in his narrative.

2 **age and country**] ancient 'Greece' (not then a country) prior to the 1st century BC.
banishment of PROTAGORAS] Ancient authorities, including Diogenes Laertius (2nd c. AD) and Sextus Empiricus, reported that the Sophist Protagoras (5th c. BC) was prosecuted in a heresy trial and banished from Athens because one of his books raised questions about the existence of the gods.
death of SOCRATES] Athenian philosopher Socrates (5th c. BC) subjected many conventional beliefs to sharp criticism. He was considered socially dangerous by the political hierarchy in Athens because of his reflections on government, morality, and religion. In a celebrated trial a jury of 501 men found him guilty of impiety for refusing to acknowledge the gods recognized by the State and of corrupting the youth of Athens. He was sentenced to death.
EPICURUS . . . EPICUREANS] Although times were troubled in Athens, Epicurus lived there undisturbed despite his unorthodox religious views. See ann. 5.1, 'philosophic sage'. Epicureans defended a view of nature that left little place for orthodox gods. They adopted an unconventional polytheism in which gods are models for living one's life even though they are distant from human affairs and exercise no providence. The Stoic view that there is a providential arrangement in the universe contrasted sharply. (See Lucian, *Zeus Rants* 3–4, 16–17, 36–51 and the works by Lucian in nn. 28–30. In

the source cited in n. 28 Lucian satirizes the idea that an Epicurean could be a priest.) Epicurus was often taken in the 18th century as a symbol of free-thinking and atheism. Hume and his critics assume this reception of Epicurus' teachings.

sacerdotal character] 'Sacerdotal' means priestly, or belonging to or pertaining to a priest or the priestly office.

every sect of philosophy] The wisest emperor is philosopher Marcus Aurelius (see ann. 10.22, 'Marcus Aurelius'), and the sects of philosophy are the four schools mentioned by Lucian in the source cited in n. 29: Platonic, Stoic, Epicurean, and Peripatetic. Lucian's character Lycinus explains that the emperor established a considerable allowance for these philosophers.

3 **bigotry . . . offspring**] Although this bigotry leads to the persecution of philosophy, it is also a product of philosophy. It occurs when religious dogmas are expressed in terms of philosophical distinctions and arguments. When allied to the fervour of religion, philosophical doctrines are turned against free philosophical inquiry.

4 EPICURUS] Epicurus' philosophy plays a significant role in the imaginary speech beginning at 11.9. Hume presents Epicurus as attempting to convince the citizens of Athens that his philosophical principles are as innocuous and acceptable as those of other philosophers.

loosen . . . the ties of morality] When Hume wrote, a connection between providence and a future state (immortality) and the peace and safety of public morals was often assumed in politics, philosophy, and theology; and Epicurus' views were commonly denigrated. In *Dialogues* 12.1 Hume has his characters debate the proposition that 'a future state is so strong and necessary a security to morals, that we never ought to abandon or neglect it'. In the larger body of his writings Hume's own position does not seem essentially different from that expressed by Epicurus here: morality does not rest on a religious foundation and should be free of religious influence.

7 **white beans . . . black one**] Beans or pebbles were used for voting in ancient Athens and elsewhere in Greece. White beans were used to signify agreement or consent; black beans signified disagreement or dissent. Beans were also used as lots by which public officers were elected; those who drew the white beans were elected. In jury trials jurors used the white bean to vote for innocence, the black for guilty.

10 **religious philosophers**] philosophical theologians who attempt to rely on reason to build doctrines of God and a defence of a particular religion, without explicit appeal to revelation. Clarke (see *EHU* n. 16) and Butler (see ann. 1.14, 'late ones, of success') were two prominent such figures in Hume's period, but many preceded them.

wise arrangement of the universe] an apparent reference to philosophers and theologians who employ the design argument for the existence of God (see Ed. Intro., § 7.2), which Hume explores at length in his *Dialogues* (esp. Parts 2–3, 5, 7). Examples of the reach of such appeals in natural philosophy, connected to a theory of providence, are found in Scottish mathematician and astronomer John Keill (1671–1721), *An Introduction to the True Astronomy*, pp. i–ii, vi (citing Cicero); Boyle, *The Christian Virtuoso* (*Works*, 5: 519–22); Grotius, *Truth of the Christian Religion* 1.7, 10–11; and Bentley, *Eight Boyle Lectures on Atheism*.

fortuitous concourse of atoms] This exact expression was often used in reference to the Epicurean system. See Collins, *A Philosophical Inquiry concerning Human Liberty*, 58; Scottish physician George Cheyne (1671–1743), *Philosophical Principles of Natural Religion* 3.2 (p. 76) and 2.1–10 (esp. p. 15); and Bentley, 'Matter and Motion cannot

Think' (second of the *Boyle Lectures*), 4. Atomism is the metaphysical theory that the universe is comprised of indivisible and indestructible particles too small to be detected by the senses. The doctrine is found in classical writers that Hume cites elsewhere, including Leucippus and Democritus (both 5th–4th c. BC), as well as Epicurus.

10 **justness of this argument**] Hume does not in Section 11 explore in detail the soundness of the so-called design argument for the existence of God—an argument based on 'the order, beauty, and wise arrangement of the universe'. He examines the adequacy of the argument more thoroughly in his *Dialogues*. Here in Section 11 Hume challenges those who defend this argument (the 'antagonists and accusers') with principles that even defenders must acknowledge to be 'solid and satisfactory'. Many modern religious philosophers have denied that the universe could have been formed from the fortuitous coming together of atoms. Some of these philosophers put the atomic hypothesis to work in defence of a divine artificer and doctrine of creation. See Bentley, *Eight Boyle Lectures on Atheism*, first lecture (pp. 8–9); and Walter Charleton, *Physiologia Epicuro-Gassendo-Charltoniana* 2.4 (pp. 125–6).

I deny a providence and a future state] This important line is integral to Hume's choice of title for Section 11. He may be using the device of a speech by Epicurus not only as a mouthpiece for his views, but also as a more subtle way of persuading readers that in the modern world, no less than in the ancient, a secular view that denies religious doctrines such as providence and immortality may include principles that 'undermine not the foundations of society'.

11 **unguided force of matter**] Epicureans held that chance, or unguided force, is the source of the order in nature. Religious philosophers (cf. Berkeley, *Alciphron*, Dial. 3, §§ 10–11) who denied that the universe could have been formed and then evolved from chance or a fortuitous coming together of ingredients play a role in Hume's *Dialogues* (see Parts 6, 8–9), though no word deriving from 'atom' is mentioned in this work.

argument drawn from effects to causes] Hume outlines the argument of those who claim that divine existence is attested by 'the order of nature'. This argument is drawn from effects to causes because one starts with what one accepts as observable effects, such as the order and beauty of the world, and then 'reasons' to the cause of these effects, namely a designing, divine creator or workman. The analogical argument is therefore from order to design, rather than from design to a designer.

12 **indulge the licence of conjecture**] give the freedom to speculate with excessive leniency.

13 **ZEUXIS's pictures**] The influential Athenian painter Zeuxis (5th–4th c. BC) was renowned for excellence in perspective, expression, and subtle use of shade and light. He also worked in sculptures. 'Statuary' here refers to sculptor, 'architect' to a planner or constructor in the generic sense.

14 **JUPITER**] the supreme deity in the Roman pantheon. Jupiter was the lord of heaven who willed the course of human history and foresees the future while serving as guardian of law, justice, and virtue. The name is apparently used here (in the context of the imaginary speech by Epicurus to the Athenians) in reference to any deity who is a supreme 'cause or author'.

16 **golden or silver age**] an ancient legendary belief that an ideal period once existed in which there were no coercive rules and laws. The early poet Hesiod (8th–7th c. BC) may be one of the unnamed poets. In *NHR* (nn. 1 and 21) Hume refers to Hesiod's

Works and Days, where a reference to the golden or silver age is found in lines 109–20.

17 **gods . . . evil and disorder . . . intractable qualities of matter**] In these passages Hume raises the question whether the existence of evil and disorder is compatible with the power and attributes of God (or the gods). The honour of gods might be saved if some aspects of the universe, such as natural laws and intrinsic features of matter, *limited* what the gods were able to do. On these themes, see Hume's *Dialogues* 10–11, where some of the problems mentioned are referred to as 'Epicurus's old questions' (10.25).

qualities . . . in the effect] It does not seem justified to ascribe qualities to a cause (here God or the gods) beyond the qualities observed in the effect (here general features of the world such as intricacy, beauty, and apparent design).

19 **doctrine . . . in my gardens**] The 'doctrine' is a reference to Epicurus' teaching, in particular his denial of the creation and the providence of a supreme governor of the world. 'My gardens' is a reference to the garden in which Epicurus taught at his house; this site was the centre of his activity until his death. 'The Garden' came to refer to the community of Epicureans.

21 **life merely a passage**] Hume here returns to the subject of a future state. In his index, he placed this paragraph under the entry 'immortality'. 'Vain reasoners' are probably the representatives of religious thought or of speculative metaphysics who expressed views about a future life.

attributes . . . never seen exerted] Hume accepts the notion that a divine being could have attributes and powers with which we are not acquainted. However, he insists that mere conjecture and hypothesis are at work in speculation about those attributes and powers, because the limited order in the universe provides no evidence to support claims of the existence of these attributes.

22 *at present*, **exert itself**] This argument about justice in divine providence rests—as do many of the arguments in Section 11—on Hume's previously established principle that in tracing an effect to its cause, nothing can be ascribed to the cause except what is necessary to produce the effect.

23 **in the field, or in the senate**] in military matters (on the battlefield), or in political matters.

in the school, or in the closet] in a public place of instruction, or in a private room or study.

24 **art**] skilled design and craftsmanship.

26 **by analogy**] Hume is interested in how arguments from design that attempt to prove the existence of God proceed by analogy. The present hypothesis is that conventional forms of analogy based on experience do not support reasoning about the attributes of God because we have no relevant experience. See also Hume's *Dialogues*, Parts 2–3, 7–8.

27 **source of our mistake**] In reasoning about the attributes of God, some philosophers make inferences to what is appropriate conduct for God based on what they believe to be reasonable. Hume is critical of the anthropomorphic and unduly speculative nature of these inferences.

apology] 'Apology' means a defence—here, the imagined defence of Epicurus' position.

disputes concerning metaphysics and religion] This reference may refer to the discussion, found at 11.2, of the banishment of Protagoras and the death of Socrates for their views on metaphysics and religion. See also the discussion immediately below at 11.28–30. Hume thinks that political concerns or outcomes should not be permitted to influence the course of disputes in philosophy.

28 **punishments on vice . . . rewards on virtue**] This statement is presumably a reference to God's judgement of people in the afterlife, a religious teaching that motivates believers to act in the interests of society during their earthly lives. Providence and a future state represent two aspects of God's governance: in the present life God governs with a scheme of 'distributive justice', as Hume twice calls it in this section. Then, in the afterlife, virtue is rewarded and vice punished.

good citizens] See 11.4 and 11.10. Hume was himself sometimes accused of presenting a socially dangerous philosophy for the reasons he mentions here. In *A View of the Principal Deistical Writers* (Letter 17 [1: 281–2]), English Presbyterian minister John Leland (1691–1766) even accused him of a 'bad influence on the community' in his arguments in Section 11 of *EHU*.

29 **tolerate every principle**] Hume is maintaining that in a political state one should be allowed the freedom to advance philosophical doctrines or views without restriction. He believes that the state will not suffer by allowing this liberty.

enthusiasm among philosophers] Enthusiasm refers to zealous belief, sometimes involving frenzied inspirations and plans by visionaries that Hume elsewhere calls fanatics (*EPM* 3.7 and 3.24; 'Of Superstition and Enthusiasm' 3, 6–8). Hume commonly links enthusiasm to religious fanaticism. However, he appreciated that philosophers can be enthusiasts in the extended sense of fanatic devotees. (At the very end of *EPM* Hume discusses a philosophical enthusiasm such as that found in Diogenes of Sinope.)

30 **have no parallel**] See the more developed arguments on this and other points in this paragraph in Hume's *Dialogues* (introduced at 2.24). The antagonists would presumably include Stillingfleet, Cheyne, Tillotson, and other 'religious philosophers', as Hume uses the term at 11.10.

cause to the effect] The views about causes and effects that Hume has expressed throughout *EHU* make it as difficult to move from a singular cause (God) to its effect (the universe) as to move from a singular effect to its cause.

SECTION 12

'What is meant by a sceptic?' (12.2). Descartes presented a type of scepticism that recommends a universal doubt of all beliefs, including beliefs about the reliability of our mental faculties. This form of scepticism is self-defeating; it can deliver no assurance of the truth or reliability of anything. Far preferable is a mitigated scepticism that scrutinizes questionable beliefs and teaches 'a proper impartiality in our judgments' while protecting us from prejudice and rash opinion (12.4).

Sceptics have often been concerned with whether our senses accurately report the nature of objects and events. For example, is the house we see really a house external to us or is it merely a perception in our minds? A sceptic with regard to the senses teaches that these objects and events are nothing but perceptions (12.9). Common belief tells us that this scepticism is unwarranted, but is common belief correct? From a philosophical viewpoint the sceptic's thesis seems warranted. None the less, there is a 'blind and powerful instinct of nature' that compels us to believe that the images that come from our senses *are* external objects. Philosophical scepticism is not sufficiently powerful to convince us that these 'external' objects are nothing but mental images.

Academic scepticism is a useful form of mitigated scepticism because it prevents us from succumbing to undue conjecture and dogmatic belief. This form of scepticism contrasts sharply with the excessive scepticism known as Pyrrhonism, which doubts everything and thus makes no contribution either to our understanding of the world or to practical affairs. The Pyrrhonian sceptic recommends a suspension of judgement about even basic beliefs—a recommendation that Hume thinks that people will be unable to follow: 'all human life must perish, were [Pyrrhonian] principles universally and steadily to prevail' (12.23). In the end human nature triumphs over deep scepticism about the existence of external objects. (For additional discussion of Section 12, see Ed. Intro., §8.)

> ACADEMICAL OR SCEPTICAL PHILOSOPHY] 'Academical' is one form of 'scep-
> tical', as the name 'academic scepticism' indicates. However, Hume may be using
> 'sceptical' in this title to distinguish academic scepticism, with which he is sympa-
> thetic, from the types of scepticism that he rejects. For the meaning of both terms,
> see ann. 5.1 and 12.21–5. Section 12 exhibits a number of parallels with *THN* 1.4.1–4,
> but also reveals many new directions of thinking.

1 **fallacies of *Atheists*]** Many philosophers of Hume's period either attempted to refute atheism or argued that there are no real atheists. The term 'atheist' was
applied not only to people who denied the existence of God, but also to people
who had no religion, denied God's providence, or denied an afterlife. When Hume
says, 'the most religious philosophers still dispute whether any man can be so
blinded as to be a speculative atheist', he may be referring to figures such as
Berkeley, who reports that 'it hath often been said, there is no such thing as a speculative atheist' (*Alciphron*, Advertisement), and Cheyne, who says, 'That there are no
Speculative Atheists . . . seems . . . evident' (*Philosophical Principles of Natural Religion*
3.1).

2 **enemy of religion]** Hume is introducing the question 'What is meant by a sceptic?',
but it is unclear at this point which sceptics he has in mind. He might mean the ancient
sceptics, the sceptics about religion discussed in the previous paragraph, or the Cartesian sceptics discussed in the next paragraph. Perhaps Hume is referring to any sceptic
whose epistemology casts doubt on religious truth-claims, and perhaps he is leading
up to his discussion of the several kinds of scepticism.

3 **scepticism, *antecedent*]** This scepticism, antecedent to investigation, is distinguished
from the scepticism consequent to investigation first mentioned at 12.5. Antecedent
doubt is not based on investigations or discoveries, but on a universal doubt that is
prior to the establishment of any basis for doubt.

CARTESIAN **doubt]** Deficiencies in our knowledge of the world and the perfection of mathematics led Descartes on a quest for knowledge that is certain. He argued that we must doubt everything. Hume denounces this Cartesian doubt,
with its antecedent scepticism about our mental faculties, on grounds that we
must use these faculties even to formulate our doubts and to find a substantial
premiss.

4 **when more moderate]** This species of scepticism embraces a milder form of doubt

than does universal doubt. Philosophers of this persuasion did not seek knowledge under the Cartesian criterion of certainty. For them reasonable or warranted belief—a form of probability—counts as knowledge. See Gassendi, *Syntagma*, Logic 2, and *Exercises Against the Aristotelians* (e.g. 2.6.5–6 on scepticism). See also French mathematician and scientist Marin Mersenne (1588–1648), *La Vérité des sciences*, Dedicatory Letter, Preface, 1.1–5, 9–15; 2.1.

imbibed from education] 'Education' here suggests absorbing second-hand opinion with the consequence that a bias is transmitted or proper learning obstructed. Scepticism can be used to promote an avoidance of such uncritical enculturation and training. This subject is treated in *THN* 1.3.9.17–1.3.10.1.

5 **scepticism, *consequent*]** Hume is contrasting this species of scepticism to what he referred to at 12.3 as 'scepticism, *antecedent* to all study and philosophy'. Consequent scepticism does not attack a class of beliefs directly (as Hume does in Sections 10–11 in discussing beliefs in miracles and natural religion); rather, it indirectly casts doubt on a class of beliefs by questioning the adequacy of the ways we have come to possess those beliefs. For example, it questions the belief that the 'objects' of perception exist in the external world by examining how we acquire this belief.

6 **oar in water . . . pressing one eye**] Compare *THN* 1.4.2.45 for the eye-pressing example; *THN* 1.4.2 treats perceptual scepticism. See also the classical arguments in Sextus Empiricus, *Outlines of Pyrrhonism* 1.36–59, 78–94, 101–11, 118–35, 140–2, 163.

9 **slightest philosophy**] See Ed. Intro., §8.4 for an explanation of this sceptical thesis.

10 **cavils**] frivolous or quibbling arguments (but cf. 'profounder . . . sceptics' in 12.14 below).

11 **caused by external objects**] Hume typically does not attempt to explain the physical or psychological conditions that give rise to impressions. He may here be criticizing Locke's causal theory of perception. See *THN* 1.3.5.2; 1.4.2; and 2.1.1.2.

13 **veracity of the Supreme Being**] Apparently a reference to 12.3 on Cartesian doubt. Descartes used his basic framework to attempt to demonstrate the existence of a veracious God, whose existence would guarantee the truth of all propositions based on clear and distinct ideas. This conclusion was then used to guarantee the accuracy of our knowledge of the nature of mind, body, and the existence of the external world. (*Meditations on First Philosophy* 1 and 6 [2: 15, 54–62].)

15 **modern enquirers**] When Hume says, 'it is universally allowed by modern enquirers', he is referring to a widespread acceptance of the view that the ideas of *secondary* qualities of objects, such as colours and the other items listed by Hume, are merely unrepresentative perceptions of the mind, whereas the ideas of *primary* qualities are representative of qualities actually *in* external objects (see entry immediately below). Locke was a prominent representative (*Essay* 2.8; 4.3.11–14). (Hume apparently thought that Berkeley and Bayle are exceptions to the position 'universally allowed'. See Berkeley, *Principles* 1.9–15; Bayle, *Dictionary*, 'Pyrrho'.)

external archetype] Some philosophers used this terminology to refer to the *object represented* in perception (by contrast to the *perception itself*).

primary qualities of extension and solidity] Primary qualities are reliably represented in perception, whereas secondary qualities (for example, those giving rise to the ideas of colour, sound, and warmth) were thought by many philosophers not to be reliably represented by ideas. Standard lists of spatio-temporal primary qualities included extension, shape, size, volume, position, and state of motion; standard lists of material primary qualities included solidity, mass, inertness, and impenetrability. Cf. *THN* 1.4.2.12; 1.4.4.5–6.

even absurd] See the discussion of abstract ideas below in ann. n. 34.

scholastic notions] These notions are either those of Aristotelian Scholastics, who held that general ideas (universals) are abstract entities and not individuals, or Platonist Scholastics, who held that general ideas are individuals that function as general ideas. 'Scholastics' is a broad category that includes Thomists, Scotists, Suarezians, etc.

n. 32 BERKELEY] Berkeley discusses primary and secondary qualities in *Principles*, especially 1.9–25, 73, 87, 102. Though Hume held Berkeley to be a true sceptic whose arguments produce no conviction, Berkeley's conclusion that sensible things are simply what we perceive often appear similar to Hume's own conclusions. See Ed. Intro., §8.4, and ann. 12.15, 'modern enquirers' and 'primary qualities of extension and solidity'.

n. 32 BAYLE] Pierre Bayle was a prominent metaphysical sceptic of the 17th century. Bayle argued that Descartes's and Malebranche's assumptions, for example, do not permit one to know that an external world exists. In an argument that anticipated Berkeley's views, Bayle argued against the Cartesians that the scepticism with which philosophers have doubted secondary properties should also lead them to doubt primary properties (*Dictionary*, 'Zeno of Elea' (B), (H)).

n. 32 **against the sceptics**] The full title mentioned by Hume of the work by Berkeley was added in the second edition (1734): *A Treatise Concerning the Principles of Human Knowledge. Wherein the Chief Causes of Error and Difficulty in the Sciences, with the Grounds of Scepticism, Atheism, and Irreligion, are Inquired Into*. Berkeley often attacked unorthodox or deviant thinking in religion.

n. 32 **in reality, merely sceptical**] This passage is another example of Hume's thesis that sceptical arguments may perplex us momentarily, but have no enduring or continual effect.

16 **contend against it**] Once matter is stripped of its primary and secondary qualities (every quality that we know in experience), nothing is left but an unknown something that some philosophers say causes perceptions in us. Hume suggests that this doctrine has been defended so poorly that no sceptic would find it worthy of refutation.

17 **sceptics to destroy *reason***] At the beginning of Part 2 Hume turns to a brief discussion of the subject of scepticism with regard to reason. A rich discussion of this topic is found in *THN* 1.4.1. However, in *EHU* 12.17–18 Hume concentrates more on material from *THN* 1.2.1–4 than 1.4.1.

18 **infinite divisibility**] See *THN* 1.2.1–4 for a detailed discussion. Hume there concludes that our ideas of space and time derive from indivisible and minimal impressions arrayed in a particular manner. Infinite divisibility, a teaching that descends from Aristotle, was widely accepted in the history of philosophy prior to Hume. In *Abstract* 29 Hume says that philosophy and common sense have, with 'regard to the question of infinite divisibility . . . wag'd most cruel wars with each other'. An influential discussion is found in Bayle, *Dictionary*, 'Zeno of Elea' (G).

n. 33 **mathematical points**] These are indivisible points without dimension. Chambers frames the controversy about mathematical points as follows: 'Many Authors are led to deny the reality of atoms, together with that of mathematical points: An

Atom, say they, either has parts, or it has none: if it have none, it is a mere mathematical point: If it have, then do these parts also consist of others, and so to infinity' (*Cyclopædia*, 'atom'). In a work known to have influenced Hume, Bayle says that 'several nothingnesses of extension joined together will never make an extension' (*Dictionary*, 'Zeno of Elea' (G)). In *THN* 1.2.2–5 Hume discusses 'disputes . . . about mathematical points' in more detail.

19 **infinite number . . . passing in succession**] The theory seems 'absurd' because if there were an infinite number of real parts of time there could not be real finite parts; the parts would themselves be infinitely divisible.

n. 34 **abstract or general ideas**] abstract (or general) ideas are general in representation, though the idea itself is of a particular item. See *THN* 1.1.7.1–6. Hume is assuming his readers' familiarity with a controversy involving Locke and Berkeley. Locke wondered how a *particular* idea (of a horse or a person, say) could represent a *class* of things (horses or persons). He maintained that this representation occurred when the mind abstracted the particular features of horses and persons (colour, weight, etc.) in order to achieve the level of generality needed for reference to all horses and all persons. By contrast, Berkeley argued that all ideas are particular; some become general not by abstraction but by the use we make of them to represent the members of a class (*Principles*, especially Introduction 12–15 and 1.5–6). Hume supports Berkeley.

21 *popular* or *philosophical*] Classical sceptics advanced these 'popular arguments', some of which Hume lists immediately below and declares weak. He takes the philosophical objections seriously; see ann. 12.22.

PYRRHONISM] On the nature of Pyrrhonism, see Ed. Intro., §8.1.

same condition as other mortals] Hume maintained that sceptical doubt would vanish as soon as philosophers ceased their moments of reflection. He thinks that some sceptics do not act on what they profess, thereby becoming a great 'subverter' of their own doctrines. It appears that Pyrrhonians and other ancient sceptics expected their doubt to have pervasive practical import and *not* to be merely philosophical. It had been reported that Pyrrho would suspend judgement about what to do even when encountering serious dangers, such as a deep precipice or a mad dog.

22 *philosophical* . . . **more profound researches**] Having now dispatched popular scepticism and Pyrrhonism, Hume returns to philosophical objections. These are presumably the sceptical problems that he takes seriously. In this *Enquiry* they have to do with various doubts about human understanding.

23 *excessive* **scepticism**] Pyrrhonism, unlike academic scepticism, exemplifies a scepticism that does not stay within proper boundaries. See the discussion of 'mitigated scepticism' at 12.24.

23 COPERNICAN or PTOLEMAIC] Astronomer Nicolaus Copernicus (1473–1543) and his defenders developed the heliocentric (sun-centred) conception of the universe in opposition to the geocentric (earth-centred) conception of Alexandrian astronomer Ptolemy (2nd c. AD). The Ptolemaic system dominated astronomy until the advent of the Copernican system. Not until the late 17th century, when the laws discovered by Johannes Kepler (1571–1630) became almost universally accepted by competent astronomers, did the Ptolemaic conception begin to lose supporters.

STOIC or EPICUREAN] For pertinent material on Stoicism, see ann. 5.1, 'philosophic sage', and 8.34, 'some philosophers . . . ancient STOICS'. On Epicureanism, see ann. 11.2 ('Epicurus . . . Epicureanism') 4 ('Epicurus').

24 **result of this PYRRHONISM**] Hume here seems to suggest that academical philosophy is a mitigated variant of Pyrrhonian scepticism. In the mitigated form common sense and reflection strip Pyrrhonism of its excessive character and confine inquiry to a study of the limits of reason, understanding, and other capacities of the mind.

25 **common life**] Hume believes that to reach correct and useful judgements we should avoid topics that promote flights of the imagination, where understanding is unsuited to attain proper conclusions. In areas of life in which we encounter ambitious flights of fancy, we would do better to confine our claim to what we know in the 'common life'. The importance of common life appears frequently in Hume's philosophy, though not as frequently as the standard of 'experience', which can correct even 'the reflections of common life' mentioned later in this paragraph.

force of the PYRRHONIAN doubt] This passage is an expression of the value that Hume sees in Pyrrhonian doubt, despite his rejection of the Pyrrhonian philosophy in general. He regards this form of doubt as helping to curb undue speculation.

27 **sophistry and illusion**] Hume is claiming that only the formal sciences, notably mathematics, *demonstrate* conclusions. Attempts to extend the methods of mathematics to philosophy (as Spinoza, Hutcheson, and others had attempted) yield sophistry and illusion rather than knowledge. Hume carries this theme down to the last line of *EHU*, which repeats the expression 'sophistry and illusion'.

squares of the other two sides] the Pythagorean theorem, perhaps first recorded in Euclid's *Elements*.

imperfect definition] This definition does not capture a true relation of ideas (see ann. 4.1) and therefore cannot be an object of *knowledge* in the strict sense.

28 **No negation of a fact can involve a contradiction**] See Ed. Intro., §5.1 and ann. 4.2.

sciences, properly so called] mathematical sciences, or those capable of demonstrations from relations of ideas. See ann. 4.1 and Ed. Intro., §5.1.

n. 35 *Ex nihilo, nihil fit*] Translation: 'Out of nothing comes nothing'. Lucretius may be the earliest source for this aphorism. He says both that 'nothing is ever by divine power produced from nothing' and that 'nothing can be created from nothing' (*De rerum natura* 1.150, 155–6).

32 *faith* **and divine revelation**] Hume need not be interpreted as endorsing appeals to faith and revelation. The appearance of this thesis in a chapter on scepticism may only be his way of presenting the claims of so-called fideism. Proponents of this view are sceptical of the capacity of reason and experience to support divinity or theology and emphasize acts of faith and appeals to revelation. From a fideistic perspective Pyrrhonism may become the ally of religious belief. Both acknowledge the weakness of human reason and both find attacks upon religion dogmatic.

33 **taste and sentiment**] This passage reflects a major theme in Hume's moral philosophy (see *EPM* 1.3–5). See above ann. 1.1; 4.1; 12.27 for further information on the point and meaning of this passage and for reasons to support Hume's claim that '[M]orals and criticism' are 'not so properly objects of the understanding'.

34 **school metaphysics**] See ann. n. 1 (Section 2), 'schoolmen'.

Glossary

This Glossary treats words in the text and notes of *EHU* that many students find unfamiliar or otherwise puzzling. Often, but not always, these words are archaic and now rarely used. Synonyms are used rather than formal definitions whenever they are simpler, less controversial, and adequate to the task of eliminating uncertainty about the text. Occasionally, however, a formal definition is needed. If Hume provides a definition in one of his works, that definition is preferred. Hume's metaphors are also explained if they have potentially puzzling meanings.

The Glossary and the annotations are mutually supplementary. Words that occur only once in *EHU* and that are defined in the annotations do not appear in the Glossary. Unlike the annotations, words in the Glossary are not indicated by markers in the text of *EHU*.

Each term in the Glossary is followed by its section and paragraph locations. When a term is used in *EHU* more than ten times with the listed meaning, the designation *passim*—'here and there'—is used to indicate frequent usage; section and paragraph numbers are not provided for these entries.

More than one meaning is listed for many terms. If a term is equivocal, the distinct meanings are segregated by numbers (1, 2, . . . , *n*), and the passages in Hume's text where the proper meanings occur are listed separately under each number. More commonly a term is not equivocal, but a family of related, English-language synonyms is helpful in the attempt to identify Hume's usage. More than one synonym or definition is often listed in explicating a single term. Several alternative synonyms or definitions can be applied to a single passage when it is unclear which term most adequately captures Hume's meaning. Rather than dictate 'the meaning' by presenting only a single possibility, a range of the possible senses of the term is provided. Of course, some listed meanings will not fit every appearance of the word in Hume's text.

Verb (*vb.*), noun substantive (*n.*), and adjective (*adj.*) forms are distinguished if needed for clarity.

Sources and Acknowledgements

The glossing has relied heavily on the following sources: Nathan Bailey (ed.), *Dictionarium Britannicum* (1730; fac. Hildesheim: Olms, 1969); Ephraim Chambers (ed.), *Cyclopædia; or an Universal Dictionary of Arts and Sciences* (London, 1728); Thomas Dyche and William Pardon, *A New General English Dictionary*, 3rd edn. (1740; fac. Hildesheim: Olms, 1972); John Harris, *Lexicon technicum* (London: 1704–10; fac. New York: Johnson Reprint, 1966); Samuel Johnson, *A Dictionary of the English Language* (London, 1755), several editions; *Oxford English Dictionary*, primarily the second electronic edition (Oxford: Oxford University Press, 1992). Although editors of glossaries often cite such authoritative sources in entries, these works have been used so extensively below that constant citation would be intrusive and unilluminating. For example, the *OED* and Dyche and Pardon have been consulted for almost every entry.

Glossary

Searches have been made of many texts in the history of modern philosophy to determine how these philosophers use various terms. The database in the Intelex PastMasters series has been particularly helpful. Finally, I have profited from the previous work of many other editors and owe a particular debt to David and Mary Norton, Edwin Curley, and P. H. Nidditch.

abstruse: deep, demanding, and theoretical. 1.3; 1.6; 1.12; 1.17; 4.23; 9.5.

absurd: unfathomable; contrary to common sense; incomprehensible. 8.32; 10.16; 10.41; 12.2; 12.15; 12.18; 12.20.

adventures (at adventures): at random; on or by chance. 3.1; 3.10.

advertisement: announcement by publication, commonly in the opening part of a book. See page 83 and also 'How to Use this Book', 3 and ann., 215–16.

affect: given to; like. 1.14; 7.22.

affection: mental state; feeling; emotion. *Passim.*

agreeable: conformable. 1.3; 1.5; 1.6; 7.28; 10.12; 10.16.

amiable: (1) agreeable; lovely. 1.1. (2) worthy; estimable. 1.5.

application: careful attention to or examination of something. 1.5; 1.15; 7.4.

artifice: strategy; crafty move. 3.12; 10.37; 11.24.

artificer: one who makes something by art or skill. 8.12; 8.17.

aspect: perspective; appearance. 1.13; 12.6.

atheism, atheist: a classification indicating not only those who do not believe in God, but also those who believe in God in an unacceptably unorthodox manner. The term can also be applied to those who fail to believe in a critical theistic belief, such as divine providence or the afterlife. 10.25; n. 25; 12.1; n. 32.

auditor: one who hears, listens, or attends to what is spoken. 10.17.

belief: See Ed. Intro., 30–1.

breast: mind; seat of the passions and affections. 10.1.

brute: lacking in reason or understanding. 4.23; 8.22; 9.5; 11.13.

canvass: survey; criticize. 10.17.

chance: See Ed. Intro. and ann., 40–1, 231–2.

character: (1) trait or quality of a person. *Passim.* (2) distinguished status or position. *Passim.*

chimerical: imaginary; visionary—and without ground of truth. 1.14.

cloaths: clothes. 5.18.

closet: a study or private room (**in the closet**: in private; in a study or private room). 11.23.

compass: extent; scope; range. 1.14; 1.15; 3.7; 3.11; 5.13; 7.2. See also ann. 1.14.

complexion: properties of a person; nature. n. 18.

complication: combination; joining or mixing. n. 20.

Glossary

composition: compounded item constituted by parts; mixing or joining of items together. *Passim*.

compounded: formed through a combination of different elements or ingredients; combined; composite. 2.6; 3.1.

comprehend: include. 3.11; 8.17; 8.34; 11.25.

conceit: fanciful conception or notion; whim. 7.2; 11.21.

concourse: flowing together or meeting of things; concurrence. 11.10.

condition: social standing; class; position. 7.13; 10.19; 12.21; 12.23.

constitution: the states, qualities, dispositions, and principles that make up a living being's nature. 8.35.

convenient: suitable; appropriate. 10.2. See also **inconvenience**.

correspondent: corresponding. 2.7; 2.8; 5.22; 7.4.

craft: trickiness, cunning, and possibly fraud. 1.11.

criticism: evaluation of literary works or discourse; art of appraising writing or oration. 1.2; 8.18; 12.33.

custom: psychological habit. *Passim*.

deceitful: misleading (deceptive), but without intent to deceive. 1.12; 12.3; 12.22.

declare: make clear. n. 25; 10.40.

delicacy: sense of what is becoming or proper. 1.5.

delicate: astute; perceptive. 1.8; 11.30.

delusive: deceptive. 10.22.

demonstration: a type of proof in which true conclusions known with certainty (undeniability) are derived from premises that are true and certain (undeniable or self-evident). n. 10; 12.18; 12.27; 12.28.

demonstrative: what is demonstrated. See **demonstration**.

destroy: counteract; neutralize; counter. *Passim*.

diffidence: distrust; lack of confidence; suspicion. 7.8; 12.18.

diffident: distrustful; undogmatic. 12.3; 12.24.

disabuse: free from error; inform truly. 11.28.

divines: ministers; those appointed to teach religion or divinity. n. 25; 12.2.

durst: dared—past tense of *dare*. n. 25.

education: beliefs acquired by acculturation, exposure, or habituation; 'opinions or notions of things, to which we have been accustom'd from our infancy' (quoting *THN* 1.3.9.17). 8.11; 9.3; n. 20; 10.15; 12.4.

eloquence: the art of oratory; the artful use of words. 1.1; 7.30; 10.18; 10.23; 10.25; 11.6.

eminent: elevated. 10.22; 10.27.

engage: (1) gain; secure. 1.1; 8.35; 9.5; 10.22. (2) influence; persuade. 4.23; 8.18; 9.17; 10.10.

enow: enough. 8.36; 10.21.

Glossary

enthusiasm: zealous or frenzied inspiration, belief, or commitment. n. 25; 11.29.

esteem: judge; consider; think. 1.14; 4.10; 4.12; 10.33.

experience: (1) empirical testing; experimental trial. *Passim.* (2) observation; accumulation of data as the basis of conclusions. *Passim.*

experiment (and experimental): See Ed. Intro., 10, 12–13.

express: explicit. 10.24.

extension: extendedness in space; space. 7.8; 12.15; 12.18; n. 33.

fabulous: legendary. 3.7; 10.40.

faculty: capacity, function, or power of the mind; mental ability such as sensation, cognition, imagination, and memory. 2.5; 5.12.

fallacious: deceptive; misleading. 5.22; 11.25; 12.22.

fallaciousness: deceitfulness or false appearance. 12.5.

false: counterfeit; pretended; feigned (not necessarily involving a false proposition). 1.12; 8.26; 10.17; 10.22; n. 18.

fancy: (1) *vb.* imagine; mentally invent. 4.8; 7.24. (2) *n.* the imagination. 3.11; 5.11; 5.16; 7.21; 10.18; n. 33.

feign: imagine; invent. 5.10.

fiat: command or order having as its object the creation of something. 7.20.

fine: subtle; refined. 1.13; 10.25; 10.34.

fly: flee. 1.11.

fond: kind; tender. 5.18; 11.23; 12.24.

frame: *n.* construction; state. 8.35; 10.20.

gaoler: jailer. 8.19.

generation: generative reproduction. 1.12; 7.21.

genius: natural disposition or aptitude. 1.9; 3.5; 9.5; 10.25; 10.26; 11.10.

grace: genteel air (as in a graceful person). n. 25; 11.21.

head: (1) topic; category. 2.2; 12.21. (2) heading. 1.13.

impertinent: presumptuous. 10.2.

impression: original perception, not merely a copy; first appearance of sensations or passions. *Passim.*

impudence: shameless boldness; foolishness. 10.17.

impulse: contact force causing motion. 4.8; 4.10; 4.12; 5.5; 5.11; 6.4; 7.6; 7.21; 7.25.

inconvenience: incongruity. 3.12.

indifferent: of no special importance; of small value or little consequence. 11.9.

indolence: insensibility or indifference (typically, towards pain). 1.12; 5.1.

indulgence: (1) admiration; appreciation. 5.1. (2) toleration. 11.29; 12.24.

in infinitum: to infinity. 5.7.

insist: dwell; reflect at length. 4.16; 8.16; 11.16; 12.6; 12.21; 12.22.

inspire: suggest to; cause in (the mind). 1.8; 12.24.

interposition: intervention. n. 23.

invention: inventiveness; faculty of inventiveness. 4.9; 4.10; 4.11; 7.4.

issue: end; termination; discharge. 8.22; 10.32; 11.23.

jealous (of): vigilant in guarding; scrupulously careful to protect. 11.4.

kindle: become excited or motivated; stir up. 3.12; 10.30.

letters: literature of the learned; learning. 1.5; 1.8; n. 25.

libertine: free-thinker; one who holds free and loose opinions about religion. 5.1; 10.26.

literature: learning; scholarship. 1.2.

mart: market-place; emporium. 10.23.

medium: (1) the second proposition in a syllogism; ground or device for reaching conclusions. 4.16; n. 25; 11.22; 12.27. (2) mid-point; middle state. 4.21; 12.6.

methodized: arranged in an orderly fashion; reduced to method or order. 12.25.

moment: cause of action; determining influence. 4.13.

moral reasoning: reasoning that is factual; having a probable conclusion based on factual evidence. 4.18; 7.2; 12.29; 12.31.

natural philosophy: what is now referred to as the natural sciences. 4.7; 4.13; 7.2; 8.27; 12.31. See also ann. 1.1; 1.5; 4.7.

nay: term used to insert a better formulated or more correct statement than one previously made. 3.1; 4.23; 10.22.

nice: subtle; precise; fine. 2.2; n. 20; 11.30.

œconomy: (1) organization, structure, or arrangement in the various parts of something (for example, of the mind). 1.15; 8.34. (2) in theology: method of divine government or administration of the world. 8.1. (3) organization or internal constitution in the major subdivisions in nature (animal economy, vegetable economy, etc.). 8.14. (4) organization or management of a home or dwelling. 9.6.

office: role; service; assigned charge. 7.13; 7.15; 10.23; n. 25.

open: clear. 1.3; 6.4.

order: species; class. *Passim.*

original: natural (prior to experience). *Passim.*

overbalance: outweigh; override. 1.12; 10.4.

parts: abilities; capacities. 1.13.

peculiar: (1) singular; particular. 1.1; 5.10. (2) special; distinctive. 3.13; 3.17; 5.12; 8.11.

penetration: an intellectual faculty or virtue of discovery by gaining access to the inner content of something. 1.13; 4.17; 7.27; n. 25.

Glossary

phænomenon: immediate object of perception; any thing or event that is perceived or observed; in natural philosophy, this term signifies any appearance or operation of a natural body. *Passim.*

philosopher (natural philosopher): person versed in or who examines natural science. 1.1; 1.14; 1.15; 7.21; 8.7; 11.29.

physic: study or practice of medicine. 12.31.

polite: polished; refined; civilized. 1.5; 1.8; 8.18; 11.6.

pompous: magnificent; grand. 5.7.

positive: sure; self-certain. 1.13; 8.34; n. 22.

precedent: preceding. 2.6; n. 1.

pretence: rationale; pretension. 4.23; 5.1; 8.18; 8.26; 10.38; 11.24.

pretend: claim; maintain. 4.15; 7.21; n. 25. See also **pretend to** and **pretension**.

pretend to: lay claim to; assert responsibility for. *Passim.*

pretension: (1) declaration; claim. 4.14; 7.10. (2) ambition; intention; aspiration. 1.15; 5.1; 10.17.

prickle: thing with which to prick. n. 25.

principle: cause; causal agent. *Passim.*

prodigy: something very strange or uncommon. 10.14; n. 25; 10.39; 12.18.

prosecute: pursue. 2.6.

prosecution: the pursuit of. 4.3.

prospect: outlook; mental insight. 1.10.

purpose: *vb.* intend; propose. 1.4.

quickening: arousing; exciting. 5.16.

receive: accept as true or correct. n. 8; 8.25; 8.27; 10.20; 10.40; 12.18.

received: widely accepted; leading. 6.4.

refined: (1) abstract. 5.1. (2) very subtle. 7.11; 10.24.

relicts: relics; items revered because they belonged to a holy person. 5.18.

run over: considered; thought about. 3.3; 3.11; 12.34.

scalenum: scalene; a triangle whose three sides are of unequal length. 7.1; 12.15.

sceptic: See Ed. Intro., 51–61.

schools (*adj.* school): Scholastic philosophers or the subject-matter taught in medieval and early modern European universities. n. 18; 8.27; 12.34.

science: a science, by contrast to an art, is a developed system or theory and a branch of demonstrated knowledge, whether formal or empirical. A list of the sciences in the eighteenth century might include grammar, logic, law, natural philosophy, morals, politics, rhetoric, arithmetic, geometry, astronomy, and music. Some writers would include history and divinity. *Passim.*

scope: purpose; aim. 10.24; 12.17.

scruple: (1) *n.* dispute; doubt. 4.16; 7.27; 8.19; 12.23; 12.25. (2) *vb.* doubt; question; question the truth of. n. 8; 10.29.

secret: concealed; undisclosed. (Does not require an intentional action.) *Passim.*

secretly: privately. 3.1.

security: confidence; assurance. 1.6; 6.3; 8.34; 11.9; 11.19.

sensible: (1) cognizant; aware. *Passim.* (2) perceivable by the senses. *Passim.* (3) noticeable; noteworthy. *Passim.*

sentiment: This term typically refers to an inner sensing, feeling, or emotion of which a person is aware—for example, anger, approval, disgust, sympathy, and compassion—but it is often used, like 'taste', to refer to judgement and opinion. Hume does not sharply distinguish sensing, judging, believing, responding, preferring, and the like. *Passim.* See also ann. 1.1.

several: distinct; separate. 1.9.

shock: collision. 7.28; 7.30; 8.4.

singly: singularly. 8.8.

solidity: good sense. 10.25.

soul: mind. 5.8; 7.9; 7.11; 7.17; 7.21; 8.22.

specious: plausible and attractive; seemingly allowable and just. 8.9; 8.34; 10.38.

spring: source or origin; cause. 1.15; 3.9; 4.12.

standish: inkstand (stand and dish). 8.20.

statuary: a person who makes or carves images in wood or stone. 11.13.

still: regularly; consistently. 1.2.

subjected: submitted. 8.32; 12.5.

subserviency: serviceableness, helpfulness, or usefulness towards an end. 1.8; 1.9.

suitable: conforming; corresponding. 8.34; 8.35; 8.36; 10.13; 11.3; 11.4; 11.16.

supine: careless; negligent. 5.1.

support: hold; maintain. 1.4; 4.16; 4.21; 12.18.

sympathy: a receptive and responsive sharing of another's opinion, distress, pleasure, or emotion. Often when Hume uses the word 'sympathy' he is pointing not to a sentiment, but to a psychological capacity to feel or arrive at sentiments. 3.11; 3.12; 3.13; 3.18.

system: organized body of principles; comprehensive philosophy. *Passim.*

taste: a properly cultivated faculty that equips us to reach good judgements and opinions regarding what is appropriate, excellent, beautiful, and the like. Hume uses both 'taste' and 'sentiment' to refer to judgement and opinion. *Passim.* See also ann. 1.1.

temper: temperament; mental constitution; disposition. 5.1; 8.7; n. 18; 8.30; 12.24.

timorous: careful; cautious. 12.4.

tract: series. 3.1.

try: test. 8.22; 11.6.

undistinguished: indistinct; confused. 12.24.

view: prospect. 1.1; 3.6; 6.3.

Glossary

violence: intensity of influence; passionate quality; commanding effect. 3.11; 8.31; 12.24.

vulgar: (1) *adj.* common; ordinary; unsophisticated. n. 13; 10.18; 11.3. (2) *n.* common or ordinary people. 7.21; 8.13; 9.5; 10.21; 10.34. See also **vulgarly**.

vulgarly: commonly; in common speech. n. 8.

References

The authors and works in this reference list are of two types: (1) works cited by Hume; (2) works cited by the editor in the annotations or introduction to this volume. The editions listed below were relied upon whenever specific references are made by the editor to the works in this list.

In the case of editions having more than one volume, the number of volumes is reported; if volumes were issued in a multi-volume edition in more than a single year, both volume numbers and individual dates of publication are reported. The title is recorded as it appears on the title-page. In a few cases involving non-standard titles, the original title and a standard translation of the title are used. Loeb Library editions are used for classical works wherever possible (abbreviated 'Loeb Library'); the dates listed are printing dates for the individual volumes or series of volumes used by the editor, not original dates of publication or dates of revised editions.

English capitalization is often normalized to modern practice. Entries for Latin and French sources follow late twentieth-century forms. These titles are accompanied by a translation of the title into English. An attempt has been made to supply more accurate translations than those found on the title-pages of many standard, published sources in English. The reader therefore should not expect the translation to follow conventional English renderings.

Entries of the form 'EHU Sect. 3.7' and 'EHU n. 21' refer to one or more locations in Hume's text where the listed work is mentioned or alluded to.

ANNET, PETER, *The Resurrection of Jesus Considered: In Answer to the Tryal of the Witnesses* (London, 1744).

ARISTOTLE, *The Metaphysics*, trans. Hugh Tredennick, 2 vols., Loeb Library (1933–5).

—— *The Nicomachean Ethics*, trans. H. Rackham, Loeb Library (1947).

—— *The Physics*, trans. Philip H. Wicksteed and Francis M. Cornford, 2 vols., Loeb Library (1929–34).

—— *The Poetics*, trans. W. Hamilton Fyfe, Loeb Library (1927). Bound with 'Longinus' and Demetrius. *EHU* n. 5.

ARNAULD, ANTOINE. See Leibniz.

—— and NICOLE, PIERRE, *Logic or the Art of Thinking*, ed. and trans. Jill Vance Buroker (Cambridge: Cambridge University Press, 1996).

AURELIUS ANTONINUS, MARCUS, *The Communings with Himself* [*The Meditations*], trans. C. R. Haines, Loeb Library (1930).

BACON, FRANCIS, *Novum organum* [*The New Instrument*], in vols. 1 and 4 of *The Works of Francis Bacon*, ed. James Spedding, Robert Leslie Ellis, and Douglas

References

Denon Heath, 14 vols. (London, 1857–74; fac. Stuttgart: Frommann, 1961–3). *EHU* n. 27.

BAYLE, PIERRE, *The Dictionary Historical and Critical of Mʳ. Peter Bayle*, ed. and trans. Pierre Desmaizeaux, 2nd edn., 5 vols. (London, 1734–8; fac. New York: Garland, 1984).

BEDE, *Ecclesiastical History of the English Nation*, in *Baedae: Opera historica*, trans. J. E. King, 2 vols., Loeb Library (1962).

—— 'The Life and Miracles of Saint Cuthbert', in *The Complete Works of Venerable Bede* (London, 1843).

BENTLEY, RICHARD, *Eight Boyle Lectures on Atheism* (London, 1692; fac. New York: Garland, 1976). Includes 'Matter and Motion cannot Think', and 'The Folly of Atheism'.

—— *Remarks upon a Discourse of Free-Thinking*, in vol. 3 of *The Works of Richard Bentley*, 3 vols. (London, 1836–8).

BERKELEY, GEORGE, *Alciphron*, in vol. 3 of *The Works of George Berkeley, Bishop of Cloyne*.

—— *A Treatise concerning the Principles of Human Knowledge*, in vol. 2 of *The Works of George Berkeley, Bishop of Cloyne*. *EHU* n. 32.

—— *Three Dialogues between Hylas and Philonous*, in vol. 2 of *The Works of George Berkeley, Bishop of Cloyne*. *EHU* n. 32.

—— *The Works of George Berkeley, Bishop of Cloyne*, ed. A. A. Luce and T. E. Jessop, 9 vols. (London: Nelson, 1948–57).

BERNOULLI, J., *Ars conjectandi* [*Art of Conjecture*] (Basel, 1713).

BIBLE, *The Holy Bible . . . The Authorized Version Published in the Year 1611* (Oxford: Oxford University Press, 1985).

BLAIR, HUGH, *Lectures on Rhetoric and Belles Lettres* (London, 1833).

BOYLE, ROBERT, *The Christian Virtuoso*, in vol. 5 of *The Works of the Honourable Robert Boyle*, ed. Thomas Birch, 6 vols. (London, 1772; fac. Hildesheim: Olms, 1966).

BRAMHALL, JOHN, *A Defence of True Liberty* (London, 1655; fac. New York: Garland, 1977).

BROWNE, PETER, *The Procedure, Extent, and Limits of Human Understanding* (London, 1728).

BURTON, JOHN HILL (ed.), *Letters of Eminent Persons Addressed to David Hume* (Edinburgh, 1849; fac. Bristol: Thoemmes, 1989).

BUTLER, JOSEPH, *The Analogy of Religion, Natural and Revealed, to the Constitution and Course of Nature*, in vol. 1 of *The Works of Joseph Butler*.

—— *Fifteen Sermons Preached at the Rolls Chapel*, in vol. 2 of *The Works of Joseph Butler* (under the title *Fifteen Sermons*).

—— *The Works of Joseph Butler*, ed. W. E. Gladstone, 2 vols. (Oxford: Clarendon Press, 1896).

CHAMBERS, EPHRAIM, *Cyclopædia; or, An Universal Dictionary of Arts and Sciences*, 2 vols. (London, 1741).

References

CHARLETON, WALTER, *Physiologia Epicuro-Gassendo-Charltoniana* (London, 1654; fac. New York: Johnson Reprint, 1966).

CHEYNE, GEORGE, *Philosophical Principles of Natural Religion: Containing the Elements of Natural Philosophy* (London, 1705).

CICERO, MARCUS TULLIUS, *Academica* [*The Academy*], in *De natura deorum, Academica*,trans. H. Rackham, Loeb Library (1972).

——*De finibus bonorum et malorum* [*On the Chief Good and Evil*], trans. H. Rackham, Loeb Library (1921). *EHU* n. 9.

——*De natura deorum* [*On the Nature of the Gods*], in *De natura deorum, Academica*, trans. H. Rackham, Loeb Library (1972).

CLARKE, SAMUEL, *The Works of Samuel Clarke, D.D.*, 4 vols. (London, 1738; fac. New York: Garland, 1978).

CLAUBERG, JOHANN, *Disputationes physicæ* [*Disputations of Physics*], in *Opera omnia philosophica* (Amsterdam, 1691).

COLLINS, ANTHONY, *A Discourse of Free-Thinking* (London, 1713; fac. New York: Garland, 1978).

——*A Discourse of the Grounds and Reasons of the Christian Religion* (London, 1724; fac. New York: Garland, 1976).

——*A Philosophical Inquiry concerning Human Liberty* (London, 1717; fac. New York: Garland, 1978).

CORDEMOY, GÉRAUD DE, *Six discours sur la distinction et l'union du corps et de l'ame* [*Six Discourses on the Distinction and the Union of the Body and the Mind*], in *Œuvres philosophiques*, ed. Pierre Clair and François Girbal (Paris: Presses Universitaires de France, 1968).

CORYATE, THOMAS, *Coryats Crudities* (London, 1611; fac. London: Scolar Press, 1978).

CURTIUS RUFUS, QUINTUS, *History of Alexander*, trans. John C. Rolfe, 2 vols., Loeb Library (1946). *EHU* Sect. 8.8.

DE MOIVRE, ABRAHAM, *The Doctrine of Chances, or, A Method of Calculating the Probabilities of Events in Play* (London, 1756; fac. New York: Chelsea, 1967).

DENNIS, JOHN, *The Critical Works of John Dennis*, ed. Edward Niles Hooker, 2 vols. (Baltimore: Johns Hopkins University Press, 1939–43).

DESCARTES, RENÉ, *Discourse on the Method*, in vol. 1 of *The Philosophical Writings of Descartes*.

——*Meditations on First Philosophy*, in vol. 2 of *The Philosophical Writings of Descartes*.

——*Objections and Replies*, in vol. 2 of *The Philosophical Writings of Descartes*.

——*The Philosophical Writings of Descartes*, ed. and trans. John Cottingham, Robert Stoothoff, and Dugald Murdoch, 3 vols. (Cambridge: Cambridge University Press, 1984–91).

——*Principles of Philosophy*, in vol. 1 of *The Philosophical Writings of Descartes*.

——*Rules for the Direction of the Mind*, in vol. 1 of *The Philosophical Writings of Descartes*.

References

DIGBY, KENELME, *Two Treatises, in the one of which, The Nature of Bodies, in the other, The Nature of Mans Soul is Looked into in Way of Discovery of the Immortality of Reasonable Souls* (London, 1644).

DIO CASSIUS COCCEIANUS, *Dio's Roman History*, trans. Earnest Cary, 9 vols., Loeb Library (1914–27). *EHU* n. 30.

DIODORUS SICULUS (DIODORUS OF SICILY), *The Library of History*, in vol. 5, trans. C. H. Oldfather, *Diodorus of Sicily*, 12 vols., Loeb Library (1933–67).

DIOGENES LAERTIUS, *Lives of Eminent Philosophers*, trans. R. D. Hicks, 2 vols., Loeb Library (1925–70).

DRYDEN, JOHN, *An Essay of Dramatick Poesie*, ed. Samuel Holt Monk, in vol. 17 of *The Works of John Dryden*, 20 vols. (Berkeley: University of California Press, 1956–71).

EPICTETUS, *The Discourses*, in *The Discourses as Reported by Arrian, The Manual, and Fragments*.

—— *The Discourses as Reported by Arrian, The Manual, and Fragments*, trans. W. A. Oldfather, 2 vols., Loeb Library (1926–8).

—— *The Fragments*, in *The Discourses as Reported by Arrian, The Manual, and Fragments*.

EPICURUS, *The Epicurus Reader*, ed. and trans. Brad Inwood and L. P. Gerson (Indianapolis: Hackett, 1994).

EUCLID, *The Thirteen Books of Euclid's Elements*, ed. and trans. Thomas L. Heath, 3 vols. (New York: Dover, 1956).

GASSENDI, PIERRE, *Exercises Against the Aristotelians*, in *The Selected Works of Pierre Gassendi*.

—— *The Selected Works of Pierre Gassendi*, ed. and trans. Craig B. Brush (New York: Johnson Reprint, 1972).

—— *The Syntagma*, in *The Selected Works of Pierre Gassendi*.

GLANVILL, JOSEPH, *Scepsis Scientifica: or Confest Ignorance, the Way to Science* (London, 1665; fac. New York: Garland, 1978).

GOODICH, MICHAEL E., *Violence and Miracle in the Fourteenth Century: Private Grief and Public Salvation* (Chicago: University of Chicago Press, 1995).

GROTIUS, HUGO, *The Truth of the Christian Religion*, trans. John Clarke (London, 1827).

HARVEY, WILLIAM, *An Anatomical Disquisition on the Motion of the Heart and Blood in Animals*, in vol. 26 of *Great Books of the Western World*, 2nd edn. (Chicago: Encyclopedia Britannica, 1990).

HERODOTUS, *History*, trans. A. D. Godley, 4 vols., Loeb Library (1921–4). *EHU* Sect. 10.28.

HESIOD, *Works and Days*, in *The Homeric Hymns and Homerica*, trans. Hugh G. Evelyn-White, Loeb Library (1936).

HIPPOCRATES, *Nature of Man*, in *Hippocrates*, trans. W. H. S. Jones, Loeb Library (1931). Bound with Heracleitus, *On the Universe*.

HOBBES, THOMAS, *Leviathan*, ed. Edwin Curley (Indianapolis: Hackett, 1994).

HOMER, *Iliad*, trans. A. T. Murray, 2 vols., Loeb Library (1924–5). *EHU* Sect. 3.11.

——*Odyssey*, trans. A. T. Murray, 2 vols., Loeb Library (1919). *EHU* Sect. 3.12.

HUME, DAVID, *A Dissertation on the Passions*, ed. Tom L. Beauchamp (Oxford: Oxford University Press, forthcoming).

——*An Enquiry concerning the Principles of Morals*, ed. Tom L. Beauchamp (Oxford: Oxford University Press, 1998).

——*A Treatise of Human Nature*, ed. David Fate Norton and Mary J. Norton (Oxford: Oxford University Press, forthcoming).

——*An Abstract of a Book lately Published; Entituled, A Treatise of Human Nature, &c.*, in *A Treatise of Human Nature*, ed. David Fate Norton and Mary J. Norton.

——*Essays: Moral, Political, and Literary*, ed. Eugene F. Miller, 2nd edn. (Indianapolis: LibertyClassics, 1987).

——*The History of England: From the Invasion of Julius Caesar to the Revolution in 1688*, 6 vols. (Indianapolis: LibertyClassics, 1983–5).

——*The Letters of David Hume*, ed. J. Y. T. Greig, 2 vols. (Oxford: Clarendon Press, 1932).

——*The Natural History of Religion and Dialogues concerning Natural Religion*, ed. A. Wayne Colver and John Valdimir Price (Oxford: Clarendon Press, 1976).

JACKSON, JOHN, *An Address to Deists* (London, 1744).

JOHNSON, SAMUEL, *Johnson's Dictionary*, ed. E. L. McAdam, Jr., and George Milne (New York: Pantheon, 1963).

KEILL, JOHN, *An Introduction to the True Astronomy*, 3rd edn. (London, 1739).

KREISER, B. ROBERT, *Miracles, Convulsions, and Ecclesiastical Politics in Early Eighteenth-Century Paris* (Princeton: Princeton University Press, 1978).

LA FORGE, LOUIS DE, *Traitté de l'esprit de l'homme* [*Treatise on the Spirit of Man*] (Amsterdam, 1666; fac. Hildesheim: Olms, 1984).

LEE, HENRY, *Anti-Scepticism: Or, Notes upon Each Chapter of Mr. Lock's Essay concerning Humane Understanding* (London, 1702; fac. Hildesheim: Olms, 1973).

LEIBNIZ, GOTTFRIED WILHELM, *The Leibniz–Arnauld Correspondence*, ed. and trans. H. T. Mason (New York: Barnes & Noble, 1967).

——*Monadology*, in *Philosophical Papers and Letters*, ed. and trans. LeRoy E. Loemker, 2nd edn. (Dordrecht: Reidel, 1976).

——*New Essays concerning Human Understanding*, trans. Alfred Gideon Langley, 2nd edn. (Chicago: Open Court, 1916).

LELAND, JOHN, *A View of the Principal Deistical Writers*, 3rd edn. (London, 1756–7; fac. New York: Garland, 1978).

LIPSIUS, JUSTUS, *Two Books Of Constancie*, ed. Rudolf Kirk, trans. John Stradling (New Brunswick, NJ: Rutgers University Press, 1939).

LIVY (TITUS LIVIUS), *From the Founding of the City* [*History*], trans. B. O. Foster, 13 vols., Loeb Library (1919–59).

LOCKE, JOHN, *An Essay concerning Human Understanding*, ed. Peter H. Nidditch (Oxford: Clarendon Press, 1975). *EHU* nn. 1, 10, 12.

LUCIAN, *Alexander, or the False Prophet*, trans. A. M. Harmon, Loeb Library (1925). *EHU* Sect. 10.22–3.

—— *The Carousal, or the Lapiths* [*The Drinking Party, or Lapithae*], trans. A. M. Harmon, Loeb Library (1921). *EHU* n. 28.

—— *The Eunuch*, trans. A. M. Harmon, Loeb Library (1936). *EHU* nn. 29–30.

—— *Zeus Rants*, trans. A. M. Harmon, Loeb Library (1929).

LUCRETIUS CARUS, TITUS, *De rerum natura* [*On the Nature of the Universe*], trans. W. H. D. Rouse, rev. Martin Ferguson Smith, Loeb Library (1975). *EHU* n. 26.

MALEBRANCHE, NICOLAS, *The Search after Truth*, ed. and trans. Thomas M. Lennon and Paul J. Olscamp (Columbus: Ohio State University Press, 1980).

MARIANA, JUAN DE, *The General History of Spain*, trans. John Stevens (London, 1699).

MERSENNE, MARIN, *La Vérité des sciences* [*The Truth of the Sciences*] (Paris, 1625; fac. Stuttgart: Friedrich Frommann, 1969).

MIDDLETON, CONYERS, *A Free Inquiry into the Miraculous Powers* (London, 1749; fac. New York: Garland, 1976).

MILTON, JOHN, *Paradise Lost*, ed. Merritt Y. Hughes (New York: Macmillan, 1985). *EHU* Sect. 3.17.

MONTGERON, LOUIS BASILE CARRÉ DE, *La Verité des miracles operés par l'intercession de M. de Pâris* [*The Truth of the Miracles Brought About by the Intercession of M. de Pâris*] (Utrecht, 1737; Cologne, 1739). *EHU* n. 25.

NEWTON, ISAAC, *Philosophiæ naturalis principia mathematica* [*Mathematical Principles of Natural Philosophy*], in *Sir Isaac Newton's Mathematical Principles of Natural Philosophy and his System of the World*, trans. Andrew Motte, rev. Florian Cajori (Berkeley: University of California Press, 1946). *EHU* n. 16.

—— *Opticks* (London, 1730; fac. New York: Dover, 1952).

NORTON, DAVID FATE, *David Hume: Common-Sense Moralist, Sceptical Metaphysician* (Princeton: Princeton University Press, 1982).

OVID (PUBLIUS OVIDIUS NASO), *Metamorphoses*, trans. Frank Justus Miller, 2 vols., Loeb Library (1960–4). *EHU* Sect. 3.7.

PLUTARCH, *Lives*, trans. Bernadotte Perrin, 11 vols., Loeb Library (1914–28). *EHU* n. 21.

—— 'The Oracles at Delphi', in vol. 5, trans. Frank Cole Babbitt, of *Moralia* [*Moral Essays*], 14 vols., Loeb Library (1927–69).

POLYBIUS, *The Histories*, trans. W. R. Paton, 6 vols., Loeb Library (1922–7). *EHU* Sect. 8.7.

POPE, ALEXANDER, 'Preface' (to the *Iliad*) and 'A General View of the Epic Poem and of the *Iliad* and *Odyssey*. Extracted from *Bossu*', in vols. 7–8, *Twickenham Edition of the Poems of Alexander Pope*, ed. John Butt (London: Methuen; New Haven: Yale University Press, 1954–9).

PORPHYRY, *On Abstinence from Animal Food*, ed. Esme Wynne-Tyson, trans. Thomas Taylor (New York: Barnes & Noble, 1965).

References

RACINE, JEAN, *Abrégé de l'histoire de Port-Royal* [*Brief History of Port-Royal*], 2nd edn., ed. A. Gazier (Paris: Société Française, 1909). *EHU* n. 25.

Recueil des miracles operés au tombeau de M. de Paris Diacre [*Collection of the Miracles Performed at the Tomb of the Deacon, Monsieur de Paris*]. Published with: *Second recueil des miracles operés par l'intercession de M. de Paris* [*Second Collection of the Miracles Performed by the Intercession of M. de Paris*]; *Réflexions sur les miracles operés au tombeau de M. de Paris* [*Reflections on the Miracles Performed at the Tomb of the Deacon, Monsieur de Paris*]; *Acte passé pardevant notaires, contenant plusieurs pièces au sujet du miracle operé en la personne de mademoiselle Hardouin* [*Act Passed in front of Notaries, containing Several Documents Pertaining to the Miracle Performed upon Mademoiselle Hardouin*]. (n.p., 1732). *EHU* n. 25.

RETZ, JEAN FRANÇOIS PAUL DE GONDI, CARDINAL DE, *Mémoires* [*Memoirs*], in *Œuvres*, ed. Marie-Thérèse Hipp and Michel Pernot (Paris: Gallimard, 1984). *EHU* Sect. 10.26.

SENECA, LUCIUS ANNAEUS, *Moral Essays*, trans. John W. Basore, 3 vols., Loeb Library (1928–35).

SEXTUS EMPIRICUS, *Outlines of Pyrrhonism*, trans. R. G. Bury, Loeb Library (1939).

S'GRAVESANDE, W. JAMES, *Mathematical Elements of Natural Philosophy*, trans. J. T. Desaguliers, 2 vols. (London, 1747).

SHERLOCK, THOMAS J., *The Trial of the Witnesses of the Resurrection of Jesus*, 12th edn. (Boston, 1809).

SORABJI, RICHARD, *Animal Minds and Human Morals: The Origins of the Western Debate* (Ithaca: Cornell University Press, 1993).

SPINOZA, BENEDICT DE, *Theologico-Political Treatise*, in vol. 1 of *The Chief Works of Benedict de Spinoza*, trans. R. H. M. Elwes (New York: Dover, 1951).

STILLINGFLEET, EDWARD, *Origines sacræ, or A Rational Account of the Grounds of Christian Faith, as to the Truth and Divine Authority of the Scriptures*, 2nd edn. (London, 1663).

STRAWSON, GALEN, *The Secret Connexion: Causation, Realism, and David Hume* (Oxford: Clarendon Press, 1989).

SUETONIUS TRANQUILLUS, GAIUS, *Lives of the Caesars*, trans. J. C. Rolfe, 2 vols., Loeb Library (1979). *EHU* n. 24.

TACITUS, CORNELIUS, *The Histories*, trans. Clifford H. Moore, 2 vols., in *The Histories Books I–III*, Loeb Library (1980); *The Histories Books IV–V, The Annals Books I–III*, Loeb Library (1979). *EHU* Sect. 8.7; n. 24.

TILLOTSON, JOHN, *The Works*, 9th edn. (Dublin, 1726). *EHU* Sect. 10.1.

VIRGIL (PUBLIUS VERGILIUS MARO), *The Aeneid*, trans. H. Rushton Fairclough, 2 vols., in *Eclogues, Georgics and Aeneid I–VI*, Loeb Library (1974); *Aeneid VII–XII, The Minor Poems*, Loeb Library (1930). *EHU* Sect. 3.12.

VOLTAIRE, FRANÇOIS MARIE AROUET DE, *La Henriade*, in vol. 21 of *The Works of Voltaire: A Contemporary Version*, trans. William F. Fleming, 22 vols. (New York: St Hubert Guild, 1901). *EHU* Sect. 3.11.

References

WATTS, ISAAC, *The Works*, 6 vols. (London, 1810).

WILKINS, JOHN, *Of the Principles and Duties of Natural Religion* (London, 1675).

WILSON, FRED, 'Is Hume a Sceptic with regard to the Senses?', *Journal of the History of Philosophy*, 27 (1989), 49–73.

WINTERS, BARBARA, 'Hume on Reason', *Hume Studies*, 5 (1979), 20–35.

WOLLASTON, WILLIAM, *The Religion of Nature Delineated* (London, 1724; fac. New York: Garland, 1978).

WOOLSTON, THOMAS, *Six Discourses on the Miracles of our Saviour* (London, 1727–30; fac. New York: Garland, 1979).

WRIGHT, JOHN P., *The Sceptical Realism of David Hume* (Manchester: Manchester University Press; Minneapolis: University of Minnesota Press, 1983).

XENOPHON, *Hellenica, Books I–V*, trans. Carleton L. Brownson, vol. 1 in *Xenophon*, 4 vols., Loeb Library (1918–25).

Index

This index encompasses the entire book while emphasizing names, titles, and concepts in Hume's text (pp. 87–211). Entries for *book titles* are limited to titles (or authors of those titles) mentioned or intimated by Hume. Entries of *authors* are limited to persons mentioned either by Hume (in the text of *EHU*) or by the editor (in the annotations and suggested supplementary readings).

281

Index

Index

Johnson, Oliver 68, 74, 77
Johnson, Samuel 233, 264
judicature 183, 252
justice 50, 193–4, 196, 252, 256–8
justification 21, 30, 52, 54, 56, 73, 75
justness 122, 189, 256

Kant, Immanuel 71–2
Keill, John 255
Kepler, Johannes 262
King, James 69–70, 78
Klibansky, Raymond 65
knavery 180, 185
knowledge:
    of causal relations 25, 103, 109–13, 156,
      165, 191, 194–6, 222, 236
    and certainty 24, 108, 209, 224, 227
    of God 50
    Hume's use of the term 22
    and instincts 167
    Locke on the basis of 10–11, 16, 32, 233
    in memory, senses, and experience 129,
      151, 202
    probability and 22, 24, 227, 232–3, 246, 260
    and types of reasoning 115, 117–18, 120–1,
      123, 149
Kuypers, Mary Shaw 70

Laelius 128, 230
La Forge, Louis de 236
Laird, John 68–9
language:
    as jargon 19, 52, 92, 99, 216
    and meanings of words 96–7, 99, 125, 131,
      135, 144, 146, 148, 160, 209
    and problems in fixing meanings 99, 148,
      160, 209, 220, 238–9, 242
    and the theory of meaning 19–23, 35–7
    see also definition
lassitude 104
laws:
    causal 26, 40, 101, 126, 132, 141, 162–3,
      192, 226, 233, 247
    deists and 49–50
    experience and knowledge of 184, 195
    free will and 148–64, 238
    of gravitation 12, 233
    of human behaviour 42–3
    irregularities in 152–4
    miracles as violations of 45–7, 173, 185,
      245, 247

of nature 10, 38–40, 43, 46, 110, 226, 231,
    233, 254, 257
    political and judicial 122, 155, 160, 197,
      252
    scientific 10, 12, 112, 149, 219, 228, 262
    see also canons and canon law; causation;
      determinism; miracles
Lee, Henry 235
Le Franc, Anne 250
Leibniz, Gottfried Wilhelm 10–11, 39, 66, 231,
    233, 235, 238–9, 246
Leland, John 258
Lennon, Thomas 66
Lesher, James 73–4
Letter from a Gentleman (Hume) 63–4
Leucippus 256
Leviathan (Hobbes) 66, 242
Levine, Michael P. 75–6
liberty:
    in Aristotle 103, 222, 231, 239
    in Bramhall 239–41, 243
    in Collins 239, 241
    definition of 39–40, 148–9, 158–9, 238, 242;
      see also verbal disputes
    in Hobbes 39, 239–40, 242
    in Leibniz 39, 231, 239
    in Locke 39, 239
    and necessity 34, 38–41, 74–5, 148–62, 220,
      238–9, 242
    reconciling theory of 39, 158, 242
    in Spinoza 239
    in Watts 242
    see also free will
licence 190, 196, 256
Lipsius, Justus 243
literature 9, 87, 217–18, 221, 268
liveliness in impressions, ideas, and beliefs 17,
    30, 51, 96–8, 125, 128–9, 228; see also
      belief; impressions
Lives (Plutarch) 172, 223, 247–8, 252
Lives of the Caesars (Suetonius) 178, 229
Livingston, Donald 69–70, 78
Livy (Titus Livius) 178, 185, 248, 253
Locke, John:
    his attacks on schoolmen 242
    on the basis of knowledge 10–11, 16, 32,
      233
    Berkeley's criticisms of 57, 61, 262
    on determinism and freedom 39, 239
    on God and natural religion 11, 48
    his influence on Hume 10, 20, 220–1, 234

Index

Index

Index

Index